SOLZHENITSYN IN EXILE

CRITICAL ESSAYS AND
DOCUMENTARY MATERIALS

SOLZHENITSYN IN EXILE

CRITICAL ESSAYS AND DOCUMENTARY MATERIALS

Edited by
JOHN B. DUNLOP
RICHARD S. HAUGH
MICHAEL NICHOLSON

Hoover Institution Press
Stanford University, Stanford, California

Hoover Press Publication 305
First printing, 1985
Manfactured in the United States of America
89 88 87 86 85   9 8 7 6 5 4 3 2 1

Library of Congress Cataloging in Publication Data
Main Entry under title:

Solzhenitsyn in exile.

Bibliography: p.
1. Solzhenitsyn, Aleksandr Isaevich, 1918-   —Criticism and
interpretation—Addresses, essays, lectures. I. Dunlop, John B.
II. Haugh, Richard S. (Richard Stanley), 1942-
III. Nicholson, Michael (Michael A.)
PG 3488.04Z8865   1985   891.73'44   84-10821
ISBN 0-8179-8051-2

Contents

III. DOCUMENTARY MATERIALS

IV. BIBLIOGRAPHY

Preface

The publication of *Solzhenitsyn in Exile* is intended to reflect an abiding interest in Solzhenitsyn, the writer and the man. It was conceived as a sequel to *Aleksandr Solzhenitsyn: Critical Essays and Documentary Materials,* a collection first published in 1973 and reissued in expanded form in 1975, but unlike its predecessor it contains only critical essays specifically written for inclusion in *Solzhenitsyn in Exile.*

The volume is divided into four parts. The first, entitled "Receptions," treats the reactions to Solzhenitsyn the public figure in the United States and Europe since 1974. Part two, "Critical Essays," concentrates upon his published writings during the same period. None of the documentary materials which make up the third section has hitherto been available in English: they include an important memoir by dissident novelist Lidiia Chukovskaia, a lengthy interview in which Solzhenitsyn discusses his literary views, and a polemical exchange on the subject of his *Lenin in Zurich.* A bibliographical section brings the book to a close.

Finally, the editors would like to thank Alexis Klimoff and Georges Nivat for their generous assistance. John Dunlop is grateful to the Oberlin College Committee on Research and Development and Michael Nicholson, to the Humanities Division of Colgate University for grants in aid of their work on the volume. And we thank our families for their encouragement and support.

J.B.D.
R.H.
M.N.

PART ONE

Receptions

Solzhenitsyn in the British Media

ROBERT CONQUEST

Before Solzhenitsyn's expulsion from the Soviet Union the main feelings expressed about him in Britain were of admiration for his courage and his talent. The appearance of his work in English and the other Western languages starting with *One Day in the Life of Ivan Denisovich* in 1962, was an enormously different phenomenon from the mere "translation" of a "writer" in the ordinary sense. For the barrier between ourselves and the Russia of the present day is not merely linguistic or literary. It is a matter of witness being borne about a culture, a political culture, which is from our point of view almost unbelievably strange; a culture which we can only begin to understand by a constant effort of the imagination.

Work like Solzhenitsyn's which helped us, or even forced us, into that understanding was and is therefore crucial to our real grasp of the world today, of the very springs of policy—in fact of the preservation of our own future. The reception of his work in the West, as much as in the USSR itself, seemed to prove that the point was taken—and at some deeper level than mere persuasion.

He was first a witness for the dead—the tens of millions of innocent and helpless victims of the regime. Secondly, he was witness for the truth against what Pasternak described as "the inhuman power of the lie." The present rulers still suppress all the facts of the Terror there. Indeed, nowadays, not even lies are told—though they are told about Solzhenitsyn.

Among the weapons they brought to bear on him was a vast disinformation effort by the KGB. This had been in operation long before his expulsion from the USSR. Whispering campaigns were conducted to the effect that he had been sentenced in 1945 as a deserter or spy, that his rehabilitation was a mistake, and so on and so on.[1]

None of this greatly affected British opinion. Nevertheless, even before his expulsion from the USSR critical, and even hostile opinions, not all of them from pro-Soviet sources, were voiced in this country as well as favorable ones. It will be convenient, however, to start this brief conspectus by looking at what was said at the moment when his fate dominated the world's headlines—that is, when he was arrested on February 12, 1974, and deported to the West the following day. In a leader on February 13, as soon as the arrest became known, *The Times* summed up the international significance of the case:

> The Soviet authorities have created an almost insoluble problem for themselves by their treatment of Solzhenitsyn. First they precipitated publication in the West of *Gulag Archipelago*, his account of Soviet prison camps, by seizing a copy of the manuscript and thereby removing his main reason for delaying publication, which was to protect individuals mentioned in the book. Then they launched an extremely noisy campaign of abuse which attracted maximum attention throughout the world. Then they summoned him to the State prosecutor's office, perhaps failing to anticipate his refusal.
>
> Now they have taken him by force . . . the real question in detente is the nature of the country with which the West is being asked to seek a new type of relationship. If it is a country which cannot face facts about its past and suppresses human rights which are taken for granted in the West this is bound to put severe limits on any new forms of relationship between these two very different worlds. The next moves in the confrontation with Solzhenitsyn will therefore be watched with deep concern not only for the person of Solzhenitsyn but also for the broader trends of Soviet policy.

Other papers, while sharing this general view, nevertheless already combined it with an element of criticism of Solzhenitsyn himself. *The Guardian* (13 February 1974) commented:

> In recent months a new bitterness has come into Solzhenitsyn's voice. More and more he has appeared to be a lonely, cussed, and at times arrogant man. But all this is understandable for someone living under the perpetual strain and tension which the Soviet authorities have deliberately imposed on him. . . . Whatever reservations Western critics may have about this or that detail of Solzhenitsyn's views, the Soviet leadership has ensured that the West is united in

supporting his right to think and publish what he likes. An academic discussion of Solzhenitsyn's strong and weak points is made irrelevant by the stark injustice of his plight.

Solzhenitsyn's expulsion from the USSR the day after his arrest similarly produced general support for the writer and condemnation of the Soviet regime. *The Times* (15 February 1974) thoughtfully noted that the expulsion was particularly sad for one who "is about as far as one could imagine from the salon intellectual dabbling in foreign ideas. He draws his entire spiritual strength from the Russian soil." *The Times Literary Supplement* (15 February 1974), rather more critically, put the point as follows:

> Whether or not one accepts Solzhenitsyn's analysis, whether or not one would wish to qualify its implacable generality, it is essential that one grasps the underlying stance. It is that of a Slavophile and moral transcendentalist, or even mystic, in the tradition of Dostoevsky and Berdyaev. There is nothing of a western democratic programme, of western enlightenment about Solzhenitsyn's position.

This theme was to be developed, often in a very hostile fashion, over the following years. Meanwhile we may note, in a column in *The Guardian* (14 February 1974) by Stanley Reynolds, the first overt attack on Solzhenitsyn.

> Solzhenitsyn, I am afraid, is not one of us. That is to say he is not a liberal. I don't know what exactly he is, but whatever it is it is most peculiar.
> He was converted to the Russian orthodox church which really won't win him many votes in Hampstead. He also seems to have a soft spot for the Tsar.... Then, too, you can pick paragraphs out of his Nobel Prize speech which sound very much like moral rearmament propaganda: "The old same primitive urges rend and sunder our world—greed, envy, licence, mutual malevolence, though they now adopt euphemistic pseudonyms as they go, such as 'class struggle,' 'racial struggle,' 'the struggle of the masses,' 'the struggle of organised labour.'"
> In fact, Moral Rearmament—so aptly named Moral Regurgitation by Michael Frayn and which has not been heard of very much since its heyday a decade ago when it was telling us we could spot the queers in our midst by their green clothes and suede shoes—in fact, the MRA quoted Solzhenitsyn in an advert in the Times the other day.

At other times Solzhenitsyn sounds like something out of Aims of Industry or seated upon a Tory backbench: "Whenever any group of workers seize a chance to grab something extra—never mind if they don't deserve it, never mind if it's more than they need—they up and grab it and ruin takes society."

Snide in tone (and smearing by association), this was to be the precursor of many such. Not long after, Alan Brien (*Sunday Times*, 10 March 1974) attacked Solzhenitsyn's "Letter to the Soviet Leaders"—developing further the theme of the reactionary crackpot:

Is Alexander Solzhenitsyn a crank? His open, un-opened, letter to the Soviet Government certainly bears a superficial resemblance to those lengthy screeds which flop on to the desk of every journalist from time to time, even down to the passages underscored and printed in capitals, full of contradictory assertions, obsessive fears, Falstaffian escalations of statistics, personal experiences insecurely generalised, all carried along on a flow of deep, genuine emotion. . . . The Soviet treatment of Solzhenitsyn, indeed of all its artists and intellectuals and of anyone there who really wants to know, say, just the true history of its Revolution is an abomination and an obscenity. But Solzhenitsyn must do better than this collection of inflammatory half-truths. If the Soviet rulers were as clever and clear-sighted as he imagines, they would print it, uncut, in Pravda.

The Observer, in an editorial (17 February 1974), summed up the tone of such attacks admirably:

An affinity has been growing up between some Western journalists and those intellectuals in Moscow and Warsaw who, while proclaiming themselves liberals and not men of the regime, speak debunkingly of the leading Soviet dissidents. Their line on Solzhenitsyn is identical.

He is a brave man and no doubt admirable, but. . .and then they make the fact that he has become a Christian imply that he is also an apologist for the Orthodox church (whereas he has openly criticised its present Patriarch for his political subservience); his use of Western newsmen and book publishers to make his views heard and gain a temporary immunity from Soviet persecution is deplored as obviously bound to be disastrous; his plea that Western intellectuals should take as much interest in the repressive acts of the Soviet regime as in those of non-Communist dictatorships is twisted to suggest that he actually sympathises with the latter; his nostalgia for Russian history is represented as a soft spot for the Tsar, and so on.

It is easy to see why would-be liberals among Soviet writers may wish to belittle Solzhenitsyn and Sakharov. If these heroic men were accepted as wholly admirable, their lead ought to be followed in some degree. And any non-hero can easily understand the embarrassment of that situation. But how explain the eagerness of writers here to reduce, on such shaky evidence, the reputation of a man known for his extraordinary achievement in thinking his own thoughts and uttering them in the face of one of the most repressive systems of State control ever devised?

It is appropriate, nevertheless, to note honest and respectful disagreement, as voiced by Francis Hope in *The New Statesman* (22 February 1974):

> I deeply disagree with much of what I can discern of Solzhenitsyn's political views... But...I must pay attention to what he says. Even when I have made allowances for the unchecked folklore of the prison camps, for the religious beliefs which I do not share, for the rhetorical exaggerations and the unreal aspirations (and yes, I do think all these things are to be found in *The Gulag Archipelago*), I am left with something which cannot be absorbed even into my own privileged view of the world.

While the themes thus far noted were to be the constant and central issues raised over Solzhenitsyn and his views or supposed views, it seems worth noting at this point some of the odder and more peripheral of the comments to be made—all of them more or less representative of strands of lay opinion in this country. First, the notion (expressly repudiated by the writer) that injustices in our society are just as bad as those of the USSR, or nearly so. For example, a letter in *The Times* (19 February 1974) from a clergyman interested in penal reform (a Mr. Graham Dowell), said:

> There is, however, another danger, directed more at the voice of prophecy itself. It would be tragic if we in the West should be tempted to use the powerful denunciations of an oppressive system as mere propaganda for the superiority of our social democratic processes. That would be nothing but to prostitute the prophet and to ignore the evils which wash over all of us.

It is likely that Solzhenitsyn would be an irritant in any society. It is greatly to be hoped that if he settles in Western Europe he will open our eyes to the erosion of our civil liberties, the dehumanizing and self-defeating nature of our penal system. . . .

In a more partisan context, a similar point was made in the *Sunday Times* (17 February 1974) by a Mr. J. M. S. Brown:

I would like Alexander Solzhenitsyn to accept Mr. Heath's invitation to come to Britain. Then, when he has a day or two to spare, I would like him to pop over to Northern Ireland, to try writing about The Maze, Britain's political internment camp. I doubt whether he would have much success publishing his findings in Britain, although I'm sure Russia would oblige.

I find it impossible to condone the attitude of the Russian authorities, but equally impossible to join with the hypocritical smugness of the Western world. We do not so much turn a blind eye, as close our eyes completely to our own political injustices.

Some, on the other hand, assumed Solzhenitsyn to be already equally critical of Western and Soviet abuses. For example, Mr. David Storey, the writer, had a letter in *The Times* (15 February 1974), in which he said,

The deep humanism of his socialist beliefs, his insistence on acting as a christian witness, are not merely qualities which we can admire from a distance but those we can practise in our daily lives. His persecution is an indictment not only of the Russian people but of those forces in society, whether directed from Washington or Moscow, which seek to devalue the individual. . . .

Then there was the notion that we should not judge the USSR by our own standards—again invoking the "double standard" idea Solzhenitsyn had so strongly condemned. A letter in *The Times* (21 February 1974) from a Mr. Stephen Scoffham was typical:

Without wishing to detract from Solzhenitsyn's reputation, I would suggest that such thinking is mistaken in that it transfers the values of the West to a Soviet context. In Britain, democracy is one of our (rightful) boasts. We are heirs to a long tradition of tolerance and individualism. By contrast, it would seem that the values of Russian society are somewhat harsher than our rather gentlemanly and ill-defined notions.

Individualism does not, and never has, counted for much. In Russia a sense of duty and of community appear to be more important—the "autocratic" virtues are given a high rating. Against this background free speech is something of an anathema.

Given this position, the Soviet government is justified in deporting Solzhenitsyn. It is important to try and understand the event and to see it as the expression of a coherent philosophy. We may not agree with the Russian action; but at least let us exercise our gift of tolerance, and respect the integrity of a government which is prepared to stand up for its values (as ours so often is not).

Such reactions at least reveal the variety and confusion of attitudes to Solzhenitsyn, to the Soviet Union, to justice, to morality, which are to be found among literate sections of the British public, and seem worth recording for that reason (as the editors of the papers publishing them no doubt felt). But one should note that—unlike the more orchestrated "liberal" response—they were exceptional; and that they were invariably answered with cogency and force by more representative voices. Of these I will content myself with a single example, a rebuttal by Mr. Jonathan Guinness (*The Times*, 28 February 1974) of the letter quoted earlier from Mr. Graham Dowell, though to some degree also applicable to the others.

Solzhenitsyn's denunciations of tyranny must certainly, as the Reverend Graham Dowell says, not be used as "mere propaganda for the superiority of our social democratic processes." To take daily sadism and atrocity as the norm against which our imperfect though comparatively humane society should be measured would indeed be the royal road to complacency.

But to suppose that Solzhenitsyn, after 40 years of surviving the worst that the worst tyranny in history can inflict, is going to bother himself with the comparatively minor injustices in Western society is to assume that a retired mountaineer will spend his time scaling molehills; and to describe these injustices as "evils which [Solzhenitsyn] has so bitterly and eloquently denounced in the society which has rejected him," is to compare the shortcomings of British magistrates with the fundamental falsehood of Soviet "justice," or the petty tyranny of British screws with the institutionalised sadism of Siberian camp guards.

Solzhenitsyn has nothing to do with our necessary reforms; to

think of him in this context is only to blind ourselves to what needs
to be done here. His message is different. It is that the verbiage of
equality and the social conscience leads to gross oppression when it
is allowed to sweep away, rather than reform and revitalise, the
system as it is.

So far, the critical or hostile voices we have quoted have, however
unfairly or uninformedly, been directed at Solzhenitsyn's public
character. We should note, however, that already at this early stage
there could be seen the beginnings of a more personal attack. The
Sunday Times (17 February 1974) published a long article by George
Feifer. (Feifer, joint author of a book on Solzhenitsyn which relies
in part on the author's estranged first wife Natal'ia Reshetovskaia,
was denounced for this as a "rascal" by Solzhenitsyn.) He now,
after professing enormous admiration, first put the case that Solzhenitsyn is nevertheless too "implacable": "The conviction of his
appointment as a divine agent is probably responsible for his impa-
tient intolerance not only of the 'exclusive clique of people' who
tyrannise Russia, but also of less disciplined, less heroic democrats...." and so on and so on. However, he goes on to raise the
question of Solzhenitsyn's former marriage. Since Solzhenitsyn's
lawyer has forbidden Western publishers to publish his letters to
her (in our law, of course, he owns the copyright), this is represented
as a contradiction of his stand on liberty of publication: "As with
many national heroes born in a struggle against despotism, he seems
unfamiliar with the notion of a press free enough to print not only
him, but opinions and versions of events contradicting his." Purely
private matters are here confused with public. (But it is worth adding
that Solzhenitsyn also reserved the right not to publish his own non-
personal work—e.g., *The Feast of the Victors*. The right to publish
is in any case not the compulsion to publish!)

After the first weeks of exile the immense public interest in
Solzhenitsyn not so much subsided as became less vocal. Over the
years which followed, his words and actions remained news. But
until he came to London in 1976 to appear on television, there was
no longer a great deal of comment, and what there was largely
duplicated what had been said in the high moment of his first appearance in the West. It will therefore be convenient at this point to
consider the arguments thus far put forward against him in the

media, but in particular those which publicly and frequently misrepresented his views.

He had, it is true—and even by British standards—the enormous power of the fact that his remarks about the Soviet Union, and about Communist rule everywhere, were totally authoritative. First of all, they were quite obviously true; and then, they were the product of a profound experience accessible in no other way to his audience. Those who nourished various delusions about the USSR had no valid retort, and could do little but nurse their resentment and hope for a later opening.

On the other hand the authoritative, prophet-like, tone often used by Solzhenitsyn is alien to the traditional British tendency to understatement. The matter is trivial enough. (Indeed the tone and stance of almost any foreign writer may tend to grate on most British readers in the long run.) Nevertheless, it went some way to lending credence to the tendency we have noted to criticise Solzhenitsyn as "authoritarian"—not in the sense of a supposed political attitude, but merely in reaction to the *tone* of his public pronouncements. These were, it is true, made with an air of complete conviction, and a certainty of the wrong-headedness of other views. But it is, of course, a logical fallacy to suppose that intensity of conviction, let alone of a mode of expression, is the same as or automatically implies any "authoritarian" desire to silence others. This could indeed have been seen from Solzhenitsyn's warmly expressed approval of Academician Sakharov in spite of his public disagreement with many of his ideas.

This view of his "authoritarianism" merged into attacks on his supposed hostility to democracy, together with his supposed predilection for Tsardom. This is, of course, a complete misrepresentation of Solzhenitsyn's position. What he did say was that the instant democratization of March 1917 did not have long-term beneficial results or lead to the establishment of a stable democracy: on the contrary, it was paid for by (so far) sixty years of virulent tyranny. Solzhenitsyn (noting too that Hitler also came to power in conditions of democracy) suggested that in Russia's case the gradual progress toward liberty since the 1860s bore more solid promise than resulted from the dissolution of the old state. He asserted, in fact, that conditions under the limited autocracy were better than those resulting from its overthrow. This is far from attributing any supreme virtue to Tsardom. If he says that the last half-century of Tsardom was better than the first half-century of Leninism, it is like saying that measles is preferable to leprosy—not an all-out endorsement of measles, but a statement of preferability: a statement, moreover, easily provable. Solzhenitsyn quotes figures on executions under the two regimes. Let me add some from Soviet sources: The *Small Soviet Encyclopedia* (first edition) in its article on "Capital Punishment" tells us that Russia had 94 executions in the years 1866-1900. Andrei Vyshinskii, in his *Prisons of Capitalist Countries*, Moscow, 1937, gives the maximum number of prisoners in Tsarist times as 183,949 (in 1912). Stalin's executions ran into millions, to say nothing of deaths procured by other means. The numbers in his Gulag were well over fifty times greater than those imprisoned under the Tsars. But a residual notion first that Tsardom was terrible in itself, and secondly that Stalinism was, in its bad aspects, no more than a continuation of Tsarist tradition, is very prevalent among those with little knowledge of Russia, and is easily exploited to show that when Solzhenitsyn speaks approvingly (as Sakharov also does!) of the comparative decency of life under post-Emancipation Tsardom, he is merely siding with another and similar despotism.

The other aspect of Solzhenitsyn's supposedly reactionary attitude is to be found in the charge that he is a "nationalist."

It is plainly true that he identifies himself with his country's fate. But the suggestion, often made implicitly or explicitly, that he in any way supports Russian domination over subject peoples, let alone the further expansion of Russian power, is entirely false. He has always spoken for the liberation from Moscow of the Soviet periphery. And while identifying himself with the "Russian and Ukrainian" (on one occasion adding "Belorussian") peoples and clearly hoping that once free they could live together amicably under some political arrangement, he has nevertheless said that the Ukraine must have the right to full independence if it so wishes.

Then his "nationalism" is often characterized as "Slavophile." If this means no more than the fact that he is more traditionalist— in particular more attached to Russian Orthodoxy—than a number of his contemporaries, this is certainly true. And it is also the case that he is sceptical of the solution of Russia's problems by the simple application of Western forms. But far from his having any hostility to the Western culture as such, he has spoken warmly of its strengths and potentialities.

Like all Russians, Solzhenitsyn is the product of his country's past—that Russian history which, as Chekhov put it, weighs down on every Russian like a huge rock. Like many Russians, he is upheld by the hope that the nation's fearful sufferings may bear positive fruit and make Russia's contribution to the world something unique.

But the admirable qualities he sees in traditional Russia are those incompatible with the despotic elements in Russia's history. He turns to Novgorod and Pskov, to the Zemskii Sobor, the free Cossacks, the Old Belief, the village mir, and warmly attacks the St. Petersburg bureaucracy, serfdom, the elements of *unreconstructed* Tsardom in general. He is a traditionalist who does not oppose the Enlightenment; a Russian conservative who admires the "brilliance," as he puts it, of the Western democratic tradition.

For the next couple of years after the great drama of his arrest and expulsion, Solzhenitsyn was naturally less heard of in our media. Still, the denigrations continued to trickle out. On 27 March 1975 *The Times* published an article by George Feifer which, though expressing an unctuous admiration, made unpleasant and false suggestions about Solzhenitsyn's moral position. The ordinary *Times* reader would be unaware that personal unpleasantness already existed between the two men. It might have been franker if Feifer had at least alluded to this, and perhaps justified the conduct Solzhenitsyn had found reprehensible. In any case, the substance of Feifer's charges was particularly disgraceful, especially as it was easy to prove false. He wrote that when a prisoner, Solzhenitsyn "submitted to some of the vicious pressures to collaborate and inform." This, if it means anything, means that he actually did "collaborate and inform." "Collaborate" may be a vague word, but "inform" is not. For this Mr. Feifer relied on Vol. III of *The Gulag Archipelago*, pages 353-360. But these merely show that Solzhenitsyn was trapped into signing a declaration that he would inform, but that, quite specifically, he did not in fact do so. Again, Mr. Feifer imputed a lack of public courage to Solzhenitsyn in the post-1956 epoch. All that he could adduce was the fact that Solzhenitsyn's name was absent from the signatories protesting against the Siniavskii trial. Solzhenitsyn has, it so happens, told us (in his *The Oak and the Calf*) of his decision not to become involved in individual campaigns, in the interests of the assembly of *The Gulag Archipelago*. But his "Letter to the Fourth Congress of the Union of Soviet Writers" (May 1967) calls, as one of its major points, for its intervention in favour of persecuted writers; he was violently attacked for it; he defended it forthrightly and "impermissibly" before the massed ranks of his opponents; was expelled from the Writers' Union; and was under constant attack—making constant counter-attacks—throughout the period.[2] Moreover, he several times lapsed from his decision on individuals—publicly attacking the psychiatric imprisonment of Zhores Medvedev, for example.

From time to time he was in the news in Britain in a more indirect way—through President Ford's reluctance to meet him, later through the Harvard speech. For instance, at the time of the Ford contretemps in July 1975, *The Guardian* (15 July 1975) printed a piece by its Washington correspondent, Simon Winchester, which fully matched in irresponsible snideness some of its earlier (and later) contributions to the debate. He spoke of "the talkative exile," who "believes that all international relations should be forged on the basis of an intense personal morality—his own," a "kind of talk" which, Mr. Winchester said, "has gone down very well with this society's more Neanderthal brothers and sisters," so that "overnight, it seems fair to say, this man who, via the Book of the Month Club (which has ensured that millions of unread copies of *The Gulag* be on coffee tables from Scarsdale to Sausalito) and the kind of media blitz so popular in this country, has become the darling of the redneck population." When Solzhenitsyn addressed the AFL-CIO Mr. Winchester put it that the "shaggy author" (also the "hairy polemicist") went so far as to "talk non-stop for an hour and a half" to his audience of 2,400 "sagging beer bellies." Winchester concluded that if President Ford invited Solzhenitsyn to the White House it would mark a lapse from "reality and integrity," and as to Solzhenitsyn himself, he claimed astonishment that certain people have "expressed hurt disbelief that some observers had actually had the temerity to query the hysterical author's mental stability."

This extraordinary tirade was vigorously answered by Bernard Levin in *The Times* (17 July 1975), who treated it as the beginning of the overt campaign, without the disguise of pretended admiration, which he had long expected from "exponents of American radical-chic and their modish equivalents in this country." But in fact it remained exceptional on this side of the Atlantic, at least in more or less literate journals.

Controversy nevertheless sputtered continually over the ensuing years, till a new high point came in the Spring of 1976, following the famous BBC television interview on March 1, and the recorded sound broadcast put out on March 24.

The immediate reaction to the interview was overwhelming. Though not given much advance publicity, it was seen by five million, and its repeat by fifteen million. The Chairman of the BBC Board of Governors, Sir Michael Swann, spoke of the "intense response" to the interview, and there is virtual unanimity that the impact was tremendous.

The conclusion reached by Sir Michael, and by other commentators, was that the British people were seriously worried by what they saw as evils and dangers at home and abroad, tired of listening to easy and reassuring promises, and glad to hear for once a voice speaking not in day-to-day calculation but from the profundities of the moral issues. As an early letter in *The Times* (4 March 1976) from Mr. D. Bernard Hadley put it,

> How small our national leaders look before the towering figure of Solzhenitsyn. How petty our internal problems seem in the face of the fundamental questions which he poses about the very survival of our way of life.
>
> I was moved by Solzhenitsyn in his interview on BBC 1's *Panorama* as I have never been moved by any politician or philosopher living.

In the same issue, on the other hand, Mr. Andrew Stallybrass felt obliged to write, "we condemn him to silence, with a mild 'Tut, he does so exaggerate; a fine man of course. Sad. But then he's no longer news, is he? Always banging the same drum.' Silence and cynical skepticism can yet calm our slight sense of unease."

For, at least among the media community, the phenomenon aroused unease, and was found hard to handle. *New Society* indeed (4 March 1976) had to say,

> At lunch with Alexander Solzhenitsyn, first impression is one of vitality. He has nothing of the dolefulness that his photographs convey: he is a smaller, less burly man than he appears from pictures. He is clearly rushed...as he moves from person to person. His concentration alternates with moments of relaxation. He summons up the former to deal with every question, even when it might seem quite irrelevant, to offer a reasoned answer.

The purposiveness with which he projects his uncomfortable moral dilemmas is personally direct and makes him the difficult, unassimilable literary figure that he is. A clear perspective and a determination to leave nothing unsaid slices into the ambiguity of western attitudes. This, more than anything else, helps to account for the way in which people react to his name instead of the content of what he has to say.... Yet Solzhenitsyn is unassuming—not exactly surprised by the attention he commands, though certainly invigorated by it. There is no sense in which he might be said to play the role of "the great man" and he does not seek adulation: rather, where people defer to him, as they do, his personality half-consciously expands into the vacuum so created.

And the left-wing *New Statesman*, in a television column by Dennis Potter, reported,

It would be a grotesque indecency to respond to such a figure as Alexander Solzhenitsyn with anything less than proper respect and tension. But it was an uncomfortable and a salutory experience to watch him on Monday's *Panorama* (BBC-1) rebuking the writers and journalists of the West for throwing away 'their sense of responsibility before history and their own people.' Almost any convenient aphorism, or a whole junior common room full of aimless chatter, seemed to be preferable to such an onerous charge, so terrible was the thought of a 'responsibility' so bitterly won.... A writer who can keep such a steady gaze while talking in absolute terms about 'the spirit of the age,' or who can insist without any sign of egotism that his own future is inseparably linked with the fate of his country, is indeed one of the most noble and unfamiliar and unsettling species ever to come on to our screens. Pray God we too never have to make words, words, words the very marrow of our bones instead of the marks on the side of the tube of the sixteenth brand of toothpaste now on sale. Facetiousness is also a way of avoiding another's pain, of course...

But such modesty and self-questioning were rare. In *The Guardian* (5 March 1976) Mr. Peter Jenkins said, "he exaggerates dreadfully," and disagreed with his view of Soviet advance in the Third World. In the *New Statesman* (12 March 1976) Mervyn Jones criticised his views on Angola as being much the same as Ronald Reagan's. Edward Crankshaw in *The Observer* (7 March 1976) took issue with the idea that the USSR would pursue expansionist policies. Clive James in *The Observer* (7 March 1976) departed from his usual understanding of the issues. While ironically noting "Talking to us about moral regeneration, he sounds like Dr. Arnold of Rugby. A bit dated. After all, we've got beyond all that. We're all the way up to Hugh Hefner," he fell into the trap which troubled superficial analysts at the time of our struggle with Hitler:

> To be worried about the KGB doesn't mean that we should stop being worried about the CIA. In fact being worried about the CIA is probably the most effective way of being worried about the KGB, since the West will never be able to defeat totalitarianism by going totalitarian—it will always arrive second—but might possibly stand a chance by remaining liberal.

In *New Society* (11 March 1976) Mr. Nick Anning asked indignantly, "Would he also call the Ellsberg Papers and Agee's *CIA Diary* irresponsible journalism?" (The answer is, of course, "Yes.")

The What-about-Chile note appeared in various places—a letter from the Rev. Paul Oestreicher in *The Times* (6 March 1976) for example. Mr. James Cameron, in an article in *The Guardian* (8 March 1976) took a personal tone, speaking of "Solzhenitsyn, the one-man Armageddon," and "the pop-politics of the Solzhenitsyn show," and saying "I am getting tired of being patronized by Mr. Solzhenitsyn"; "I think Mr. Solzhenitsyn seeks more public engagements as the Prophet-in-Exile"; "He suffered bitterly and cruelly and unjustly at the hands of his countrymen; he would therefore have his countrymen suffer in return." (Perhaps the most gross perversion of Solzhenitsyn's attitudes ever put forward!)

Bernard Levin in *The Times* (19 March 1976) commenting on such commentators, retorted,

> We who have just seen the greatest man now alive, and have found ourselves responding to him immediately and without equivocation, on the level at which he was addressing us...find our mood so misjudged and the measure of the man so signally missed, by most of those who have, so to speak, accidentally been entrusted with the task of speaking for us; it is a precipitate descent indeed to go from Solzhenitsyn's demand for a moral content in politics to the spectacle of such a giant being patronized by Mr. Peter Lennon, instructed in clarity of thought by Mr. Clive James, compared with Ronald Reagan by Mr. Mervyn Jones, and offered suggestions for the improvement of his character by Mr. James Cameron.

and he sums up interestingly that "even as he speaks of external dangers he forces his hearers to look within themselves for the ultimate causes of those dangers, and since that truth is unbearable (like, alas, most truth), the only defence available is the belittlement of the accuser."

In one sense, it may be thought, Mr. Levin is being a little unfair. It is, or so it may be argued, the duty of the intellectual to try to remain aloof, to stand outside, to criticize even the most compelling of moral statements. Still, we might agree that some critics took iconoclasm to inappropriate lengths.

Solzhenitsyn's radio talk, broadcast on March 24th, criticized Western and specifically British faults and weaknesses in a way that aroused far greater resentment in some quarters. He attacked, certainly, in unqualified, even intemperate terms, what he saw as the apathy of this country towards its own liberties and towards the danger of world catastrophe.

Such rhetorical tropes as "Britain's position in the world today is of less significance than that of Rumania, or even Uganda" went down badly with the *Daily Mirror* (25 March 1976) which, in true Jack Moron style, ran a column headed "Solzhenitwit," describing him as "Britain-basher" and refuting him by naming some foreign stars who liked life in Britain; its editorial asked "what does this millionaire Russian exile expect of us, . . . Solzhenitsyn has become the Cold War prophet. . . . The man who wants the West to become a mirror image of Soviet ruthlessness."

The Guardian (25 March 1976) had an article by Mella Pick to the effect that Solzhenitsyn had "developed a special hatred for Britain," and much else in the same tone. (The same paper, on 8 April 1976, quoted Zhores Medvedev, now become hostile to him, as saying "Apart from a few religious fanatics no one thinks of his political views in a positive way," and the *Sunday Times* [28 March 1976] published a hostile article by the other Medvedev twin, the "Leninist" dissident Roy, partially justifying the Soviet experience as against Solzhenitsyn's criticisms.) However, *The Times* (2 April 1976) noted that "All that Solzhenitsyn asks of us is that we should have faith in our own beliefs and in ourselves. That is all he asks, but it still seems to many people to be asking too much"; while the *Daily Telegraph* said, in a leader,

You could call Mr. Solzhenitsyn's reflections on our country and the West an "attack"—our headline yesterday did so. But it is an attack delivered with such obvious reluctance and unmistakable affection, with such anguish and regret, as to cause not the slightest offence but rather deep misgivings and heartsearchings. He speaks of Britain as once "the core, the very pearl of the Western world," giving expression "with particular brilliance" to Western civilisation. This is the peak from which in his view we have fallen. He laments that Britain's voice in the world is no longer heard, "its character gone, its freshness faded . . . British commonsense, so lucid, so universally acknowledged seems to have failed now." He suspects that our strength, our will to defend ourselves has been even more sapped than that of other Western countries. An enemy would rejoice in these symptoms. Not he—his words are part terrible warning, part tender elegy, alas.

He criticises us; with the same love and respect, we may criticise him. Indeed, his expectations of us and the West were touchingly but unreasonably high. They were bound to be disappointed. He justly condemns our frequent failure to act in a morally intelligible way. But is he not sometimes inclined to neglect or undervalue the necessity for prudence, without which moral stances become mere posturing? He chides us for placing at times our own interests first. Would we be justified in criticising, say, a civilised Russian Government for acting always in accordance with enlightened self-interest?

Enough: the recent conduct of our affairs has often been a disgrace, never more so than now. We have been neglectful, guided by no consistent or secure morality, by no prudence or commonsense, the cause of humiliation to ourselves, of grief to our friends and joy in our enemies. We should not be resentful, but most grateful for Mr. Solzhenitsyn's passionate concern about us, and for the courage and candour with which he has expressed it.

And in part it is easy enough to show that, as he put it in the television broadcast, "I am not a critic of the West. I am a critic of the weakness of the West." He and his friends had "looked upon the West as being the sun of freedom, a fortress of the spirit, our hope, our ally." Or, as he had put it in a talk in Paris on April 11, 1975, "it is not your liberty I am criticizing, but the way you surrender that liberty step by step." All this is, of course, relevant to charges that his views were anti-democratic or anti-libertarian.

None of this is to say that Solzhenitsyn's own views, especially on Western internal matters, were sound in every way. Even allowing for the emphasis of rhetoric, the rousing power of the unqualified

statement, which way he thought defensible in prophecy or sermon—
both in themselves perfectly legitimate ways of speaking—it is
not difficult to find errors of detail, exaggerations of fact, and at
least dubious estimates of reality. All the same, it is one thing to
listen smugly to an account of other people's failings, quite another to
have to hear of our own. But it was not in Solzhenitsyn to adjust his
tone to the new material.

Of course, when he spoke of the weakness of the Western political
will, the short-sightedness of Western attitudes in foreign policy, he
antagonised an important interest group. Few others could have
thought his charges *wholly* inaccurate; yet those whom he now made
his antagonists had a disproportionate influence in the media, and
their animus now lay in wait for him.

When he spoke of social ills of the West, of the spoilt attitudes
of the "Me society," he equally antagonized small sections of
"liberal" opinion. More importantly, it was clear that most of his
knowledge in this sphere cannot have been first-hand: and though
that is not exactly a criterion of its validity one way or another, he
could be made to appear to be parlaying his huge general reputation
into a claim to authoritativeness in fields where it was at least less
applicable. When he expressed doubts about the possibility of the
recovery of Western morale, or the persistence of the old values
behind the more unpleasant modern phenomena, he was clearly on
shakier ground yet—as was pointed out even by such devoted supporters as Mr. Bernard Levin, who was asked on BBC Radio: "But is
Solzhenitsyn, perhaps, basing all his judgments on an intellectual
minority in Britain today? Do you feel that the heart of the people . . .
the man in the pub, do you think that he is as lacking in all the virtues
as Solzhenitsyn seems to think he is?" Levin replied:

> No, I don't. And this is what I should like to say to Solzhenitsyn.
> That it is absolutely certain that the heart of the people, as you put it,
> is absolutely as sound as ever it was, and I can tell you this, when I
> have written in the last few weeks about Solzhenitsyn, I have had a
> flood of letters, the theme of which, all the time, has been: 'Thank
> God somebody has said this, somebody has expressed what *we* are
> feeling, rather than these unrepresentative people who command so
> much of the public voices in this country.' Let me read you a short
> excerpt from one of the letters, an absolutely representative letter—I
> have received scores and scores and scores. The writer says: 'Solzhe-
> nitsyn spoke on *Panorama* and somehow the world of communication

has been changed. The power of the little men, our pundits, evapo-
rated. No use their complaining about Solzhenitsyn's pessimism or
ignorance, or lack of subtle understanding of our nuances: we saw the
measure of the man, and we silently and almost unconsciously compared it with the others, and the clear superiority of the one over the
many was as obvious as the difference between day and night.'
    That's the voice of the British people. (*Listener*, 1 April 1976)

Mr. Levin commented elsewhere (*The Times*, 19 March 1976)
on the difference between the popular and the media attitude to
Solzhenitsyn, that the public

> ... understand what he is saying, which is that men who do not value
> freedom, and who divorce it from morality, will not long possess
> it.... Whenever before did *The Listener* (it carried a substantial
> chunk of the interview) have to be reprinted to meet public demand?
> When did *Panorama* serve as such a focus for the feelings of millions
> and such a trigger for their release? When, if it comes to that, did a
> single man, commanding no armies and disposing of no votes, last
> compel the world to listen to him, to take him seriously, and to
> wrestle with the dark angel he has raised among them—an effect
> achieved by nothing other than the force of his character and the iron
> strength of his moral purpose?
>   Never, I think. And what is so heartening is that, clear and bell-
> like above all the febrile jeers and the expressions of incomprehen-
> sion, has come the people's voice. I wrote my own column about
> Solzhenitsyn's interview, and my meeting with him, on the day the
> programme was shown, before I had had any opportunity to gauge
> the reaction of others. Yet it is already clear that I was speaking for
> a vast army in the words with which I concluded, and which I find
> even more apposite for my conclusion today: "Alexander Isayevitch,
> do not despair just yet. We understand."

Further evidence in the same or a similar sense may be found
in the fact that three volumes of *The Gulag Archipelago* became best
sellers in both hard-back and paper-back. The phenomena described
were not, in principle, new to the British reading public. But this time
they had behind them the established prestige of the author; and
secondly they were presented with a vivid authenticity, and a cumu-
lative power, which swept the reading public. (It is not quite the case
that what occurred in France—the effective destruction of the Marx-

ist power in the intellectual world—resulted here. But short of that, the result was unprecedented.)

One might follow the press on the theme of Solzhenitsyn over the ensuing years, but little new would emerge. The two cruxes of his expulsion and his television triumph were focuses of all the views ever to be expressed, and it would serve little purpose to go on from here. All the arguments, reservations, support, slander are covered by the examples we have given above.

What we have examined may, in particular, make us think of what Bernard Levin meant when he said (*The Times*, 19 March 1976),

> It cannot, I think, be healthy for a society to be flawed by a massive gulf between what is felt by those who do not have to offer any public comment and those who are professionally obliged to say something and who, having nothing of their own to say, rummage through the tired fashions of our tired time to find some pat, pert comment with which to sustain in themselves the fading illusion that they are still alive. Yet that is what has just happened in the case of the Solzhenitsyn interview.

Perhaps I may conclude with a comment of my own (*Daily Telegraph*, 17 April 1976):

We are told that Solzhenitsyn does not understand the West. This is belied to quite a fair extent by the nature of some of the attacks on him and his principles, which resemble nothing more than carefully contrived proofs of his allegation that all too many Britons resent being told what it is like out in the cruel hard world. All the same, it is naturally the case that Solzhenitsyn knows less about Britain than he does about Russia. Mr. Bernard Levin has commented on the BBC, I think rightly, that Solzhenitsyn has underestimated the reserves of moral strength in the country; though the mere fact of his addressing us is in itself an appeal to such qualities. But, paradoxically, if he has made our position out to be even worse than it really is, this would be due to his having unavoidably gained most of his impressions from the Press, especially the liberal Press. Indeed, it is surprising that he doesn't go a good deal further in a diagnosis of extreme decadence, if he has relied on most of our self-appointed leaders of opinion.

On his major theme, in any case, the precise degree of decadence we have reached is not really the point. A doctor, a cholera expert, coming here from a cholera-infected country, pointing out that the plague is sweeping eastward, and recommending measures which could protect us, would hardly be thought to have been refuted by someone noting that he had misunderstood a few details about the inefficiency of our Health Service. On the contrary, we would queue to accept his cholera shots, however painful.

Of course there are those who prefer to close their eyes in the hope that danger will go away. And if not, perhaps at least the bearer of uncomfortable news will vanish if one is rude enough to him. But he doesn't seem to, does he?

Notes

1. See Leopold Labedz, ed., *Solzhenitsyn: A Documentary Record* (London: Allen Lane, Penguin Press, 1970).

2. *Ibid.*

Solzhenitsyn's Reception in the United States

JOHN B. DUNLOP

> I have been in the dragon's belly, in its redhot innards. It was unable
> to digest me and threw me up. I have come to you as a witness to what
> it is like there, in the dragon's belly.[1]
>
> —Speech at an AFL-CIO sponsored
> luncheon in July, 1975

In the half decade since his forced departure from the Soviet
Union, Aleksandr Solzhenitsyn has exerted an influence on the political life of America which has perhaps been unequalled by any other
foreigner in the two hundred year history of the United States. This
essay will concentrate on reactions to Solzhenitsyn the public figure
in America and will eschew treatment of responses that are primarily
literary in emphasis, though, and this should be stressed, his writings
have had a singular impact of their own. Each of his major novels was
on the best-seller lists, and nearly three million copies of the first
volume of *The Gulag Archipelago* were sold in the United States.[2]

My aim in this article will be twofold: first, to deal in more or less
chronological fashion with the major landmarks of the "Solzhenitsyn
affair" in America, and, second, to summarize and analyze the
debate over Solzhenitsyn as it simmered and occasionally boiled up
on the pages of the press.

On February 13, 1974, Solzhenitsyn was formally charged with
treason and expelled from the USSR. The same day, Secretary of
State Henry Kissinger said at a press conference that Solzhenitsyn
would be welcome to reside in the United States if he so wished.
In a cautious and somewhat opaque statement, Kissinger continued:

> The United States has always looked with sympathy and appreciation
> at the expression of freedom of thought in all societies. We have
> regretted some of the manifestations that interrupted this. We do not
> know enough about the circumstances of the departure of Mr. Sol-

zhenitsyn and the only problem that we have seen here is the extent
to which our human, moral and critical concern for Mr. Solzhenitsyn
and people of similar convictions should affect the day-to-day conduct
of our foreign policy.[3]

Other nations, including Great Britain, extended similar offers to
the exiled Nobel prizewinner.

As is common knowledge, Solzhenitsyn chose Zurich as his
initial place of residence (he was not to move to the United States
until two years later, during the summer of 1976). Six days after
the writer's arrival in West Germany, Senator Jesse Helms (Republican of North Carolina) introduced a resolution into Congress that
Solzhenitsyn be made an honorary citizen of the United States.
The text of the resolution read: "Resolved by the Senate and the
House of Representatives of the United States of America in Congress assembled. That the President of the United States is hereby
authorized and directed to declare by proclamation that Aleksandr
I. Solzhenitsyn shall be an honorary citizen of the United States
of America."[4] Helms culled his language from the 1963 congressional
resolution which conferred honorary citizenship on Winston Churchill. (The only other instance of such an award was the citizenship
bestowed on the Marquis de Lafayette by the legislatures of Virginia
and Maryland during the period of the Articles of Confederation.)
It is noteworthy that the twenty-four co-sponsors of Senator Helms'
resolution spanned the political spectrum e.g., Bayh of Indiana,
Brock of Tennessee, Dole of Kansas, Hatfield of Oregon, Javits of
New York, Ribicoff of Connecticut, Thurmond of South Carolina.

In a letter to Solzhenitsyn acquainting him with the text of the
resolution, Senator Helms wrote: "Mr. Solzhenitsyn, we are very
glad to see you here with us in the West. You are a citizen of the
world. . . . You would do us an honor if you would visit this country
to meet with the co-sponsors of this resolution. I would like to extend
to you an invitation to come first to my State of North Carolina. . .
and then to Washington to meet with your Senate supporters."[5]
In his reply, dated March 5, Solzhenitsyn expressed warm appreciation for the action of Helms and his colleagues but stated that he was
unable to come to the United States at the present time.[6]

At approximately the same time, two Democratic congressmen,
Benjamin Rosenthal of New York and Donald Fraser of Minnesota,
both members of the House Committee on Foreign Affairs, wrote

the novelist soliciting his views on *détente* and U.S.-Soviet relations. Solzhenitsyn responded with a detailed letter, dated April 3, in which he argued against "pseudo-*détente*" and for a "truly guaranteed *détente*." How, he wondered, can one ascribe "sacramental significance" to the signatures of rulers who have never observed their own constitution? The United States was engaged in making "real concessions" while the Soviet Union was offering "a certain number of smiles." No *détente*, Solzhenitsyn warned, is possible with a country which continually perpetrates "acts of cruelty and brutality" against its own citizens and neighboring peoples, since such actions testify to the true essence of that country.[7]

Also during this period, Solzhenitsyn received an invitation from George Meany, President of the AFL-CIO, to tour the United States as a guest of the powerful labor organization.[8] Solzhenitsyn had to decline this offer, too, for the time being.

As the events just described clearly attest, Solzhenitsyn did not intrude into the political life of the United States. Rather, he was *asked in* by influential members of Congress and by the leader of the American trade union movement. How is one to account for this unusual interest in the opinions of an exiled Russian writer?

Solzhenitsyn's expulsion from the USSR came at a critical point in modern American political life. The trauma of Vietnam was just beginning to recede, while that of Watergate was in full bloom. In addition, the Kissinger-Nixon policy of *détente* with the Soviet Union was coming under increasing fire in the Congress. Solzhenitsyn arrived in the West at a time when a demoralized and somewhat volatile America was groping around for a proper response to a perceived "Soviet threat." The appearance at this juncture of the celebrated Nobel laureate and dissident, who had quite literally put his life on the line in a mesmerizing duel with the Soviet authorities, inevitably attracted the interest of influential Americans, especially those such as Senator Helms and George Meany who had their doubts about *détente* as practiced by Kissinger and Nixon, and those, such as Rep. Fraser, who maintained a strong personal commitment to safeguarding human rights throughout the globe.

Additional testimony concerning the interest aroused by Solzhenitsyn's arrival in the West is provided by the journey which CBS-TV anchorman Walter Cronkite, "the most trusted man in America," made to Zurich to interview the writer on June 17. Under Cronkite's friendly but probing questioning, the novelist elaborated upon his previous criticism of the Western mass media (he champions freedom of the press, but also responsibility of the press), clarified his views on democracy (he is an admirer of decentralized, "noiseless" Swiss democracy), and explained why he felt required to criticize various aspects of the American political system: "...It's untrue that I have not noticed the good sides of American democracy. I have noticed many good sides. But when we converse, or when we speak publicly, are we endlessly to praise one another?"[9] Perhaps loosened up by Cronkite's legendary bonhomie, Solzhenitsyn then offered some fulsome praise on behalf of the United States:

> ...America has won two world wars. America has twice raised Europe up from devastation. And it defended Europe several times from Stalin after the Second World War. For twenty-five years, it constantly stopped the communist onslaught in Asia and defended many countries which would otherwise now be in slavery. That is what the United States has done. And in so doing, it has never asked for repayment of debts, has never placed conditions. That is, it has manifested exceptional generosity, magnanimity, and disinterestedness. And how has the world reacted? What has America received in return? The name of America is everywhere reviled.[10]

During the interview, Solzhenitsyn also prophesied the imminent fall of South Vietnam, an event which did in fact shortly occur.

In the spring of the following year, 1975, Solzhenitsyn decided to accept some of the proferred invitations: he agreed to deliver two addresses to the AFL-CIO, one in Washington and one in New York, and to meet with Senator Helms and other Senate supporters in Washington. This visit to the United States in the late spring and early summer of 1975 initiated a period of extraordinary influence by a foreigner in the political life of America, a period which was to last through the summer of 1976. The trip also served to bring him into direct conflict with the most powerful Secretary of State since John Foster Dulles, Henry Kissinger, the architect of *détente*.

In late June, apprised of Solzhenitsyn's forthcoming arrival in Washington, Kissinger, through his executive assistant George Springsteen, sent the following memorandum to President Ford's National Security Advisor, Brent Scowcroft. Due to the unusual importance of this document, the text is quoted here in full:

George Meany has invited the President to attend a June 30 banquet in honor of Solzhenitsyn, which will be an occasion for outspoken anti-Soviet rhetoric. The Soviets would probably take White House participation in this affair as either a deliberate negative signal or a sign of Administration weakness in the face of domestic anti-Soviet pressures. We recommend that the invitation to the President be declined and that no White House officials participate.

During Solzhenitsyn's Washington visit (June 27-July 1) another problem may arise: Pressure may be generated by Meany, members of Congress or others for the President to receive Solzhenitsyn in the White House. He is a Nobel Prize Winner, he is widely admired in the United States and the Senate has passed a resolution granting him honorary United States citizenship (if the House follows suit he would be the only person except Churchill so honored). Advocates of a meeting would argue that the President has received a whole range of Soviet visitors ranging from journalists and trans-polar fliers to the Minister of the Food Industry. They would ask: since the White House doors are open to Soviets of this sort, why not also to Solzhenitsyn, the most admired of all Russians? The arguments against such a meeting are as compelling as those against accepting the banquet invitation, but more difficult to defend publicly.

Solzhenitsyn is a notable writer, but his political views are an embarrassment even to his fellow dissidents. Not only would a meeting with the President offend the Soviets but it would raise some controversy about Solzhenitsyn's views of the United States and its allies (as expressed, for example, in the attached *New York Times* article). Further, Solzhenitsyn has never before been received by a Chief of State and such a meeting would lend weight to his political views as opposed to his literary talent.

We recommend that the President not receive Solzhenitsyn. If significant pressures develop which make it imperative that the White House do something for Solzhenitsyn, we would suggest inviting him to any large social function taking place at the White House while he is in town, or arranging for him to be at a social function attended by the President during that period.[11]

The text of this memorandum was eventually "leaked," much to Secretary Kissinger's displeasure, one may be sure, to George Meany, who made it public in testimony before the Senate Foreign Relations Committee in December, 1975.[12] "So there it is in black and white," Meany commented gruffly to the senators, "We didn't want to offend the Commissars—so we spit in the face of the man our State Department refers to, perhaps sarcastically, as 'the most admired of all Russians.' And—most incredible of all—we must not give the Soviets a sign of weakness. Weakness in standing up to the Soviets? No, weakness in standing up to the *anti*-Soviets at home.''[13] To Meany's angry but generally apt words one might add that the memorandum implicitly conveys an intention to thwart the Senate's effort to make Solzhenitsyn an honorary American citizen.

Presumably acting on Kissinger's advice, Ford turned down the AFL-CIO's invitation to attend the June 30 banquet and also resisted an offer from Senators Helms and Strom Thurmond to meet with the writer. Ford's ''snub'' of Solzhenitsyn, as it soon came to be called, became national news and generated immense negative publicity for the President.[14] Almost five hundred letters and telegrams were received by the White House concerning the incident, not one of them supporting Ford's action. The President was also subjected to severe and uncomplimentary attacks in the press and Congress. To take a representative day, on July 11, the *Washington Post* carried a column by George Will opening with the words, ''The United States government may have to expel Aleksandr Solzhenitsyn from the republic, not only as a hands-across-the-barbed-wire gesture of solidarity with its *détente* partner, the Soviet government, but also to save the president and his attendants from nervous breakdowns,'' and concluding, ''*Détente* has conferred upon Brezhnev veto over the appointments calendar of the President of the United States.'' The same day Senator Ernest Hollings, terming Ford's sidestepping of Solzhenitsyn an ''embarrassment'' to the United States, introduced a resolution that the writer be invited to address a joint session of Congress.[15]

Under such unsparing and virtually uniform criticism, the White House decided to backtrack. It seems to have begun to make indirect approaches to Solzhenitsyn as early as July 12, and on the 15th no fewer than four attempts were made through intermediaries to arrange a meeting. By this time, however, Solzhenitsyn had become uninterested in an encounter which promised to have a purely cosmetic character.[16]

During his news briefings, Ron Nessen, Ford's press secretary, attempted to justify the President's failure to meet with Solzhenitsyn, first by citing his crowded schedule and then by asserting that Ford preferred meetings of ''substance.'' Since Ford had just met with the famous soccer player, Pelé, this latter explanation elicited mirth on the part of the press. As Bill Moyers was to write in *Newsweek:* "Pelé, the soccer player, had just been there to be photographed with the President. So had other athletes, beauty queens, celebrities and assorted hustlers and cause pushers. But to this literary giant whose cause is freedom, the President said no . . . "[17]

On July 16, at a press conference in Milwaukee, Kissinger, under some pressure from reporters, was induced to admit that he personally counselled the President not to see Solzhenitsyn because the "symbolic effect" of such a meeting would have been disadvantageous to United States foreign policy.[18] Kissinger's admission unleased new criticism at his and the President's expense.[19] Summing up the entire unhappy episode, one columnist, Anthony Lewis, wrote: "The decision not to invite Aleksandr Solzhenitsyn to the White House has been deplored by now from all points of the ideological compass. For sheer political ineptitude it was in a special class. . . . Men will remember and read Aleksandr Solzhenitsyn when Gerald Ford is a footnote to history . . . . "[20]

In subsequent years, both Ford and Kissinger came, at least publicly, to regard the "snub" as an error. In February, 1977, while a visiting Chubb Fellow at Yale, Ford told a history class that it was "regrettable" that he had failed to invite Solzhenitsyn to the White House. He then proceeded somewhat to obfuscate matters by maintaining that the decision had been not so much a "policy problem" as a "logistics problem."[21] Ford's assertion flies in the face of the evidence, which points to the decision's having been precisely one of policy, taken on the advice of Secretary Kissinger.

As for Kissinger, he permitted his confidant, conservative columnist William Buckley, to reveal in the late summer of 1976 that he now considered his judgment to.have been "defective" in recommending that President Ford snub the novelist.[22] Kissinger's disclosure was probably at least in part intended for conservative Republican consumption, in light of the approaching presidential election.

Let us now return to the June 30 AFL-CIO banquet, held at the Washington Hilton. On this occasion, Solzhenitsyn addressed an audience of 2,500, which, despite Kissinger's wishes, included two cabinet officers, Secretary of Defense Schlesinger and Secretary of Labor Dunlop, as well as Daniel P. Moynihan, Ambassador to the United Nations.[23] Absent, on the other hand, was one of Solzhenitsyn's staunchest supporters, Senator Helms, who was not given an invitation since he is not regarded as a "friend of labor."[24] Another conservative supporter, Senator James Buckley of New York, received an invitation only after Solzhenitsyn's intercession.[25]

In his introductory remarks, George Meany said:

> ...today, in this grave hour in human history, when the forces arrayed against the free spirit of man are more powerful, brutal, and more lethal than ever before, the single figure who has raised highest the flame of liberty heads no state, commands no army, and leads no movement that our eyes can see.... We heed this voice, not because it speaks for the left or the right or for any faction, but because it hurls truth and courage into the teeth of total power when it would be so much easier and more comfortable to submit and embrace the lies by which that power lives....

And he concluded: "We need echoes of his [Solzhenitsyn's] voice. We need to hear the echoes in the White House. We need to hear the echoes in the Congress and in the State Department and in the universities and in the media, and...in the United Nations."[26]

In his address, Solzhenitsyn warned a largely approving audience of the perils contained in the policy of *détente* as currently practiced. "Today," he warned, "they don't say, 'We are going to bury you,' now they say '*Détente*.' Nothing has changed in communist ideology. The goals are the same as they were...."[27] The essential purpose of Solzhenitsyn's speech was to alert his listeners to the expanding communist menace. "From our experience," he asserted, "I can tell you that only firmness makes it possible to withstand the assaults of communist totalitarianism. History offers many examples... You, in 1948, defended Berlin only by your firmness of spirit, and there was no world conflict. In Korea in 1950 you stood up to the communists, only by your firmness, and there was no world conflict. In 1962 you forced the missiles to be removed from Cuba. Again it was only firmness, and there was no world conflict."[28] By hearkening back to the principled decisiveness of two Democratic presidents, Truman and Kennedy, Solzhenitsyn sought to waken his audience from a trance induced by the Vietnam tragedy.

As in his earlier comments to Walter Cronkite, Solzhenitsyn was profuse in his praise of the United States, though he also stressed the magnitude of America's world responsibility:

> The United States has long shown itself to be the most magnanimous,

the most generous country in the world. Wherever there is a flood, an earthquake, a fire, a natural disaster, an epidemic, who is the first to help? The United States. Who helps the most and unselfishly? The United States. And what do we hear in reply? Reproaches, curses, 'Yankee Go Home.' ...But none of this takes the load off America's shoulders. Whether you like it or not, the course of history has made you the leaders of the world. Your country can no longer think provincially.[29]

And Solzhenitsyn ended his address with a plea: "Ordinary working men of America...do not let yourselves become weak."[30]

On July 9, Solzhenitsyn delivered a second speech at a luncheon in his honor, hosted by the AFL-CIO in New York. One thousand guests were in attendance. In his introductory remarks, Lane Kirkland, then Secretary-Treasurer of the AFL-CIO, proclaimed: "He [Solzhenitsyn] stands as a living, monumental reproach to all those statesmen and leaders who today raise the practice of abstention on basic moral issues to the level of high national policy..."[31] During his one-and-a-half hour speech, Solzhenitsyn stressed the "unscientific" and specious nature of Marxism-Leninism, as well as its lethalness, and renewed his attack on pseudo-*détente*. "The Cold War—the war of hatred," he underlined, "is still going on, but only on the communist side."[32] America, he admonished, must "pay a tax" for the freedom it enjoys: you cannot love freedom for yourselves alone..."[33]

Reaction in the press to Solzhenitsyn's two AFL-CIO addresses was mixed, tending toward the negative. "Americans who hearken to his [Solzhenitsyn's] message," cautioned Joseph Kraft, "are at least half-looking for the simple answers of the cold war."[34] Columnist Peter Lisagor dissented from the novelist's message in cruder fashion: "Solzhenitsyn sang for his supper, all right, to the delight of Meany and every other unrequited cold warrior in the vast ballroom...."[35] But some, such as Roscoe Drummond, writing in the *Christian Science Monitor*, supported what Solzhenitsyn had to say: "His [Solzhenitsyn's] guiding premise is that firmness in dealing with the communists is least likely to lead to war; that weakness and one-sided concessions are the road to war."[36] And one of the numerous readers who chose to write in to the *Washington Post* echoing support for the writer reflected: "We all laugh at Solzhenitsyn's simpleness when he expounds upon the evils of communism, forgetting that Solzhenitsyn is, if anything, overly educated in communism, and is therefore not simple, but *wise*—wiser than Joseph Kraft will ever be—and has much good counsel for us . . ."[37] It will be noted that Solzhenitsyn's supporters put the stress on the reality and danger of Soviet expansionism, while his detractors emphasized the pitfalls of an over-reaction to that threat.

On July 13, Solzhenitsyn was interviewed on NBC-TV's "Meet the Press" program.[38] The panelists—Peter Lisagor of the *Chicago Daily News*, Norman Cousins, editor of *Saturday Review*, and Hedrick Smith of *The New York Times*—were all to varying degrees hostile to the novelist's message. Lisagor had, as we have seen, already flayed Solzhenitsyn in a column appearing on July 5;[39] Cousins was shortly to author two highly critical assessments of the writer's thought;[40] and Hedrick Smith would write disparagingly of him in his book, *The Russians*, which was published in 1976.[41] One wonders why NBC chose to assemble such a one-sided panel. The episode obviously did not serve to better Solzhenitsyn's opinion of the American media.

Whatever the antipathy toward Solzhenitsyn in the press, the Congress continued to exhibit an unflagging interest in his views. On July 15, he addressed an audience of 70-80 congressmen at a reception in his honor held in the Senate Caucus Room. The meeting was sponsored by twenty-five senators representing a variety of political views: e.g., Henry Jackson, Frank Church, John Glenn, Hubert Humphrey, Adlai E. Stevenson, Richard Stone, Clifford Case, James Buckley, Ted Stevens. In his invitation asking Solzhenitsyn to address the congressmen, Senator Jackson had written:

> As elected representatives of the American people, we would like to convey their admiration and respect and our own for your literary work and your courageous support for human rights. For the people of the United States . . . your devotion to individual liberty has been particularly stirring. It would be an honor for us to express to you personally . . . our appreciation for the way your efforts have enriched the life and fortified the spirit of all freedom-loving peoples.[42]

"Your country," Solzhenitsyn told the assembled congressmen, "has just recently passed through the extended ordeal of Vietnam, which exhausted and divided your country. I can say with certainty that this ordeal was the least of a long chain of similar trials which awaits you in the near future."[43] At the conclusion of his remarks, the members of Congress lined up to shake Solzhenitsyn's hand, and a few collected his autograph.[44]

In early October, the Senate unanimously adopted Senator Helms' resolution to confer honorary citizenship on Solzhenitsyn.[45] The resolution then went to the House Committee on the Judiciary for its recommendation. It was at this point that the State Department stepped in to block the initiative. On December 17, Robert McCloskey, the Department's Assistant Secretary for Congressional Relations, wrote the chairman of the Judiciary Committee, Peter Rodino, strongly recommending against the resolution, which was being sponsored in the House by Rep. Larry McDonald of Georgia. In his letter, McCloskey noted that only one foreigner, Winston Churchill, had been so honored previously, whereas there had been many persons around the globe whose courage had served to inspire Americans. The Nobel Prize was "an appropriate confirmation of his [Solzhenitsyn's] exceptional place among exceptional men and women of letters." Churchill and Lafayette, on the other hand, had manifested a "commitment to aid and affect America's destiny," while "there is no evidence that Solzhenitsyn...has made such a commitment or even desires to do so."[46] (In light of the two AFL-CIO speeches, this statement is singularly disingenuous.)

House supporters of the resolution were understandably furious. Rep. McDonald wondered acidly how Churchill's devotion to the American way of life jibed with his being "a fervent monarchist."[47] But McCloskey's letter (and, presumably, some behind-the-scenes maneuvering) proved effective, and the resolution "died" in the Committee on the Judiciary, a result which prompted Senator Helms to fulminate the following August: "I am ashamed that the Judiciary Committee of the House of Representatives, under Democrat Chairman Peter Rodino, has deliberately stalled the proposal to pay America's respects to this great citizen of the world."[48]

The defeat of the resolution on honorary citizenship was an important victory for Secretary of State Kissinger against the best known critic of *détente*. Earlier in the same month of December, however, Solzhenitsyn had drawn some blood of his own when he published his essay "Schlesinger and Kissinger" in *The New York Times*.[49] This polemic represented Solzhenitsyn's first explicit attack on Kissinger. Angered over the dismissal of Secretary of Defense James Schlesinger, "a man of steadfast, perceptive and brilliant mind," who, in Solzhenitsyn's opinion, had exemplified firmness in the face of communist expansion, the novelist alluded to rumors that Kissinger had Schlesinger removed. "Defending his policy of unending concessions," Solzhenitsyn wrote, "Kissinger repeats the one and same argument almost like an incantation: 'Let our critics point out the alternative to nuclear war!'" Solzhenitsyn mocked Kissinger's "celebrated Vietnam agreement" and bemoaned his failure to understand that peace must be the opposite of violence and coercion, not simply of war.

The important election year of 1976, which was also to be America's bicentennial, dawned, and Solzhenitsyn, though living in Switzerland, continued to play a signficant role in American political life. On March 25, William Buckley showed Michael Charlton's March 1 BBC interview with Solzhenitsyn on his public television program "Firing Line."[50] Though broadcast, at least in some areas, in an inauspicious time slot—Channel 13 in New York scheduled it for six p.m. on a Saturday[51]—the program nevertheless managed to create quite a stir (in Britain, it had been raptly watched by twenty million viewers). As Benjamin Stein wrote in *The Wall Street Journal*: "...I have never seen anyone on television express so strongly the abhorrence of the Soviet communist system, its fundamental evil, and the danger it poses to the West....the Solzhenitsyn interview is one of the most important pieces of TV journalism ever, and is spellbinding besides."[52]

In April, Republican presidential hopeful Ronald Reagan went on record as stating that Solzhenitsyn "would be welcome to eat dinner anytime at the Reagan White House."[53]

At approximately the same time, Solzhenitsyn, unable to find the privacy he desired in Zurich, and undoubtedly motivated by other considerations as well, decided to move to the United States. In June, he applied for a permanent United States resident visa, which was quickly granted by the immigration authorities, and in August he officially moved to a fifty-acre tract of land in Cavendish, Vermont.[54]

During the same month of August, Solzhenitsyn's name was very much on the tongues of the drafters of the Republican platform meeting in Kansas City. (A Solzhenitsyn plank had been "quietly rejected" by the Democratic drafting committee the previous month.[55]) A heated fight reportedly broke out between the Ford and Reagan forces over whether to include a Solzhenitsyn plank in the Republican platform. Ford eventually backed down rather than risk a divisive floor fight over the issue, a decision which is said to have greatly angered Secretary Kissinger, causing him to threaten to resign.[56] (Here, once again, one sees the intense opposition of Kissinger the policy maker to any mention of the Soviet Union's most noted dissenter, showing that the thinking behind the "Ford snub" remained operative one year after that fiasco.) The text of the Solzhenitsyn plank which was adopted reads: "We recognize and commend that great beacon of human courage and morality, Aleksandr Solzhenitsyn, for his compelling message that we must face the world with no illusions about the nature of tyranny. Ours will be a foreign policy that keeps this ever in mind."[57]

Solzhenitsyn's name also cropped up twice at the convention itself. "...listen," exhorted John Connally on August 17, "to one of the world's great spokesmen for freedom. Listen to what Aleksandr Solzhenitsyn says about freedom in the United States. He says of us... 'You have the impression that democracies can last. But democracies are islands in an immense river of history...and the water is always rising.'"[58] And in his speech seconding the nomination of Ronald Reagan for president, Senator Jesse Helms repeatedly invoked the writer's name:

> When Solzhenitsyn visited me in Washington last year, he said: 'Cannot your people perceive the advancing tide of communism? Can they not somehow be led to act, before it is too late?' History will remind future generations that welcoming the wisdom of just one Solzhenitsyn would have been far more important to the survival of freedom in the world than a thousand-mile procession of soccer players, monarchs, diplomats, politicians, and entertainers who seem unwilling to understand the threat of totalitarianism—let alone to restrain it.
>
> Logic tells us, now, that we will ignore the warnings of Solzhenitsyn at our own peril—and at the peril of generations to come....[59]

The Reagan forces, of course, went down to defeat at the 1976 convention, and President Ford subsequently lost a close election to the former governor of Georgia, Jimmy Carter. One might speculate about how much the Kissinger-Ford "snubs" of Solzhenitsyn cost Ford in political terms. Certainly their cold-shouldering of the writer served to dampen the enthusiasm for Ford among the Reagan forces, thereby to some extent lessening their willingness to work energetically during the election campaign. Not unmindful of this

Just for you...

You can request your own

lesson on how to use the

library's computer catalog.

Learn how to find books,

videos, tapes, and CDs,

as well as current articles

from magazines and journals

danger, Secretary of State Kissinger seems to have tried to send a signal to such persons through his conservative friend William Buckley. "Henry Kissinger," Buckley wrote in a column appearing on September 2:

> shortly after Gerald Ford became President, sat down to read a chapter or two from *Gulag Archipelago*, having up until then read only Solzhenitsyn's *Cancer Ward*. He found the book so engrossing, he ended by reading it all. He then read through *Ivan Denisovich*, and *First Circle*. He then took *Gulag* to President Ford with the recommendation that he read it. One does not know whether Mr. Ford did so.[60]

During his campaign, Jimmy Carter, undoubtedly aware of strong anti-Solzhenitsyn sentiment in the ranks of liberal Democrats, shied away from mentioning the novelist. Once elected, however, he appears to have seriously entertained the idea of a meeting with Solzhenitsyn. Thus when Rep. Malcom Mabry of Mississippi, a Republican follower of Reagan still smarting over the Ford "snub," wrote Carter suggesting an invitation to the writer, Carter replied: "I do intend to meet with Mr. Solzhenitsyn (no time set). Thank you."[61] And at a press conference in February, 1977, Carter scored Ford's and Kissinger's failure to invite Solzhenitsyn to the White House.[62] However, apparently due to political considerations, Carter never did get around to extending an invitation.

Throughout 1977 and the first half of 1978, Solzhenitsyn remained ensconced in south central Vermont, working on his multi-volume historical novel. Then came the unexpected announcement that he would deliver the commencement address at Harvard University on June 8, 1978. Solzhenitsyn at Harvard! A media event of the first magnitude, one would have thought, but the commercial television networks thought otherwise, and the address was broadcast on public television. On that commencement day an estimated 15,000-20,000 guests sat through the rain and drizzle to hear some extremely frank comments on the state of the West. Press reaction to Solzhenitsyn's speech was prompt and intense. In terms of publicity, only the "Ford snub" three years previously came close to rivalling this episode.

In his address, Solzhenitsyn took off the gloves in speaking to his largely liberal establishment audience. Gone were the balancing comments concerning America's generosity and magnanimity and past "firmness" which had characterized the AFL-CIO addresses. "The Western world," Solzhenitsyn began, "has lost its civic courage..."[63] Why? Because of its narrowly legalistic mentality ("...a society with no other scale but the legal one is less than worthy of man."[64]); because of a press which "miseducates" public opinion and fails to provide the in-depth analysis which society needs; and because of its numbing popular culture ("...TV stupor...intolerable music"[65]). But primarily because of its loss of religious faith, a process which has been ongoing since the Renaissance, and which has found "political expression" since the Enlightenment.[66] Echoing a theme elaborated in much of Dostoevskii's writings, Solzhenitsyn scored the spiritual consequences of anthropocentricity. In its irreligion and materialism, the West draws close to the communist East, but in competition between these two societies, the wavering, flaccid West must inevitably succumb. "Humanism which has lost its Christian heritage cannot prevail in this competition."[67]

For this bold airing of his views, Solzhenitsyn was pounded unmercifully in the press. As he later complained: "I had not expected it [the press] to be so unreceptive to criticism: I was called a fanatic, a man possessed, a mind split apart, a cynic, a vindictive warmonger; I was even simply told to 'get out of the country'..."[68] The fallout continued throughout the summer of 1978, and then gradually abated.

Solzhenitsyn surfaced once again, briefly, in the spring of 1980, when he published a lengthy indictment of America's policies vis-à-vis the Soviet Union in *Foreign Affairs*. In the article, he appeared in particular to be exercised by the widely held belief in the West that there is "an indissoluble link between the universal disease of communism and the country where it first seized control—Russia."[69] Solzhenitsyn also focused on the important issue of *how* the United States forms its opinions of the USSR (a subject which he had earlier broached in an address at the Hoover Institution in May, 1976), discussing the often unhelpful role of American scholars, diplomats, and foreign correspondents, and of recent émigrés from the Soviet Union.[70] He likewise pointed to major failings in the Russian-language broadcasts of the Voice of America. Implicitly referring to Kissinger's recent neo-conservative public statements, he also spoke ironically of what he called the "Kissinger syndrome":

I will note here a tendency which might be called the 'Kissinger syndrome,' although it is by no means peculiar to him alone. Such individuals, while holding high office, pursue a policy of appeasement and capitulation, which sooner or later will cost the West many years and many lives, but immediately upon retirement the scales fall from their eyes and they begin to advocate firmness and resolution. How can this be? What caused the change? Enlightenment just doesn't come that suddenly! Might we not assume that they were well aware of the real state of affairs all along, but simply drifted with the political tide, clinging to their posts?[71]

Before passing on to a discussion of the debate over Solzhenitsyn in the American press, I should like to deal briefly with several questions concerning the depth of Solzhenitsyn's knowledge of the United States which are often raised by critics. In 1978, former Librarian of Congress Archibald MacLeish complained in comments solicited by *Time* magazine apropos of the Harvard speech: "He [Solzhenitsyn] sees few Americans, speaks little English, and what he knows of the Republic he knows not from human witnesses but from television programs... If Solzhenitsyn had talked to us—to a few of his neighbors in that village in Vermont...—he would not have spoken those sentences at Harvard."[72] As far as I am aware, Solzhenitsyn's English is quite serviceable, and he seldom if ever watches American television (as he told Walter Cronkite in 1974, he keeps up with events by listening to Russian-language short-wave broadcasts, as he did when living in the USSR[73]). Were MacLeish a reader of the *Black River Tribune* (Ludlow, Vermont), he would have learned of the writer's unannounced appearance before a town meeting of two hundred Cavendish citizens in 1977, during which he apologized for the fence on his property. "I ask both categories of people [hunters and snowmobile drivers]," he said, "to forgive me..."[74] The fence, he explained, was necessary to keep out curiosity-seekers, who pestered him unceasingly when he lived in Zurich, hindering the progress of his work. He went on to explain that he had chosen Cavendish as a place to live because he favored the countryside with its simplicity of human relations. And he continued: "And I like the climate with the long winter and snow which reminds me of home." When he had concluded his remarks, his neighbors gave him a "boisterous, standing ovation."

In the late spring of 1977, a reporter for the *Christian Science Monitor* traveled to Cavendish and learned that Town Manager Quentin Phelan had recently spent an hour and a half chatting with

Solzhenitsyn, during which "...Solzhenitsyn asked many questions about local government."[75] The *Monitor* account also reported that Solzhenitsyn had had dinner with Vermont's lone congressman, James Jeffords, and that "a friendship is fast developing." "We are proud he [Solzhenitsyn] chose our town to find what peace he can," said one Cavendish resident, "The word 'affection' is not too strong to describe the way they feel about him here."[76] In a July, 1978 interview with Hilton Kramer, Arts Editor of *The New York Times*, Solzhenitsyn spoke of his Cavendish neighbors as "wonderful people who have been very helpful and kind to us."[77] Clearly, Archibald MacLeish's criticism of the writer is rather wide of the mark.

A related charge—one, like MacLeish's, rooted in a kind of populism—concerns Solzhenitsyn's alleged ignorance of the American countryside, of the "real" America. "If he could get on a Greyhound bus," the *Christian Science Monitor* wistfully editorialized, "and take himself unobtrusively across the country, brushing up against grass-roots Americans, he might find a great deal less 'moral poverty' than he now believes is there."[78] One must conclude that the *Monitor* editors are not familiar with Solzhenitsyn's AFL-CIO speeches. "I have traveled enough," he told his audience

> through the different states of your country and its various regions to have become convinced that the American heartland is healthy, strong and broad in its outlook.... Yet, when one travels in your country and sees your free and independent life, all the dangers which I talked about today seem imaginary. I've talked to people, and I see this is so. In your wide-open spaces even I get a little infected, the dangers seem somehow unreal.[79]

During the period 1975-1976, Solzhenitsyn made two trips across the American continent. The first, preceding his AFL-CIO addresses, took him to Alaska, Oregon, California, the Middle West, the Virginia countryside, and Washington and New York. In Alaska, he conversed with simple fishermen and with Orthodox Christian Indians, who inducted him into their clan.[80] He was impressed with the "firmness and strength" which he encountered in the Middle West,[81] and in the Washington area, he visited the historic sites connected with the nation's beginnings. The following summer, i.e., in 1976, he and his wife drove from Palo Alto, California, to Vermont, a trip which became known when Natal'ia Solzhenitsyn picked up a speeding ticket in Kansas.[82] Thus, while he has not traveled about on a Grey-hound bus, Solzhenitsyn has seen a goodly share of the country and has made contact with "grass-roots" America. The problem, how-ever, as Solzhenitsyn seems to see it, is that the healthy elements in the United States have little influence over the way the country is run.

A third criticism which is sometimes made concerns the degree of Solzhenitsyn's understanding of the theoretical underpinnings of American democracy. In a sharp attack on the writer, Norman Cousins wrote that, before criticizing America's institutions, Solzhe-nitsyn should "familiarize himself with the central ideas that have gone into the making of the United States," and he counseled him, in particular, to read the writings of Jefferson, Franklin, Thomas Paine, and John Adams.[83]

I am not aware of the extent to which Solzhenitsyn has studied the writings of the Founding Fathers, but as both the AFL-CIO and Harvard speeches attest, he clearly has at least some familiarity with this subject. "Let me remind you," he told his AFL-CIO lis-teners at one point, "that the great Washington did not agree to recognize the French convention because of its savagery."[84] (This in contrast with Franklin D. Roosevelt who bestowed recognition on the USSR in 1933.) And elsewhere he observed to his labor audience: "It makes one think that the men who created your country never lost sight of their moral bearings. They did not laugh at the absolute nature of the concepts of 'good' and 'evil.' Their practical policies were checked against that moral compass."[85] He returned to this theme in a more philosophical key in his Harvard address:

> ...in early democracies, as in American democracy at the time of
> its birth, all individual human rights were granted on the ground that
> man is God's creature. That is, freedom was given to the individual
> conditionally, in the assumption of his constant religious responsi-
> bility. Such was the heritage of the preceding one thousand years.[86]

Obviously, Solzhenitsyn has done some study of the Founding Fathers and their thought.

The debate over Solzhenitsyn in the American press took on an ever more sharply defined ideological cast in the period 1974-1980. Liberals, whom we shall discuss first, had begun to have doubts concerning Solzhenitsyn even before he was forcibly exiled in early

1974. The publication of *August 1914*, which appeared in English translation in 1972, alarmed such writers as Mary McCarthy and the late Philip Rahv with its religious and nationalist sentiments.[87] The real watershed for liberals, however, was probably Solzhenitsyn's "Letter to the Soviet Leaders," which was published a month after the writer came to the West. As Harry Schwartz wrote in *Saturday Review/World*:

> For over a decade now Western liberals and conservatives have debated uneasily about which camp could legitimately claim Aleksandr Solzhenitsyn as its own... Now all doubt has been resolved. In his "Letter to the Soviet Leaders"...the greatest living Russian writer removes all ambiguity. In the strict sense of the word, he is a reactionary, a proud throwback to the nineteenth-century Russian Slavophiles... No one who reads this letter attentively can doubt that if Solzhenitsyn had been an American citizen in 1972 he would have voted for Richard Nixon against George McGovern...[88]

And in a *Newsweek* article, entitled "For God and Mother Russia," Richard Boeth observed: "Whether the West will pout because one of its leading ideological heroes has turned out to be a nonpolitical holy fool is yet to be seen. But whatever else he is, Solzhenitsyn is the most unblushing poet-lover-priest of Mother Russia since Tolstoi himself..."[89]

Liberals, it soon became clear, were worried by Solzhenitsyn's critique of American democracy—a situation which put them in the unfamiliar role of "patriots"—as well as by his effort to curb Soviet expansionism, which for them raised the specter of a new "cold war." And they were concerned over his program for a renewed Russia, particularly its religious and "authoritarian" aspects. A lengthy editorial, "The Obsession of Solzhenitsyn," which appeared in *The New York Times* following the writer's Harvard address in 1978, represents a kind of summa of the liberal indictment against Solzhenitsyn. "Yes," *The Times* wrote:

> our laws are used by the rich and the powerful to gain more wealth and power; our press is often irresponsible; television is a swamp of nonsense; pornography does flourish; and, yes, the nation is in thrall to material things. But given all that, Mr. Solzhenitsyn's world view

seems to us far more dangerous than the easygoing spirit which he finds so exasperating.[90]

The Times went on to explain why:

> The argument he [Solzhenitsyn] raises is not new; it goes back to the beginnings of the Republic and has never disappeared. At bottom, it is the argument between the religious Enthusiasts, sure of their relationship to the Divine Will, and the men of the Enlightenment, trusting in the rationality of humankind.
>
> Although Mr. Solzhenitsyn comes out of a very different tradition, he has this in common with the Enthusiasts: he believes himself to be in possession of the Truth and so sees error wherever he looks... The trouble is, of course, that life in a society run by zealots like Mr. Solzhenitsyn is bound to be uncomfortable for those who do not share his vision or ascribe to his beliefs...

Moving on to Solzhenitsyn's criticism of *détente*, *The Times* cautioned:

> As to this country's relations with the communist states, we fear that Mr. Solzhenitsyn does the world no favor by calling up a holy war... Much as we have been instructed and inspired by Mr. Solzhenitsyn, his willingness to set aside all other values in the crusade against communism bespeaks an obsession that we are happy to forgo in this nation's leaders.

And *The Times* reminded its readers of the "terrible damage, to others and ourselves," resulting from the American involvement in Vietnam.

For *The Times* and the liberal establishment for which it presumes to speak, Solzhenitsyn represents an irrational and potentially dangerous man ("religious Enthusiast," "zealot," "holy war," "obsession") who foolishly dares to criticize the inherent good sense of the American system, a legacy of the Enlightenment. *The Times* rejects Solzhenitsyn and his message *in toto*.

A number of other liberal commentators have voiced similar views. Solzhenitsyn's ideal, warned Arthur Schlesinger, Jr., "has nothing to do with liberal democracy... His ideal is a Christian

authoritarianism governed by God-fearing despots without the bene-
fit of politics, parties, undue intellectual freedom or undue concern
for popular happiness."[91] He sounds "rather like General Le May on
Vietnam, like *Pravda* on American pornography and like Spiro T.
Agnew on the American press."[92] Having invoked these bugbears,
Schlesinger then went on to note that Solzhenitsyn's message is
"close to that of the Puritan divines who once preached in Harvard
Yard."[93]

Hans Morgenthau sternly questioned Solzhenitsyn's competence
as a political philosopher. The American legal system, he underlined,
"is based upon, and permeated by, moral principles..."[94] And in
his column, "A Russian at Harvard," James Reston, while appearing
to agree with certain of Solzhenitsyn's strictures against materialism,
"TV stupor," and the press, excoriated the writer for his views on
Vietnam:

> He [Solzhenitsyn] suggests that it was the spiritual bankruptcy and
> physical cowardice of the United States that led to what he calls 'the
> hasty Vietnam capitulation.' Hasty? After a generation of slaughter?
> Lack of courage? It was precisely because the American people still
> heard some echoes of their spiritual heritage and belief in the sanctity
> of human life that they rose up against the genocide that Mr. Solzhe-
> nitsyn condemns.[95]

At times, some liberal columnists were wont to take the low road,
proclaiming that Solzhenitsyn was a sham, devoid of literary talent.
Thus Jimmy Breslin: "...I came up with only two [literary people]
who claimed to have waded through any of Solzhenitsyn's last few
books. They did not do it for the simple reason that it can't be
done."[96] *Boston Globe* columnist Mike Barnicle put it more crudely
still: "...it has been common knowledge for some time now that the
Russian [i.e., Solzhenitsyn] was incapable of writing his way out
of a paper bag."[97] To such aspiring literary critics, one might cite the
words of John Leonard, formerly editor of the *New York Times Book
Review*: "...Solzhenitsyn is not a Evtushenko, a hula-hoop... The
person who wrote *One Day in the Life of Ivan Denisovich*, *Cancer
Ward*, and especially, *The First Circle* belongs in the first rank of the
world's writers, period."[98]

In addition to assailing Solzhenitsyn in the press, American liberals have also attempted to ignore him, as writer Tom Wolfe charged
in an article appearing in *Harper's* in 1976:

Solzhenitsyn's tour of the United States last year [i.e., 1975] was like an enormous funeral procession that no one wanted to see. The White House wanted no part of him. The *New York Times* sought to bury his two major speeches, and only the moral pressure of a lone *Times* writer, Hilton Kramer, brought them any appreciable coverage at all. The major television networks declined to run the Solzhenitsyn interview that created such a stir in England earlier this year (it ran on some of the educational channels).

And the literary world in general ignored him completely. In the huge unseen coffin that Solzhenitsyn towed behind him were not only the souls of the *zeks* who died in the Archipelago. No, the heartless bastard had also chucked in one of the last great visions: the intellectual as the Stainless Steel Socialist glistening against the bone heap of capitalism in its final, brutal, fascist phase. There was a bone heap, all right, and it was grisly beyond belief, but socialism had created it.[99]

Self-styled moderates, including the so-called "Ford wing" of the Republican Party, generally agreed with the liberals in rejecting Solzhenitsyn's views on *détente*. A good summary of their criticisms was provided by Secretary of State Kissinger at his July 16, 1975 Milwaukee press conference. "...if I understand the message of Solzhenitsyn," Kissinger stated on that occasion, it is not only that *détente* is a threat, "but that the United States should pursue an aggressive policy to overthrow the Soviet Union." Which prompted him to conclude: "...if his [Solzhenitsyn's] views became the national policy of the United States, we would be in a period—we would be confronting a considerable threat of military conflict."[100]

Conservatives, on the other hand, tend to be favorably inclined both toward Solzhenitsyn and his message. If they disagree with certain of his strictures, they appear willing to forgive all in light of his articulate exposure of Soviet expansionist intentions. In the Democratic Party, such conservatives appear to be in the minority; in the Republican Party, the conservatives are in the ascendancy.

Republican conservatives in Congress have frequently lent strong support to Solzhenitsyn's interpretations of Soviet aims. Thus Representative Jack Kemp of New York: "Realities have not changed through *détente*. The Soviet hierarchy remains an instrument of oppression. It still remains a means through which subversion of free societies is fostered throughout the world. By marked contrast

Aleksandr Solzhenitsyn offers a voice of freedom and hope."[101] Former senator James Buckley put it this way: "Aleksandr Solzhenitsyn's message...is simply this: Do not let the policy of *détente* deceive you into believing that the Soviet Union has relented in the slightest in the long-term determination to overthrow the West, the United States included. Do not, through your trade, provide the Soviet tyranny with the tools with which to tighten its repression of the Soviet Union and of the satellite nations...."[102] Thus, while liberals see Solzhenitsyn as calling up an *offensive* "holy war" against the USSR, conservatives see him summoning the West to *defend* itself against ongoing and increasing communist expansionism. The two perceptions could hardly be more dissimilar.

Conservative columnists have, in the main, been highly supportive of Solzhenitsyn. Patrick J. Buchanan, for example, wrote this concerning the Harvard address:

> Hard words for Harvard Yard. But are they not true? Did not the best and the brightest crack in the cauldron of Vietnam? Did not the anti-war movement contribute mightily to the communist victory and thus, directly, to its horrid consequences?[103]

And Buchanan continues: "Our material splendor does indeed co-exist with moral squalor. Our prosperity and freedom have produced a society awash in violence, eroticism, and crime." Which leads him to conclude: "Aleksandr Solzhenitsyn is...a prophet sent to the West as a final warning that unless its ways are altered, the end is not far distant."

Another conservative columnist, George Will, chose to disagree with *The New York Times* editorial, "The Obsession of Solzhenitsyn," discussed previously. "*The New York Times*," he wrote, "whose specious skepticism extends to all values except its own, considers Solzhenitsyn dangerous and a zealot because he believes himself to be in possession of the truth. The *Times* wishes he were more like the American founders who, the *Times* forgets, committed treason and waged an eight-year war on behalf of the truth they considered self-evident."[104] Solzhenitsyn's ideas on the essential political problem of the era are, Will notes, "broadly congruent with the ideas of Cicero and other ancients, and those of Augustine, Aquinas, Richard Hooker, Pascal, Thomas More, Burke, Hegel, and others."

Wills' sentiments were seconded by Michael Novak, writing in the *Washington Post*: "He [Solzhenitsyn] learned that criticizing the American people for their hedonism is for liberals only. It's all right for James Reston and the editors of the *New York Times* to look down blue noses at hoi polloi. It is not right for a foreigner who is a 'religious Enthusiast.' (This is how the editors of the *Times* tried to demean him.)"[105]

One of the most attentive Solzhenitsyn-watchers has been columnist William Buckley, who has called the novelist "...the outstanding human figure of the century,"[106] and "the noblest man alive."[107] A friend of Henry Kissinger as well as an admirer of Solzhenitsyn, Buckley several times attempted to mediate between the two adversaries on the pages of his columns. "What Kissinger says," he pointed out, presumably alluding to private conversations with the diplomat, "isn't, 'We must have *détente* because the alternative is a nuclear war.' What he says is 'The American people (by which he means the American Establishment) will not stand up and resist. Under the circumstances, the only alternative is to maneuver.'" Buckley then offered his own opinion: "I agree with Solzhenitsyn, not Kissinger, that the American people if roused will do better than they have done."[108] Buckley believes that the "Ford snub" was not a matter of defective judgment, as Kissinger claims, but of defective policy: "You cannot fete the most eloquent critic of the Soviet Union while carrying on *détente* with the Soviet Union. It is, simply, a matter of incompatible policies."[109]

Buckley is one of the few commentators to have noted that Solzhenitsyn cannot easily be placed within the American political spectrum. Responding to an attack on Solzhenitsyn by the editors of *Newsweek*, he recalled the writer's criticism, made during one of his AFL-CIO speeches, of "the burning greed for profit" which has led Western businessmen to prop up the USSR's faltering economy. "Far right talk," Buckley chortled, "to the editors of *Newsweek*..."[110] Solzhenitsyn speaks of the decadence of Western society, but so do *The New York Review of Books*, Noam Chomsky and Herbert Marcuse. As for *Newsweek*'s charge that Solzhenitsyn glorifies rural life, Buckley reminds the magazine's editors that Thomas Jefferson, "the founder of the Democratic Party," did so as well.

Before concluding this survey of the debate over Solzhenitsyn, one might mention that Solzhenitsyn is admired by many American

Catholics and Protestants, who particularly appreciate his conversion from fervent Marxism-Leninism to the Christian faith. In a comment solicited by *Time* magazine, Theodore Hesburgh, the president of Notre Dame University, spoke warmly of the "ageless" spiritual themes contained in the Harvard speech,[111] while evangelist Billy Graham cited his name approvingly during a crusade in Europe.[112]

What can one conclude concerning the "Solzhenitsyn affair" as it has unfolded in the U.S.? While it is still too early to evaluate the over-all impact of Solzhenitsyn, I can offer the following observations. The issue which most clearly separates Solzhenitsyn's admirers from his detractors is his view of how the United States should deal with the Soviet Union. As historians of U.S.-Soviet relations have shown, such a domestic debate over Soviet intentions is hardly new; differences of opinion emerged following the Bolshevik coup in 1917 and were sharpened during, and particularly after, the Second World War. While serving as Secretary of State, Henry Kissinger, for example, seems to have believed that Solzhenitsyn's perception of the USSR represented a threat to world peace. A number of Solzhenitsyn's supporters, on the other hand, see him as a prophet rallying a demoralized and dispirited America to meet a growing Soviet challenge. Solzhenitsyn insists that all he wants is for the West to regain the steadfastness with which it thwarted previous Soviet adventures in Berlin, Korea, and Cuba. For the Kremlin, he stresses, *détente* is not a policy but a tactic; the regime's goals, fueled by Marxist-Leninist ideology, remain as malign as ever. Modern totalitarianism, when unchecked on its own soil, has a natural tendency to expand abroad.

For myself, I tend to agree with Solzhenitsyn (and such recent exiles as Andrei Amal'rik and Vladimir Bukovskii) that the Soviet threat is real and growing. I concur with the writer's view that only firmness will impress the Soviet leadership, and that such steadfastness, rather than leading to a nuclear war, will be a pledge of peace and stability in the future.

In addition to being depicted as a latter-day cold warrior, Solzhenitsyn has often been accused of being enamored of the past and of being a "Slav mystic." Those who, on the basis of a misreading of "Letter to the Soviet Leaders," believe that Solzhenitsyn wants a return to a pastoral never-never-land have not succeeded in grasping his thought. A physicist and mathematician by training, with a strong interest in cybernetics, Solzhenitsyn has a healthy respect for the capabilities of modern technology. What he wants is a modern civilization shorn of as many of its unsavory traits as possible—pollution, urban blight, etc.—not a return to primordial bliss. As for the novelist's promotion of a return to Russian Orthodoxy, those who find this absurd are perhaps unacquainted with the religious renaissance which has been taking place for over two decades in the Soviet Union.

Similarly, those who together with Kissinger's former high-ranking assistant Winston Lord, consider Solzhenitsyn "just about a Fascist,"[113] have failed to understand his programmatic views concerning Russia's future. Solzhenitsyn believes, correctly in my opinion, that it would be exceptionally dangerous for present-day Soviet Russia to move in unprepared fashion from despotism to American-style democracy. This does not mean, as he has repeatedly made clear, that he opposes democracy as a form of government. Likewise, critics of "Letter to the Soviet Leaders" often forget that the letter really was addressed to the leaders of the USSR, i.e., was meant as a pragmatic attempt to turn today's tyranny into a moral social order.

Solzhenitsyn's ideas may seem bizarre, perhaps even frightening, in New York or San Francisco, but in Soviet Russia his attempts, and those of his co-contributors to the collection *From Under the Rubble* (1974), to find a "third way" between the extremes of Western capitalism and Eastern communism enjoy considerable support. It is simply a fact that far more Soviet citizens think like Solzhenitsyn than like Andrei Sakharov or Roy Medvedev.[114] The novelist fits securely within the mainstream of a major ideational current known variously as "neo-Slavophilism" or the "Russian national and religious renaissance." In a number of recent publications, I have argued that Russian nationalism is the ideology most likely to replace an increasingly discredited Marxism-Leninism as the ruling ideology of the Soviet Union.[115] Part of the reason that Solzhenitsyn's views are distorted and, at times, caricatured in the press lies in the nearly total ignorance concerning neo-Slavophilism among many journalists reporting on the USSR.

A related point: it is risky at best to attempt to peg Solzhenitsyn within the American political spectrum. I would hazard a guess that in certain spheres Solzhenitsyn's thought is close to that of conservative liberals, such as the AFL-CIO leadership, and of Republican "neo-conservatives" in that he advocates a strong national defense while favoring "people-oriented" reforms on the domestic scene.

But would such persons agree with his radical ecological views and espousal of a "zero-growth" economy? Hardly. The fact remains that Solzhenitsyn is *outside* the American political spectrum—any attempt to evaluate him in American political terms is inevitably distorting.

Up to this point, I have concentrated upon misrepresentations of Solzhenitsyn's views. To be fair, I should add that the novelist has upon occasion harmed his own chances of getting a hearing. The problem is one of style: the vigor with which he presses an argument and the unqualified certainty of his tone runs counter to the prevailing manner of dealing with issues. Furthermore, though he may be wrong on details, he is frequently right concerning the essence of a problem. Solzhenitsyn's understanding of America is usually less distorted than America's understanding of him.

To conclude, Solzhenitsyn is an important guest in the United States—not simply because he is a very gifted writer but, more significantly, because he represents a major, potentially dominant current of thought and sentiment in the Soviet Union. He is, in fact, an *ambassador* of that current. My suggestion would be that we give him a hearing, attempting not to caricature his words and always bearing in mind that he does not fit within the American political spectrum. This does not mean that we should deem him above criticism or make him a cult figure, but it does imply a willingness to listen.

Notes

The author would like to acknowledge the generous bibliographical assistance which he has received from professors Alexis Klimoff of Vassar College and Michael Nicholson of Oxford University. Professor Klimoff and Mr. Duncan Clark, LL.B., kindly read through the manuscript and made a number of useful suggestions. The final responsibility for the text is, of course, mine alone.

1. Alexander Solzhenitsyn, *Warning to the West* (New York: Farrar, Straus and Girous, 1976), p. 53.

2. *Time*, 28 July 1975, p. 41.

3. *International Herald Tribune*, 14 February 1974.

4. Senator Jesse Helms, "Honorary Citizenship for Solzhenitsyn," *East Europe*, July, 1974, p. 5.

5. *Ibid.*, p. 3.

6. *Ibid.*, pp. 2-3. The Russian text of Solzhenitsyn's letter is on p. 4.

7. Text available from the House Committee on Foreign Affairs. For the Russian original, see *Russkaia mysl'*, 23 May 1974, p. 2.

8. *New York Times*, 15 March 1974, p. 12.

9. A. Solzhenitsyn, *Mir i nasilie* (Frankfurt/Main: Possev Verlag, 1974), pp. 91-92. For an English transcript of the broadcast, see *Congressional Record-Senate*, 27 June 1974.

10. *Ibid.*, pp. 92-93.

11. *Statement of George Meany, President, American Federation of Labor and Congress of Industrial Organizations Before the Senate Foreign Relations Committee on Foreign Policy Choices for the 1970's and 80's, December 8, 1975*, pp. 5-6.

12. *New York Times*, 9 December 1975.

13. *Statement of George Meany*, p. 6. Meany italics.

14. The following is a condensed version of a summary of this episode which I published as part of my article "Solzhenitsyn in Exile," *Survey*, 21, No. 3 (1975), pp. 133-154.

15. *New York Times*, "Notes on People," 12 July 1975. Hollings' resolution eventually "died."

16. *New York Times*, 18 July 1975, and Rowland Evans and Robert Novak, "Snub and Countersnub," *New York Post*, 19 July 1975.

17. *Newsweek*, 28 July 1975, p. 72.

18. *New York Times*, 17 July 1975, p. 10, and *The Times* (London), 17 July 1975, p. 5.

19. E.g., the editorial in *The New York Times*, 24 July 1975, and David S. Broder, "Kissinger's Advice on Solzhenitsyn," *Washington Post*, 23 July 1975.

20. "Life Without Dreams," *International Herald Tribune*, 5 August 1975, p. 4.

21. *New York Times*, 8 February 1977, p. 1, and *Time*, 21 February 1977, p. 45.

22. William F. Buckley, "Some Points Concerning Solzhenitsyn," *International Herald Tribune*, 2 September 1976. Reprinted in *National Review*, 15 October 1976, pp. 1140-1141.

23. *New York Times*, 10 July 1975, p. 31.

24. *Ibid.*

25. William F. Buckley, "On the Right," *National Review*, 15 August 1975, p. 900.

26. *Warning to the West*, pp. 3-6.

27. *Ibid.*, p. 14.

28. *Ibid.*, p. 42.

29. *Ibid.*, p. 27.

30. *Ibid.*, p. 50.

31. *Ibid.*, pp. 51-52.

32. *Ibid.*, p. 87.

33. *Ibid.*, p. 72.

34. *Washington Post*, 3 July 1975.

35. *New York Post*, 5 July 1975.

36. *Christian Science Monitor*, 23 July 1973.

37. Letter of Kristen E. Carpenter. *Washington Post*, 12 July 1975, p. A11. Italics in original.

38. See Norman Cousins, "Brief Encounter with A. Solzhenitsyn," *Saturday Review*, 23 August 1975, pp. 4-6.

39. *New York Post*, 5 July 1975.

40. See the item mentioned in note 38, and his column in the *Christian Science Monitor*, 21 June 1978.

41. Hedrick Smith, *The Russians* (New York: Quadrangle, 1976), pp. 417-438.

42. *Congressional Record-Senate*, 16 July 1975, p. S12715.

43. *Warning to the West*, p. 94.

44. *Washington Post*, 16 July 1975.

45. *New York Times*, 5 October 1975.

46. *Daily Telegraph* (London), 18 December 1975, p. 1. It is curious that this incident was reported in the British press only.

47. *Ibid.*

48. *Statement of Senator Jesse Helms (R-NC) Seconding to the Nomination of Ronald Reagan to be the Republican Presidential Candidate for 1976. Kansas City, Missouri, August 18, 1976*, p. 1.

49. *New York Times*, 1 December 1975.

50. For a transcript of this interview, see *Warning to the West*, pp. 99-122.

51. *New York Times*, 25 March 1976, p. 63.

52. *Wall Street Journal*, 26 March 1976.

53. *New York Post*, 12 April 1976.

54. *New York Times*, 9 September 1976, p. 50.

55. Robert Evans and Rowland Novak, "The Hostility Toward Solzhenitsyn," *Washington Post*, 2 September 1976, p. A15.

56. *Ibid.*

57. *Text of 1976 Republican Platform*.

58. *Remarks of Honorable John B. Connally Before the Republican National Convention*, p. 12.

59. *Statement of Senator Jesse Helms* . . . , pp. 1-2.

60. *International Herald Tribune*, 2 September 1976. Reprinted in *National Review*, 15 October 1976, p. 1140.

61. Rowland Evans and Robert Novak, "Carter and Solzhenitsyn," *Washington Post*, 5 February 1977, p. A13.

62. *New York Times*, 9 February 1977, p. A16.

63. Aleksandr I. Solzhenitsyn, *A World Split Apart* (New York: Harper and Row, 1978), p. 9. This volume is now out of print. For an available version, see Aleksandr I. Solzhenitsyn, *East and West* (New York: Harper and Row, 1980), pp. 37-71. For a useful collection of responses to the Harvard address, see Ronald Berman, ed., *Solzhenitsyn at Harvard* (Washington, D.C.: Ethics and Public Policy Center, 1980).

64. *A World Split Apart*, p. 17.

65. *Ibid.*, p. 37.

66. *Ibid.*, p. 47.

67. *Ibid.*, p. 55.

68. Aleksandr Solzhenitsyn, "Misconceptions about Russia Are a Threat to America," *Foreign Affairs*, Spring, 1980, p. 830. Book edition: *The Mortal Danger: How Misconceptions about Russia Imperil America* (New York: Harper and Row, 1980).

69. *Ibid.*, p. 797. See also Solzhenitsyn's essay on communism in *Time*, 18 February 1980, pp. 48-49.

70. See Solzhenitsyn's "Remarks at the Hoover Institution, May 24, 1976," *The Russian Review*, 36, No. 2 (1977), pp. 184-189.

71. Solzhenitsyn, "Misconceptions . . . ," pp. 806-807.

72. *Time*, 26 June 1978, p. 35.

73. *Mir i nasilie*, p. 56.

74. *Black River Tribune*, 2 March 1977.

75. *Christian Science Monitor*, 20 June 1977.

76. *Ibid.*

77. *New York Times Book Review*, 2 July 1978, p. 14.

78. *Christian Science Monitor*, 12 June 1978.

79. *Warning to the West*, p. 81.

80. *Novoe russkoe slovo* (New York), 5 June 1975.

81. *New York Times*, 10 July 1975, p. 31.

82. *New York Times*, 14 July 1976, p. 43.

83. *Christian Science Monitor*, 21 June 1978.

84. *Warning to the West*, p. 18.

85. *Ibid.*, p. 80.

86. *A World Split Apart*, pp. 49-51.

87. See their contributions to John B. Dunlop, Richard Haugh, and Alexis Klimoff, eds., *Aleksandr Solzhenitsyn: Critical Essays and Documentary Materials*, 2nd ed. (New York, 1975).

88. Harry Schwartz, 'Solzhenitsyn Without Stereotype," *Saturday Review/World*, 20 April 1974, p. 24.

89. *Newsweek*, 18 March 1974, p. 122.

90. *New York Times*, 13 June 1978, p. A18.

91. "The Solzhenitsyn We Refuse to See," *Washington Post* (Sunday *Outlook* section), 25 June 1978, p. D1.

92. *Ibid.*

93. *Ibid.*

94. *New Leader*, 3 July 1978, p. 12.

95. *New York Times*, 11 June 1978, p. E21.

96. "Solzhenitsyn and the Rubes," *Boston Globe*, 23 July 1975, p. 15.

97. "A Fancy Con Job at Harvard," *Boston Globe*, 9 June 1978.

98. "Solzhenitsyn as a Media Creature," *New York Times Book Review*, 3 March 1974, p. 39.

99. Tom Wolfe, "The Intelligent Co-ed's Guide to America," *Harper's*, July, 1976, p. 34.

100. "Kissinger Sees Perils in Solzhenitsyn's Views," *New York Times*, 17 July 1975, p. 10.

101. *Congressional Record-House*, 8 July 1975.

102. *Congressional Record-Senate*, 16 July 1975.

103. *The Philadelphia Enquirer*, 18 June 1978.

104. *Washington Post*, 18 June 1978.

105. *Washington Post*, 21 June 1978.

106. *National Review*, 23 January 1976, p. 53.

107. *National Review*, 15 October 1976, p. 1141.

108. *National Review*, 23 January 1976, p. 53.

109. *National Review*, 15 October 1976, p. 1141.

110. *New York Post*, 31 July 1975.

111. *Time*, 26 June 1978, p. 34.

112. *International Herald Tribune*, 4 August 1975.

113. Rowland Evans and Robert Novak, "The Hostility Toward Solzhenitsyn," *Washington Post*, 2 September 1976, p. A15.

114. As evidence, one could cite the fifty-million-member Russian Orthodox Church

or the All-Russian Society for the Preservation of Historical and Cultural Monuments, a voluntary organization with fourteen million members.

115. E.g., the concluding chapter of my book *The New Russian Revolutionaries* (Belmont, Mass.: Nordland, 1976). See also *The Faces of Contemporary Russian Nationalism* (Princeton: Princeton University Press, 1983).

Solzhenitsyn in the West German Press Since 1974

BIRGIT MEYER

Publicity surrounding the hitherto secret documentary work *The Gulag Archipelago* by the Nobel Prize-winning Soviet author Aleksandr Solzhenitsyn unleashed a violent controversy at the beginning of 1974, and this was directly reflected in the political press of the Federal Republic of Germany. Since 1974, the name of this critic of the Soviet system has become synonymous with a whole range of problems, far exceeding those immediately affecting his person, and in this sense we are justified in speaking of a "Solzhenitsyn affair." In the first five years of his exile, the debate over the Solzhenitsyn affair tended to be concerned less with its actual news value, than with mirroring the warring political attitudes in the Federal Republic towards East-West confrontation.[1] The present essay will consider the course and extent of this crystallization process and the way in which political opinions shifted over the five-year period. The aim is to bring out the social and political substance of the various arguments and their relative significance, to elucidate and contrast individual attitudes toward Solzhenitsyn (from acclaim to antagonism), and to show how such attitudes evolved. It follows that the history of Solzhenitsyn's reception in the West German press from 1974 to 1979 is simultaneously a history of the domestic political tensions and controversies arising from the Federal Republic's *Ostpolitik*.

Solzhenitsyn's charges against Stalin and the Soviet system became an immediate bone of contention. In early 1974 the first volume of *Gulag* was enthusiastically greeted in some quarters and rejected in others, even before anyone had had an opportunity to read it. Enthusiasm was displayed by those who are ever on the lookout for abuses in Eastern Europe which might be used as ammunition against the Soviet Union, while tending towards a correspondingly more lenient view of the failings of the West. Negative reactions came from those who are wont to dismiss any criticism of the Soviet

Union as "capitalist rabble-rousing," yet are all the more swift to pillory the sins of the capitalist West. The discussion acquired further, and more distinctly political, dimensions in February 1974, following the Soviet authorities' action in expelling Solzhenitsyn from his homeland, and this date forms the starting point of the present survey.

In tracing the history of Solzhenitsyn's reception, we will draw upon utterances in the West German press which were prompted by his person, his family, his activities in the West, his speeches in exile, and the works which were published here: the three volumes of *The Gulag Archipelago*, *The Oak and the Calf*, and *Lenin in Zurich*. The first part of the essay describes the materials on which the study is based and the political positions reflected therein. This is followed by an analysis, with illustrations, of how the press went about reporting on Solzhenitsyn. The main strands in his reception are brought out and followed chronologically. The third section clarifies and comments upon the analysis, while the last attempts an evaluation and draws certain conclusions of a more broadly political nature.

I

By and large, each political standpoint in the Federal Republic of Germany has its corresponding organ, and these publications may be divided, at least as far as the reception of Solzhenitsyn is concerned, into four groups. Among the various gradations in the political and publishing scene in Germany, we can distinguish a liberal Center and the twin extremes of a conservative Right and a marxist Left. Each of these groupings in its turn may be variously subdivided. Upon closer scrutiny, the Left is seen to break down into an orthodox, pro-Soviet faction, politically geared to the German Communist Party (DKP), and an unorthodox or neo-marxist faction, which is critical of the Soviet Union and has no party affiliation. Similarly, West Germany's conservatives fall into two groups: an extreme Right which still stands in the traditions of Nazism, and a moderate Right which seeks to distance itself from Nazism and Communism alike. The newspapers of the radical Right responded with an aggressive and predictable uniformity which precludes serious discussion; accordingly, it is only the moderate Right which will figure in the following pages as representative of the conservatives. In terms of party affiliation, this would be the position taken by the national-liberal and Church-oriented tendency within the CDU/CSU (Christian Democratic Union/Christian Social Union). The liberal position is here conceived in very broad terms and may be identified with that of the "Center" in general. Within the political spectrum of the German Federal Republic, liberals are taken to be those who disassociate themselves from strict conservatives, on the one hand, and from marxists, on the other, while advocating the most far-reaching reforms within the bounds of the existing system. Their numbers are not confined to formal membership of the FDP (Free Democratic Party), but include reformist elements within the CDU as well as those Social Democrats who, over the last decade, have remained aloof from the ideas of the emerging "New Left." This division largely coincides with the groups' own assessment of their standpoints, as expressed during the debate over Solzhenitsyn. Each of these group interests and attitudes, which we have reduced to four broad political positions, has at its disposal specific publications in which it regularly finds expression.

West Germany's national conservative newspapers include the dailies, *Die Welt* and the *Frankfurter Allgemeine Zeitung*, and the major weeklies, *Welt am Sonntag, Deutsche Zeitung, Christ und Welt*, and the *Rheinischer Merkur*. The *Frankfurter Allgemeine Zeitung* may be assigned to the liberals, since in its discussion of the Solzhenitsyn affair it opened its pages to a range of political opinions from reformist to progressive. The liberal voices offer the widest variety of viewpoints and express them in numerous newspapers and political magazines. Those examined here include the dailies, *Süddeutsche Zeitung* and the *Frankfurter Rundschau*, together with the weekly newspaper, *Die Zeit* and the political magazines, *Der Spiegel* and *Stern*.

As for the groups which are defined more in terms of party adherence than of that broader world view and intellectual perspective which we saw in the case of the conservatives and liberals, they are represented in the following publications: the DKP daily, *Unsere Zeit*, the "Antifascist Weekly *Die Tat*," and the magazine, *Kürbiskern*. The various publications associated with the position of the "New Left" are those which encourage critical voices in general, such as the political magazines *Konkret, Sprit* (later renamed *das da*), *Pardon*, and *Der Spiegel*, the newspaper of the SPD (German Social-Democratic Party), *Vorwärts*, and the daily *Frankfurter Rundschau*.

II

1. The Conservatives

The conservative newspapers of the Bundesrepublik—and especially *Die Welt*, which for reasons of space will here be examined as a representative example—were already displaying by the early 1970s three significant and clearly developed tendencies in their reports on Solzhenitsyn. First of all, they paid particular attention to Solzhenitsyn in their articles on Soviet dissidents, an explicable preference, for they were able to demonstrate that Solzhenitsyn had certain conservative traits in common with them. In these reports, Solzhenitsyn is commended to the immoral West as a moral authority worthy of emulation, an accolade which includes his political testimony, directed as it is against the USSR. *Die Welt* praises the courage with which Solzhenitsyn "seeks the truth and proclaims it out loud in a land where objective reporting is viewed as treasonable subjectivity, to be fought against and punished as a criminal offense" (2 February 1974). In attempting to classify Solzhenitsyn politically, *Die Welt* furnishes him with epithets appropriate to the newspaper's own self-image: "conservative," "Christian," and "anti-Revolutionary." At the same time, it emphasizes that Solzhenitsyn is in no wise to be thought of as "right-wing," "reactionary," or "anti-national." "For as non-communist he is a Christian, and as Christian he is a Russian patriot" (3 April 1974).

Other descriptions of Solzhenitsyn as a "towering literary figure," an "heroic champion of civil rights," an "exemplary Christian," and "non-marxist conservative" abound on the pages of *Die Welt* and clearly define the newspaper's own concept of excellence. Solzhenitsyn thus comes to symbolize *Die Welt's* own political values. Both the author and the newspaper portray themselves as entrusted with a kind of higher mission: an unfinished opus, in Solzhenitsyn's case, and a moral role as "custodian" of conservative values, in the case of *Die Welt*. And in both cases a pessimistic attitude towards the state of Western culture is matched by an unyielding anti-socialist critique of the Soviet system.

Secondly, Solzhenitsyn stands, in the eyes of *Die Welt*, for all those values whose decline in the West is deplored by conservatives.

Die Welt sees him not merely as a writer, but as "a moral force, (...) something unfathomable in purely political terms" (16 February 1974). As early as 1970 *Die Welt* had stressed the social and moral task which a writer must face: "The Nobel Prize characterizes (...) the writer's position (...): freedom from society, and hence for society; rebellion, even where rebellion is doomed; patriotic adherence to the truth; mistrust of prescribed articles of faith; and primacy of conscience" (15 October 1970). Solzhenitsyn is consistently depicted as guardian of a Russian tradition reaching back to Tolstoi, the social and religious voice of the Russian peasantry, and to Dostoevskii, the epitome of literary greatness and suffering humanity. The writers most frequently mentioned in the same breath as Solzhenitsyn for their exhortations to a moral and political *volte-face* are Siniavskii, Daniel' and Maksimov: "It has long been apparent that it is from the land where you live, and from people such as you that Hope comes, a Hope which goes beyond the ephemeral concerns of the day" ("Open Letter to Aleksandr Solzhenitsyn," 23 September 1972).

A third characteristic feature of conservative reporting of the Solzhenitsyn affair is *Die Welt*'s long-standing practice of locating such items in its *political* section, rather than following the example of other newspapers, which continued to write about him in the pages of their cultural supplements. Even before 1974, *Die Welt* never fails to regard Solzhenitsyn as, at least in part, a political writer, bearing political witness, albeit in literary form, to the lawlessness and brutality of Soviet socialism. His moral integrity implicitly guarantees the quality of his political judgement. "Not only does Solzhenitsyn the man offer hope to the whole of mankind (...) but as a writer (...) he also holds out hope for literature, which, by following his example, could once again become worthy of its finest epithet—the adjective 'dangerous'!" (27 January 1974).

In his expulsion from the Soviet Union *Die Welt* sees its own consistent portrayal of Solzhenitsyn as a political phenomenon amply confirmed: "Here the writer is silent, here the accuser's voice is heard!" (5 January 1974). The paper stresses the documentary character of *The Gulag Archipelago* and the independence of its author: "Solzhenitsyn accuses—communism. Its brutality. Its utter disregard for human dignity. Its ruthlessness. Its omnipotent despotism. This documentary settles accounts with the communist terror system" (5 January 1974). New arguments enter the picture at this point, arguments of importance for *Die Welt*'s overall treatment of Solzhenitsyn. Having made him out to be intimately familiar with the Soviet system, the newspaper goes on to cast him in the role of supreme judge. *Gulag* is seen as the final showdown, and the position it takes up as a *ne plus ultra*. Solzhenitsyn's portrait, as sketched by *Die Welt*, is that of a stern champion of liberty and justice, a hero of our time. To the conservatives he embodies the highest values of the individual in a bourgeois society, representing "the selflessness of the volunteer," "the ethics of the individual," and "the patriotism of a loving heart" (27 January 1974). At the same time, the moral force of his judgement is built up to the point where this analysis becomes unassailable.

No less explicit is *Die Welt*'s anti-communist posture. It speaks of the communist "system of terror and repression," which no man can fail to reject. Unprecedented in its vehemence and clarity is the position which the newspaper adopts, on the occasion of Solzhenitsyn's expulsion, towards Soviet communism, socialism, and the entire intellectual legacy of marxism. In the debate over Solzhenitsyn, all the social systems of communist lands are starkly contrasted with their non-communist counterparts; any transition between them is impossible, and one side (that of the communist states) poses a constant threat to the very survival of the other. World socialism or marxism is presented not only as an external, but also as an inner menace to all non-communist states:

> The worldwide triumph of fanaticism and ideological delusion, which marxists in East and West so jubilantly prophesy, will not come, and Solzhenitsyn will have contributed more to its collapse and to the victory of freedom and human dignity than any man alive and any man before him. (21 January 1974)

Solzhenitsyn's moral warnings are offered as political insights into the ultimate impossibility of realizing the communist idea. *Die Welt* identifies itself with his anti-socialist position (clearly expressed in his "Letter to the Soviet Leaders" of 1974). *Die Welt* directs its polemics against marxism, communism and Soviet socialism, tending to equate the terms and use them interchangeably. Any criticism of the USSR is fashioned into an attack upon socialism and socialist thought as a whole. At the same time, the newspaper uses Solzhenitsyn in its attempts to refute socialists of whatever hue, "all these obfuscating advocates of the third way (. . .) who maintain that one can mix elements of Western social order with a dash of communism and end up with the Promised Land of true socialism'' (21 November 1974).

It follows that attacks upon pro-socialist, left-oriented West German intellectuals should become a further feature of the debate surrounding Solzhenitsyn in the first years of his exile. *Die Welt* uses Solzhenitsyn's words to bolster and morally fortify its own criticism of left-leaning intellectuals. "For quite some time now our trend-setting leftist intellectuals (. . .) have been wondering just what to do with this Solzhenitsyn character (. . .). Now the European Left is becoming decidedly uneasy about him" (21 November 1974). *Die Welt* gives its readers the impression that solidarity with Solzhenitsyn in effect guarantees the survival of Western freedom, and links the survival of such values with the survival of the group it represents, the "conservatives" and "non-marxists" of the Bundesrepublik. "The help which Russian dissidents afford to us non-marxists [is] exceedingly important for the survival in this country of political freedom and freedom of public expression" (23 March 1974).

The conservatives frequently emphasize the commanding position occupied by Leftists in the cultural and political arenas. In so doing, they dramatize the role of the conservatives as that of a threatened minority. On this basis, *Die Welt* elaborates a community of interests between Soviet dissidents and West German conservatives: "In the intellectual life of the West today, these new arrivals from the Soviet Union offer the most substantial counterbalance to the hitherto dominant leftist trend" (3 April 1974). In the eyes of *Die Welt*, the main threat to political freedom comes from West German intellectuals and social democratic writers. Its principal targets are the authors Heinrich Böll (not easy to assail ever since Solzhenitsyn was his guest in February 1974, but frequently attacked for all that) and Günter Grass. They are dismissed as "official hypermoralists" (6 February 1974), and Grass, in particular, as "government spokesman for the intellectual Left" (17 February 1974).

By stressing the need for Soviet dissidents and the Springer Press (which controls *Die Welt*) to create a common front against marxists in East and West, the newspaper reveals its fundamental intellectual motivation: a criticism of socialist ideas, sustained by a pessimistic, critical attitude towards the state of Western culture. Simultaneously, *Die Welt* introduces a simplistic division into friends and foes which marks its whole treatment of the Solzhenitsyn affair. Two steps are involved: the first is to insinuate that the rulers of the USSR and representatives of the West German Left share essentially the same political objectives. "The result attained by our reformists would not differ substantially from what Russia's dissidents are risking life and liberty to resist"(23 March 1974). The second is to conclude, on the basis of this alleged identity of political aims, that Soviet dissidents and West German leftist intellectuals can have nothing in common. "The legend of an intellectual opposition in East and West is (. . .) reduced to a pile of ashes" (17 October 1974).

At the end of 1974 an argument arose over the new Russian émigré journal, *Kontinent*, which was to be published by the Ullstein publishing house, a subsidiary of the Springer-Concern. This served as the occasion for a sharp attack upon the West German Left. In an "Open Letter", Günter Grass reproaches Solzhenitsyn and Siniavskii with "playing into the hands of an empire (. . .) whose reactionary intolerance reflects the same mentality, with ideological variants, as that which roused you to protest and resistance in the Soviet Union" (10 October 1974). Siniavskii, in his reply, did not beat about the bush: "without going into the affairs of this 'Concern,' (. . .) I should like to point out that [it] has yet to execute a single writer, or send him to a concentration camp. Your comparison of the 'Springer group' with (. . .) the ruling state system for the destruction of dissidents is disgraceful" (12 October 1974). *Die Welt* comments at length on the controversy and is vehement in its criticism of the entire "intellectual Left," a blanket term covering literary figures, philosophers, students and scholars. The intellectuals, as "Fifth Estate," are alleged to have been preaching "preceptorial violence" (27 October 1974) for years. Socialist attitudes are condemned as "heresy" and "under the sway of the Eastern myth." Whereas the intellectuals of Eastern Europe have, since 1968, "learned in the hard school of reality," those in the West still suffer from the same "crazy notions." "Reality could teach them nothing, for they have never made contact with it" (17 October 1974). West German leftists are lumped together indiscriminately, with no account taken of their political background, arguments and goals. Their criticisms are dismissed as "unjustified bellyaching," as "the political dabbling of pseudo-esthetes," and as "sheer love of negation." "As the persecuted revolutionaries, which they longed to be but were not, they had, vampire-like, to suck the blood of the living, to bask in the radiance of martyrdom which fell from their friends in the East" (17 October 1974).

Central to the entire debate over Solzhenitsyn is the issue of *détente* and the West's *Ostpolitik* as it affects relations with the Soviet Union. For the newspapers published by Springer, the Solzhenitsyn affair marks the culmination of this issue. Previously, *détente* had already been termed a "cynical farce" (27 January 1974), but now the Nobel Prize winner's expulsion from the Soviet Union is taken as a sign that "international morality and humanity" have been brought to the brink of extinction as a result of the "corruption" and "ethical narcosis of *détente*."[2] The logical conclusion is clear enough: any rapprochement with Eastern Europe is illusory, and relations with those states should be broken off. "All right, now that Aleksandr Solzhenitsyn is free, by dint of our strength, we shall (. . .) break off cultural relations with a regime that has no culture to exchange with us."[3] Advocates of *détente* are described by the conservatives as "credulous" and "obtuse": "anyone who, in his euphoria, enters into '*détente*' with a regime such as this, is not simply guileless; he displays all the acumen of a hippopotamus" (14 February 1974).

During 1975 and 1976, the stereotypes which we have seen exemplified in *Die Welt* recur in the conservative press's presentation and treatment of the Solzhenitsyn affair. In 1975, for instance, the speeches which he gave before the American Trades Union association AFL-CIO are reprinted in a number of conservative newspapers.[4] His warnings against *détente* are exploited to the full in the publications of the Right, and his words are used to "spread awareness of the true dimensions of the conflict in the world today" (21 December 1975).[5] Solzhenitsyn, we are told, is "a present-day prophet, and never has the present day stood in greater need of prophecy." Thus, Solzhenitsyn's "moral force" fulfills more than one function for the conservatives: not only does it discredit the Kremlin, but it also provides a basis on which to argue and rally public opinion against the socially liberal policies of the West German government, i.e., its *Ostpolitik* and support for *détente*.

In 1976, the conservative press focuses more intensively upon Solzhenitsyn's increasingly explicit and fierce criticism of the West. They identify themselves with his criticism of the moral decline of the West,[6] and especially with its abuse of freedom. The underlying tenor of Solzhenitsyn's criticism is conservative and it has elements of a backward-looking utopianism. It is in this spirit that the conservatives seize, too, upon his Harvard Commencement Address of June 1978, in which he argues vehemently in defence of the ethical strength and obligations of the free individual.[7]

Taking up Solzhenitsyn's "flaming appeal" (10 June 1978), even *Die Welt* itself now takes issue with his objections to the extensive use of the vested democratic rights to strike and to enjoy freedom of the press:

> Liberalism and the market economy can be noble concepts, as too can social security and worker participation in management. (...) [However,] the Russian's condemnation of the Western press, with its sensationalism and its habit of passing over the truly significant issues in favor of inflated pseudo-problems, can only be described as devastating. (10 June 1978)

Solzhenitsyn's words are taken as an exhortation to restore traditional social, spiritual and ethical values. At the same time, they are accompanied by a reminder of the theory of cultural decline, so characteristic of the conservative standpoint, and so influential in shaping its response to Solzhenitsyn.

> What kind of a world do we live in, when the ideas of loyalty, Fatherland, home, even family (let alone God!) are no longer used except ironically and in quotation marks? There are many things that Solzhenitsyn has correctly understood. His words should give us food for thought. (10 June 1978)

2. Liberals

In West Germany, the liberal image of Solzhenitsyn is neither as unambiguous as that held by the conservatives, nor does it show the same stability during the first five years of his exile. Quite the contrary, one is struck above all by the changes which his reception undergoes. One important feature of this difference is already present in the reports of his deportation: while the conservatives link the literary form of Solzhenitsyn's utterances with their political content, seeing in his competence as writer and moralist proof of his political credibility as historian and prophet, the liberals attempt to keep these two spheres distinct.

Liberal critics, especially the authors among them, stress Solzhenitsyn's literary significance and moral integrity: "None the less, it is not the material that makes the writer, but the writer who makes the material (...). And we owe this artistic mastery not to the angry moralist, but to Solzhenitsyn the writer."[8] This implies for the liberals neither agreement with his political convictions, nor acceptance of his tactics. Accordingly, praise of his literary works may go hand in hand with criticism of his political views.

The liberals subject Solzhenitsyn's political statements to detailed scrutiny, and the first criticisms of his competence as a historian are raised in connection with *The Gulag Archipelago*.[9] Rudolf Augstein, publisher of *Der Spiegel*, challenges the work at the most fundamental level. He regrets the author's failure to come to grips with Marxism-Leninism, which, he holds, arose as a historical necessity,[10] and sees his position as that of a "moralizing bourgeois intellectual," who in the final analysis is merely defending the principles of a bourgeois elite:

> Freedom of expression is not of equal importance to all social strata and to all individuals (...) In Mao's China there is less freedom of expression than before, but the country is incomparably better ruled (...) the author is calling for a moral world-order (...) an enlightened marxist is quite right to maintain that this is just another of those theatrical props which have ever adorned the stage of the ruling classes. (*Der Spiegel*, 11 February 1974)

The liberals question Solzhenitsyn's credentials as a critic, and consider the possibility that his arguments may be the expression of particular class interests. Augstein—and this is true of other liberals—approaches Solzhenitsyn with a mixture of sympathy and reserve.

They disagree with Solzhenitsyn's view, in that they do not, in principle, exclude the possibility of internal reforms in the Soviet Union. The Soviet Union's "efforts to distance itself from Stalin are genuine, even though they only work in a series of dialectical leaps" (*Der Spiegel*, 11 February 1974). In their dealings with Solzhenitsyn, the liberals make clear their interest in preserving the Soviet system and liberalizing it in the spirit of a humane socialism.

> No intelligent person in the world can favor an overthrow in the Soviet Union, but all must hope for change.[11]

> What is important for the future of Soviet society (...) is that the
> rights of all its citizens should be increased, but not beyond the point
> where the social system as constituted breaks down.[12]

It was the liberals who first reproached the conservatives of the
Bundesrepublik with having usurped Solzhenitsyn's name in order to
promote their own political objectives. The conservatives duly returned the charge. Such was the political atmosphere in which the
debate proceeded, that the protagonists often seem to be chiefly
afraid of accidentally saying the same thing as their ideological
opponents, while meaning something different. They fear ''applause
from the wrong side.''

> I suppose that I must at this point say something about the
> problem of applause from the wrong side. I have repeatedly (...)
> distanced myself from the vituperative pens of the Springer press,
> (...) they know that I find their praise more loathsome than their
> blame.[13]

For the liberals, the very fact that the conservatives support Solzhenitsyn precipitates a crisis of identity. Their sympathy for Soviet
dissidents turns into a cautious tightrope walk between the position of
the conservatives or ''cold warriors,''[14] and that of the pro-Soviet
German Communist Party.

At the end of 1974, the argument over the journal *Kontinent*
developed into another major cultural and political controversy,
which was fought out between liberals and conservatives in a variety
of West German publications. Günter Grass's argument was that
criticism organized by the West and supported by ''intolerant, anti-
Soviet forces'' should be rejected in no uncertain terms. Questionable
as Grass's remonstrances may seem from a wider perspective,
they did not fail to have their effect in West Germany. When the
Springer-owned newspapers reacted sharply to Grass's open letter,
other liberals came forward to share his position—in support of
Soviet dissidents, but against the conservative publishing-house.

> The anti-Communism of many of *Kontinent*'s authors is not
> identical with that of the Springer Concern, the former is based on
> personal experience of a violent system, (...) the latter seeks to
> defame anything in the Bundesrepublik which so much as smells of
> socialism and the Left.[15]

Conservative attempts to blur the distinctions between their own anti-intellectual campaign in the Bundesrepublik and the integrity of writers from Eastern Europe, are vigorously repudiated by the liberals, as is the conservative stratagem of declaring Solzhenitsyn "sacrosanct" and thereby maneuvering liberal critics into an impossible position.

> For Solzhenitsyn has not called for the restoration of private capitalism in the West, he has spoken out against the abuses and arbitrary power of communist state capitalism.[16]
> Arm in arm with the authors of *Kontinent*, and sustained by their moral integrity, our new avant-garde, the Springer Concern, sallies forth to do battle with all that motley leftist literary rabble which hitherto has eluded it. (*Die Zeit*, 25 October 1974)

Over and above the immediate issues of the *Kontinent* debate, the liberals are anxious to make the point that criticism of Western democracies remains possible and legitimate, and that it need not forever be tempered as a result of the Russian exiles' criticisms of Soviet socialism. "If the horrors of Stalinism are to be the only standard for judging suffering in the world, then Chile becomes a mere trifle, as do the problems of France, the Bundesrepublik and the USA."[17] Those of Solzhenitsyn's goals with which liberals could identify at the beginning of 1974 were determined in the first instance by the struggle against Soviet repression. At the same time, the liberals resisted efforts to enlist Solzhenitsyn as "propagandist against the treaties with Eastern Europe" or in any other domestic political issue (*Die Zeit*, 8 February 1974).

In consequence, the liberal image of Solzhenitsyn underwent a change during 1975. He came to be regarded with ever greater reserve—a process which has persisted to the present day. Liberal criticism of Solzhenitsyn was intensified after his visit to America in June and July of 1975, when he expressed his admiration for the United States and its people and urgently warned the Western world against cooperation with the Soviet Union. His attacks on *détente* and Western policies towards the countries of Eastern Europe bewildered and alienated many liberals. This change in attitude is reflected in all their publications, but, for reasons of space, it will here be traced largely with reference to *Die Zeit*.

In 1974 there was still a feeling of solidarity with Solzhenitsyn "due to the exceptional circumstances in which the writer found himself" (*Süddeutsche Zeitung*, 9 February 1975). But after his speeches to the AFL-CIO there was growing disillusionment with his political pronouncements and his "apocalyptic visions" (*Frankfurter Allgemeine Zeitung*, 11 July 1975). The moment Solzhenitsyn intervenes in the current debate over *détente* and sees himself as bearer of a political warning, the liberal response is critical and unsympathetic. This is particularly apparent in a series of major articles published about the time of the SALT Conference in Helsinki.[18]

Solzhenitsyn is described as "a Russian gloom-monger," "an Old Testament prophet of doom," who "glimpses the world through blinkered eyes" (*Die Zeit*, 25 July 1975). "Solzhenitsyn cast himself in the role of witness and prophet.(...) Rarely has a New York audience listened so patiently, politely and approvingly to the prophecy of its own destruction" (*Frankfurter Allgemeine Zeitung*, 11 July 1975). The liberals attempt to preserve their respect for Solzhenitsyn's appeal at least on moral grounds, but in political terms they so hedge about and qualify his statements as ultimately to reject them altogether. At the end of 1975, *Die Zeit* responds to Solzhenitsyn's *New York Times* article "Schlesinger and Kissinger" by firmly rebutting what it regards as his short-sighted and politically uninformed analysis. "He is no liberal. Let us make no mistake about that" (*Die Zeit*, 5 December 1975). "His notion of *détente* translates into nothing short of a new Cold War" (*Die Zeit*, 23 April 1976). The conclusion is an unqualified rejection of Solzhenitsyn: "There is such a thing as the immorality of the moralist. Let us be on our guard against it!" (*ibid.*). Solzhenitsyn's warnings about Soviet intentions are put down to the extreme subjectivity of his own experience, to which one should pay no heed when formulating a policy towards Eastern Europe: "If Solzhenitsyn were to be right, then our only alternative would be the Apocalypse" (*ibid.*). Even the liberal-conservative newspaper *Frankfurter Allgemeine Zeitung* distanced itself from Solzhenitsyn's American pronouncements.

> The dominant feature of Solzhenitsyn's speeches (...) is superficial rhetoric and verbal gesticulation. They are, for the most part, a chain reaction, a series of forcefully expressed short circuits (...). Consequently, it is impossible to accept many of his prophecies and prognoses without reservation. (8 November 1975)

It should be said, however, that the attitude of the *Frankfurter Allgemeine Zeitung* towards Solzhenitsyn changed in line with the newspaper's increasingly sceptical assessment of the outcome of the CSCE Conference. Thus, by mid-1976 it could write that the "black picture" painted by Solzhenitsyn today seems "closer and more tangible," since *détente*, to our mind, is "nothing but a pipe-dream" (5 May 1976).

This whole controversy flared up once again in summer 1978, and with essentially the same disposition of forces, in the wake of Solzhenitsyn's Commencement Address at Harvard University. In the Bundesrepublik, Solzhenitsyn's vehement criticism of the West is given a sceptical and unsympathetic reception by all save the conservatives. The *Frankfurter Allgemeine Zeitung* likens him to "one crying in the wilderness" (14 June 1978), though elsewhere his words are taken as "a critique which frequently rings true, and which deserves to be taken seriously." Some liberal voices emphasized the tragedy of Solzhenitsyn's position. He was, after all, an involuntary exile, living off his "experiences with Russian communism and the resulting tendency to measure every injustice in the world by the Soviet yardstick and to belittle it proportionately" (*Süddeutsche Zeitung*, 11 December 1978). The same article described Solzhenitsyn's fate as "the great tragedy of a man, (. . .) whose best place was in his own homeland, if only because it was there that he could hope to achieve the most." For many liberals Solzhenitsyn is, in the West, a great but misunderstood figure, "involuntarily enlisted in the conservative opposition within the Bundesrepublik" (*Frankfurter Allgemeine Zeitung*, 13 February 1975).

Thus, during the first five years of Solzhenitsyn's exile the liberals lost no opportunity to debate his arguments and views. In so doing, they also gave space to other voices from the Soviet Union which were not always in agreement with Solzhenitsyn: for example, that of the socialist critic of the Soviet regime, Roy Medvedev, six of whose essays on Solzhenitsyn appeared in the liberal *Die Zeit* between 1974 and 1976. After the Harvard Speech, the liberals' distance from Solzhenitsyn was established explicitly, in their published reactions, and implicitly in their growing tendency to ignore him. For the present Solzhenitsyn is ever less an object of controversy to the liberals. He has no new political insights to offer them, his basic standpoint is unambiguously conservative, and he arouses correspondingly fewer responses. In the words of the left-liberal *Frankfurter Rundschau*:

The longer the Russian writer Aleksandr Solzhenitsyn lives in the West, and the more speeches he gives there, the quicker his moral and political influence seem to evaporate, and with it the authority which he won by his merciless indictment of the Soviet labor camp system. (30 September 1976)

3. West German Communists

Throughout the period under consideration, the attitude of West German communists towards Solzhenitsyn, an established critic of the Soviet system, is shaped by their traditional, fraternal links with the Communist Party of the USSR. The sharply hostile way in which the Soviet Union reacted to Solzhenitsyn, culminating in his deportation, sets the trend for the West German communist response and leaves its mark upon their every pronouncement. By the beginning of 1974 their image of Solzhenitsyn is firmly established, and it varies not a jot in the five years which follow.

Solzhenitsyn is appraised almost exclusively from a political perspective, with purely literary and esthetic considerations playing scarcely any role. At most, literary criteria are invoked in order to divest Solzhenitsyn of "the claim to literary and moral significance which once he had with his *Ivan Denisovich*."[19] As *Die Tat* put it: "We are not dealing here with a literary work, still less with that tired old war-horse 'artistic freedom'" (*Die Tat*, 19 January 1974). Solzhenitsyn is termed a "counter-revolutionary" and "Great Russian nationalist," who denies the real achievements of the October Revolution and all positive developments in the USSR, even though he himself has enjoyed them to the full. He is reproached with having profited from the benefits of socialist society, while refusing to honor his obligations by expressing his solidarity with that society.[20] He is presented as a "hypocrite" and "opportunist," who has knowingly gambled away his right to be a member of a socialist society, an argument equally prominent in the Soviet campaign against Solzhenitsyn.[21]

He is further charged with displaying the egoism of a bourgeois individualist, ready to enrich himself at the expense of socialist principles, but not to acknowledge them or give them due credit. Moreover, he is a reactionary: "Everything progressive arouses his loathing.''[22] Other stereotypes include Solzhenitsyn, the "traitor": "He is a literary Vlasovite, (...) a traitor in the eyes of Soviet patriots."[23] Or Solzhenitsyn, the tool of West German "cold warriors" who are fanning the flames of anti-communism in the Bundesrepublik: "No wonder the cold warriors are yelling for more ammunition—Solzhenitsyn's the man for them" (*Die Tat*, 26 January 1974). Great play is made in this connection with the positive response to Solzhenitsyn on the part of the conservatively inclined West German press and of international "neofascist newspapers." Here, once again, the West German communists merely parrot the Soviet press: "We might add that Solzhenitsyn's book [*The Gulag Archipelago*] is being praised to the skies by both the newspapers of the Franco regime and the radio stations of the South African Republic.''[24]

Not only do Solzhenitsyn's books serve to promote anti-socialist propaganda in the Bundesrepublik, but their author is used by West German anti-communists to distract attention from the current crisis of capitalism:

> The reason that Solzhenitsyn's name flickers across the TV screen so often is to leave less room in the programs and in the viewers' thoughts for the really important things: questions of peace and security, the consequences of a failed energy policy, inflation and the scourge of unemployment. Any thought that this system might be changed (...) has to be suppressed. (*Unsere Zeit*, 19 January 1974)

Hence, in a word, Solzhenitsyn is a "hit" in the Bundesrepublik. When he compares the way in which the Soviet Union after Stalin faced up to its past, with the German experience after Hitler, this is used to discredit him as nothing short of a defender of Nazism: "Solzhenitsyn's anti-communist bestseller [*The Gulag Archipelago*] warms the hearts of all old Nazis" (*Dlan*, No. 3, 1974). He is depicted as someone not even worth arguing with:

> *The Gulag Archipelago* is just another of those anti-Soviet works which so distort historical processes and contexts by jumbling together truth and distortion, prejudice and accurate statistics, that it would be absurd to repudiate them in point of detail. The only answer to inflammatory, belligerent writing is to fight it. In fact, the very reason why texts like this are circulated is to forestall any serious discussion.[25]

As we shall see, the Solzhenitsyn affair splits the ranks of the political Left in the Bundesrepublik into those "for" and those "against." The DKP-affiliated communists, for their part, neither criticize his expulsion from the Soviet Union, nor treat his later statements from the point of view of the ominous mutual escalation of dissidence and repression in the Soviet Union. Instead, the same attacks on Solzhenitsyn are repeated after his AFL-CIO speeches and after his warnings about Soviet intentions at Harvard in 1978. The attitude of orthodox marxists in the Bundesrepublik towards Solzhenitsyn is consistently and thoroughly hostile; at the same time, he is used to brand any criticism of the Soviet Union as neo-fascist propaganda.

4. The New Left

Apart from the pro-Soviet communists in the Bundesrepublik, the Solzhenitsyn debate attracted the attention of a group which also described itself as socialist, but which had its own, distinctive attitude towards the dissident movement and developments in the Soviet Union. These West German socialists, who gave themselves the title "New Left" during the 1960s, stand out from the pro-Soviet communists on the one side, and the social democratic reformists on the other.

In tackling the Solzhenitsyn affair, the New Left begins by relating it to the question of the opposition within the Soviet Union. As a main representative of this opposition, Solzhenitsyn is seen, in political terms, as a "disillusioned socialist," "true to the communist party line" in his youth, but moved by years of suffering to seek his own individual alternative to the officially prescribed socialism of the Soviet Union.[26] Rudi Dutschke, a representative of the undogmatic wing of the West German Left, and a prominent spokesman in this debate, refers to Solzhenitsyn as a "former socialist" who, after years of toeing the "party line," is today inclined to "damn the Revolution altogether."[27] Solzhenitsyn's evolution from socialist to critic of the system, and thence to anti-socialist, seems understandable to these representatives of a critical communism: they lay the blame not upon him as individual, but upon errors in the development of Soviet socialism. Socialism in the Soviet Union is seen as bureaucratic and dictatorial, a fundamental perversion of the socialist idea. "The Party installed itself in place of the Class, and the Bureaucracy in place of the Party. It is the Bureaucracy that determines what is to be in the interests of Party and Class."[28] The existence of a persecuted, underground intellectual opposition in the Soviet Union is felt to be symptomatic of the deep-seated failings of the system, and these must be exposed by "reactivating our critical awareness."[29]

Although the socialist critics note certain differences between Solzhenitsyn's ideological and political position and their own, they consider it their bounden duty, in view of the critical attitude towards the Soviet system which unites them, to show their solidarity with him. This thinking is especially marked at the time of his deportation, but is voiced on later occasions as well. "What matters now is not our differences with Solzhenitsyn, but the need to stand up for this threatened, isolated, lonely comrade in suffering."[30] In 1975, it is true, the New Left intensifies its criticism of Solzhenitsyn. The marxists reproach him for his nationalism, his irrational retreat into Russian Orthodoxy, and his renunciation of socialism. Furthermore, they reject his criticisms of the West's policy of *détente*. Even so, as a former socialist and an exile, he continues for a time to be entitled to a certain, not uncritical solidarity, if only for domestic political reasons: "Nevertheless, the Western Left must not do the Right a favor by renouncing Solzhenitsyn" (*Vorwärts*, 10 July 1975).

In the course of 1976, and especially 1978, the New Left modifies its image of Solzhenitsyn ever more. The position he adopts towards Chile and Indonesia (welcoming the overthrow of a communist regime in the former and of an attempted Putsch in the latter), and towards Portugal (where he interprets the supersession of the Salazar dictatorship exclusively as a boost to Soviet power and a threat to the West) is not allowed to go unchallenged:

> His declaration of war on Soviet communism was hitherto justi-
> fied in view of the repression endured there by minorities, political
> dissidents and non-conformists of all kinds, but now his struggle with
> communism has become a *condicio sine qua non*, which can, in its
> turn, justify bloody repression. (*Frankfurter Rundschau*, 30 October
> 1976)

This is, ultimately, the reason why the non-orthodox marxists of the Bundesrepublik became gradually more alienated from Solzhenitsyn.

III

Solzhenitsyn's reception in West Germany, as outlined above, can be represented as falling broadly into three phases, each of them associated with significant events in his career. The four groups which we have distinguished each react differently to these events. The first phase begins in January 1974 with the announcement of the German edition of *The Gulag Archipelago* and extends to the middle of 1974, when the "Letter to Soviet Leaders" was published. Thematically, this could be termed *the phase of irritation and solidarity with Solzhenitsyn*. The second phase runs from the end of 1974 to the end of 1976 and covers the *Kontinent* debate, Solzhenitsyn's "Speeches to the Americans," the appearance in Germany of the second volume of *Gulag* and *The Oak and the Calf*, his BBC talk, published as "A Warning to the West," through to his move to the United States and the publication of the last volume of *Gulag*. This is *the phase of political alienation or of political exploitation*, the phase when attitudes towards Solzhenitsyn are more sharply defined. The third phase begins at the end of 1976 and, in effect, continues throughout the 1970s. After Solzhenitsyn's move to Vermont, his activities in his newly chosen abode, and notably his Harvard speech, were not only geographically far removed from West Germany, but aroused a generally cool response there. Hence, the third phase is characterized by a degree of *aloofness* between established antagonistic positions, or in many cases by a *return to indifference*. At the same time, there were those who made constant reference to Solzhenitsyn's words during this period, if only in order to press them into the service of their own political sympathies.

The way in which West German perceptions of Solzhenitsyn changed during these different phases had much to do with the basic political attitudes of the groups responding to him. It is no less evident that the Solzhenitsyn affair provided unusual scope for generalizations about the forms of political debate in the Bundesrepublik.

Solzhenitsyn's increasingly explicit elaboration of his political position—as a conservative with a warning message, a self-imposed historical mission to convince the West of the brutality of the Soviet regime—was variously received. The liberals and neo-marxists were forced to revise their initial assessment of him. His attacks on *détente* disconcerted them and aroused their strong reservations. For the conservatives and orthodox marxists, on the other hand, Solzhenitsyn's anti-communist profession of faith and his call for a spiritual and political about-face, seemed to legitimize their basic attitude towards him. The conservatives could now declare that they had been right all along in interpreting Solzhenitsyn as anti-communist, while the DKP communists could claim that they had "always known" him to be on the side of capitalism, conservatism and the anti-Soviet campaign in the Bundesrepublik.

Four principal tendencies were discerned in the response to the Solzhenitsyn affair. Together they spanned the range of political groupings in West Germany.

1. The conservatives endeavored to identify themselves with Solzhenitsyn's moral position. For them the Soviet dissident symbolized the abortiveness of any attempt to implement socialism. They entertained a consistently positive image of him and harnessed it for their own political ends.

2. The liberals assured the persecuted writer of their support at the beginning of his exile and criticized the Soviet variety of socialism much in the same way that he did. At the same time, they were resolved not to engage in hero-worship and reserved the right to disagree with him. His criticism of *détente* and the West's *Ostpolitik* gradually estranged them from him.

3. The communists affiliated to the German Communist Party followed the Moscow line. They defended the official policy of the Soviet Union and attacked Solzhenitsyn as a "traitor to socialism" and "capitalist lackey." Their hostile stance towards him remained constant over the years.

4. The New Left declared its solidarity with Solzhenitsyn and took his case as an occasion for demonstrating its own, unorthodox conception of socialism. It accused the Soviet Union of having distorted the ideals of socialism, and simultaneously criticized anti-democratic tendencies in capitalist countries. The New Left, too, moved gradually away from Solzhenitsyn as a result of his conservative, anti-democratic comments.

At the beginning of Solzhenitsyn's exile, in particular, the debate which he trigggered in the daily press and in the literary and political periodicals of the Bundesrepublik developed into a public clash of opinions. The Solzhenitsyn affair stirred up emotions and confirmed stereotyped images of political foes; it was instrumental in strengthening the ideological borders between one group and another. In short, the Solzhenitsyn affair ceased to be a topic of discussion in the

West; it became, instead, the medium for a debate, whose course Solzhenitsyn himself was soon unable to influence, and to which he was involuntarily subjected. Eventually, the tide of the debate turned against Solzhenitsyn, something which would not have been possible for as long as he lived in the Soviet Union. *Before* his deportation, the substance and level of the debate was determined solely by his actions and utterances. *After* his exile, he soon became just one more factor in the political deliberations of the West, which had at first focused upon the question of lending him moral support, then upon the consequences of the expulsion and his speeches in the West against *détente*, but which eventually became an autonomous dispute over political nuances and lines of demarcation.

IV

The predictions of early 1974, that Solzhenitsyn would soon find himself much more lonely in the West than he had been in the East, have, tragically, been fulfilled. Whereas in the East he came to occupy the role of a martyr, he was peddled in the West as an irksome prophet. It is his tragedy to be able to speak in the West, but not to be properly heard, to be isolated as a non-émigré among ever greater numbers of voluntary emigrants from the Soviet Union, to be subordinated here to the various political options of the day, and to have underestimated the mass lethargy of the world democracy which he invoked. In the first five years of his exile, Solzhenitsyn was unable to effect any significant changes. After his exile, he was no longer a cause, but a medium through which existing conflicts in the political structure were fought out, a medium for expressing political tendencies which were already present.

Solzhenitsyn was never more popular among the intellectuals of the Bundesrepublik than at the time of his deportation. His fate never stimulated such a protracted and intensive debate among left intellectuals here as it did, for example, in France: in Germany it would take a more local furor, the controversial and extremely influential political ideas of Rudolf Bahro, to achieve a comparable effect. Soviet calculations would seem, tragically, to have been borne out: the West's appetite for sensation has passed on from Solzhenitsyn to other topics.

—Translated from the German by Michael Nicholson.

Notes

1. See the present author's earlier work on the reception of Soviet dissidents in the Federal Republic of Germany: "Der Fall Solschenizyn im Spiegel der westdeutschen Presse," MA, Munich 1976, and the recently completed PhD dissertation on "Die Darstellung der sowjetischen Dissidenten-Bewegung in der Presse der BRD."

2. *Welt am Sonntag*, 17 February 1974.

3. *Ibid.*

4. E.g. *Bayernkurier*, 9 August; *Welt am Sonntag*, 20 July; *Rheinischer Merkur*, 25 July; *Deutsche Tagespost*, 29 July; *Sudetendeutsche Zeitung*, 8 August—all 1975.

5. An example is publisher Axel Springer's New Year's greeting to his readers, entitled "Only Firmness Helps against Violence." The message consists of a quotation from Solzhenitsyn's address to the AFL-CIO, placed underneath pictures of him and Springer.

6. In particular with his speech of 1 June 1976 at the Hoover Institution in California, upon the occasion of receiving the Friendship Prize of the American Freedom Foundation.

7. Reprinted in *Welt am Sonntag*, 11 June; *Rheinischer Merkur*, 16 June; *Bayernkurier*, 24 June; *Die Welt*, 8 July; *Frankfurter Allgemeine Zeitung*, 14 July—all 1978.

8. Heinrich Böll in *Frankfurter Allgemeine Zeitung*, 9 February 1974.

9. Rudolf Augstein, "Solschenizyn oder die Ehre Gottes," *Der Spiegel*, 7 January 1974.

10. See *Der Spiegel*, 7 January; 11 February; and 18 February 1974.

11. Heinrich Böll in *Frankfurter Allgemeine Zeitung*, 9 March 1974.

12. Rudolf Augstein in *Der Spiegel*, 11 February 1974.

13. Heinrich Böll in *Die Zeit*, 11 January 1974.

14. Böll, *ibid.*, 14 February 1975.

15. D.E. Zimmer, "Grass hat recht behalten," *Die Zeit*, 25 October 1974.

16. Günter Grass in *Frankfurter Rundschau*, 19 February 1974.

17. Heinrich Böll in *Die Zeit*, 6 December 1974.

18. E.g. "Was gilt uns Solschenizyn?" *Die Zeit*, 25 July 1975; "Wo irrt Alexander Solschenizyn? Die moralische und die politische Perspektive der Entspannung," *ibid.*, 1 August 1975; and "Die Unmoral des Moralisten. A. Solschenizyn und die Entspannung," *ibid.*, 5 December 1975.

19. Friedrich Hitzer in *Kürbiskern*, No. 2, 1974, p. 129.

20. E.g. in *Elan*, No. 3, 1974; and *Unsere Zeit*, 17 December 1974.

21. Cf. the collection *Der letzte Kreis* [*The Last Circle*] (Moscow: Novosti, 1974); and *Sowjetunion Heute*, 1 March 1974.

22. Hitzer, *loc. cit.*, p. 134.

23. Hitzer, p. 135.

24. "Solschenizyns Claqueure," *Sowjetunion Heute*, 16 February 1974.

25. Hitzer, *loc. cit.*, p. 133.

26. Hans C. Buch, "Abschied von gestern. Warum *Archipel GULAG* die Illusionen vieler Linker zerstören kann," *Pardon*, March 1974.

27. Rudi Dutschke, "Solschenizyn und die Not der Linken," *Vorwärts*, 28 February 1974. Dutschke's article may be regarded as typical of the position of the New Left.

28. Jochen Steffen in *Sprit*, 4 October 1974.

29. Ernest Mandel in *Alternative*, February 1975.

30. Gerhard Zwerenz in *Südwestfunk*, 13 January 1974.

Solzhenitsyn in France After 1974

PIERRE DAIX

During the summer of 1973, Solzhenitsyn became the object of political speculation in France, for it was then that the French Communist Party took up the campaign launched against Solzhenitsyn and Sakharov in the Soviet Union. The communists regarded the criticisms of Soviet handling of this affair published in *Le Monde* and *Le Nouvel Observateur* as an "outburst of anti-Sovietism," and they responded by mobilizing their own supporters and producing special issues of their newspaper *l'Humanité*. It is significant that not the slightest attempt was made to examine what Solzhenitsyn and Sakharov were actually saying. Instead, they were presented as "enemies of *détente*," engaged in a "campaign to denigrate the socialist countries." It was in this precise direction that the French Communist Party bent its efforts—ostensibly in order to "make the truth about the socialist countries known by all available channels of information and debate."

With the publication of the Russian edition of *The Gulag Archipelago* in Paris in December 1973, the campaign against Solzhenitsyn in *l'Humanité* was intensified still further. Taking as its pretext the appearance of excerpts from *Gulag* in *Le Monde* and *l'Express*, the communist newspaper printed, with great fanfare, an article by a member of the Central Committee of the French Communist Party, Léo Figuères. Its title was "On Solzhenitsyn and Vlasov, a Rehabilitation Attempt Insulting to Every Patriot."[1] The strategy could hardly have been simpler: *Gulag* was presented exclusively through a montage of quotations relating to the case of Vlasov, a Russian general who had sided with the Nazis against Stalin. Figuères duly concluded that Solzhenitsyn was, indeed, trying to rehabilitate Vlasov. "As for the view," he wrote, "that the reasons for Vlasov's treason, and for that of his followers, are to be sought in Soviet society, we might just as well be told that the King of Norway is responsible for Quisling's crimes, the King of Belgium for those of Degrelle, and the French people for Laval's or Darnand's treason." And the article calls upon "all of France's Resistance members and patriots" to condemn any such rehabilitation attempt. For good measure, the same issue of *l'Humanité* presents a compilation of reactions drawn from the West German press, under the title, "Neo-Nazis in Ecstasy."

In the days which followed, *l'Humanité* returned to the fray, wondering disingenuously whether Solzhenitsyn's "defense of Vlasov" might just be a "blunder," only to conclude that Solzhenitsyn is "firmly embedded in the political struggles of the day. His political conservatism places him shoulder to shoulder with the reactionary political forces of the West, with those who decided, in concert with Solzhenitsyn, when to launch his book, which had apparently been completed several years before. For in these times of crisis, the reactionaries are sorely in need of a new version of this desperado [Vlasov]."

As can be seen, the communist journalists did not allow reality to inhibit them in their all-out effort to discredit Solzhenitsyn in the eyes of the French public. "Solzhenitsyn's plan," *l'Humanité* sums up, "is to blacken Soviet society as a whole. The errors of the past are for him no more than an excuse for joining in the ideological struggle against socialism."

The themes of the campaign were firmly established, and were later to be taken up by the communist parties of other French-speaking countries as well—those of Switzerland and Belgium. Solzhenitsyn is seen as part of a plot directed against international *détente*, and concocted in order to divert attention away from the global crisis now rocking capitalist society. Even the Soviet authorities' action in deporting Solzhenitsyn moved these same responsible communists to no more than the merest token gesture of disapproval, and the day after his arrival in Zurich *l'Humanité* did not hesitate to run the headline: "Solzhenitsyn Vacationing in Switzerland."

Probably the most noteworthy feature of this preventive campaign, which raged so violently, and almost without interruption, from August 1973 to February 1974, was its abysmal failure. In fact, when the French translation of the first volume of *Gulag*[2] went on sale in May 1974, it enjoyed instant and massive success. The question of Soviet labor camps had been widely discussed in France at the time of the Cold War and, too, some twenty-five years before, when

David Rousset had called upon the former inmates of Nazi concentration camps to enquire into their existence in the Soviet Union. Since then it had never really been reopened, due chiefly to Khrushchev's de-Stalinization, but also to de Gaulle's policy of *détente*. Even the appearance of the French translation of *One Day in the Life of Ivan Denisovich* in 1963 had failed to revive the debate, partly because the story had been officially published in the Soviet Union, and partly because the very fact of its literary quality disappointed those who were expecting a brutal account of the horrors of the Gulag.

Thus, *The Gulag Archipelago* reached new generations of readers, who had hitherto kept themselves aloof from the debate and who had a dim notion that Stalinist repression was a thing of the past, constituting some kind of accident in the development of the Soviet revolution. This was the thesis spread abroad by the Communist Party, but also one accepted by the Left as a whole and by those parties of the ruling majority which were anxious to maintain good relations with the Soviet authorities.

These specific features of French politics, which coincided, by and large, with the period of the Fifth Republic, contributed greatly to the shock people felt when they discovered *The Gulag Archipelago*; they also explain why the book has been so important in France ever since. We might sum up by saying that the discussion now shifted away from the analysis of Stalinism—When did the deviation occur? Was it in 1929? Or 1934, as Khrushchev claimed? and so forth—and towards more general problems concerning the Soviet revolution, such as the question of Lenin's responsibility, the connection between the emergence of the Gulag system and the development of the Bolshevik Party, and the transformations which the Soviet regime has undergone.

In a country whose communist party has enjoyed mass support (especially since the days of the Popular Front and the Resistance), but has been, at the same time, one of the most thoroughly Stalinized parties and the last to stop dodging the issue of de-Stalinization—in such a country, the fact that questions like these were actually raised at all promptly became a political event in itself. More especially since the Socialist Party, constrained by its obligations to the Union of the Left, tended to adopt an extremely wary approach to problems of this kind. From the summer of 1975 on, the French Communist Party had to acknowledge, however grudgingly, that the de-Stalinization file could not be considered closed. In 1976, it was compelled to condemn the existence of concentration camps in the present-day Soviet Union, and also the use of psychiatric hospitals as instruments of political repression. Finally, it had to disassociate itself from the "dictatorship of the proletariat." All of this can be attributed to the dramatic upset in French public opinion, particularly among the Left, occasioned by the reading of *The Gulag Archipelago*.

Yet, attempts to discredit Solzhenitsyn did not cease for all that. For example, *l'Humanité* was one of the papers which alleged that he was intending to visit Chile following General Pinochet's seizure of power. And when Solzhenitsyn appeared on the French TV program "Apostrophes" in April 1975, a great deal of the discussion centered upon his hostile attitude towards the communist regime in Vietnam. His statements on Spanish TV were likewise denounced as virtually endorsing dictatorship in that country. It is striking to note, in retrospect, how many of these controversies have been overtaken by events themselves, and how often Solzhenitsyn has turned out to be right: the oppressive character of the North Vietnamese regime is a case in point, and the democratization of Spain is another.

As a result of all this, the specifically literary works by Solzhenitsyn which were published in France during the same period have tended to be underestimated and to be treated merely as an extension of the political debate. This applies, among others, to *The Oak and the Calf*, *August 1914* and, even more, to *Lenin in Zurich*. The latter two works, in particular, contradicted the accepted French image of both tsarist Russia and the revolutionary movement. In addition, *Lenin in Zurich* was the subject of an historical analysis by Boris Souvarine, a survivor of the French revolutionary movement, and one of the founders of the French Communist Party expelled by the Comintern in 1924.[3]

Souvarine's highly critical study is the definitive attempt to raise the question both of Soviet expurgation of historical sources relating to the history of the revolution, and of its ideological approach to history, and by so doing to draw attention to Solzhenitsyn's own unconscious conditioning. This, Souvarine argued, was a result of his being cut off from Western thinking on these issues, and also a result of the impossibility of meeting reliable witnesses in the Soviet Union who were able to speak freely, even of the experiences of the Bolshevik Party. This essay can be regarded as one of the most significant contributions to the discussion of Solzhenitsyn's works in France.

A complete bibliography of works about Solzhenitsyn published in France is to be found in *Soljénitsyne*, a recent book by the Slavist, Georges Nivat.[4] Certain items may be singled out as representing significant stages in the study of Solzhenitsyn's writings. Such are: the volume in the series "Cahier de l'Herne" published in 1971, which assembled more or less all of the information about him that was then available;[5] my own essay of 1973, *What I Know about Solzhenitsyn*, which attempted to mobilize public opinion in defence of the writer at a time when his life and liberty were under threat;[6] and Michel Heller's study, *Soviet Literature and the Concentration Camp World*, which appeared in 1974 and took stock of the whole problem of Gulag.[7] In 1975, André Glucksmann's book *The Cook and the Cannibal*[8] marked a shift in the attitude of the Leftists of 1968 under the influence of Solzhenitsyn's works: many of them now rounded upon oppressive communist regimes, be they Soviet or Maoist. This was the beginning of a development which has taken on ever sharper and more radical contours, especially in view of the invasions of Cambodia and Afghanistan. Nivat's book, a general study of remarkable intelligence, provides a detailed picture of French reactions to Solzhenitsyn's works. It is, in this sense, not only an evaluation, but a thoroughly well-informed guide to the subject.

—Translated from the French by Michael Nicholson.

Notes

1. *L'Humanité*, 1 February 1974.

2. *L'Archipel du Goulag* (Paris: Seuil, 1974).

3. Boris Souvarine, "Soljénitsyne et Lénine," *Est & Ouest*, vol. 28, No. 570 (1-15 April 1976), pp. 1(121)-16(136); English in *Dissent*, Summer 1977, pp. 324-36. See also Solzhenitsyn's response to Souvarine in the documentary section of the present volume.

4. Georges Nivat, *Soljénitsyne* (Paris: Seuil, "Ecrivains de toujours," 1980).

5. Georges Nivat and Michel Aucouturier, eds., *Soljénitsyne* (Paris: Herne, 1971).

6. Pierre Daix, *Ce que je sais de Soljénitsyne* (Paris: Seuil, 1973).

7. Michel Heller, *La Littérature soviétique et le Monde concentrationnaire* (Lausanne: L'Age d'homme, 1974).

8. André Glucksmann, *La Cuisinière et le Mangeur d'hommes* (Paris: Seuil, 1975).

Yugoslav Reactions to Solzhenitsyn

DUŠAN PUVAČIĆ

In view of the unique relationship existing between Yugoslavia
and the Soviet Union, one might have expected the Yugoslav response to Solzhenitsyn's fate and writings to have attracted particular
attention. In fact, it appears that no comprehensive survey or bibliography of that reception has ever been published. For that reason
the present essay begins not in 1974, but twelve years earlier, at the
time of Solzhenitsyn's literary debut.

In its November issue for 1962, the Soviet literary monthly *Novyi
mir* published *One Day in the Life of Ivan Denisovich* by Aleksandr
Solzhenitsyn. This story by an unknown writer was a literary as well
as a political sensation, and not only in the Soviet Union. Its echo
quickly spread to Yugoslavia. Everyone who was lucky enough to get
hold of a copy of *Novyi mir* was staggered by the story's outspoken-
ness in describing the inhumanity of the regime under which political
prisoners suffered and perished in Stalin's labor camps. The Yugoslavs, who had their own unsettled accounts with Stalin dating from
1948, the year of their break with Moscow, were quick to welcome
and accept Solzhenitsyn as a natural ally in their "ideological struggle" against the remnants of Stalinism.

On 23 November 1962, the most influential Yugoslav newspaper,
the Belgrade daily *Politika*, published the first installment of *One
Day*.... The political importance of the story was not only clearly
stated in a short introductory note, but it was further indicated
by the position in which the first installment was actually printed.
In Yugoslav newspapers the first five or six pages are usually taken
up with important foreign and domestic news. The first part of *One
Day*...was printed on page four. Amazed by the content of the story,
Politika's editors almost neglected its author. "A. Soljenicin" was
mentioned in the introductory note only once, and in subsequent
installments his name was for some time omitted altogether. It was

mentioned again in the sixth installment (28 November), but in the same misspelt form. Not until 5 December did *Politika* finally print his name in its correct spelling: "A. Solženjicin." At the same time, *Politika* was serializing another important "anti-Stalinist" novel, Iurii Bondarev's *Silence*. When the publication of *Silence* ended, *One Day*...was duly moved to the back pages, where novels in *Politika* are normally serialized, and where its serialization was completed on 28 December 1962.

But *Politika* was not the only Yugoslav paper to serialize *One Day*.... In late 1962 and early 1963 it came out in Slovenian, both in the Maribor evening paper *Večer*[1] and in the Ljubljana weekly *Tovariš*,[2] while a Hungarian translation appeared in the Novy Sad daily *Magyar Szo*[3] and an Italian one in the Rijeka weekly *Panorama*.[4]

Among the first articles about Solzhenitsyn published in the Yugoslav press—which relied heavily on information provided by Soviet sources and which were written either by Yugoslav correspondents in Moscow or by dedicated observers of the Soviet literary scene in Yugoslavia—one was in certain ways unique. It was France Klopčič's article on *One Day*..., which was printed in *Tovariš* together with the last installment of his translation of the story. What distinguished it from everything else written about Solzhenitsyn in Yugoslavia so far was not its emphasis on the truthfulness and authenticity of Solzhenitsyn's prose, but Klopčič's ability to pass judgment with the authority of a man who had shared the same kind of experience. Between September 1937 and November 1945, Klopčič himself had spent 2,981 "such days," and he was the first Yugoslav witness, who had passed through the same circle of hell as Ivan Denisovich, to speak in support of Solzhenitsyn's claims.

On 23 December *Politika* reported on an interview with Aleksandr Tvardovskii which had been printed in the Moscow *Literaturnaia gazeta*, and in which he announced the publication of two new stories by Solzhenitsyn. "Matrena's Home" was serialized in Yugoslavia immediately after its appearance in the January 1963 issue of *Novyi mir*, both in Serbo-Croat[5] and in Slovenian.[6] "Incident at Krechetovka Station" was published in two daily papers in two different translations into Serbo-Croat,[7] as well as in Macedonian.[8] Furthermore, it was later serialized in Slovenian in the newspaper *Večer*, after having appeared together with *One Day*... and "Matrena's Home" in the first Slovenian collection of Solzhenitsyn's stories.[9] However, the first book-edition of these three early stories to appear in Yugoslavia in any language was that issued in late 1963 by the "Kultura" publishing house, Belgrade.[10] In 1964 a further story, "For the Good of the Cause," was included in an anthology of contemporary Soviet prose.[11] Thus, Yugoslav readers had ready access to those early published works on which Solzhenitsyn's reputation at home and abroad was based.

Among the first critical comments and reviews published in various Yugoslav daily papers and literary journals during the first wave of the Solzhenitsyn furor, two contributions to Solzhenitsyniana deserve to be mentioned here: Duško Car's essay entitled "Between Two Starry Nights"[12] and Mihajlo Mihajlov's essay "Dostoevskii's and Solzhenitsyn's *House of the Dead.*"[13] Car assessed *One Day...* primarily as a document, a first truthful utterance about Stalin's "paradise"; but he was also the first in Yugoslavia to suggest that Solzhenitsyn's story deals with the same kind of "moral dilemma" as that which concerned Dostoevskii in his *House of the Dead.* Although Dostoevskii was undoubtedly the greater artist, the moral dilemma illuminated by Solzhenitsyn was the more tragic because it informed a literary work which was "an artistic document" about a whole epoch. Even though its "horrible truths" had occasionally "exceeded" Solzhenitsyn's creative powers, his work was seen by Car as "a diamond in a period of darkness."

Mihajlov started off where Car left off: "by examining the living reality" of Solzhenitsyn's *One Day...* and Dostoevskii's *House of the Dead*, he established "the similarities and differences between two worlds—that of the nineteenth and that of the twentieth century." In his essay Mihajlov treated Solzhenitsyn as a "great artist," retracting his earlier opinion (one shared by some other Yugoslav critics), that Solzhenitsyn was "unfortunately, on the whole, probably not a 'born writer'. (...) What he has written this far is extraordinarily talented reportage, but it is likely that the moment he has described all that has happened in his life, his pen will dry up."[14]

In early 1965 an essay by György Lukács on "Socialist Realism Today" was published in the February issue of the Novi Sad monthly *Letopis Matice Srpske.* It stressed the importance of Solzhenitsyn's work in a wider theoretical context and described "the critical settling of accounts" with Stalinism as the "central problem of socialist realism today." In his review of a collection of Isaak Babel's short stories, published in a Sarajevo monthly,[15] the writer and critic Risto Trifković elaborated on the theme of Solzhenitsyn as a turning point in the development of Soviet literature. Having portrayed Babel' as a writer who "in the pre-Stalinist period was a precursor of that springtime of socialist literature" which, "for well-known reasons," never came about, Trifković went on to assert that Solzhenitsyn was merely taking up where Babel' had been forced to stop on his path to the truth. If Babel' had survived his confinement in labor camp, he would probably have written his own version of *One Day*..., because "he was predestined to write it." It would have been "a logical culmination" of his life and his literary career. Therefore, "Solzhenitsyn is the Babel' of today," concluded Trifković, wishing him "luck, courage and better conditions that those granted to Babel'."

During 1966 and 1967, Solzhenitsyn's initial disagreements with the Soviet Writers' Union and its Secretariat were only sparsely, sporadically, and factually reported in the Yugoslav press. But in 1968 the responses to Solzhenitsyn's difficulties with the Soviet literary authorities were greater in number and scope. In three issues (1-3 June) *Vjesnik* carried Solzhenitsyn's letter of 12 September 1967 to the Secretariat of the Writers' Union and the text of the discussion at the meeting between Solzhenitsyn and the Secretariat of the Union held on 22 September 1967. Both the letter and the transcript of the debate were translated from the Italian texts published in *Il Giorno*, while *Le Monde*, *Time* and *Rinascità* were quoted as sources for an article on "Solzhenitsyn's Suffering," published in *NIN* on 13 October 1968. It gave a survey of his life, putting particular emphasis upon his conflict with literary bureaucrats, the mysterious publication of *Cancer Ward* Part 1 in the West, and the writer's denial that he had been responsible for sending the manuscript to foreign publishers.

Although the editors of *NIN* were informed about the publication of *Cancer Ward* in the West, it seems that they were unaware that it had already been published in Yugoslavia as well. It had even been very favorably reviewed in *Borba* on 12 October,[16] only one day before the appearance of the article in *NIN*. *Cancer Ward* Part 1 was published in late summer of 1968 by a Rijeka publishing house.[17] It appeared in Yugoslav bookshops at the height of the Yugoslav-Soviet rift caused by the Warsaw Pact countries' invasion of Czechoslovakia. And so, once again, Solzhenitsyn and his works were given additional political significance within the Yugoslav-Soviet ideological conflict. On 5 September 1968, practically as a reply to the Soviet tanks then rolling through the streets of Prague, *Borba* began to serialize those pages from *The First Circle* in which Solzhenitsyn portrays Stalin's encounter with Abakumov and their discussion about the possibilities of assassinating Tito and other Yugoslav leaders. Between 5 September and 6 October, thirty-two installments of *The First Circle* were published in *Borba*. Only three days after this serialization had ended, *Borba* again turned its attention to Solzhenitsyn. Between 9 and 16 October it carried a series of documentary materials about him entitled "My Fate." Urged to publish more about Solzhenitsyn by constant readers' demands, *Borba* included in this series such pivotal documents as the 1967 interview with Bratislava journalist, Pavel Ličko, Solzhenitsyn's letter to the Fourth Congress of the Soviet Writers' Union (16 May 1967),[18] and others of his letters to the Secretariat of the Writers' Union and to its rank-and-file members. Yugoslav commentators were eager to explain the Solzhenitsyn "affair" within a wider ideological context. *Borba*'s Moscow correspondent, Slobodan Vujica, reported on 14 September 1968 that a new "ideological offensive" was being mounted in the Soviet press against those writers who, like Solzhenitsyn, "spoke out sincerely and forcefully about the Stalinist era"; he stressed that the most recent developments in literature were only a reflection of certain "general trends" in Soviet life.[19]

The first reviews of *Cancer Ward* appeared in 1968. They demonstrate that for Yugoslav critics it was no easy task to distinguish between Solzhenitsyn the artist and Solzhenitsyn the moral and social force, the centre of a politico-literary controversy. This dichotomy in the approach to Solzhenitsyn would mark many attempts at a literary evaluation of his works.

In his review published in *Borba* (12 October) the poet Mića Danojlić praised the novel highly, but did not let slip the opportunity to mention the "exceptional, dramatic circumstances" under which Solzhenitsyn's works were being read. He expressed admiration especially for the way in which Solzhenitsyn portrayed his female characters, but concluded that the author of *Cancer Ward* (he was reviewing only the first part of the novel) was "a traditionalist writer" who "rarely reaches, and never surpasses" the achievements of the Soviet writers of the 1920s and 1930s—of Pil'niak, Babel', Bunin and Olesha.

In an article entitled "All for the Sake of the Truth," published in November in the Zagreb literary paper *Telegram*,[20] another poet, Slavko Mihalić, laid greater emphasis upon the political aspects of

Solzhenitsyn's novel than had Danojlić. The first question that anyone reading *Cancer Ward* has to ask himself, according to Mihalić, is what kind of political system it is that for years has refused to allow a work such as *this* to be published, and has even persecuted its author "to the brink of despair and death." In *Cancer Ward*, which embodies a "deep and passionate striving for humanism," Mihalić finds nothing that could be proclaimed as anti-socialist. Solzhenitsyn made many "concessions" in his attempts to have the book published, but according to the Croatian poet, he made one essential miscalculation: he believed that Stalin was really dead. That was not so. Dogmatism in the Soviet Union had continued to grow; it had become more and more rigid; and its bureaucratic forms had "recently" triumphed in the campaign against the freedom of the Czechs and Slovaks. Mihalić tried to find an answer to the question of why the book was refused publication in the Soviet Union, but he despaired at the task, because "censorship is not something that can be comprehended by a normal human mind." Solzhenitsyn's problem was that he did not want to tell "commissioned and well-paid fairy tales" as official Soviet writers did. "He thinks that the task of a writer is to tell the truth, and all the more so if that truth is not accessible to all." Only by making the truth known, Mihalić maintained, could we ensure that the errors of the past would not be repeated.

In a review of *Cancer Ward* published in the Sarajevo monthly *Izraz*, under the title "Literature of the Truth,"[21] Risto Trifković related the novel to conditions in the Soviet Union and ventured the opinion that Solzhenitsyn "has even anticipated certain phenomena in Soviet society which have been more strongly and more obviously manifested recently—a certain revival of Stalinist methods in both the domestic and foreign policy of the country." These three articles, by Danojlić, Mihalić and Trifković, set the tone for more or less everything that was to be written about Solzhenitsyn in Yugoslavia in the next few years.

As time went by, and particularly between 1969 and 1972, interest in Solzhenitsyn increased and the support of Yugoslav intellectuals for his lonely battle with the Soviet authorities was unanimous. An illuminating example of such support was a commentary by the Slovene dramatist Bojan Štih, published in the Ljubljana literary newspaper *Naši razgledi*[22] shortly after Solzhenitsyn's expulsion from the Writers' Union. Extolling both the artistic virtues of Solzhenitsyn's works and the moral vitality of his personality, Štih concluded that "to stand side by side with Solzhenitsyn today is one's duty both as a writer and as a human being."

As a consequence of this interest and sympathy, Yugoslavia was in the early 1970s the only Communist country where more or less all of Solzhenitsyn's works had been translated and published—and, moreover, in all the main languages spoken in its different regions.

For example, the second part of *Cancer Ward*, published in Serbo-Croat as *River with No Estuary*, appeared in 1969.[23] The second edition of the novel, now complete in one volume, came out in the following year, not long after the author was awarded the Nobel Prize for Literature. The Slovenian edition, in two volumes, was brought out in 1971.[24] As for *The First Circle*, it was published in 1969 in Serbo-Croat,[25] and in 1970 in both Slovenian[26] and Macedonian.[27] But as early as 1968 a private, "independent edition" of the original Russian version had appeared in Belgrade, published by the poet Marija Čudina, the painter Leonid Šejka and the architect Slobodan Mašić. Their series has since become a popular vehicle for Yugoslav writers wishing to publish their books privately.

In 1971 a new translation of Solzhenitsyn's stories appeared in Belgrade.[28] Along with the three early stories, which had been included in the first collection of Solzhenitsyn's works, this new volume also contained "For the Good of the Cause," "Zakhar-Kalitá," and the cycle of "Sketches." The translator, Mira Lalić, won the "Miloš Đurić" Prize, awarded by the Association of Translators of Serbia for the best translated book of the year. Solzhenitsyn's two plays, *Candle in the Wind* and *The Lovegirl and the Innocent*, were also brought out in 1971.[29] The following year a book entitled *The Fire and the Ants* was published:[30] it contained Solzhenitsyn's "Sketches," of which the title story is one, his autobiographical note and 'Prayer," "The Ninth Day" (commemorating the death of Aleksandr Tvardovskii), "How People Are Reading *One Day...*," the "Letter to Three Students," and various other letters. The second Slovenian edition of Solzhenitsyn's stories was issued in 1971, now enlarged to include "For the Good of the Cause," "Zakhar-Kalitá," the "Sketches," and a wide selection of documents concerning the Solzhenitsyn "affair."[31] Finally, in 1973, *August 1914* appeared in the three major Yugoslav languages, Serbo-Croat,[32] Slovenian,[33] and Macedonian,[34] respectively.

Daily and weekly newspaper, literary journals and news magazines have all sustained an inexhaustible interest in Solzhenitsyn's
works. Almost all of his writings which were eventually published in
book form had previously appeared, in part or in full, in various
periodicals; many other items, which were not included in book
editions, were likewise published in the periodical press, not only
in the main languages of the country, but also in Albanian, Hungarian, Romanian, Slovak and Turkish.[35]

Further evidence of Solzhenitsyn's celebrity in Yugoslavia came
in January 1971, when the Belgrade monthly *Savremenik* published
a special Solzhenitsyn issue, with the intention of assessing his
books—testimonies of "human suffering in the hell of a false humanism"—"in the light of literature, psychology and morality," over and
above their political context. At the beginning of February 1971 the
theater in the Serbian town of Šabac produced a dramatization of
Cancer Ward which the Belgrade press proudly hailed as a "world
premiere." It was even reviewed for *Borba*[36] and *Politika*[37] by Belgrade theater critics, an honor rarely bestowed upon provincial
theaters in Yugoslavia.

More than fifty essays, reviews, commentaries and topical
articles on various aspects of Solzhenitsyn's works and career were
published in the country in the period 1969-1972. They expressed a
wide range of opinions. But all these writings were pervaded by a
common idea: that Solzhenitsyn was fighting for an "ethical socialism," and that his struggle was thus essentially similar to the one
that the Yugoslavs themselves had been waging. The award of the
Nobel Prize for Literature to Solzhenitsyn in October 1970 and its
aftermath provided Yugoslav critics with an excellent opportunity
to re-assess Solzhenitsyn's works, to give him additional support
in his fight, and to express their complete loyalty to a writer who, in
spite of his precarious position, had been bravely challenging, as the
Yugoslavs saw it at the time, the remnants of Stalinism in his own
country.

Perhaps the response most indicative of the sympathy that
surrounded Solzhenitsyn and his works in Yugoslavia in those years
was an article published in October 1970 in *Komunist*,[38] the official
paper of the League of Communists. Entitled "Obsessed with Truth"
and written by Risto Trifković (two of whose earlier articles have
already been referred to), it vividly illustrates the Yugoslav view of
Solzhenitsyn at the time and contains certain statements which help

in understanding why the attitude of the Yugoslav press towards the Russian writer was later—particularly after his Stockholm press conference in December 1974—to become so relentlessly hostile.

Although the decision of the Swedish Academy of Sciences was "not quite free" of political implications, wrote Trifković, the 1970 Nobel Prize for Literature had "gone to deserving hands." He stated unequivocally that Solzhenitsyn was "no opponent of socialist ideas" and "no anti-Communist"; rather, he was a product of Russian literature and of the Russian spiritual climate, which compelled writers to "live at the edge of individual and general martyrdom." "This means," added Trifković, "that one must not only write, but also preach and struggle for one's own ideas and principles, one must victimize oneself and, if necessary, perish in such a struggle! The infusion of the truth—this is Solzhenitsyn today." Although at present he stood "isolated in his own country, like a lighthouse," the time would come when his work, like that of Babel', Bulgakov and Pil'niak, would be accepted: "With open arms! History still has much to teach us." In his effort to reveal the "final truth" about Stalinism, which "degraded, darkened and destroyed hopes for socialism," Solzhenitsyn had, according to Trifković:

> turned against *any* system designed to subjugate human beings and humanity as a whole, against *any* system designed to suffocate freedom. This means that Stalinism has become only a symbol. His condemnation reaches the roots of *any* aggression against humanity. The author is not to be blamed in the least for the fact that he has used his own case as an example, nor for the fact that all this happened in the country in which he was born. In other words, Solzhenitsyn attacks every inconsistency based on a "lofty goal"—be it ideological, religious, racial or political.

Even though the picture he paints "is not nice"—sometimes "it is perhaps too one-sided and caustic"—it is not Solzhenitsyn "who is to be blamed for the fact that the truth he describes has been so dark! The facts are indeed dark, and he has not invented them."

It is beyond the scope of this essay, and of the present volume, to discuss in detail all of the major Yugoslav reactions to Solzhenitsyn in the period up to his expulsion. But, in concluding this preliminary survey of the reception of his works in Yugoslavia before 1974, it should be pointed out that, despite the general acceptance of Solzhenitsyn's ideas and a shared understanding of the moral and literary qualities of his writing, various—and often conflicting—views about his contribution to Soviet literature were published. They ranged from the opinion of Sveta Lukić that Solzhenitsyn, by his work and career, "announces the end of socialist realism" and "opens a new chapter in the history of Soviet Russian literature,"[39] to the claim by Pavle Ivić that, contrary to "the legend that there remains only one true writer in the Soviet Union," Solzhenitsyn is "neither the most talented Soviet writer, nor is his criticism of Soviet society the most profound one."[40]

The first volume of *The Gulag Archipelago* was published in Paris on 28 December 1973. On 6 January 1974 the initial stage of the official Soviet press campaign against Solzhenitsyn began with a summary in *Pravda* of an attack on the book by the East German Communist newspaper *Unsere Zeit*. Six days later, on 12 January, the Belgrade *Večernje novosti* ran a TANJUG dispatch entitled "Solzhenitsyn Severely Criticized." The Moscow correspondent of the official Yugoslav news agency reported that so far the Soviet press had carried only a selection of opinions from the East European press and the Communist papers of the West, but that an "atmosphere has been created, or is being created, in which a severe and more comprehensive reponse to Solzhenitsyn's activity is to be expected on the part of Soviet political institutions." On 10 January *Politika* had reported the official Soviet reaction to *Gulag*: the paper's Moscow correspondent, Risto Bajalski, stressed that the only Western comments being publicized in the Soviet press were those which agreed with the Soviet line. A similar report by the Moscow correspondent of the Zagreb daily *Vjesnik*, Drago Buvač, was printed on 13-14 January under the title "Solzhenitsyn's Cold War." Neither of these reporters permitted himself any personal comments.

On 14 January *Pravda* published an article by I. Solov'ev headed "The Path of Treachery," and the next day both *Politika* and *Vjesnik* quoted extensively from this, the first authoritative Soviet attack on Solzhenitsyn in the new campaign. *Politika*'s correspondent further mentioned the critical remarks made by Iurii Zhukov on Moscow television, as too did *Vjesnik* in its report of 13-14 January.

The first indigenous Yugoslav comment on *Gulag* (which also turned out to be the first unequivocal condemnation of Solzhenitsyn) was printed on 17 January by *Vjesnik* under the title "Solzhenitsyn." Željko Brihta, the newspaper's foreign editor, severely criticized him for smearing both socialism and Lenin, and for changing from "a critic of individuals" into "a critic of the system." Solzhenitsyn had become, Brihta wrote, "whether he wanted to or not, a supporter, an emblem and standard-bearer of notorious anti-Communists and anti-socialists (...) of those people who would like to see the ruin of the Soviet and of any other socialist society." The article was, however, careful to make the point that "Yugoslav Communists do not object to anti-Stalinism, but rather to anti-socialism; they object to the fact that some people automatically and in every case identify Stalinism with socialism and in so doing identify (...) Stalinism with Communism. One does not oppose mention of Stalin's camps, nor consider it essential; what is of the essence is the attitude shown toward socialism."

Despite its strongly critical tone, Brihta's article stopped short of unqualified support for the Soviet authorities' treatment of Solzhenitsyn. That such support did not exist is obvious from the coverage in Yugoslav papers of the events preceding and following Solzhenitsyn's expulsion from the Soviet Union. Although at first the Yugoslav press carried only short news items, they included not only interpretations of the official Soviet view of the Solzhenitsyn "affair," but also reports from Western news agencies, unofficial Soviet responses (Evtushenko's protest telegram to Brezhnev and his letter to friends in the West), and the comments of those Western Communist parties which were critical of the Soviet decision to expel Solzhenitsyn. The first Yugoslav comments were published rather belatedly, but by two influential weeklies, the Belgrade *NIN* (24 February) and the Zagreb *VUS* (27 February), as well as by the Ljubljana daily *Delo* (23 February). In Ljubljana on 8 March, the fortnightly newspaper *Naši razgledi* published an interview with Heinrich Böll on the expulsion of Solzhenitsyn, which had previously appeared in *Der Spiegel*, as well as an article by Giorgio Napolitano taken from *Rinascità* and written from the Italian Communist point of view.

The two Yugoslav reactions, by Zoran Žujović and Drago Buvač, respectively, are worth considering in some detail. Writing in *NIN*,[41] Žujović, the first to translate *One Day*...into Serbo-Croat, began by summarizing the main themes of Solzhenitsyn's major works, then went on to describe his conflicts with the Soviet authorities and the measures taken against him in February 1974, culminating in his expulsion. Žujović maintained of *Gulag* that it "has a documentary character" since it is based on the "oral and written testimony of 227 persons, themselves former prisoners, convicts and camp inmates."

He cited Solzhenitsyn's assertion that in his book "there are no fictitious persons or fictitious events," and that "people and places are
called by their real names." After a brief survey of the main chapters
of *Gulag*, Žujović turned his attention to those passages in the book
which treated the case of General Vlasov and his army, contesting
more by implication than in so many words the official Soviet version,
according to which Solzhenitsyn "glorifies treason and traitors—
Vlasov and the Vlasovites, as his supporters were called—as well
as German fascism and Hitler's army." The *NIN* article pointed out
that Solzhenitsyn, too, believed that "these traitors deserve condemnation—as traitors. But he also raises the question: how was it possible that hundreds of thousands of people could have chosen the
path of treason, betraying their own country?" The answer to this
question Solzhenitsyn finds in the conditions prevailing in Russia
after the October revolution. Žujović further emphasized that Solzhenitsyn did not accept the view that Stalin was responsible for distorting Leninist theory and practice, but saw Stalin merely as Lenin's
successor. Žujović's "comment" on this claim by Solzhenitsyn is
an exclamation mark.

Later in his article Žujović reviewed the various official responses
to Solzhenitsyn's expulsion, not only in the Soviet Union and elsewhere in the East, but also in the West, concluding with an analysis
of the positions taken by those West European Communist parties
which, despite their disagreement with some of Solzhenitsyn's views,
had been critical of his expatriation. Finally, Žujović mentioned the
attitudes of Roy Medvedev and Evgenii Evtushenko. Medvedev was
quoted as saying that "all the major facts" in Solzhenitsyn's book,
and "all the details about the life and suffering of prisoners," are
absolutely true, but that he nonetheless disagreed "with certain
judgments and conclusions," notably Solzhenitsyn's allegation that
Stalin was merely Lenin's successor. Evtushenko's letter, published
in *Il Giorno*, was reproduced in part (including Evtushenko's claim
that he had sent a letter of protest to the Soviet leadership, that his
poetry reading on Moscow television had then been cancelled, and
that he had been officially advised to condemn Solzhenitsyn publicly).
The same story was mentioned in *Vjesnik*: in a report of 24-25 February entitled "What Did Evtushenko Want," the paper's Moscow
correspondent quoted Evtushenko as saying that he was worried
that Soviet youth would be insufficiently informed about "the darkest
consequences of Stalin's personality cult," because of the decelera-

tion of the process of de-Stalinization. *Vjesnik's* correspondent also mentioned the opinion of some "malicious Muscovites" who claimed that the real reason for Evtushenko's protest was not his disagreement with the action taken against Solzhenitsyn, but his supposed desire to turn attention to himself because of his waning popularity.

It was the same author, Drago Buvač, who discussed the Solzhenitsyn "affair" in *VUS*, in what was the second major Yugoslav press response to the expulsion. In an article entitled "Making Play with Soviet Dissidents,"[42] Buvač alleged that "certain Western circles have been trying to exploit Soviet dissidents as a means of exerting pressure upon the Soviet Union, a kind of ideological payment for economic cooperation," but he also pointed out that Soviet dissidents were not simply a creation of Western propaganda: "this would be only half of the answer, since dissidents are a product of the internal political development of the Soviet Union." In addition, Buvač reviewed the forms of dissent in the Soviet Union, providing a list of prominent dissenters, emphasizing the absence of a common political platform among those affiliated to various "movements" and explaining their methods and their unauthorized publishing activities. He also quoted two opposing opinions, namely that dissidents had appeared as a result of de-Stalinization, and that they had emerged as a consequence of the deceleration in de-Stalinization. However, Buvač concluded, "there is, frankly speaking, another judgment which could be made with regard to Soviet dissenters: if Soviet society had a slightly wider margin for free public expression and polemics with those [whose] stands are 'out of line'—but in essence neither negative, nor anti-socialist—the number of dissidents would be much lower."

This article, with its suggestion that a relaxation of censorship would reduce the number of dissidents, is by far the most outspoken attempt to lay the blame for the increased number of dissenters in the Soviet Union on the restrictive character of the Soviet regime itself. Similar views about the intellectual climate in the USSR had been voiced in Yugoslav literary journals and magazines in earlier years, but this kind of political justification of the dissident movement carried special weight in the present case, since it was carried on the pages of an influential daily paper with a large circulation.

In late February and early March Western news agencies reported from Belgrade that two Zagreb publishing houses, Naprijed and Znanje, had applied for an option to publish *The Gulag Archi-*

pelago in Serbo-Croat. It was speculated that this initiative was connected with the attack by Vladimir Bakarić, the leading Croat politician, and some other Croat leaders on Stalinism and a "Stalinist
faction" in Yugoslavia. It was assumed that *Gulag* could provide an
effective additional weapon with which to fight any "Stalinist faction" in the country. At the same time, doubt was expressed as to
whether Solzhenitsyn would agree to the deletion from his work of
any references to Lenin's responsibility for Stalin's subsequent
crimes, a contention that the Yugoslav authorities would have
found repugnant. On 19 March DPA, the West German news agency,
carried a report from Belgrade based on an interview between a DPA
correspondent and a spokesman for the Znanje publishing house: the
spokesman was reported as saying that the YMCA Press in Paris,
publishers of the original Russian edition of *Gulag*, had failed to
answer Znanje's request to examine Solzhenitsyn's new book and
that, therefore, Znanje now considered its request withdrawn. According to DPA, Naprijed was continuing its efforts to obtain the
original of *Gulag* for study. A Naprijed representative was quoted
as saying that, since widely divergent views were held about the
book, a decision on its publication could be made only after the editors had had a chance to see the original. However, on 8 April Reuters stated in a report from Zagreb that the "Croatian Communist
Party has recommended that Aleksandr Solzhenitsyn's controversial
book (...) should not be published in Yugoslavia because of its
'extreme anti-Soviet views.'" According to Reuters, the Party's
ideological commission had made its recommendation to Naprijed
and the decision on whether or not to publish *Gulag* now lay with
Naprijed's editorial board. The report also claimed that "word that
Naprijed was seeking an option on the work brought an immediate
Soviet protest."

To a good many Western journalists, Soviet pressures on the
Yugoslav authorities often appear to be the most obvious explanation
for certain Yugoslav actions. There is no doubt that such pressures
have been, and continue to be exerted, or that in many instances they
influence specific decisions whereby individual and factional interests
in Yugoslavia are sacrificed for the sake of interests of state. But, as
far as *The Gulag Archipelago* is concerned, the reported Soviet
pressure was not the crucial factor in the decision against publication.
Rather, it was Solzhenitsyn's own "offence," as the Yugoslav author-

ities saw it, in "defaming" Lenin, as well as his general "anti-socialist" position. Solzhenitsyn had now clearly demonstrated to Yugoslav officials that their previous defence of him had been based on a false presumption: he was not only an anti-Stalinist, he was an anti-Communist. And his anti-Communism was not to be tolerated.

It should be remembered that the main reason for banning the Belgrade magazine *Delo*, in which Mihajlo Mihajlov's *Moscow Summer* had been serialized in 1965, was his implicit indictment of Lenin as the one responsible for opening the first labor camps in the USSR. Even to the present day, Stalinism, "bureaucratic socialism" and the "cult of personality" can be attacked in the Yugoslav press without restraint, but Lenin's image must not be smeared. In all other respects *Gulag* would have been welcomed, particularly given the fact that anti-labor camp literature had been officially encouraged in Yugoslavia since the 1950's. Not only Western revelations about that gruesome episode in modern Russian history,[43] but even some Yugoslav treatments of the same theme, were published. The most outspoken of the latter was Karl Steiner's *Seven Thousand Days in Siberia*, which appeared in installments in *NIN* between February and June 1971. In 1972, after it had been published as a bulky volume,[44] Steiner's book was awarded a distinguished literary prize as the book of the year.[45] The announcement of this award was made in the middle of 1972, only one day before an official visit by Tito to Moscow. In 1977 the same prize was given to another Yugoslav book with a similar theme. This was a collection of short stories by Danilo Kiš, entitled *A Tomb for Boris Davidovich*,[46] which gave a moving account of the misfortunes of several characters who perished in Soviet labor camps or died in the USSR as the victims of blind forces of terror. One of Kiš's stories—in which authentic documents serve as the basis for the fiction—is dedicated to Karl Steiner.[47]

Despite their disagreement with Solzhenitsyn's attitude towards Lenin, Yugoslav newspapers were still not openly hostile to him. But December 1974 brought a new event, which introduced a further element of discord between Solzhenitsyn and his Yugoslav commentators. At a press conference in Stockholm following the delayed presentation of his Nobel Prize, Solzhenitsyn spoke out on behalf of Mihajlo Mihajlov, who had been arrested two months earlier for allegedly spreading anti-Soviet and anti-Yugoslav propaganda. In response to a question, Solzhenitsyn said that President Tito was

leading a "cruel and heartless" Communist regime, and that Mihajlov found himself in the same situation as did Soviet political prisoners.

Yugoslav papers were quick to reply. On 20 December *Borba*
carried an article entitled "In Springer's Service," in which it was
said that Solzhenitsyn had "crudely slandered Yugoslavia" and
falsified its reality by "well-established methods." Pointing out that
"the activities of this author increasingly transcend the bounds of
literature and assume an unconcealed anti-Communist character,"
Borba particularly criticized Solzhenitsyn for contributing to the
émigré periodical *Kontinent*. *Borba* reminded its readers that Solzhenitsyn's connection with *Kontinent*, which was published by right-
wing West German publisher Axel Springer, had elicited a "sharp
reaction from the West German liberal intellectuals Günter Grass
and Heinrich Böll." This was the first in a series of similar strongly-
worded articles in which Solzhenitsyn's "messianic ambition,"
his "Christian socialism" (which he supposedly shared with Mihajlov), and his appeals to the West to start an "ideological crusade"
against the Soviet Union and socialist countries in general were
singled out for criticism.[48] Sakharov's rejection of Solzhenitsyn's
"nationalism, isolationism and patriarchal and religious romanticism" was quoted with approval.

Among the articles published between late December 1974 and
March 1975 there was only one in which a tone of virulent hostility
towards the "new" Solzhenitsyn was lacking. This was Predrag
Matvejević's essay "Confrontation with Solzhenitsyn," which
appeared in the Sarajevo monthly *Izraz*.[49] Matvejević is an influential
Croatian literary critic and a professor of French literature at Zagreb
University. In the last few years he has played an important part in
directing and co-ordinating literary developments in Yugoslavia and
can almost be said to have assumed a semi-official role. Since his
essay was probably written about two months prior to its publication—as contributions to literary magazines usually are—it is illus-
trative of the manner in which the Yugoslav critical establishment
treated Solzhenitsyn *before* his "anti-Yugoslav outburst."

Matvejević contended that, after the publication of *The Gulag
Archipelago* and the author's expulsion from his homeland, Yugoslav
attitudes towards him had been expressed exclusively in the form of
quotations from foreign news agency reports. He wondered if this
were not a result of "insufficiently defined views" and suggested

that it might be necessary to formulate critical judgments, however divergent, which would come "from the social and cultural climate which characterizes the *individuality*" of Yugoslavia and its chosen path. He proceeded to attempt to do exactly that. Solzhenitsyn "disappointed" Matvejević because in his later books he had not fulfilled the expectations aroused by his early stories. What was more, Matvejević noticed in *The First Circle* an "inversion of certain socialist realist procedures" and voiced surprise that György Lukács should have described it as a "temporary pinnacle of contemporary world literature."[50] Matvejević concentrated his analysis, however, upon three of Solzhenitsyn's works: *August 1914*, "Letter to the Soviet Leaders" and *The Gulag Archipelago*.

Throughout his essay Matvejević maintained a moderate tone, trying to be both objective and reasonable in his comments. He described *August 1914* as a "vast historical fresco," modelled partly on Tolstoi's *War and Peace*. Devoid as it was of any direct political reference to present-day conditions in the Soviet Union, it was only in its "general implication" that this novel suggested an analogy with Stalin's disastrous unpreparedness for war in 1941. Solzhenitsyn's aim in *August 1914* was to expose "the true face of history, its misery more than its glory," but in so doing he had resorted to techniques well-known in West European and American novels. While recognizing that it is a difficult task to judge a work which remains unfinished, Matvejević nevertheless admitted that he found in *August 1914* "a certain homogeneity" and that he had read it with interest. However, Solzhenitsyn's artistic mastery, according to Matvejević, had not reached the level of Sholokhov, nor surpassed that of Leonov; Bulgakov, by contrast, was much closer to contemporary aesthetic sensibility.

Matvejević defined the "Letter to Soviet Leaders" as a "short work which brings explicitly to light Solzhenitsyn's political, philosophical, historical and religious attitudes and ideas." It testified, among other things, to Solzhenitsyn's isolation from "many developments of contemporary thought" and illustrated "his effort to judge new times by old, traditional criteria." Matvejević went on: "While fully respecting Solzhenitsyn's right to hold and to express his beliefs, one might at this point ask how the ancient Orthodox faith, in which this author sees a repository of values and the only salvation for his country, could become historically and socially relevant in our times, when it was unable to change even the old

Russia into a modern and just country and to save it from its own glaring contradictions?'' And what about the non-Russian and non-Orthodox peoples and regions of the Soviet Union?—asks Matvejević rhetorically, concluding that Solzhenitsyn's views are "anachronistic, conservative and provincial."

As far as *Gulag* was concerned, Matvejević accepted one French critic's description of it as an "historical pamphlet," and asserted that "testimony" and "pamphlet" were two layers of this book which continuously intertwine. Solzhenitsyn's treatment of Lenin as the man responsible for the terror and for the camps in post-revolutionary Russia Matvejević explained as reflecting his Christian ideas of non-violence. "The writer of *Gulag* does not accept and does not approve of any revolution, because it is by definition an 'expression of violence.' Therefore, he cannot accept that the measures which the Soviet authorities had to undertake in order to establish and sustain their power were necessary revolutionary acts; rather he sees in them repressive and anti-human crimes." That was why Solzhenitsyn so readily and unreflectingly identified those acts with Stalin's methods in the period when resort to violence, repression and lawlessness was no longer necessary, since power had already been won. In the parts of *Gulag* dealing with the period of the "cult of personality" Matvejević saw nothing that would not already have been known and read about in Yugoslavia, but he affirmed that the writer's testimony was "extraordinary" and "convincing." The Vlasovites, he emphasized, were "a special problem in the book." Solzhenitsyn justified their predicament by reference to Stalin's indifference towards human beings and explained their treason as a struggle for survival. Their fate following repatriation to the Soviet Union *was* "horrible," but while "all this probably goes some way towards explaining why the Vlasovites were so numerous," Matvejević "nevertheless could not see how one can justify those most brutal crimes which they themselves committed in their Nazi uniforms," thereby implying that Solzhenitsyn had done so. In conclusion, Matvejević described *Gulag* as a "painful" book, and therefore of the kind likely to cause "misunderstandings" and "conflicts" between politics and art. Although Solzhenitsyn's testimony cannot "leave us indifferent, we are aware that the issues raised by this man and writer are slaves of his own bitterness."

An escalation of hostilities against Solzhenitsyn on the part of the Yugoslav press took place in July 1975, and ever since then

Yugoslav responses to his various political statements have been characterized by a complete rejection of everything for which this "new" or "second" Solzhenitsyn—as some Yugoslav commentators have described him—now stands. On 2 July TANJUG reported from Washington in terms that are typical of the way in which Solzhenitsyn has been treated in Yugoslavia in the mid- and late-seventies. His speech at an AFL-CIO banquet given in his honor in Washington the day before was described as "his fiercest outburst of anti-Communist and reactionary feelings to date." In his condemnation of the United States "for recognizing the USSR in 1933 and for allying herself with its 'totalitarian regime' in 1941," TANJUG claimed, Solzhenitsyn "has surpassed even the most sinister reactionaries." The following day most Yugoslav newspapers published this report.

In mid-July one of Yugoslavia's "heavies" entered the polemics. In response to Solzhenitsyn's short essay "The Third World War," recently printed in *Le Monde*, the Yugoslav press carried an article by Josip Vidmar, literary critic and president of the Slovenian Academy of Arts and Sciences, which had originally been written for the Ljubljana daily *Delo*. A translation of Vidmar's article, entitled "Dark Irresponsibility," appeared in *Politika* on 13 July. Summarizing Solzhenitsyn's vision of the "third world war," Vidmar took particular exception to his assertion that the Vietnam War had ended with thousands of executions and with the establishment of huge new concentration camps. Dubbing Solzhenitsyn "this Christian alchemist of the West," Vidmar insisted that the Vietnam War had brought a "splendid victory to the Vietnamese people" who, inspired by "unprecedented bravery," had won in spite of the "unscrupulous interventionist army of the United States." According to Vidmar, "the world has probably never read anything more deplorable" than Solzhenitsyn's *Le Monde* article: his "philosophizing" was "horrible," and Vidmar discerned in it a "blind and fanatical hatred." The Slovenian critic recalled the appeals sent by Leonid Andreev to the Western powers from his Finnish sanctuary after the First World War and which were as futile as was the actual military intervention against the young Soviet state. To launch the same kind of appeals today, Vidmar thought "ridiculous." He admitted that Solzhenitsyn had suffered "a great injustice in the past," but that, in his view, did not give him the right "to look upon the revolution as a terrible nightmare, an act of senseless violence inimical to mankind," or to belittle the peoples "who have been fighting for their place in the sun."

The last paragraph of Vidmar's article was addressed to those P.E.N. Clubs which "have Platonically guarded and protected" Solzhenitsyn hitherto. "Would some of these P.E.N. Clubs," wondered Vidmar, "inform him, in accordance with their charter, that blind and fanatical hatred does not befit a writer?"

On 31 July 1975 *Večernje novosti* (Belgrade) published an editorial entitled simply "Solzhenitsyn." Even though the paper is printed in Cyrillic, the title of the leader was in Latin script, as an indication of the author's "moral fall." The writer, Milivoje Glišić, reviewed Solzhenitsyn's activities since his expulsion and asked why the younger Yugoslav intellectuals, who had in the past rightly sympathized with Solzhenitsyn's struggle for greater freedom of expression, were now so "drowsily silent." It seemed to Glišić that "in Yugoslavia it was only the octogenarian Academician Vidmar" who had publicly analyzed "the pathology of this turn to the right." In fact, such an analysis had already been published in the July issue of the Belgrade literary journal *Književna reč*. It was in the form of an "Open Letter to Solzhenitsyn" by Dževad Sabljaković, a young man better known in Yugoslavia as a television news-reader than as either a writer or a critic. As the cause of what he described as his "sad anger," Sabljaković cited Solzhenitsyn's "morally unacceptable behavior, which jeopardizes the whole creative and intellectual personality of an inspired and brave" writer. "To tell the truth about the events of an epoch in one's own country, even when that truth is as bitter as gall, when it impugns leaders, throws whole periods of politics and ideology into question—this is a great task for a writer; but to promote war, enslavement and colonialism marks a precipitate moral, spiritual and creative decline."

This tone of solemn invective was disturbed in September. Writing under the pseudonym A. Ljubimov in his regular column in the Belgrade review *Duga*, Brana Crnčević, one of the most popular Yugoslav satirists, ridiculed the pretentiousness and pomposity of Sabljaković's "letter."[51] In his usual sarcastic manner Crnčević proclaimed Sabljaković's letter "the event of the season" and explained that, "before taking a stand on the whole matter," he would like to know something more about the nature of this conflict between "the great powers." Therefore, he was impatiently awaiting Solzhenitsyn's reply which, he hoped, would explain what it was all about.

After 1975 there was no love lost between Solzhenitsyn and the Yugoslav press. Readers in Yugoslavia were duly informed about the escalation of Solzhenitsyn's anti-Communism and his opposition to the policy of *détente*, in factual reports following his speeches in July 1975 to the AFL-CIO in New York and to a gathering of US Senators and Congressmen. Both President Ford's disinclination to receive Solzhenitsyn in the White House and the myth-enshrouded refusal of the Kenyan government to issue him an entrance visa that same year were greeted with sympathy and approval.[52]

In the late seventies the tenor of Yugoslav comments was set by an interview which Erich Fromm granted to the Italian review *Panorama*. The sections referring to Solzhenitsyn were reprinted in Serbo-Croat in *Večernje novosti* on 3 November 1975. This short piece, entitled "Solzhenitsyn—Man of Hatred," described the Russian writer as a "dangerous man," who was directly or indirectly encouraging a process which could lead only to nuclear catastrophe. Portraying Solzhenitsyn as a "fanatic" and a "typical demagogue with almost Nazi-like illusions of being the saviour of the world," Fromm pointed out that Solzhenitsyn's "wish to destroy Communism was much stronger than his wish not to destroy humanity in a nuclear war." The same interview was quoted again in *Večernje novosti* of 3 April 1977. Under the headline "Solzhenitsyn behind the Iron Curtain," the article depicted his "American idyll" in the Vermont town of Cavendish and described Solzhenitsyn as a near-maniac, closeted behind an iron fence and protected by closed-circuit television cameras. This article displayed the same kind of bitter cynicism as an earlier dispatch filed by the TANJUG correspondent in Madrid and published on 31 March 1976 in the Ljubljana daily *Delo*. Entitled "Solzhenitsyn the Crusader," it castigated Solzhenitsyn for the television interview which he had given during a recent trip to Spain. A few other reports from Madrid were published in connection with the same visit,[53] but in subsequent years the number of comments has sharply decreased. Thus, in February 1977 *NIN* was again severely critical of Solzhenitsyn, but this time it lumped him together with the whole "third wave of the Russian emigration."[54] In June 1978 his Harvard speech was censured in terms as predictable as the ones which Solzhenitsyn himself had been using in recent years.

That this bickering will continue in years to come, unless there are dramatic changes either in Yugoslavia or with Solzhenitsyn, is clearly indicated by a report which appeared when this survey was almost completed. Commenting on an essay by Solzhenitsyn published in *Time* magazine on 18 February 1980, *NIN*[55] discovered in

Solzhenitsyn's "anti-Communist crusade" "a few characteristically new accents." The first of these was a "pathetic effort" to defend the Russian national spirit against "unidentified accusations of collaboration with Communism." The second was the argument—put forward long before him and "with more persistence and consistency" by "some of his bitterest ideological opponents"—that only one "model" of Communism exists, and that within the leadership of one party there can be no diverging views. Thus, Solzhenitsyn had come to a conclusion with which not even the most "exemplary Stalinist" could find fault. According to *NIN*, there was also a third new "accent": Solzhenitsyn had claimed that the West was making an historical mistake in seeking an ally in Communist China; more than that, "it is a mad, suicidal policy." Solzhenitsyn had, *NIN* contended, come "full circle." He was now adopting a position very close to the official policy of the country from which he had been expelled.

Judging both by Solzhenitsyn's *Time* essay and by these comments on it, we may safely conclude that we have not heard the last of the Yugoslav commentators' quarrel with Solzhenitsyn's "messianism."

Notes

1. *Večer*, 3 January to 6 February 1963.

2. *Tovariš*, 31 December 1962 to 2 March 1963.

3. *Magyar Szo*, 28 November to 5 December 1962, and 1-20 January 1963.

4. *Panorama*, vol. 12, Nos. 8-12, 1963.

5. *Večernje novosti*, 23 January to 6 February 1963.

6. *Večer*, 5-22 March 1963.

7. *Politika*, 23 January to 7 February 1963; and *Vjesnik*, 6-21 February 1963.

8. *Nova Makedonija*, 6 January 1963.

9. *En dan Ivana Denisoviča in še dve noveli* (Ljubljana: "Državna zalozba Slovenije," 1964); *Večer*, 26 April to 26 May 1966.

10. *Jedan dan Ivana Denisoviča. Dogadaj na stanici Krečetovka. Matrjonina kuča* (Belgrade: "Kultura," 1963).

11. Aleksandar Flaker, ed., *Suvremeni sovjetski pisci*, vol. 4 (Zagreb: "Naprijed," 1964), pp. 233-85.

12. "Između dvije noći zvjezdane...," *Kolo*, vol. 1, No. 3 (New Series), 1963, pp. 357-68.

13. "Mrtvi dom F.M. Dostojevskog i A. Solženjicina," *Forum*, vol. 5, No. 6, 1964, pp. 906-28. English translation included in Mihajlov's *Russian Themes* (London: Macdonald; and New York: Farrar, Straus & Giroux, both 1968), pp. 78-118.

14. "Suvremena ruska proza na raskrsnici," *Vjesnik*, 2 October 1963. English in *Russian Themes*, pp. 304-10.

15. "Od Babelja do Solženjicina," *Izraz*, vol. 17, No. 5, 1965, pp. 483-87.

16. Mića Danojlić, "Birokrata koji boluje od raka," *Borba*, 12 October 1968, p. 12.

17. *Odjel za rak* (Rijeka: "Otokar Keršovani," 1968).

18. The letter to the Fourth Writers' Congress was also published in *Kolo*, vol. 6, No. 12, 1968, pp. 577-81.

19. "Obračun sa 'literaturom obračuna'," p. 9.

20. "Sve zbog istine," *Telegram*, 8 November 1968, p. 4.

21. "Literatura istine," *Izraz*, vol. 24, No. 12, 1968, pp. 553-56.

22. "Aleksander Solženicin," *Naši razgledi*, 21 November 1969, p. 667.

23. *Rijeka bez ušća* (Rijeka: "Otokar Keršovani," 1969).

24. *Rakkov oddelek*, 2 vols. (Ljubljana: "Delo," 1971).

25. *U prvom krugu* (Rijeka: "Otokar Keršovani," 1969).

26. *Prvi krog*, 2 vols. (Ljubljana: "Mladinska knjiga," 1970).

27. *Vo prviot krug*, 2 vols. (Skopje: "Nova Makedonija," 1970).

28. *Pripovetke* (Belgrade: "Srpska književna zadruga," 1971).

29. *Sveća na vetru. Jelen i logorska lepotica* (Belgrade: "Obelisk," 1971).

30. *Vatra i mravi* (Belgrade: "Obelisk," 1972).

31. *En dan Ivana Denisoviča. Povesti, črtice, dokumentacija* (Ljubljana: "Državna založba Slovenije," 1971).

32. *Avgust četrnaeste*, 2 vols. (Belgrade: "Srpska književna zadruga," 1973).

33. *Avgust štirinajstega*, 2 vols. (Ljubljana: "Mladinska knjiga," 1973).

34. *Avgust četirinaestata*, 2 vols. (Skopje: "Nova Makedonija," 1973).

35. See, for example: *Jeta e re*, vol. 12, No. 6, 1970, pp. 959-73; *Rilindja*, 5 November 1970; 7 *Nap*, 23 October 1970; *Libertatea*, 18 October 1970; *Nový život*, vol. 23, No. 4, 1971, pp. 325-36; and *Sesler*, vol. 6, No. 52, 1971, pp. 115-20.

36. B. Bulatović, "Odlazak kulturne provincije," 18 February 1971, p. 8.

37. Mirko Miloradović, "'Točak' za Borisa Kovača," 15 February 1971, p. 11.

38. "Opsjednutost istinom. Uz Nobelovu nagradu Solženjicinu," *Komunist*, No. 709, 22 October 1970, p. 28.

39. "Jedan pogled na teoriju i praksu socijalističkog realizma" (Part IV), *Delo*, vol. 17, No. 1, 1971, pp. 67-85.

40. "A. Solženjicin: *U prvom krugu*," *Gradina*, vol. 5, No. 3, 1970, pp. 29-39. Ivić held that both Ovechkin and Tendriakov were Solzhenitsyn's superiors.

41. "Slučaj Solženjicin," 24 February 1974, pp. 30-32.

43. For example: Margaret Buber-Neumann, *Under Two Dictators*; Georgy Klimov, *The Terror Machine*; A. Weissberg-Cybulski, *Conspiracy of Silence*.

44. *7000 dana u Sibiru* (Zagreb: "Globus," 1970).

45. The "Goran" Prize, awarded by the Zagreb daily *Vjesnik*.

46. *Grobnica za Borisa Davidovica* (Zagreb: "Liber"; Belgrade: "BIGZ" 1976). English translation (New York: Harcourt Brace Jovanovich, 1978).

47. Steiner, an Austrian by birth, came to Yugoslavia in the early 1920s, joined the Yugoslav Communist Party and later went to the Soviet Union. He was arrested there in 1936. After his death sentence was commuted to life imprisonment, he spent "seven thousand days" (between 1936 and 1956) in various Soviet labor camps. After the reconciliation between Belgrade and Moscow he was released and returned to Yugoslavia. His story of his days in Siberia was written with the intention of telling the whole world, but above all "my party comrades and friends, all the terrible things that I experienced," in order that "many illusions, lies and deceptions could be destroyed."

48. Miodrag Marović, "Transformacija jednog pisca," *NIN*, 29 December 1974; Miodrag Marović, "Solženicin včeraj in danes," *Naši razgledi*, 7 February 1975; France Klopčič, "Dva Solženicina," *Naši razgledi*, 21 March 1975.

49. "Solženjicin pred nama," *Izraz*, vol. 37, No. 2, February 1975, pp. 160-68; reprinted in the Skopje daily *Nova Makedonija*, 9 March, and the Titograd daily *Pobjeda*, 31 March-8 April 1975.

50. Lukács's book *Solženjicin* was published in Belgrade in 1971 by "Klub čitalaca Komunista."

51. "Jedan letnji zapis," *Duga*, 6 September 1975, p. 28.

52. The Kenyan episode was reported as "Solženjicinu zabranjen ulazak u Keniju," *Politika*, 25 July 1975, p. 2, and was also carried in the Western press. The story arose from an invitation apparently extended to Solzhenitsyn for him to attend a meeting in Nairobi of the International Council of Christian Churches. There seems to be some doubt as to whether Solzhenitsyn received any such invitation, let alone accepted it. The Kenyan government appears to have rejected in advance a visa application which might never have been made.

53. See *Nova Makedonija*, 13 April 1976 and *Vjesnik*, 14 April 1976.

54. Miodrag Marović, "Treći ešalon," *NIN*, 13 February 1977, p. 41.

55. "Biće skoro propast sveta," *NIN*, 24 February 1980, pp. 44-45.

Solzhenitsyn: Effigies and Oddities

MICHAEL NICHOLSON

The survey which follows is concerned less with the "real" Solzhenitsyn than with certain versions and images which have been
fashioned in recent years.[1] Ever since his literary début almost
twenty years ago, Solzhenitsyn has repeatedly emerged as catalyst
or litmus, figurehead or irritant. His works have been translated
into at least thirty-five languages and have sold more than thirty
million copies throughout the world.[2] His fate has seemed to impinge
upon that of whole governments, not least in the Soviet Union. Students of the political career of Nikita Khrushchev in particular have
good reason to dwell on the First Secretary's decision in 1962 to allow
the publication of *One Day in the Life of Ivan Denisovich*, while the
list of other Soviet dignitaries who have found themselves constrained to utter Solzhenitsyn's name in public (with varying degrees
of repugnance) is headed by Brezhnev, Kosygin, Podgornyi and
Furtseva. Outside the Soviet Union the award of the Nobel Prize for
Literature in 1970 led to the discomfiture of Swedish Prime Minister
Olof Palme and charges that his government's reluctance to assist
in the formal presentation of the prize in Moscow amounted to scandalous pusillanimity. In 1974 the West German Bundestag was the
scene of impassioned debate when Willy Brandt faced criticism for
allegedly having connived at Solzhenitsyn's expulsion from Soviet
territory by making a premature offer of sanctuary. The European
Parliament, in session in Strasbourg, was another of the august bodies which set aside time for discussion of his forcible removal from Soviet soil, and shortly afterwards the Secretary-General of the United
Nations had to defend himself against the embarrassing accusation
that "the embargo imposed upon Solzhenitsyn's writings in his
native land has been, with exquisitely indicative irony, reproduced
on the international territory of the United Nations—the organization
charged with defending the free expression for which Solzhenitsyn

was ready to give his life."[3] As for the response from the American body politic, suffice it to say that its amplitude was such as to span the near-conferment of honorary citizenship in 1975 and a public rebuke three years later from the First Lady of the Land.[4]

Spokesmen of all political persuasions, a veritable gallery of intellectuals and eminences, have been ready to testify, in sympathy or animosity, to the impact Solzhenitsyn has made, and we have come to take such attention for granted. No longer are we startled that the Soviet Nobel laureate Mikhail Sholokhov should once have likened him to a Colorado beetle,[5] or that the present heir to the throne of the United Kingdom should speak in his support before the Australian Academy of Science.[6] After all, those who have quoted or passed comment upon Solzhenitsyn by now include at least one Pope,[7] Hitler's architect,[8] several of France's "nouveaux philosophes,"[9] and a member of the Baader-Meinhof Gang.[10]

It is scarcely surprising that amongst these diverse and voluminous responses there are not a few which incline towards the curious or the extravagant. Thus, at the end of the 1970s the representative of one American firm which specializes in T-shirts depicting cultural and historical personalities estimated that of all the subjects not offered by his company the most frequently requested were Solzhenitsyn and the culinary expert Julia Child.[11] In 1975 when evangelist Billy Graham spoke warmly of Solzhenitsyn, he did so, we are told, "from a flower-bedecked podium, with the support of choirs, an organ and a piano," while preaching to a crowd 10,000 strong in a Brussels sports stadium.[12] In 1976 the British press reported that a former foreign minister, apparently intoxicated by the spirit of Solzhenitsyn's appearance on television the night before, had announced to assembled journalists his intention of retiring from the Labour Party, had declared himself henceforth for "the army of Solzhenitsyn and Sakharov," and had, more or less simultaneously, fallen over, muttering: "Oh God, I knew this was going to happen."[13] In spring of the same year a sample of American high school pupils was asked to name the public figure it admired most. Topping the poll with 19.5% was Aleksandr Solzhenitsyn.[14] (The President of the United States managed barely a quarter of that figure.) Ironically, though, even as the poll was being mounted, authorities at a high school in Milton, New Hampshire, were obliged to withdraw an obscene item from the school library: the offending copy of *One Day in the Life of Ivan Denisovich* was duly burnt.[15]

There is a danger that all the reactions to and images of Solzhenitsyn cited in the pages which follow may be seen, by association, as trivial or grotesque. Yet, while certain of them richly deserve both epithets, they are offered not as a mere catalogue of curiosities and ephemera, but in the belief that a fresh, if somewhat oblique, view of Solzhenitsyn's stature and influence upon his contemporaries may be gained by focusing upon those considerable mythopoeic energies which have been expended in his honor, or at his expense.

Adaptations

That Solzhenitsyn's fiction should have attracted the attention of scriptwriters and film producers is hardly cause for surprise. Had it not been for a rapid shift in the political climate, *One Day in the Life of Ivan Denisovich* would have been filmed in the Soviet Union in the early sixties.[16] As it was, Caspar Wrede's later version with Tom Courtenay in the title role was widely seen and generally well received in the West. *The First Circle* fared less well in Alexander Ford's film adaptation of 1973. In addition, *Cancer Ward* has been dramatized for the benefit of German television viewers and the short story "Incident at Krechetovka Station" for their Swedish counterparts. In some cases individual motifs, rather than whole works, have been adapted, as in the case of P. Murav'ev's story "The Birch Fungus," with its acknowledged debt to *Cancer Ward*.[17]

More noteworthy in the present context, however, are transmogrifications of a bolder kind. Consider the following description:

> The human mass flows across from one wing to the other. People are slithering round in a circle, dragging themselves along on their elbows, gripping each other's heels, thrashing about like fish in a frying pan, scorched by the frozen earth, and, falling, they pause motionless, a plastic image of slow, unending, unendurable suffering.(...)
> An interesting part in this episode is danced by yet another character, the guard. He appears to be majestically neutral, no less cruel towards the "criminals" than he is towards the "politicals." Yet the delicacy of the choreography allows us to sense a certain magical connection between the guard and the "criminals."[18]

The performance recorded here by N. Shiller is not quite a ballet of *Ivan Denisovich*. What it is is an eighteen-minute choreographic essay based on motifs from Solzhenitsyn's works and entitled "One Day in Their Lives." The work, created by the French-born Wladimir Oukhtomsky, was performed under his direction by a student dance troupe of the Boston Conservatory in May 1974. Shiller, who was in the audience, owns to having felt considerable misgivings before the curtain rose: he feared that he was about to be subjected to yet another balletic "speculation" suggested by an established literary work. In the event he was disarmed and moved by this unfinished, but vigorous and sincere performance. "The work must see a major professional stage," he wrote. "It deserves to."[19]

No less deserving in its own way is a musical adaptation of the same subject matter, the choral suite "A Day in a Life," based, of course, on Solzhenitsyn's *Ivan Denisovich*. Music and lyrics were composed by two teachers at an English high school. Wrenched from their settings the texts may cause a smile:

> I'm just a number, you're just a number,
> He's just a number, we are all numbers,
> Counted like pigs and sheep at a market,
> We are numbers, not men!
> (...)
> Pass up the trowel, the hod and the trowel,
> Then slap on the mortar and down with a brick;
> Check with the plumb-line and stretch out the thin twine,
> Then knock into shape with a chop and a flick.[20]

That the enterprise is, in fact, far from a flippant one is made clear in the composers' preface to the sheet music:

> (...) we hope that the songs will be found appealing without being condescending. There is no attempt to make something "jokey" out of what is a fairly grim subject, and we have already found that children respond with conviction to the songs and their words.

Judged on the basis of an amateur recording of the work, made under adverse acoustic conditions at a school concert, this optimism does not seem especially farfetched.

Adaptations may sometimes go badly awry. The following excerpt is purportedly "based on" *One Day in the Life of Ivan Denisovich*:

TYURIN (*at window*). There's a dark form, lying in the snow, near the barbed-wire! I can just—see it through the snow.

DENISOVICH (*fearfully*). Gopchik?

TYURIN. The fence-patrol guard. Dead before he could cry out.

DENISOVICH (*exultant*). They've made it over the wire!

TYURIN. Their luck's still holding!

(. . .)

ALYOSHKA. Oh, Heavenly Father, grant them this further grace that they may reach the tracks in safety! (*The ugly wail of a siren starts to rise off Left. The search beacons flash light frenziedly across the window Downstage Left.*)

DENISOVICH (*sitting up in his bunk, tension at its height*). Tyurin! Was there time?

ALYOSHKA. Pray God!

CAESAR (*violently*). Pray God they are caught and dragged back to serve their own fifteen days in the cold cell. Pray God!

ALYOSHKA. Forgive him, Lord! (*In the near distance off Left a burst of machine-gun fire is heard. There is a horror-stricken pause in which everyone stands motionless in grim tableau. Then comes another burst of machine-gun fire. Another pause. (. . .) The wild flashings of light become the old slow, intermittent flashings. The wail of the siren descends and stops.*)

TYURIN (*turning from the window, head bent, moving slowly toward his bunk Upstage Right Center*). It was only a million to one chance.[21]

Attentive readers of this one-act adaptation by Robert Brome may detect that it departs from Solzhenitsyn's story in certain points of detail. Solzhenitsyn's Gopchik had no urgent need to break out of camp and escape the imminent amputation of his frostbitten hand, if only because his hand did not happen to be frostbitten. Buinovskii, an impetuous but loyal communist as Solzhenitsyn conceived him, makes an unlikely ally in this race for the nearby railway tracks (which, incidentally, are a further product of Brome's imagination). In the original there *was* no escape attempt. If there had been it would not have been jeopardized by Caesar (Tsezar' Markovich), an unheroic figure, but decidedly *not* the notorious camp informer of Brome's creation. No camp guard was murdered—least of all using Ivan Denisovich's knife. No lights flashed wildly, no sirens wailed. The machine-guns kept their peace. The crescendo is all Brome's, and with it the paroxysmal stage-directions. Solzhenitsyn's story has survived thanks to its studiously unsensational, understated

treatment of a "sensational" theme. Impending violence and sub-
dued tragedy cast their shadow over the whole work, but it relies for
its pathos on Solzhenitsyn's rigorous restraint, his ability to make
eloquent the undramatic features of the *zek* routine. Robert Brome's
adaptation systematically violates the letter and spirit of the original.
It is a "dramatization" only in the cheapest sense of the word.

Good intentions are notoriously compatible with travesty. There
was no doubting the sincerity of Mary Ward's admiration for *The Oak
and the Calf* when she described its author as "the soul struggling for
surcease, somewhat as Captain Ahab pursued the White Whale,
Moby Dick," then went on:

> His tragic sense (...) sounds across the psyche of the reader like
> a wolf's howl in the midnight blackness of the frozen steppes of
> Siberia. It haunts, it strikes chill into the heart.[22]

Likewise victim of his own enthusiasm was John Lukacs who, in a
recent book about the year 1945, intoned:

> (...) something happened in 1945, in a most unlikely place: in the
> pine forests of East Prussia, forsaken by God, surrounded by the
> debris of war, under the cap of a Soviet captain, into the gray fur of
> which the metallic red star was deeply impressed. Something had
> crystallized in his head. A cold and crystalline thought which,
> through the mysterious alchemy of the human mind, was produced
> by the passionate heat of intensity. It eventually led this man far, far
> enough to reject the entire mental system of the world in which he
> was born and in which he lived, to the point where the very rulers
> of that enormous empire began to worry about him and to fear him,
> while to millions of other people he became that new thing, a Light
> from the East. Truly a single event in a single mind may change the
> world. It may even bring about—and not merely hasten—the collapse
> of the Communist system, which is inevitable, though only in the long
> run. If so, the most important event in 1945 may not have been the
> division of Europe, and not the dawn of the Atomic Age, but the
> sudden opening and the sudden dawning of something in the mind of
> a ragged Soviet officer, Alexander Solzhenitsyn, in the East Prussian
> marshes and woods, an event compared to which the two flashes of
> the two atomic bombs were but ephemeral feats of technology.[23]

It might reasonably be supposed that bad writing of such a high order
could not be sustained for long, but there is one work in which

adulation of Solzhenitsyn has attained to monumental form. Harrison
E. Salisbury's 400-page novel *The Gates of Hell*[24] may be regarded as
an "adaptation" to the extent that it fuses fictionalized biography
with a pastiche of *The First Circle*. Regardless of its author's sincerity
and his qualifications as a student of Soviet affairs, this enterprise
seems likely to warm the hearts of Solzhenitsyn's more subtle denigrators.

In the first line of *The First Circle*, State Counselor Volodin
absent-mindedly notes that: "The ornate hands of the clock showed
five past four." As Salisbury's novel opens, another Soviet dignitary
"glanced at his watch. The sweep second hand was just coming up
to ten o'clock."[25] The sense of déjà vu is allowed to persist. In both
novels a privileged representative of Soviet power waits alone in his
luxurious office, lost in thought. From tall windows he glances down
into the street to where the scurrying mass of humanity passes by,
indifferent to the worries of that powerful, yet vulnerable figure
above them. But Salisbury's clock-watching official is no Volodin.
When Volodin heeds his conscience and risks office and well-being in
order to thwart the schemes of the State Security forces, he triggers
off urgent processes of detection which justify the introduction of
progressively higher "circles" of power, and which provide one of
the mainsprings in the plot of a novel otherwise largely episodic in
construction. Salisbury ushers us into these same circles some twenty
years on through the agency of Andropov, real-life head of the KGB,
a man who is alert to the dangers of life at the apex of power, but who
has no intention whatever of joining the ranks of the victims.

The Andropov chapters, though dispersed throughout the novel,
focus upon the intractable problems posed by a celebrated dissident
writer, and upon the Politburo deliberations and KGB investigations
aimed at defusing the situation which this malcontent has engi-
neered. The chapters thus form a world functionally akin to that
inhabited in *The First Circle* by Iakonov, Oskolupov, Sevastianov,
Abakumov and Stalin himself. In place of the comparatively leisurely
and retrospective treatment of the inmates of the Mavrino special
scientific prison, Salisbury offers the life story of the troublesome
writer from his childhood up to the moment in 1974 when this biographical plane intersects that of the frenetic narrative present
occupied by Andropov and his colleagues.

Salisbury's protagonist Andrei Ilych Sokolov had become an
overnight celebrity when his labor camp novel *Taishet 303* was

published with Khrushchev's blessing in a famous literary journal. Now, as Andropov's minions attempt to seize the disgraced author's explosive new masterpiece, Sokolov is living in the Peredelkino dacha of a distinguished composer. Here, as throughout *The Gates of Hell*, the simplest of transpositions allow the reader to reconstitute a barely fictionalized Solzhenitsyn and it comes as no surprise when Sokolov is finally arrested and forced aboard a plane bound for Frankfurt, there to tell waiting journalists: "I am beyond the borders of my country. But I have not left Russia in spirit."[26]

Solzhenitsyn figures in various disguises in at least two other recent novels.[27] But in each of them his personality is subordinated to an obtrusive overreaching fictional design and he is beset with fanciful characters and events. Even the informed reader is thus free to feel entertained or insulted by these creations without being seriously concerned about the relationship between the Ersatz-Solzhenitsyns and the actual one. *The Gates of Hell* does not spare the reader this distraction. For the bulk of the book fictional resources are used in an attempt to flesh out what is known of Solzhenitsyn's life, to fill in the gaps with plausible episodes—not least intimate ones—and emotional nuances. *The Gates of Hell* thus tends to read as a novelization rather than a novel, and at its worst it becomes mawkish and trite.

No less distracting is the strategy adopted by Harrison Salisbury in respect of personal names. Andropov, Brezhnev, Khrushchev, Kosygin and other political luminaries figure in the novel under their own names and with greater or lesser credibility. In addition well-known literary contemporaries of Sokolov-Solzhenitsyn are engaged as extras, among them Evtushenko, Akhmadulina, Simonov and Kochetov. Arriving at the Kremlin for a reception at which he is to be introduced to the guests by Khrushchev, Sokolov notices "Erenburg in a corner, a saturnine smile on his face and a tumble of cigarette ash down the vest of his excellently tailored gray English tweeds."[28] The principle appears to be that characters drawn from life forfeit their names and undergo a greater degree of fictionalization in measure as they approach Sokolov's orbit. This provides the reader with a certain amount of harmless entertainment: a figure clearly based on the cellist Rostropovich masquerades as the composer Aryutinyan, Heinrich Böll turns up as Hans Koch, and Arthur and Inge Miller lurk somewhere behind the hardbitten Morgan couple. At one point, however, vertigo sets in. The role played in

Solzhenitsyn's literary career by the editor of *Novyi mir,* Aleksandr Tvardovskii, is closely paralleled in Salisbury's novel by that of the editor Boris Stasov. When the real Tvardovskii died in 1971 Solzhenitsyn made a demonstrative appearance at his funeral. In *The Gates of Hell* Stasov passes away on cue, but as Sokolov arrives for the obsequies, the reader is startled to glimpse among the mourners "Tvardovsky, Stasov's staunch supporter and the editor of *Novy Mir.*"[29]

For Russian-speaking readers *The Gates of Hell* is memorable at least for the surpassing illiteracy of its Russian names and phrases. The foremost Soviet literary journal of the day is here named, with scant regard for the elements of Russian grammer: *Novy Zhizn.* Salisbury's characters never touch homebrew (*samogon*), preferring the non-existent *samogan*, which they regularly drain to the toast *do adna* (rather than *do dna*). On the first day of January they wish each other "snovem godem, snovem schastya" (something like "Happily Newyur"), and earnestly encourage their children to follow suit. Even when provoked, they abhor the Russian expletive *svoloch'*, and stun their foes instead with the neologistic *swolich*. Particularly unfortunate in view of these gaffes (which are endemic in the novel rather than occasional) is the oddly-worded assertion in a biographical appendix that the author "has spent almost half of his life *in and out* of Russia since the days of World War II (. . .)."[30]

Stat magni nominis umbra

The Gates of Hell marks a transition from versions of the oeuvre to versions of the man, and, as it turns out, Solzhenitsyn's very name lends itself to incantation. At the same time, the difficulties which it poses for speakers and writers of English are notorious. In 1974 the *New York Times* ascribed copyright for an excerpt from *The Gulag Archipelago* to one Aleksandr I. *Solzhenitsky*,[31] while three years later the publishers of a journal of African affairs claimed to have featured interviews with Ian Smith, Moamar Gaddafi and *Solzhezni-tsyn*.[32] More recently, Alan Watkins, political columnist of the London *Observer*, or perhaps his compositors, achieved a dubious record with the combination—De Tocqueville, Rudyard Kipling and *Solzh-entitsyn*.[33] These examples make slightly less farfetched Clarence

Brown's cartoon in the *Village Voice* which had President Ford not only hopelessly unable to spell Solzhenitsyn's name, but also curious to know what position he played on the football field.[34]

Even the most innocent slip may gain resonance in the re-telling. In 1967 Georgii Markov, a Soviet writer and official of irreproachable orthodoxy, told how, while on a Siberian lecture tour, he had received a note from a member of the audience asking: "When is this *Dolzhenitsyn* going to stop insulting Soviet literature?"[35] Markov related his anecdote at a meeting between Solzhenitsyn and the Secretariat of the Board of the Soviet Writers' Union with the transparent intention of belittling, as local and ephemeral, the furor which the Solzhenitsyn affair had aroused. The episode is far more telling as an example of those conditioned ideological reflexes, as remote from personal experience as they are from critical judgement, which have always been indispensable adjuncts of any well-run Soviet witchhunt. In England a decade later Clive James was among those who made merry over Margaret Thatcher's inability to utter the name which she professed so to admire, dubbing the phenomenon "The Case of Torynitskyn":

> The pronunciation 'Solzhenitskyn' was invented last year by Margaret Thatcher, who thereby suggested that she knew nothing about Solzhenitsyn's writings beyond what she had heard from her advisers, who in turn had apparently mixed him up with Rumpelstiltzkin.[36]

In order to conjure with a name one must be able to reproduce it accurately. Such journalistic tags as "the Solzhenitsyn Syndrome"[37] and "Solzhenitsyns of other lands,"[38] or the proposition that "it may be too soon to look for a Chinese Solzhenitsyn"[39] demonstrate an artless, but effective enough metonymy. Satirists favor a more incongruous transposition or distortion. In a Soviet skit on Tvardovskii and his journal *Novyi mir* the editor is made to confuse the patronymic of Ivan Sergeevich Turgenev with that of another figure close to his thoughts, and to refer to the author of *Rudin* and *On the Eve* as "Ivan Denisovich."[40] Again, Ivan Shukhov, hero of Barry Collins's play "The Strongest Man in the World," was so named with serious ironical intent,[41] and it was in a spirit very far from banter that the Novosti Press Agency chose to call one of its collections of anti-Solzhenitsyniana *The Last Circle*.[42] Solzhenitsyn's surname too has provided scope for distortion of an imaginative rather than accidental kind.

"Solzhenitsyn" is a name intriguing even to the professional onomastician. Its phonetically most likely derivation is from *solo-ženica* ("malt-maker"), a form which has not, however, been recorded.[43] In any case, popular etymology has sought its inspiration in areas less drab than that of malt-production. While Solzhenitsyn's photograph was revered in some circles almost as an icon, one waggish avant-garde Russian artist, choosing to derive the writer's name from *sol'* ("salt"), created a bas-relief of Solzhenitsyn's head, fashioned from the appropriate substance. This he juxtaposed with a comparable replica of Academician Sakharov, suitably saccharized. The ensemble, he assured at least one visitor, would assist blind art-lovers, who could now distinguish the two images by licking them.[44]

There were other, more serious derivations of the name. The famous pun "Solzhenitsyn ne solzhet" ("Solzhenitsyn won't lie" or "Solzhenitsyn's no liar"), while not coined by Iurii Kariakin, was given currency by him in 1966 at a writers' meeting in Moscow which demonstrated the support Solzhenitsyn then enjoyed among rank-and-file members of the Writers' Union.[45] Kariakin apologized for the pun, though not for the sentiment behind it. No such apology was forthcoming when, a full seven years later, the voice of official indignation found its ponderous way to a cognate play on words. In one of the hundreds of letters ritually abominating Solzhenitsyn at the time of his deportation from his homeland a Hero of the Soviet Union wrote:

> Your name will doubtless become a common noun. The significance of your present position is implicit in its etymology. It means 'liar' [*solzhets*], one who participates in falsehood. Yes, you are a liar; together with all the most villainous anti-Soviet elements you prostrate yourself [*past' nits*] and obsequiously lick the boots of Fascist remnants and Vlasovite traitors. This too is reflected in your surname, *-nitsyn*. Indeed, there is no need to look for names to insult you with. You are—Solzhenitsyn. That says it all.[46]

To appreciate the comparative restraint of this obloquy one should recall that the same campaign threw up a poem about a whore called Mme. Solzhe, who preferred to euphemize her métier as "dissidence."[47]

Non-Russian punsters have on the whole failed to impress. An exception must be made for Frederic Raphael, one of whose feather-brained heroines speaks with awe of "that prolific Russo-American author and TV personality, *Sol G. Nitzkin*."[48] Otherwise, contributions from Britain have ranged from the dull to the moronic. One Scotsman proposed in a letter to the Director of the BBC that the querulous Russian be renamed "Solzheni*sin*" in recognition of his many transgressions, a gem which only the Moscow *Literaturnaia gazeta* deemed worthy of repetition.[49] In 1975 the London *Daily Mirror* sought to immortalize another pun with a headline in 1½-inch capitals proclaiming: "SOLZHENIT-WIT!" Credit for this jeu d'esprit was given to a Mr. Hiroshi Iseki, a 55-year-old London-based Japanese waiter, described by the *Daily Mirror* as one of those exiles who had mobilized to "slap down Britain-basher Alex."[50]

What matters in all this is less the name itself than the attitude of the nomenclator, and this leads on with depressing inevitability to another, more morbid abuse of names. When David Markish was visiting Argentina in the mid-1970s he met an elderly Jew whose first question about Israel was:

> "How's that, you know, what's his name... Solzhenichkin, Shmol-zhenichkin...that writer. How's he getting on over there? Does he go to the synagogue every day?"
> I was somewhat taken aback.
> "Solzhenitsyn is a Russian," I said, "and a devout Christian. He's living in Switzerland."
> "Don't give me that!" replied the old man with a sly wink. "No use defending him! I know for sure!"[51]

The serenity of the old man's conviction, which, as Markish at once recognized, neither argument nor evidence could ruffle, is the stuff of which anti-Semitism is made. In the Soviet Union, where the tapping of anti-Semitic sentiment for political ends is a routine official procedure, "Solzhenichkins" had begun to spring up from the late 1960s on. Zhores Medvedev describes an ideological lecture in Moscow in which the speaker was consistently critical of the writer *Solzhenitser*. When challenged from the floor, he asserted that Solzhenitser was indeed the real name of the Jew, Aleksandr Solzhenitsyn.[52] In the best traditions of official Soviet anti-Semitism the Yiddish echoes of "Solzhenitser" or "Solzhenitsker" were allowed to reverberate through the lecture halls of the land even as the speakers were appending their statutory disclaimer—"not that this matters in our country, of course."[53]

The appearance of *August 1914* with its thinly disguised picture of the Solzhenitsyn family tree raised hopes in interested quarters that the first name of Solzhenitsyn's father might reflect Jewish provenance, rather than the then common Russian affection for Biblical Christian names. As Solzhenitsyn recounts:

> A special major in the State Security Service named Blagovidov dashed off to check through the personal files of every Isaakii in the archives of Moscow University for the year 1914, in the hope of proving that I was a Jew. (...) Alas, these racist researches came to nothing: it turned out that I was Russian.[54]

Indeed, were any documentary evidence of Jewish lineage to exist, it hardly seems likely that it would not by now have been turned to advantage within the public or covert reaches of the campaign against Solzhenitsyn. This is not, however, an area in which either facts or logic tend to carry much weight.

Solzhenitsyn and the Jews

To those suitably predisposed an authoritative juggling with consonants in the course of a lecture may have been sufficient to establish Solzhenitsyn as a crypto-Jewish alien element. The press of the Soviet Union and other synchronized East European propaganda services had to observe international niceties and make do with a label such as "double-dyed counter-revolutionary and *Zionist*."[55] As an elegant variation, Solzhenitsyn could be presented—in a tradition which reaches back to the *Protocols of the Elders of Zion*—as a well-oiled cog in the worldwide Masonic conspiracy. Since, according to this particular demonology, world Masonism is in any case nothing less than the fifth column of Zionism and is bent on speeding Zionist domination of the globe, the terms become virtually interchangeable:

> At present the Masonic movement is widespread in the West, particularly in Scandinavia and South America which is why they are nice to Israel. Masons head governments. The Swedish Prime Minister

Palme is a Mason and that is why he invited the Mason Solzhenitsyn to come to him [*to receive the Nobel Prize*—MN]. In our country Kerensky and all his government were Masons, so Solzhenitsyn weeps for him.[56]

The official and semi-official image of Solzhenitsyn as Jewish-Zionist-Mason could presumably be expected to elicit a visceral anti-Semitic response from sections of the populace. It also made contact with less mealymouthed criticism of Solzhenitsyn from the extreme right of the Russian nationalist spectrum in the Soviet Union, and from émigré Russian anti-Semites of various hues. In the 1970s, however, and particularly after 1974, the Soviet media and information services adopted a second triad of epithets. Solzhenitsyn, the erstwhile Jewish russophobe, became Solzhenitsyn, the "monarcho-fascist-chauvinist"[57] and, for export purposes at least, the virulent anti-Semite. The latter motif was vigorously promoted by the Novosti Press Agency in the years following Solzhenitsyn's deportation, both through film[58] and through the tainted memoirs of former acquaintances.[59] One of Novosti's deathless contributions to legendry consists in having sponsored two mutually exclusive versions of how Solzhenitsyn came to have a scar on his forehead. The Agency's overall strategy, however, was far from inept, for there were troubled foreign waters to be fished.

Suggestions that Solzhenitsyn is anti-Semitic had begun to appear in the Israeli press in the early 1970s, and a brisk exchange on the subject was in progress by the time he was deported. Recent émigrés from the Soviet Union figured on both sides of the debate, which continued in Jewish, Russian émigré and American periodicals into the second half of the seventies.[60] Considering the nature of the issue, there was less stridency and recourse to personalities than might have been expected. In most cases Solzhenitsyn's public statements, together with his selection and treatment of Jewish figures in *The Gulag Archipelago* and his fictional works, were used as evidence of wider sympathy or antipathy. By the end of the 1970s this debate was overshadowed by broader discussion of Solzhenitsyn's nationalism, in which, however, the "anti-Semitic" note continued to resound.[61] Variations in the background and attitudes of the contributors were appreciable, and this was even more true of the standard of argumentation: the voguish equation of Solzhenitsyn's aspirations with those of the Ayatollah Khomeini[62] by no means represented the nadir, while even more sober critics, who conceded that Solzhenitsyn's variety of Russian national sentiment was of itself essentially innocuous, expressed fears lest it open the door to neo-fascist elements, whose anti-Semitism and general xenophobia were explicit and programmatic.[63]

In the controversy over Solzhenitsyn's alleged anti-Semitism the occasional instances of vitriol and bluster are less curious than those moments when polemic slips the bonds of reality altogether. Since the Soviet information agencies owe allegiance to no principle higher than expediency, it is inappropriate to expect them to be inhibited by any sense of the absurd: for them Solzhenitsyn will be an anti-Russian Jew or an anti-Jewish Russian, or both, as the occasion demands. At the extreme fringes of this issue there remain writers for whom facts exist only to confirm their passionately held beliefs. Mikhail Grobman, who initiated the Israeli press debate over Solzhenitsyn as anti-Semite, was also perhaps the least cogent contributor to it. In one of his pieces he accused Solzhenitsyn of anti-Semitism in *Cancer Ward* on the grounds that:

> If one discounts a single faint hint, the novel is free of Jews, and this in the work of a realist-author against a background where the medical profession is one of the "Jewish" professions. (. . .) One must harbour considerable antagonism towards Jews not to refer to them in this context.[64]

Yet two years earlier in the Soviet Union the pseudonymous, extreme right-wing nationalist, Ivan Samolvin, had inveighed against the blatant Judaeophilia of *Cancer Ward*, a novel whose most positive character is "a Jewish surgeon with hairy hands" and whose villain bears the name Rusanov, no doubt from the adjective *russkii* ("Russian").[65]

The diametrically opposed views of Grobman and Samolvin converge on a plane which lies somewhere beyond argument and reason. Another denizen of that eery land is Grigorii Klimov, author of a work entitled *Case No. 69. On Psychological Warfare, Mad-Houses, the Third Jewmigration and the Forces of Darkness*.[66] Klimov, a Russian of the second emigration now living in the United States, has elevated his anti-Semitism to the level of a cosmology: to the clichés of the world Jewish conspiracy he adds kitchen psychiatry, "scientific degenerology,"[67] the Kinsey Report and a dash of black magic. The role apportioned to Solzhenitsyn in the resulting apocalyptic extravaganza is no meagre one.

Klimov's Solzhenitsyn is a half-Jew, married first to a half-Jewess, then to a full Jewess, son of a suicide, and himself prey to a martyr complex. In the guise of a Russian and an Orthodox Christian he "proclaims the total dismemberment of Mother Russia and, like the Antichrist, crows over her ruin, echoing the dreams of all Russia's foes."[68] We now begin to understand why Solzhenitsyn has become a hero of the Third Emigration. Not only is Klimov able, with the aid of statistics, to demonstrate that no less than 111% of all Jews are mentally abnormal, but he also abundantly characterizes the Soviet 'dissidents,' and those of the Third Emigration in particular: they, it turns out, are essentially mad Jews of an intellectual or artistic bent, with strong self-destructive urges, who form a satanic cabal cemented by homosexuality, with oral sex functioning as a kind of Masonic handshake. Klimov clinches his argument by alerting us to the sinister code implicit in certain sexual expletives in *One Day in the Life of Ivan Denisovich*.

Would that this crazed horde could remain confined within the bounds of the Soviet Union, their lusts and dementia subversively fanned by the CIA. But Soviet government and KGB officials— apparently paragons of perspicacity in a world of myopia and decay— have boldly excised this festering menace and passed it on to their adversaries, among whom there could be no organism more receptive than the United States, with its Kinseyan 37% of open and latent homosexuals and its 18.5% of mentally abnormal citizens. All doubts crumble before Klimov's inexorable statistics:

> If we compare this 18.5% with Dr. Kinsey's 37%, we find that it is exactly half; that is to say, every second legionnaire in Dr. Kinsey's Legion is also mentally abnormal. If we take the population of the United States as a round figure of 200 million, then we are left with a Kinseyan Legion of 74 million, of whom 37 million are psychopaths to boot. Quite a substantial legion! Look, for example, at the millions upon millions of American hippies.[69]

Only now, with the drooling dissident legions flooding in from the East to swell the ranks of America's native degenerates, with civilization as we know it entering its paroxysmal *Totentanz*—only now do we recognize in the "Russian prophet" Solzhenitsyn the grinning mask of Antichrist, of decadence, insanity and death.

Phantasmagoria

Klimov's book is beyond travesty. It may, however, encourage us to loosen our grip on reality and to surrender briefly to the charm of certain Doppelgänger and homunculi, to say nothing of preternatural manifestations.

Among the daemonic visions of the "doom-faced writer"[70] Solzhenitsyn is Elizabeth Hardwick's presentiment of meeting "the striding Armageddon on the road, glowing as I imagine him to be with eschatological fires and accompanied by menacing dogs."[71] Yet, others have put their faith in Solzhenitsyn's power to combat the forces of darkness and to frustrate the evil eye. During the World Chess Championship in the Philippines in 1978 the challenger, Viktor Korchnoi, felt troubled by the obtrusive presence of an alleged Soviet parapsychologist among Karpov's entourage. It became imperative that these evil emanations be neutralized.

> So the Korchnoi camp counter-attacked. Petra Leeuwerick, leader of Korchnoi's group, began sitting next to Dr. Zoukhar, staring at him and ostentatiously showing him a copy of Solzhenitsyn's book *Gulag Archipelago*.[72]

The efficacy of this measure is not recorded, and Ms. Leeuwerick was eventually removed from the hall for plunging a ball-point pen into the sinister doctor's arm and stamping on his foot. She appears, nevertheless, to have been the first person ever to wield Solzhenitsyn's works as a cross before a vampire.

Almost this-worldly by comparison was the item which greeted students of Solzhenitsyn's career in the May 1975 number of the magazine *Prediction* (incorporating *Weekly Horoscope* and *Fantasy*). Taking pride of place in an issue which included "The Seance: A Personal Experience" and "Onions for Romance and Leeks for Luck" was Joan Rodgers's reconstruction of Solzhenitsyn's solarscope.[73] Biographers laboring with inadequate and unreliable data must have rejoiced to see pioneered a new, astral route to their subject, especially one which afforded such insights as the following:

> In appearance, Solzhenitsyn is tall and very thin, and in many ways his looks coincide with what we know of Sagittarius. (. . .)

> The young Alexander was a good student and went to Rostov University where his subjects were mathematics and physics. We can attribute this to the good positions of Mercury and the exalted Mars, both in Capricorn. (...)
> Finally, we come to the Moon in Pisces. It is in close square to Venus and exactly sextile Mars in this chart, and from this we may deduce that Solzhenitsyn's mother was gentle and sweet.[74]

Who but a sceptic devoid of fantasy could question the essential congruence between the ectomorphic Sagittarius and the not-so-ectomorphic Solzhenitsyn, especially since the latter's life—or at least his recent reception—has undeniably "been full of 'duality,' typical of the Sagittarian"?[75]

Indeed, under a bombardment of myth and speculation his reputation has been made to exhibit signs of ontological instability. Which is the real Solzhenitsyn? How many of him are there? Are there in fact any? When Georgii Vladimov's *Faithful Ruslan* began to circulate in *samizdat* in the early 1960s, journalistically amplified rumour, inspired by the labor-camp motifs in the story, promptly attributed it to Solzhenitsyn.[76] Upon the publication in 1966 of Boris Mozhaev's controversial *From the Life of Fedor Kuz'kin*, dispatches from Moscow reported a widespread conviction in literary circles that the true author was Solzhenitsyn.[77] Since Mozhaev was an established living writer, reality was not long in asserting itself, but three years later, at a time when the Soviet press and information network was diligently encrusting Solzhenitsyn in defamatory gossip and innuendo, the spectres seemed to gain brief, but all-too-human flesh. Friends of the author finally succeeded in running to earth a passable double, who had been making his raucous and lecherous way round Moscow, bragging that he was the world-famous writer Solzhenitsyn.[78] There seems little doubt as to where pseudo-Solzhenitsyn was incubated, and the Police displayed a predictable lack of eagerness to prefer charges. The Doppelgänger was seen no more, having perhaps, like Gogol's disconcertingly sturdy wraith, bent his steps towards the Obukhov Bridge and vanished into the gloom of night.

That the bridge in question stands not in Moscow, but in Leningrad, traditional haunt of Russian ghosts and doubles, could not seriously incommode the well-travelled apparitions with which we are concerned. "Solzhenitsyn in Calcutta" was the title of a lengthy article published in 1976 by a Slovenian-language émigré journal based in Buenos Aires.[79] However narrow its readership, *Meddobje* managed on this occasion to cause a ripple of consternation among those attempting to keep track of Solzhenitsyn's extensive travels and numerous public statements in the mid-1970s. A sample translation of the text suggested that, far from being merely a piece on the Indian response to Solzhenitsyn's recent utterances, this was nothing less than an interview granted by the writer shortly after his arrival in Calcutta:

> I offered him a genuine Burmese cigar which helps reduce perspiration, but he declined; however, he kept on chewing the candy that Böll, his friend from Frankfurt, had put in his pocket.
>
> "I was expecting you with your wife Natal'ia and with your little boy Ermolai on your shoulders, the way I first saw you on the back of the paperback edition of *One Day in the Life of Ivan Denisovich*. Perhaps you'd come back from Kazakhstan?"
>
> "No, that photo was taken in Riazan'. I like it too. But my Ermosha is a bit too heavy for my shoulders now. He's at school in Switzerland and Natal'ia Svetlova is handling my affairs while I chase around the world."[80]

A ten-page interview in a comparatively obscure publication and an inconvenient language, with a Solzhenitsyn who ought not to have been within a thousand miles of the scene of the interview, was unnerving to the bibliographer. Happily, a more systematic reading revealed that this was yet another imaginative projection: Jože Cukale had met Solzhenitsyn in the spirit, not in the flesh.

Among such titles as "The Real Solzhenitsyn,"[81] "Solzhenitsyn and Reality,"[82] "The Spiral of Solzhenitsyn's Contradictions,"[83] "Solzhenitsyn and the Secret Circle"[84] and "The Sakharov-Solzhenitsyn Fraud,"[85] a special place is occupied by "The Riddle of Solzhenitsyn."[86] For it was under that title in 1971 that Nikolai Ul'ianov made short work of this plethora of Solzhenitsyns, whether corporeal or ethereal, by demonstrating that there *was* no Solzhenitsyn, but only the composite product of a KGB Hexenküche working to infiltrate and disarm anti-Soviet circles in the West. While it would be easy to dismiss such suspicions as simply a reflex of émigré paranoia, there is no doubt that the combination of prolificacy, insubordination and apparent immunity which marked Solzhenitsyn's public image at that time strained the credulity of a number of his seasoned émigré readers. Ul'ianov's hypothesis came to enjoy a limited vogue in Russian and Polish émigré circles in the early seventies,[87] and at one time even Vladimir Nabokov was far from dismissing it out of hand.[88] More tenacious adherents clung to a minimally modified version of the "riddle"-theory even after Solzhenitsyn had arrived in the West: there might indeed exist a man named Solzhenitsyn, but whose creature was he and with what mission had he left the Soviet Union? It was fascination with this riddle that launched the Russian émigré journal *Niva* on its brief Icharus-flight from obscurity in 1978. The extravagances of *Niva*, published in Mobile, Alabama, had already been something of an embarrassment even to émigrés who shared its unyielding anti-Bolshevik platform.[89] It outdid itself, however, by publishing what purported to be a photograph of Solzhenitsyn in mourning beside the corpse of Stalin. The accompanying diatribe reads in part:

AT THE COFFIN OF THE BEAST OF THE APOCALYPSE
Stalin lies in his coffin.
Beside Stalin's coffin stands Solzhenitsyn.
How glad they would be, both the Soviet government and Solzhenitsyn, if this photograph did not exist. But it does exist. We are seeing it.[90]

But were we seeing it? At first glance the open-air setting did not even resemble Stalin's funeral. And why did Solzhenitsyn look scarcely any older at the time of *Niva*'s sensational disclosure than he did on a photograph supposedly taken a quarter of a century earlier? As for any inherent incongruity about Solzhenitsyn's presence at the funeral this was anticipated and effortlessly dispelled by *Niva*: after all, he had long been a pawn of the Soviet government and had now been sent out by his devious masters to spearhead the Third Emigration in its bid to subvert the few surviving exclaves of the true Russia. But why should a prematurely aged *Novyi mir* critic, Vladimir Lakshin, also feature among those paying their last respects to the tyrant? *Niva*'s dramatic solution to the riddle of Solzhenitsyn was thus in itself something of a puzzle—albeit a lame one. For what we were in fact seeing had nothing to do with apocalyptic beasts and everything to do with a fairly artless fake. The well-publicized original of the photograph in question had been taken at the Novo-Devichii Cemetery on December 21, 1971, at the funeral of Aleksandr

Tvardovskii (whose widow and daughter are, incidentally, prominently visible among the mourners).[91] By techniques of retouching or photomontage, a simple head-transplant had been performed upon the undeserving Tvardovskii—but performed not by the culpably obtuse *Niva*. The "forgery" had originally appeared five years earlier on the front cover of William Buckley's *National Review*,[92] whence *Niva* had reproduced it without acknowledgement. The shift in context was decisive, for *National Review* had used the picture to highlight an issue containing a long excerpt from the Stalin-chapters of *The First Circle* and a sympathetic essay on its author. However gross a lapse of taste the original publication may have represented, it was neither calculated to, nor in context likely to deceive. *Niva* subsequently compounded its offense by publishing what must rank among the most grudging retractions in the history of journalism, accompanied as it is by such charges as: "The West—Zionist, Marxist, Freudian, depraved, godless, amoral, and profoundly hostile to all things Russian—has acknowledged and accepted Solzhenitsyn as its next of kin."[93] Nonetheless, Ul'ianov's and *Niva*'s basic contention—that Solzhenitsyn has been manipulated from hostile centres of espionage and subversion—received unexpected confirmation in 1979 with the publication of a Soviet book revealing how systematically over the years the writer's career had been guided and his works ghosted by—"experts on sabotage, 'writers,' and 'scholars' *from the CIA.*"[94]

Proto-Solzhenitsyn

The proliferation of Solzhenitsyns with its gothic hint of doubles and Jekyll-and-Hydery reflects concerns of a less whimsical nature which have arisen with increasing frequency during the 1970s. In the preceding decade images of Solzhenitsyn, while often mutually exclusive, did tend to be *cohesive*. Today the emphasis seems to be upon disjuncture. Birgit Meyer, for example, finds that the debate in the Western news media which followed his expulsion from the Soviet Union rapidly took on an autonomous quality: instead of being the subject of discussion in any participating role, Solzhenitsyn was henceforth passively subjected to it.[95] Norman Cousins, in whose view Solzhenitsyn's words, though "full of zest and allusion, (...)

don't nourish the sequential intelligence," concludes that: "The man has become more important than his platform. The symbolism supersedes the message."[96] Others have defined the supposed rift in generic terms, distinguishing with Grigorii Svirskii between the "immortality" of Solzhenitsyn's literary achievements and his decidedly "mortal" publicistic ventures.[97]

But among Solzhenitsyn's harsher critics are some who claim to see discontinuities in his bibliography, and in his literary and ideological evolution, in which he is actively and reprehensibly implicated. In 1975 Vladimir Lakshin, author of the most celebrated defense of *One Day in the Life of Ivan Denisovich* to be published in the Soviet Union, reacted angrily to the appearance of *The Oak and the Calf.* He accused Solzhenitsyn of a teleological approach to his own biography, a tendency to project his present views and aspirations back onto the canvas of his earlier career in a bid to persuade himself and others that his mature life has been seamlessly consistent:

> (...) I remember him as I knew him throughout the sixties and I wonder: did we, too, really fail so utterly to understand him? Or did he act out his role impeccably and make fools of us? Or perhaps, after all, he is dissembling *now*; perhaps in the past he was rather a different person?[98]

Francis Barker introduced his recent study of Solzhenitsyn with the words:

> To follow the development of the writing of Alexander Solzhenitsyn is to record a process; it is to chart the degeneration of a radical opposition to the Soviet bureaucratic regime into an authoritarian moralizing.[99]

While cautioning against a "rigidly linear" approach,[100] Barker points to 1967 as a fairly abrupt turning-point in Solzhenitsyn's political thinking. The transition from such works as *One Day in the Life of Ivan Denisovich, The First Circle,* and *Cancer Ward* to the later *August 1914* and *The Gulag Archipelago* is one "from knowledge to belief, from egalitarianism to religious authoritarianism" and from "historical fiction" to "fictional historiography."[101] Interviewed in 1979, Zhores Medvedev added to these ingredients imputations of textual fraud. Medvedev appears to regard the authorized editions of Solzhenitsyn's works which he began to publish in 1973 as concoctions reflecting his newly reactionary outlook:

> Today, however, Solzhenitsyn feels that these works are not as they should be, and has set about rewriting them, claiming that he was labouring under an 'inner censorship' at the time of their composition. He has already produced a fresh version of *One Day in the Life of Ivan Denisovich*, to make it more anti-Soviet. He now plans a new version of *The First Circle*, with thirteen [*sic*] new chapters (. . .) The meaning of the novel is transformed in a way that makes it clear that Solzhenitsyn is no longer writing so much for a Russian audience as for his own messianic vision of future generations. It is inconceivable that Solzhenitsyn had the views he now expresses in the late 50's, when he was an absolutely different person. He is rewriting his own history.[102]

It is altogether salutary that Solzhenitsyn's biographers and students of his works should have to confront and evaluate objections of this sort, and particularly those which are made in good faith or which offer supporting evidence. At the same time, it must be noted that charges based on the more or less dramatic transformations undergone by an alleged proto-Solzhenitsyn are more easily made than tested. The volume of independent biographical material relating to the period before 1967 grows very slowly and is not free of KGB-inspired pollutants. Scarcely any of Solzhenitsyn's reminiscences and statements of belief reached the public domain before the mid-sixties, and we have almost nothing in the way of correspondence or diaries. Moreover, the textual basis for studying the fiction itself has undergone considerable changes since the middle of the 1970s, and most of what we know about the chronology and history of the texts stems from their author, rather than from independent scholarship. Francis Barker numbers *The First Circle* among the works of Solzhenitsyn's "democratic" period, basing his judgement on a text close to the one which Solzhenitsyn claims to have drastically revised for possible publication in the Soviet Union in 1964. It is at least theoretically possible that Barker would have found the earlier versions, written without regard for the censorship, to be as "elitist," "authoritarian," "moralizing" and "artistically flawed" as, in Barker's opinion, is the later *August 1914*. The authorized, 96-chapter version of *The First Circle* (discussed elsewhere in this volume) is described by Solzhenitsyn as a somewhat modified variant of the 1968 redaction which essentially restored the text to its pre-1964 state. Although such publications are of the greatest scholarly importance, it is clear that decisive and independent textological adjudication in the matter of Solzhenitsyn's literary continuity is not yet feasible. Thus, even areas of Solzhenitsyn studies remote from the lunatic fringe may prove hospitable to plausible and tenacious simulacra.

* * *

Cast in bronze, set to music, choreographed, subject of poems, jokes and novels, of dozens of monographs, a score of American doctoral dissertations, innumerable articles, and even a scatological sally in *Hustler* magazine,[103] parodied and plagiarized, quoted and interpreted in countless incompatible combinations—Solzhenitsyn has produced an impact which, in its extensity, if not its intensity, has been equalled by no other writer in recent times. Two of his compatriots, Lev Tolstoi and Maksim Gor'kii, earned fame and opprobrium within and far beyond the boundaries of Russia for reasons only partly connected with literature. But, for all that the world was then a larger place and media coverage less exhaustive, the phenomenon of Solzhenitsyn's reception seems to be of a different order. If the present survey has emphasized the unusual, the nugatory and the miasmic, then it was not in a bid to deny Solzhenitsyn's life and writing either greatness or continuity. At the same time, it does us no harm to be reminded that individual images are not exclusively the product of direct intellectual or spiritual cognition, but many entail processes of an altogether gaudier kind.

Notes

1. Many individuals have generously shared bibliographical information with me over the years, but especially great is my debt to Martin Dewhirst of the University of Glasgow, Patricia Blake, and Alexis Klimoff of Vassar College. In addition,

Alexis Klimoff and John B. Dunlop made valuable comments on the typescript. Responsibility for the substance of this survey remains my own.

2. For this, by now extremely conservative, estimate see "How World Rights Work for the Solzhenitsyn Industry," *Publishers Weekly*, 10 May 1976, pp. 25-26.

3. Shirley Hazzard, "'Gulag' and the Men of Peace," *New York Times*, Book Review Section, 25 August 1974, p. 35. A letter from the Spokesman of the Secretary General of the United Nations Organization was printed, together with Hazzard's vigorous and persuasive reply, *ibid.*, 6 October 1974, pp. 42-43.

4. Rosalynn Carter's remarks were cited with strong editorial approval in "An Eloquent Answer," *The Constitution* (Atlanta), 22 June 1978. On the citizenship episode and the American reception of Solzhenitsyn as a whole, see John B. Dunlop's essay elsewhere in this volume.

5. Sholokhov deplored the survival of Colorado beetles among the ranks of Soviet writers and anticipated their speedy eradication, in the course of a speech to the Third All-Union Congress of Collective Farmers in November 1969, not long after Solzhenitsyn's expulsion from the Writers' Union: "Schast'e zhit' sredi takogo velikolepnogo naroda!" *Literaturnaia gazeta*, 3 December 1969, p. 2.

6. Speech by H.R.H. the Prince of Wales for the induction as a Royal Fellow of the Academy of Science, Canberra, 26 March 1979. Much of the relevant section is cited in "Prince Warns on 'Loss of Courage,'" *Daily Telegraph* (London), 27 March 1979, p. 5.

7. Pope Paul VI quoted from *Cancer Ward* in the course of an audience in the Vatican in 1970.

8. In an interview, Albert Speer named Solzhenitsyn as a present-day bearer of Acton's warning about the corrupting effect of power: James P. O'Donnell, "Charlie Chaplin, Adolf Hitler and Napoleon," *Encounter*, vol. 50, No. 6 (June 1978), p. 28.

9. See, e.g., André Glucksmann, *La cuisinière et le mangeur d'hommes: Essai sur les rapports entre l'État, le marxisme et les camps de concentration* (Paris: Seuil, 1975) and Bernard-Henri Lévy, *La barbarie à visage humaine* (Paris: Grasset & Fasquelle, 1977).

10. After reading *The Gulag Archipelago*, Holger Meins wrote: "Most intellectuals are vermin, and Solzhenitsyn belongs to this rot." Cit. in Melvin J. Lasky, "Ulrike Meinhof and the Baader-Meinhof Gang," *Encounter*, vol. 44, No. 6 (June 1975), p. 11, f.n. 3.

11. Historical T-Shirts & Totes (Cambridge, Mass.) was kind enough to provide this informal estimate.

12. *International Herald Tribune*, 4 August 1975. Solzhenitsyn had met and talked with Graham in Stockholm the previous year: "Solzhenitsyn Talks Religion with Graham," *New York Times*, 10 December 1974, p. 53.

13. The episode was given front-page coverage on 3 March 1976 by *The Times*, *The Guardian*, *The Daily Telegraph* and *The Daily Express*. The lines quoted are from *The Times* and *The Daily Express*, respectively. Issues of propriety were raised in an exchange of leading articles: "An Honest Man's Warning," *Times*, 4 March 1976, p. 15 and "The Picture and the Story," *Guardian*, 5 March 1976, p. 12.

14. "Amerikaner bewundern Solschenizyn," *Frankfurter Allgemeine Zeitung*, 4 May 1976.

15. "Personalities," *Washington Post*, 16 March 1976, p. B2, repr. in *Index*, vol. 5, No. 3 (Autumn 1976), p. 96. It should be noted, in all fairness, that the English translation introduces four-letter terms of abuse which are absent from the Russian original, or else are presented in veiled form.

16. A Soviet journalist who interviewed Solzhenitsyn barely one month after the appearance of *Ivan Denisovich* wrote that the author had already received one proposal to film it: Viktor Bukhanov, "U Solzhenitsyna v Riazani," *Literaturnaia Rossiia*, 25 January 1963, p. 8, col. 4. In a posthumously published essay a well-known Soviet film director spoke of the considerable challenge which such a venture would pose: Vladimir Skuibin, "Glubinnoe postizhenie zhizni," *Sovetskoe kino*, No. 2, 1964, p. 56.

17. P. Murav'ev, "Berezovyi grib," *Novyi zhurnal*, No. 126 (1977), pp. 23-28.

18. N. Shiller, "'Odin den' iz ikh zhizni," *Russkaia mysl'*, 5 September 1974, p. 9.

19. *Ibid.* Oukhtomsky had created his essay for the Indiana University Dance Theatre, where it had its world premiere in March 1973. In the program notes to the Boston production Oukhtomsky writes: "The struggles and suffering described by Alexander Solzhenitsyn are (...) almost beyond the limits of Dance expression itself. Always mindful of this terrible suffering, my students and I have tried to create moods rather than to depict actual happenings." The movements are entitled: "The frozen ground. Solitary. Confinement and forced labòr. Remembering the past, faith and hope. Common criminals. Power and conscience. Message of hope: Silent, unending, merciless struggle between truth and lies." The staff of the Albert Alphin Main Library of the Boston Conservatory of Music kindly located two further reviews of the performance, both of them favorable: Kathleen Connell, "Boston Dance Theatre's Three Innovative Programs," *Christian Science Monitor*, 14 May 1974 and Iris M. Fanger, "Advocating Dance," *Jewish Advocate* (Boston, Mass.), 23 May 1974.

20. Keith Swanwick and Patrick Lee, *A Day in a Life: A Choral Work (Unison Voices and Piano, with Optional Instruments) for Stage or Concert Presentation* (Oxford University Press, 1977). In addition, at least two songs have been composed about Solzhenitsyn himself. In 1975 a Soviet journal translated and partially reproduced in facsimile a satirical song, "Russischer Arbeiterchor" (Chorus of Russian Workers) by the West German communist Dieter Süverkrüp: "Zhurnalist" (pseudonym), "Oruzhiem satiry," *Sovetskaia muzyka*, No. 6, 1975, p. 123. The German original is included in Horst Tomayer and Valland, eds., *Lachend in die 80-er? Satire im bürgerlichen Deutschland* (W. Berlin: Verlag für das Studium der Arbeiterbewegung, 1976), pp. 122-23. The workers' chorus, in mock confession and with a refrain of "Holy Saint Solzhenitsyn," acknowledges its error in having cast off the slavery and misery of the tsarist regime "which matched so well our Russian temperament," and having so forgotten its traditional hospitality as to repulse the allied intervention of 1919 and Hitler's invading armies. The song ends with the verse:

> Now we are hapless victims of *our* might.
> Now Socialism's end is not in sight.
> No power on earth, alas, can bring to us
> Solzhenicynicism's joy and bliss.

So what's to do? Who cares! We'll be all right!
Holy Saint Solzhenitsyn...

(Nun sind wir Opfer unsrer eig'nen Stärke.
Nun hört der Sozialismus nimmer auf.
Denn welcher Macht der Welt soll's noch gelingen,
den Solschenizynismus uns zu bringen?
Was bleibt uns da? Wir pfeifen einfach drauf!
Heiliger Sankt Solschenizyn...)

The second song, "Mother Russia" by the group "Renzissance," was included in the album "Turn of the Cards" and has been explicitly dedicated to Solzhenitsyn in the course of a live performance: "Renaissance Live at Carnegie Hall." Sire Records, 2XS 6029. The following lines indicate its dominant sentiment:

Mother's son, freedom's overdue.
Lonely man, he thinks of you.
He isn't done, only lives for you,
Mother Russia, can't you hear him too?

Finally, there is a *chastushka* (rhyming couplet or quatrain in the folk idiom for singing or declaiming) devoted to Solzhenitsyn, which could be approximately rendered as:

No use murmuring, mighty meadow,   (Ne shumi, shiroko pole,
With your ripe wheat glistening.   Speloiu pshenitseiu.
Our kolkhoz is much too busy   My chitaem vsem kolkhozom
Reading Solzhenitsyn.   Povest' Solzhenitsyna.)

V. Kabronskii, ed., *Nepodtsenzurnaia russkaia chastushka* (New York: Russica, 1978), p. 90.

21. Alexander Solzhenitsyn's *One Day in the Life of Ivan Denisovich*, A Play in One Act, translated by Max Hayward and Ronald Hingley, adapted as a play by Robert Brome (Chicago: The Dramatic Publishing Company, 1963), pp. 35-36. The phrase "based on" is used in the copyright attribution at the foot of p. 2. (Brome drew on the existing Hayward and Hingley translation, but the translators were involved in this adaptation in no way whatsoever.)

22. Mary Ward, "Litany of an Anguished Soul," *News-Press* (Santa Barbara, Cal.), 10 May 1980.

23. John Lukacs, *1945: Year Zero* (New York: Doubleday, 1978), pp. 243-44.

24. Harrison E. Salisbury, *The Gates of Hell* (New York: Signet paperback, 1976). All subsequent references are to this edition. First editions were by Random House (New York, 1975) and Hutchinson (London, 1976). Reviews include: Anthony Astrachan, "The Gates of Hell," *New York Times*, Book Review Section, 2 November 1975, p. 16; Richard R. Lingeman, "The Banishment of Sokolov," *New York Times*, 27 December 1975, p. 15; and Jane Miller, "The Prophet Motive," *Times Literary Supplement*, 6 August 1976, p. 975.

25. *The Gates of Hell*, p. 1.

26. *Ibid.*, p. 441.

27. As Nikolai Kubiatshev in Robert B. Asprey, *Operation Prophet* (New York: Doubleday, 1977) and as Ignat Issaakowitsch Wetrov in Harry Thürk, *Der Gauk-*

ler, 2 vols. (Berlin: Verlag das Neue Berlin, 1979). Both are discussed in my forthcoming article, "Solzhenitsyn, Harry Thürk and the CIA/KGB Connection."

28. Salisbury, *The Gates of Hell*, p. 370.

29. *Ibid.*, p. 400.

30. *Ibid.*, "About the Author," p. 442 (emphasis added). Salisbury is not, of course, responsible for the wording of this note.

31. "Excerpt from 'Gulag Archipelago' on Law in Soviet Union Today," *New York Times*, 13 February 1974, p. 12, col. 1. The attribution immediately follows the italicized introductory paragraph.

32. Undated publisher's advertisement circulated in early 1977 and inviting subscriptions to *To the Point International* (Antwerp), "The International Weekly with the sharpest eye on Africa and the Third World."

33. Alan Watkins, "Saint Francis of the Lame Ducks," *Observer*, 6 May 1979, p. 9.

34. Clarence Brown, "Hereafter," *Village Voice* (New York), 4 August 1975, p. 38.

35. Appendix to Aleksandr Solzhenitsyn, *Bodalsia telenok s dubom: Ocherki literaturnoi zhizni* (Paris: YMCA Press, 1975), p. 512. English ed.: *The Oak and the Calf: Sketches of Literary Life in the Soviet Union* (New York: Harper & Row; London: Collins & Harvill, 1980), p. 476 (emphasis added).

36. Clive James, "Case of Torynitskyn," *Observer*, 9 April 1978, p. 35. Another listener transcribed the pronunciation as *Solzhenitskin* in a letter to the *Guardian*, 8 April 1978 (under the subtitle "Pronounced Palindromic Points").

37. Used by Shaun Usher in "The Man Who Slapped America in the Face," *Daily Mail*, 10 May 1979, to characterize Aleksandr Ginzburg's alleged ingratitude to the United States for securing his release from captivity. Pierre Daix had earlier observed that: "Il y a un effet Solschenizyn," cited after Helen von Ssachno, "Solschenizyn in Frankreich: Zu einer Pariser Diskussionsrunde," *Süddeutsche Zeitung*, 30 September 1978. Nikita Struve has since discussed the "Solzhenitsynskii kompleks" in an editorial in *Vestnik RKhD*, No. 131 (I-II, 1980), pp. 3-4. The similarity between these three items does not extend beyond their use of Solzhenitsyn's name to evoke a broader phenomenon.

38. The title of a television review in the London *Sunday Times*, 10 March 1974, p. 52.

39. The opening words of an article, "Novels on Mao Rule Horrors," *Daily Telegraph*, 11 November 1978, p. 6. P. Varnai discusses József Lengyel as "The Hungarian Solzhenitsyn" in *Canadian Slavonic Papers*, vol. 8, 1966, pp. 260-66.

40. P. Nikodimskii, "Piat' novogodnikh interv'iu," *Voprosy literatury*, No. 1, 1964, pp. 224-25.

41. Victoria Radin, "Tackling the God-problem," *Observer*, 6 July 1980, p. 32, based on an interview with Collins.

42. *The Last Circle* (Moscow: Novosti, 1974), distributed in the major European languages, but apparently not in Russian.

43. O. N. Trubachev, "Iz materialov dlia etimologicheskogo slovaria familii Rossii (Russkie familii i familii, bytuiushchie v Rossii)," in Zh.Zh.Varbot *et al.*, eds., *Etimologiia 1966. Problemy lingvogeografii i mezh"iazykovykh kontaktov* (Moscow: Nauka, 1968), pp. 48-49; and B. O. Unbegaun, *Russian Surnames* (Oxford University Press, 1972), pp. 124-25. Solzhenitsyn's own predilection

for etymologically evocative names has been frequently commented on and is the subject of Eckhard Ruttner's uneven article, "The Names in Solzhenitsyn's Short Novel: *One Day in the Life of Ivan Denisovich*," *Names*, vol. 23, No. 2 (1975), pp. 103-11.

44. There appears to be no published iconography relating to Solzhenitsyn, except for the brief selection of photographs noted in Elisabeth Markstein and Felix Philipp Ingold, eds., *Über Solschenizyn: Aufsätze, Berichte, Materialien* (Darmstadt and Neuwied: Luchterhand, 1973), p. 344. Apart from many hundreds of published photographs, cartoons and caricatures, Solzhenitsyn has been represented in bronze by the Yugoslav Drago Cherina ("Solschenizyn in Bronze," *Münchner Merkur*, 29 April 1975, with illustration), sculpted by Hungarian émigré Zoltan Glattner (*FCI—Features and News from behind the Iron Curtain*, Special Document No. 959, April 1976, with illustration), sketched by the unofficial artist Vadim Sidur (an illustration accompanies the article, "Torzhestvo pravdy i chestnosti," *Possev*, No. 11, 1970, p. 18), and included—in labor camp uniform, complete with number—in a huge and highly controversial canvas, "Mystery of the Twentieth Century," by the Soviet artist Il'ia Glazunov (O. Galin, "Misteriia XX veka," *Possev*, No. 8, 1977, pp. 54-57, with illustration; see also the particularly clear detail in *Khudozhnik i Rossiia* [Düsseldorf: "Grad Kitezh," 1980]). Included in an exhibition of paintings and sculptures by Hungarian artists at the Drian Gallery, London in January 1981 was one painting "bristling with portraits of Solzhenitsyn, one for every year spent in captivity," see Waldemar Januszczak, "Hungarian Dissidents," *Guardian*, 12 January 1981. Of considerable biographical interest is a pencil portrait of Solzhenitsyn as he appeared in the winter of 1949-1950. The artist is Ivashev-Musatov, prototype of Kondrashev-Ivanov in *The First Circle* (*Solzhenitsyn: A Pictorial Autobiography* [New York: Farrar, Straus & Giroux, 1974], p. 33). In addition, a portrait of Solzhenitsyn by Elena Nikolaevna Rus'ian is described and reproduced in T. Panshina, "Portret Solzhenitsyna," *Russkaia mysl'*, 24 June 1976, p. 12, while a photograph of Ely Beliutin's "Homage to Solzhenitsyn" (oil on canvas, 1969) may be found in Enrico Crispolti and Gabriella Moncada, eds., *La Nuova Arte Sovietica. Una Prospettiva non ufficiale* (catalogue of an exhibition sponsored by *Gazzetta del Popolo* and the Biennale di Venezia, 1978), p. 50. Fabio Traverso's unusual representation of Solzhenitsyn appears under the title "When Liberty Dies" in Luigi Stefani, *Sradicati: József Mindszenty e Alexandr Solzenitcyn* (Florence: "Lo Sprone," 1974), facing p. 224. Among the works of art inspired by Solzhenitsyn's books are the widely acclaimed drawings of Mikhail Shemiakin on themes from *The Gulag Archipelago*, John Cornfield's sculptures devoted to the same work, and Feliks Topolski's illustrations to *August 1914*.

45. Aleksandr Solzhenitsyn, *Sobranie sochinenii v shesti tomakh*, vol. 6, 2nd ed. (Frankfurt/Main: Possev, 1973), p. 270.

46. Vladimir Karpov, "Solzhets antisovetchikov" (general heading: "K pozornomu stolbu!"), *Literaturnaia Rossiia*, 1 February 1974, p. 17.

47. Iurii Barzhanskii, "Madam Solzhe," *Krokodil*, No. 7, March 1974, p. 11.

48. Frederic Raphael, "Whatever Happened to Lolita?", sketch on the BBC television program, "Word for Word," broadcast July 14, 1979.

49. Dzhon Lo (John Lowe?), "Pis'mo iz Shotlandii," *Literaturnaia gazeta*, 26 May 1976, p. 9, with editorial introduction.

50. *Daily Mirror*, 25 March 1976, p. 5. Note also the punning title "Solschenizyni-

smus" (Solzhenicynicism) used to announce a translation of Tvardovskii's letter of January 1968 to Konstantin Fedin in *Neues Forum* (Vienna), vol. 16, No. 183 (1), March 1969, p. 149, Dieter Süverkrüp's satirical use of the same word (see note 20), and the vulgarly familiar form "Solzy" affected by Neal Travis in his column, "Publishing Notes from All Over," *New York Magazine*, 24 July 1978, p. 6.

51. David Markish, "V strane moloka i miasa," *Sion* (Tel Aviv), No. 12, 1975, pp. 116-17.

52. Zh. A. Medvedev, *Desiat' let posle "Odnogo dnia Ivana Denisovicha"* (London: Macmillan, 1973), p. 115.

53. Solzhenitsyn, *Bodalsia telenok s dubom*, p. 335 (English p. 310); also his interview of 30 March 1972, *ibid.*, pp. 565-66 (English p. 506); and Tatyana Babchin-Herzenberg, "Solzhenitsyn and the Jews," details in note 60 (the Russian version of her article gives the form "Solzhenitser," the English—"Solzhenitsker").

54. Interview of 30 March 1972, *Bodalsia telenok s dubom*, pp. 567-68 (English p. 508). Trubachev (see note 43) concludes that "Solzhenitsyn" may be regarded as an "indigenous Southern Great Russian" surname.

55. Karel Dobeš, "Sionismus nástroj kontrarevoluce," *Život strany*, No. 6, 1977, p. 31. Emphasis added.

56. "The Soviet Version (2): Jews and Judaism," transcript of a lecture by Candidate of Economic Sciences, V. I. Emel'ianov at the Scientific-Research Institute of the Rubber Industry on February 19, 1974, *Insight: Soviet Jews* (London), vol. 2, No. 6, 1976, p. 7. (All the more grotesque in this light is Aleksandr Ianov's recent description of Emel'ianov as one of Solzhenitsyn's "followers": see his "D'iavol meniaet oblik [SSSR: liberalizatsiia ili stalinizatsiia?]," *Sintaksis*, No. 6 [1980], p. 100.) In 1980 it was reported that Emel'ianov had been expelled from the Party for publishing his latest anti-Semitic opus abroad without permission, that he had subsequently quarrelled with his wife, murdered her and attempted to dispose of the corpse by burning it, and, finally, that he had been found guilty but insane and committed to a prison psychiatric hospital for ten years: Reuben Ainsztein, "The Fall of an Anti-Semite," *New Statesman*, 11 July 1980, pp. 44-45; and "Antisemit—ubiitsa," *Novoe russkoe slovo*, 31 October 1980, p. 1.

57. Guram Gldaneli, "Ten' v pustyne," *Literaturnaia gazeta*, 24 May 1978, p. 14, col. 3. The variant "inveterate monarcho-fascist" was used at about the same time by M. Derimov and A. Povnitsa in an article with the familiar title, "Koloradskie zhuki" (Colorado Beetles), *Pravda Ukrainy*, 6 June 1978, p. 3, col. 3 of the article. Perhaps the most sustained Soviet attempt to present Solzhenitsyn as a self-serving monarchist and "holy fool" was Boris Danilov, "Bez tsaria v golove," *Literaturnaia gazeta*, 17 March 1976, p. 15.

58. One of the fullest accounts is by Robert C. Toth, "Russia Takes Aim at Solzhenitsyn. Two Films to Be Distributed in West," *International Herald Tribune*, 8 March 1975, pp. 1-2 (reprinted from the *Los Angeles Times*).

59. Notably those of his first wife, N. Reshetovskaia, *V spore so vremenem* (Moscow: Novosti, 1975) [English as: Natalya A. Reshetovskaya, *Sanya: My Life with Aleksandr Solzhenitsyn* (New York: Bobbs-Merrill, 1975)]; and those of a childhood friend, Kirill Samjonovitsj Simonjan, *Hvem er Solsjenitsyn?* (Who is Solzhenitsyn?) [Skaerbaek, Denmark: Melbyhus, 1976].

60. The principal items from the debate (listed, wherever possible, by first appearance in English or Russian) were: Mikhail Grobman, "Solzhenitsyn Does Not Deserve His Reputation As a Lover of Liberty," *Jerusalem Post* Magazine, 10 November 1972, p. 12 (Russian as "Solzhenitsyn i evrei," *Nasha strana* [Tel-Aviv], 5 January 1973); "Solzhenitsyn Defended," extracts from three letters by Michael Kahan, V. N. Malinov and K. Tannhauser, *Jerusalem Post* Magazine, 1 December 1972, p. 14; "Soviet Jewish Intellectuals Defend Solzhenitsyn," letter from David Azbel, Natan Finegold, Vitaly Rubin and Mikhail Agursky, *ibid.*, 26 January 1973, p. 15; Mikhail Agursky, "In Defence of Solzhenitsyn. He Understood Soviet Jewry," *ibid.*, 13 April 1973, p. 15 (this letter had appeared in abridged form in *Jews in the USSR—Latest Information* [London], vol. 2, No. 12 [23 March 1973], pp. 4-5); Mikhail Grobman, "Solzhenitsyn and the Jews: A Reprise," *Jerusalem Post* Magazine, 3 August 1973, pp. 15-16; two essays under the heading "The Solzhenitsyn File Reopened," one by Lucien Benda supporting Grobman, one by Gregori [sic] Svirsky attacking him, *ibid.*, 14 September 1973, p. 20 (a version of Svirskii's article appeared as "Kakovy vremena, takovy gerostraty," *Possev*, No. 11, 1973, pp. 18-20); Maurice Friedberg, "Solzhenitsyn and Russia's Jews," *Midstream*, vol. 20, No. 7 (August-September 1974), pp. 76-81; Roman Rutman, "Solzhenitsyn and the Jewish Question," *Soviet Jewish Affairs*, vol. 4, No. 2 (1974), pp. 3-16 (Russian as "Kol'tso obid. Evreiskii vopros i Aleksandr Solzhenitsyn," *Novyi zhurnal*, No. 117 [1974], pp. 178-96); Elie Wiesel, "Where Solzhenitsyn Troubles Me," *National Jewish Monthly*, November 1974, pp. 16, 18 & 20; Tatyana Babchin-Herzenberg, "Solzhenitsyn and the Jews," *Jerusalem Post* Magazine, 22 August 1975, p. 21 (Russian as: T. Babchin-Gertsenberg, "Solzhenitsyn i evrei," *Nedelia* [Tel-Aviv], 10 September 1975, pp. 5-6); Edith Rogovin Frankel, "Russians, Jews and Solzhenitsyn," *Soviet Jewish Affairs*, vol. 5, No. 2 (1975), pp. 48-68; Mikhail Agursky, "Man's Endurance," review of the third volume of *The Gulag Archipelago*, *Jerusalem Post* Magazine, 19 March 1976, p. 15 (Russian as "Konets Gulaga?" in *Nasha strana* [Tel-Aviv], 4 April 1976, p. 3); Mark Perakh, "Fakty ili selektsiia obrazov?" *Vremia i my*, No. 4, 1976, pp. 131-58 (revised English version as "Solzhenitsyn and the Jews," *Midstream*, vol. 23, No. 6 [June-July 1977], pp. 3-17); M. Sergeev, "Izrail', Solzhenitsyn i slon," *Russkaia mysl'*, 27 May 1976, pp. 6-7 (response to Perakh); Mikhail Agurskii, "K diskussii o Solzhenitsyne," *ibid.*, 17 June 1976, p. 12 (letter replying to Sergeev); Simon Markish, "Jewish Images in Solzhenitsyn," *Soviet Jewish Affairs*, vol. 7, No. 1 (1977), pp. 69-81 (Russian reportedly in *Sion*, No. 14, 1976); Max Geltman, "Solzhenitsyn in Exile," *Midstream*, vol. 23, No. 6 (June-July 1977), pp. 18-26 (particularly pp. 21-23); "Solzhenitsyn and the Jews," general heading of a letter from Leon Poliakov with replies by Mark Perakh and Max Geltman, *ibid.*, vol. 24, No. 7 (August-September 1978), pp. 78-80.

61. For a bibliography and summary of items from this controversy see the quarterly survey *Solzhenitsyn Studies* (Colgate University, New York, N.Y.), vol. 1, No. 1 (Spring 1980), pp. 10-18. For a single, more recent echo of the "anti-Semitism" debate, see Abraham Brumberg, "Solzhenitsyn Ascendant," *Washington Post Book World*, 15 May 1980, p. 12: "And why, one wonders, does Solzhenitsyn accept so readily the rumor (never confirmed) that the KGB provocateur Victor Louis is Jewish, his real name presumably Vitaly Levin? How is that different from the attempt by Solzhenitsyn's detractors to refer to him as 'Solzhenitser' or 'Solzhenitsker' (. . .)?"

62. This comparison may first have been elaborated in print in "The Talk of the Town," *New Yorker*, 12 February 1979, pp. 23-24. Certainly by the end of that

year it had become a cliché, as may be judged by the publication of and controversy aroused by: Efim Etkind, "Solschenizyn will einen Ajatollah" (Solzhenitsyn Wants an Ayatollah), interview in *Die Zeit*, No. 40, 28 September 1979, pp. 46-47; and Valerii Chalidze, "Khomeinizm ili natsional-kommunizm" (Khomeinism or National-Communism), *Novoe russkoe slovo*, 27 October 1979, pp. 5-6.

63. See, for example, one of the more interesting contributions to the debate: Grigorii Pomerants, "Son o spravedlivom vozmezdii (Moi zatianuvshiisia spor)" (A Dream of Just Retribution [My Protracted Argument]), *Sintaksis*, No. 6 (1980), particularly p. 65.

64. Mikhail Grobman, "Solzhenitsyn Does Not Deserve His Reputation...," col. 3.

65. Ivan Samolvin, "Pis'mo Solzhenitsynu," written November 1971, appended to Mikhail Agurskii, "Neonatsistskaia opasnost' v Sovetskom Soiuze," *Novyi zhurnal*, No. 118 (1975), p. 205. An English translation of the letter appeared in Michael Meerson-Aksenov and Boris Shragin, eds., *The Political, Social and Religious Thought of Russian 'Samizdat'—An Anthology* (Belmont, Mass.: Nordland, 1977), pp. 420-37.

66. Grigorii Klimov, *Delo No. 69. O psikh-voine, durdomakh, 3-i evmigratsii i nechistykh silakh. Publisistika i satanistika* (Woodridge, NY: Slavia, 1974), 105 pp., with lurid illustrations drawn largely from Peter Sadecky, *Octobriana and the Russian Underground* (London: Tom Stacey, 1971).

67. Klimov seems bent on emulating the succès de scandale of Max Nordau's book *Degeneration* (1892/1893). Nordau (Simon Maximilian Südfeld, 1849-1923) took Cesare Lombroso's celebrated theories of criminal degeneracy as the basis for a critique of contemporary culture and its leading representatives, prophesying the violent collapse of human civilization. Klimov cites both Lombroso and Nordau with approval. In his assault on Amal'rik, Anatolii Kuznetsov, Tarsis, Solzhenitsyn, Siniavskii and Daniel', he combines apocalyptic warning with systematic iconoclasm. The comparison is otherwise odious. In particular, Nordau regarded anti-Semitism as symptomatic of the sickness he was diagnosing. In this respect, he would have found Klimov's opus amply "degenerate."

68. Klimov, *Delo No. 69...*, p. 73.

69. *Ibid.*, p. 10.

70. "Pendennis" (pseudonym), "Solzhenitsyn Book Gets the Drop," *Observer*, 29 April 1979.

71. "On the Record," *Time*, 19 December 1977, p. 25 (no page number is given and adjacent pagination is inconsistent).

72. Harry Golombek, "Viktor Meditates and Suddenly All Is Not Lost," *Sunday Times*, 8 October 1978, p. 5. My account of this episode follows Golombek throughout.

73. Joan Rodgers, "The Man Who Defied the Kremlin—and Won!" *Prediction* (Croydon, England), vol. 41, No. 5 (May 1975), pp. 6-9. (By contrast, Donald R. Kelley's "Solzhenitsyn and Sakharov as Futurologists," published under the rubric "From Prophecy to Prediction" in *Futures [The Journal of Forecasting and Planning]*, vol. 11, No. 1 [February 1979], pp. 63-68 turns out to be an entirely earthbound rehearsal of the writers' views.)

74. Rodgers, "The Man Who Defied the Kremlin...," p. 7.

75. *Ibid.*, preface, p. 6.

76. H.S., "Solschenizyns 'Hunde,'" *Frankfurter Allgemeine Zeitung*, 7 August 1964; D. Burg, "O rasskaze Solzhenitsyna 'Psy,' padenii Khrushcheva i sud'be Tvardovskogo," *Possev*, No. 51 (970), 18 December 1964, p. 7; a less informative (hence less erroneous) report was "Soviet Magazine May Print New Novel by Solzhenitsyn," *New York Times*, 5 August 1964, p. 30, col 7.

78. See the account in Zh. Medvedev, *Desiat' let posle "Odnogo dnia ..."*, pp. 113-15.

77. "Ist Solshenizyn der Autor des 'Kuskin'?" *Die Welt*, 31 August 1966, p. 8, col. 1.

79. Jože Cukale, "Solženicyn v Kalkuti," *Meddobje*, vol. 15, No. 3-4 (1976), pp. 277-88.

80. *Ibid.*, p. 277.

81. Jeri Laber, "The Real Solzhenitsyn," *Commentary*, vol. 57, No. 5 (May 1974), pp. 32-35.

82. Dimitrii Panin, *Solzhenitsyn i deistvitel'nost'* (Paris: author's edition, 1975).

83. The provisional title (used by TASS in 1977) of an elusive KGB concoction attributed to the Czech writer Tomáš Řezáč, which eventually surfaced in the Soviet Union as Tomash Rzhezach, *Spiral' izmeny Solzhenitsyna* (Moscow: Progress, 1978, in a *highly* limited edition). Solzhenitsyn responds to it in his *Skvoz' chad* (Through the Fumes) [Paris: YMCA-Press, 1979], which is described on the title page as "an excerpt from the sixth supplement to *The Oak and the Calf.*"

84. Olga Carlisle, *Solzhenitsyn and the Secret Circle* (New York: Holt, Rinehart & Winston, 1978).

85. Gus Hall, *The Sakharov-Solzhenitsyn Fraud. What's Behind the Hue and Cry for "Intellectual Freedom"* (New York: New Outlook, 1973).

86. Nikolai Ul'ianov, "Zagadka Solzhenitsyna," *Novoe russkoe slovo*, 1 August 1971, p. 2. See also D. Pospelovskii's response, "Zagadka N. I. Ul'ianova," *ibid.*, 15 August 1971, p. 2.

87. Józef Mackiewicz, while not accepting Ul'ianov's thesis literally, was—as the following items from the London Polish-émigré newspaper *Wiadomości* indicate—instrumental in keeping the "riddle" alive in the early seventies: Jozef Mackiewicz, "Nierozwiązana zagadka Aleksandra Sołżenicyna" (The Unresolved Riddle of Aleksandr Solzhenitsyn), 4 June 1972, p. 3; Józef Łobodowski, "Sołżenicyn bez zagadki" (Solzhenitsyn Minus Riddle), 25 June 1972, p. 2; Barbara Szubska, "Sołżenicyn jeszcze inaczej" (Yet Another Approach to Solzhenitsyn), 6 August 1972, p. 6; Józef Mackiewicz, "Zagadek ciąg dalszy. Jesień w Zurychu" (The Riddles Persist. Fall in Zurich), 12 January 1975, p. 1; and the same author's "Przedziwne komplikacje szarady" (The Charade Grows Prodigiously Involved), 19 January 1975, p. 2.

88. See the letter from his widow, Vera Nabokova, in *Russkaia mysl'*, 6 July 1978, p. 10.

89. See, e.g., Oleg Bukov, "Na *Nive* fal'sifikatsii," *Sovremennik* (Toronto), No. 39-40 (1978-79), pp. 222-23.

90. "U groba Apokalipsicheskogo zveria," *Niva*, No. 10, 1978, pp. 37-38. The photograph is on p. 36.

91. Probably the most widely circulated print of the photograph was that published in *Life*, 14 January 1972, pp. 8-9.

92. *National Review*, 12 October 1973. It should be emphasized that the photograph is here presented tongue-in-cheek and captioned (using mock-Russian orthography): "Solzhenitsyn's Stalin (Will Mao Tse-tung's Solzhenitsyn Please Step Forward)."

93. "Pochemu my ne veruem v Solzhenitsyna?" *Niva*, No. 12, 1978, p. 35. This two-page attack was allowed to precede a quarter-page acknowledgement of the source of the picture and its spuriousness.

94. B. Bannov, "Mekhanizm diversii," *Literaturnaia gazeta*, 9 April 1980, p. 14 (emphasis added), a review of N. N. Iakovlev, *TsRU protiv SSSR* (The CIA versus the USSR) [Moscow: Molodaia gvardiia, 1979].

95. Birgit Meyer, *Der Fall Solschenizyn im Spiegel der Westdeutschen Presse: Eine Untersuchung über die Funktion and Rolle von Alexander Solschenizyn innerhalb der ideologischen Auseinandersetzung zwischen West und Ost, wie sie im Jahre 1974 in der westdeutschen Presse erscheint*, MA Dissertation, Ludwig-Maximilians Universität, Munich, 1976, p. 127.

96. Norman Cousins, "Brief Encounter with A. Solzhenitsyn," *Saturday Review*, 23 August 1975, p. 6.

97. Grigorii Svirskii, "Solzhenitsyn bessmertnyi i smertnyi," in his *Na lobnom meste. Literatura nravstvennogo soprotivleniia (1946-1976 gg.)* [London: Overseas Publications Interchange, 1979], pp. 235-52.

98. Vladimir Lakshin, "Solzhenitsyn, Tvardovskii i 'Novyi mir' (pisatel', redaktor i zhurnal)," *Dvadtsatyi vek* (London), No. 2 (1977), p. 185. One is reminded of a historical precedent: the bewilderment and vehemence with which the radical Russian critic Vissarion Belinskii repudiated the book *Selected Passages from Correspondence with Friends* (1846) by his erstwhile protégé Nikolai Gogol'. So inimical was the direction Gogol's writing had now taken that some of his former admirers could explain it only in terms of mental disorder or as a conscious betrayal of his former ideals.

99. Francis Barker, *Solzhenitsyn. Politics and Form* (London: Macmillan, 1977), p. 1.

100. *Ibid.*, p. 102, note 9.

101. *Ibid.*, p. 13.

102. Zhores Medvedev, "Russia and Brezhnev," *New Left Review*, No. 117 (September-October 1979), p. 25.

103. See the article by Jim Dawson, *Hustler*, October 1978, p. 15.

PART TWO

Critical Essays

The *Gulag Archipelago* as "Literary Documentary"

SUSAN RICHARDS

Should *The Gulag Archipelago*, Solzhenitsyn's great work of documentation, be included in a study of Solzhenitsyn's literary writing at all? To do so would seem to diminish its significance—that a Soviet Russian actually took it upon himself to write a history of the camps. As Solzhenitsyn remarks about crime: "We have no classes in our country, therefore there is no crime, and therefore you cannot write about it in the press! (. . .) It was simply announced one day that it no longer existed in our country, and from then on it became impossible to treat it or even to diagnose it."[1] In reclaiming a suppressed stratum of reality with words, Solzhenitsyn has done his part towards curing the disease.

It is for historians to assess this material, as Roy Medvedev and Robert Conquest have begun to do.[2] Commenting on the first volume alone, Medvedev estimated that even those Soviet citizens who had lived through the Twentieth and Twenty-Second Party Congresses would have known barely a tenth of the facts collected by Solzhenitsyn. To elaborate on the importance of *Gulag* as the first systematic attempt to challenge the Party interpretation of the "cult of personality" is also beyond the scope of this study. Solzhenitsyn admits that before his arrest he too thought Stalin was responsible for developments in the thirties and after. "But then Stalin died quietly—and did the ship of state change course very noticeably? The personal, individual imprint he left on events consisted of dismal stupidity, petty tyranny, self-glorification. And in all the rest he followed the beaten path exactly as it had been signposted, step by step."[3] It is this thesis, the unexploded charge behind de-Stalinization, that he develops in *Gulag*.[4] If he can show that Stalin developed out of events rather than events out of Stalin, and that mass repression can be traced back to the Revolution, he destroys the ideological ground supporting the establishment.

To discuss *Gulag* in a literary context may also seem to misapprehend its priorities, and the spirit in which it is written. In a postscript Solzhenitsyn tells how he tried to persuade others, including Varlam Shalamov, to compile the work with him; his emphasis is on the enterprise of rescuing the past, and his duty towards it, not his authorship. Yet this difference is only one of degree, for the chronicling imperative is rooted in Solzhenitsyn's whole approach as a writer: the character of Volodin's uncle (in a chapter of *The First Circle* cut from the original published edition), who keeps a secret archive for posterity in the form of apparently random piles of old newspapers, embodies a role his author has assumed.[5] We recall how clearly this priority shaped *The Lovegirl and the Innocent*, that miscast essay in dramatic form. We note, too, how closely linked in form and concept are the projects of *Gulag* and *The Red Wheel*, the documentary cycle and that of *August 1914* and the other historical novels. In both, considerations of style and genre, distinctions between fiction and documentary, are subordinated to the chronicling function. It is appropriate that in exile this self-imposed role has led Solzhenitsyn beyond the confines of authorship into launching a massive project to build up an All-Russian Memoir Library.[6]

Nor can the form of *Gulag* be discussed as if it had simply been Solzhenitsyn's to create, as in a work of fiction. The very attempt to reclaim the proscribed knowledge and memory of a nation in a century of mass communication has partly dictated the form: the work, which relies chiefly on oral sources, represents a collective act of memory. "This homegrown, homemade book,"[7] as Solzhenitsyn has called it, has also been shaped by the conditions under which it was written. Solzhenitsyn was never able, for instance, to collect together its many parts in one place. "I kept jotting down reminders to myself to check this and remove that, and travelled from place to place with these bits of paper. The jerkiness of the book, its imperfections, are the true mark of our persecuted literature."[8]

Yet, once all this has been taken into account, it must be remembered that *Gulag* is subtitled "An Experiment in Literary Investigation." We are obliged to enquire what Solzhenitsyn is trying to do which goes beyond the merely documentary, how far he succeeds, and how the "experiment" fits in with his other literary work.

The Western reader who launches into this oral harangue, that moves for 1,841 pages between high-spirited mockery, furious invective and pathos, in perpetual motion between chronicle, personal reminiscence, political commentary, thriller, psychological insight and prayer—is likely to feel confused. The nearest parallel in his literary experience is perhaps the style of the New Journalism coined by men like Tom Wolfe, Hunter S. Thompson and Norman Mailer in America of the sixties. Superficially the resemblance is striking. Like Solzhenitsyn, these writers re-examined the documentary by denying the distinction between fictional and non-fictional forms. They too eschewed the idea of a stylistic unity imposed by "the beige narrator"—to use Tom Wolfe's phrase—and chose to spike their writing with every conceivable stylistic trick.[9] The texture of their prose, with its colloquial dash, kaleidescopic changes and total assault on the reader's calm has much in common with *Gulag*'s style.

Both Solzhenitsyn and the New Journalists are engaged in experiments with anti-form, and in a limited sense the emergence of this style in different parts of the developed world in the sixties might be seen as a reaction to the growing awareness of the extent to which mass communication progressively devalues information. At about the same time Siniavskii was observing:

> In times past, man in his daily round had a much wider and stronger connection with the life and history of the universe as a whole than he has now (. . .) The amount of our information, of our knowledge, is enormous, we are overwhelmed by it, but it never changes our nature. We can go round the world in a few days—take a plane and fly round it—but without getting anything out of it for our soul except a still greater intake of information.[10]

But the New Journalists and Solzhenitsyn arrive at their styles from opposite ends. Tom Wolfe explains the development of New Journalism in entertainment terms, as the result of realisation that "readers are bored to tears without understanding why."[11] Solzhenitsyn is compelled by the need not to entertain, not even to chronicle facts, but to change reality. He suggests in his Nobel Speech that literature and art are in a unique position to do this, because they alone "can perform a miracle . . . can overcome man's detrimental peculiarity of learning only from personal experience, so that the experience of other people passes him by in vain."[12]

That is where the element of literary investigation comes in. Whenever he describes a character, or tells a story, such as that of

Tenno's escape, or the Ekibastuz uprising, he uses his power as an artist.[13] But he asks far more of *Gulag* than he does even of art: he asks not just that the reader should learn from the experiences described, but that he should so pass through them that his harrowed consciousness is irrevocably changed. It is no accident that two such sensitive commentators from behind the Iron Curtain as Mihajlo Mihajlov and Iosif Brodskii should have compared *Gulag* to the Nuremberg trial.[14] Solzhenitsyn is attempting something like exorcism, as did that trial; something more actual than literature's aim. Within a literary framework, it is what Vasilii Grossman and Anatolii Kuznetsov strive towards in *Forever Flowing* and *Babii Iar*. It is arguable that Grossman succeeds at the price of destroying his work as a novel, while Kuznetsov is caught both ways round, by the limitations of literature and those of the documentary approach. Whatever the verdict on these writers, it is safe to say that literature achieves power by drawing apart from the reality it transmutes. *Gulag*'s anarchic 2000-page tirade, on the other hand, is a sustained assault on the conventional distance maintained by any printed word. From the first page, Solzhenitsyn engages the reader in a direct relationship, one that demands involvement from him:

> How do people get to this clandestine Archipelago? (. . .) Those who, like you and me dear reader, go there to die, must get there solely and compulsorily via arrest. Arrest! Need it be said that it is a breaking point in your life, a bolt of lightning which has scored a direct hit on you? (. . .)
> The Universe has as many different centers as there are living beings in it. Each of us is a center of the Universe, and that Universe is shattered when they hiss at you: "*You are under arrest.*"[15]

From then on Solzhenitsyn bullies, teases and coaxes the reader, anticipating his criticisms and refusing to let him sink back into accepting what he is reading as "History," that is to say as something which happens in another time and place to other people. No device is too fanciful if it will overcome the distance between the reader and the reality Solzhenitsyn depicts:

> I am afraid even to think what I would have had to suffer if I had been in the position of a common convict. . . . The convoy and the transport officers dealt with me and my comrades with cautious politeness. . . .

Being a political, I went to hard labor in relative comfort—on the
transports I had quarters separate from the criminal prisoners, and
my (. . .) baggage was moved about on a cart. . . .

. . .I left out the quotation marks around the above paragraph to
enable the reader to understand things a little better. After all,
quotation marks are always used either for irony or to set something
apart. And without quotation marks the paragraph sounds wild,
does it not?[16]

He goes so far as to incite the reader to simulate the ordeals he
describes, the better to absorb his meaning. For instance, after
describing the punishment of some camp runaways, who were kept
locked up for two weeks naked in freezing conditions, he turns on
the reader: "Reader! Just try—sleep like that for one night! It was
about five degrees Centigrade in the barracks!"[17] Or again: "Well,
yes, there were tortures, home-made and primitive. They would
crush a hand in the door, and it was all in that vein. (Try it, reader!)."[18] This rebellion against the passive reception of information
is remarkably successful: the reader is never allowed to detach
himself, for his role has been written into the script. Yet Solzhenitsyn's disillusionment that the publication of the first volume in
December 1973 did not result in immediate Soviet reforms shows how
much he was taken in by his own aim: on some level he persuaded
himself that his written word could wield a power equivalent to
physical force. So much had he convinced himself of this that he is
driven to attribute its failure, in these terms, to factors beyond his
control—the delay in publication of the American edition, which
meant that the international response was not orchestrated as he
had planned.[19]

But the style of *Gulag* does more than just insist. The language
Solzhenitsyn uses represents his attempt to achieve in non-fiction
what he did in fiction with *One Day*. There, by exploring a stratum
of language new to Soviet literature, he found a voice which declared
its authenticity, as well as its immunity from control by an official
and discredited language. Here, by writing a history book in a style
based around the "I" traditionally excluded from academic and
journalistic writing, Solzhenitsyn announces his challenge to the
official Soviet monopoly of communication. We recall how Solzhenitsyn's criticisms of Sakharov's *Reflections on Progress, Peaceful
Coexistence and Intellectual Freedom* centred on the argument that

Sakharov was still in the thrall of Marxist jargon and therefore unable to maintain a consistent critical stance: the falsehood being built into the conceptual framework of the controlling ideological language.[20] Solzhenitsyn's hostility to Chalidze, founder of the Moscow Human Rights Committee, seems to have a similar foundation. He refers in his memoir to one of Chalidze's *samizdat* ventures as an "extremely boring (...) legal journal," and goes on to dismiss Chalidze's aim of defending human rights within the framework of Soviet legality with the sweeping comment: "It's a strange committee, after all, that advises the cannibals (if they ask) on the rights of their victims."[21] In non-fiction as in fiction, style remains the mirror of content for Solzhenitsyn. Solzhenitsyn's attitude to the documentary style of others may be ruthless, but he does live up to his own demand that a fresh linguistic medium be used to express values which are in opposition to the dominant ones. The fact that the figure of its author holds together the whole of this vast work of documentation establishes a close relation between *Gulag*'s style and Solzhenitsyn's fictional use of the traditional narrative techniques of *skaz*: in both, the figure of the storyteller authenticates.

In other respects, too, Solzhenitsyn defies the conventions of written form. This work is about power and evil, about the lives of sixty-six million dead, and whole nations deported.[22] It is a subject that undermines all the assumptions behind our attitude towards knowing and communicating. Some people have suggested that Solzhenitsyn has not been selective enough.[23] It would be fairer to say that he has been too selective, but that at least, as he himself points out, the limits of *Gulag* are not set by the subject or his conception of it, but by one man's ability to cope with it: "I have stopped work on the book not because I regard it as finished, but because I cannot spend any more of my life on it," as he explains in the Afterword.[24] *Gulag* is intolerably long, but, as Brodskii says, "we can only welcome the fact that he had enough aesthetic intuition—paradoxical though it may seem—to reject the 'sense of moderation' bred in us by nineteenth-century literature."[25] It is also endlessly repetitious, not only because the facts are—("The tedium of it all! Nothing but the same thing over and over again."[26])—but because Solzhenitsyn sets out consciously to counter the effects of decades of "dictated opinion, dinned into us from the electrified gullets of radio [...which] have made mental cripples of us."[27] Other inversions of the conventional manner of presenting information follow from the subject itself. A social crisis that begins and ends with the suppression of information not only brings about a reversal in the relation between the credibility of hearsay and printed fact, but between the availability of facts and their importance. The most memorable camp rebellion of all, for instance, which everyone talked about in camp, is one Solzhenitsyn can only describe like a Chinese whisper, with an added footnote that he cannot vouch for the accuracy of his account, and an appeal for more information: "Perhaps we (no, not we ourselves), shall learn at the same time about the legendary rising of 1948 at public works site No. 501 (...) They say it was led by a one-eyed Col. Voronin (or Voronov)."[28]

Not only the relation between hard fact and rumour, but between important and trivial facts comes to be reversed. Partly, this is because of the rudimentary priorities that face Solzhenitsyn: before they can be assessed, the facts must be salvaged from oblivion. In the process, perspective is destroyed because, as in an icon, anything depicted stands in the foreground, with an absolute value attaching to it as fact that would otherwise have been lost. Partly, also, the inversion occurs because Solzhenitsyn has characteristically undertaken to write a mass history of individuals, not a history of the camps. He has worn a number; he knows how little they have to do with people, and how they crush the mind: "Thus many were shot—thousands at first, then hundreds of thousands. We divide, we multiply, we sigh, we curse. But still and all, these are just numbers. They overwhelm the mind and then are easily forgotten."[29] Our memory of Gulag is significantly not of figures salvaged, but of individuals: the garage mechanic Emperor Mikhail, the "bantam rooster" Vlasov who destroyed an open trial, and Koverchenko, Hero of the Soviet Union, who ran amuck, rode his horse up two flights of stairs to demand vodka from the commissar and earned twenty-five years for his pranks.[30] Through the mass of such biographies, Solzhenitsyn's history of the camps becomes an encyclopaedia of the Russian character.

Solzhenitsyn has created an anarchic and original form whose real subversiveness lies in the fact that it seems to have arisen organically out of the stifled stratum of reality which it describes. The form declares its integrity through its difference from socialist realist writers who have also described dekulakization, for instance, but "very fluently (...) and with great feeling for its heroes (...)."[31] Rather than organize his material more tightly, Solzhenitsyn presents it as an intractable and unstoppable flow of horrors escaping from Pandora's box, through which only the personality of his narrator can coax the reader.

But what is the standpoint adopted by this narrator in the face of the torrent of raw, untreated facts? At first we assume that the dominating "I" expresses simply the most subjective, visceral impulses of indignation and pity. But it gradually becomes clear that it represents something more complex, and closer to a consistent stance. This position is reflected in the account Solzhenitsyn gives in *Gulag* of his own spiritual evolution in camp—a vital theme for anyone concerned with the development of his opinions and of the attitudes behind his fiction. He reveals with engaging and sometimes almost embarrassing frankness how his own attitudes changed from that of a member of an elite (Nemov's initial assumption in *The Lovegirl and the Innocent*), to a conscious identification with the only uncom-. promised stratum of society, the lowest. "The day when I deliberately let myself sink to the bottom and felt it firm under my feet—the hard, rocky bottom which is the same for all—was the beginning of the most important years of my life (...) From then on (...) I have been faithful to the views and habits acquired at that time."[32] Interestingly, Solzhenitsyn does not write *Gulag* from the point of view of a man of religious faith, either in his judgments or in the prominence he gives to the cause of religious persecution in the camps. Nor are the authoritarian attitudes of, say, his "Letter to the Soviet Leaders," anywhere reflected. The stance he adopts is faithful to the evolution of his views in camp. It is basically the philosophy of a man who has come to believe that "we have to keep getting banged on flank and snout again and again so as to become, in time at least, human beings, yes, human beings."[33] For all that has been said about Solzhenitsyn as the great poet of anti-Communism, in this most important work the dominant attitude is not an anti-Communist, nor even a moralist one: it is an attitude to power. However he may present his views elsewhere, *Gulag* is nothing more or less than a saga of anti-authoritarianism.[34] Solzhenitsyn offers his pen in sympathetic description of hundreds of people through *Gulag*—Communist, capitalist, believer and traitor. All they have in common is that they are victims. His attitude is summed up in a passage in which he tries to explain how he could have become friendly with a fellow exile in Kok Terek whose cowardly failure to deliver an order of retreat to a regiment during the war resulted in its being annihilated:

Logically I have no intention of defending him; logically I ought to have hated him, despised him, felt sick when I shook hands with him.

But *I had no such feelings* toward him. Because I had not belonged to that regiment, not felt what it was like to be in their situation? Because I suspected that a hundred other factors had combined to decide their fate? Because I had never seen M—z in his pride, but only when he was vanquished? Whatever the reason, we shook hands warmly and sincerely every day, and never once did I feel that there was anything disgraceful in it. One man can be bent into so many shapes in a lifetime! How different he may become, for himself as well as for others. And one of these different selves we readily, eagerly stone to death, obeying an order, the law, an impulse, or our blind misconception.

But what if the stone slips from your hand? What if you yourself are deep in trouble, and begin to look at things with different eyes? At the crime. At the criminal. At him *and* at yourself.

In this thick volume we have pronounced absolution so often. I hear cries of astonishment and indignation. Where do you draw the line? Must we forgive everyone?

No, I have no intention of forgiving everyone. Only those who have fallen. While the idol towers over us on his commanding eminence, his brow creased imperiously, smug and insensate, mutilating our lives—just let me have the heaviest stone! Or let a dozen of us seize a battering ram and knock him off his perch.

But once he is overthrown, once the first furrow of self-awareness runs over his face as he crashes to the ground—lay down your stones! He is returning to humanity unaided.[35]

It is the attitude expressed here that makes *Gulag* a work whose theme is on the same scale as its dimensions. This is not a narrowly political work: as Canetti's *Crowds and Power* is a contribution to our knowledge of crowd behaviour, so *Gulag* is to our understanding of power.[36] The concern of both writers may have begun in their personal experience of totalitarianism, but it transcends that experience.

There are, of course, definite limits to Solzhenitsyn's sympathy, but they are not whimsical or arbitrary. This is a history of those who are victims not only of physical suppression, but particularly of the suppression of information, and Solzhenitsyn makes it clear that his special concern is with those who have had no redress against their elimination from history. This may be because they were, like the so-called "kulaks," not people of the written word, or because they were particularly hard hit for ideological reasons, like the Vlasovites and civilians who collaborated with the Germans. This is one of the reasons why Solzhenitsyn stops short of championing the plight of the Trotskyites: "I am writing for a mute Russia, and therefore I have little to say about the Trotskyites; they are all people who write (...)."[37]

The other reason for his hostility to the Trotskyites extends to the criminals, trusties and orthodox loyalists, as to all pre-Revolutionary political rivals who used their identity as Communists to distinguish themselves from the mob in camp. His attitude is quite different towards "those whose Communist convictions were inward and not constantly on the tips of their tongues (...) [for] such individuals did not ordinarily hold big jobs in freedom, and in camp they worked as ordinary sloggers."[38] Solzhenitsyn condemns all the others, who continued to use what power they had in order to survive at the expense of those weaker than themselves. The distinction he draws is harsh, and he is as withering in his condemnation of the one category as he is curious and gentle in his enquiry into the other. Interestingly, the dividing line is familiar from *The First Circle*, where the breakdown of the polyphonic approach occurred, with some exceptions, on the same line between the powerful and the powerless. But what was a flaw in his novel becomes an impressive demonstration of a libertarian stance in the free form of documentary history.

Yet although the main lines of Solzhenitsyn's attitude are consistent through *Gulag*, it is not difficult to catch the author out in apparent contradictions. The seemingly ambivalent attitude to prison itself provides a striking example of this. Opposition to Solzhenitsyn as a proponent of the cult of suffering and repentance is widespread, and has been particularly vocal in *samizdat* in recent years.[39] When we find Solzhenitsyn declaring without hesitation: "*Bless you prison*, for having been in my life!"[40]—such criticism seems justified. But then comes the third volume and Solzhenitsyn's rapturous account of the Ekibastuz rebellion (in which he took part), and his championship of the heroes of the Kengir uprising. His attitude to the thieves and their long unquestioned right to tyrannize the "politicals" and steal their possessions offers another instance of this contradictory spirit of resistance. "Keep as few things as possible," Solzhenitsyn advises in the first volume, "Give them up without a struggle (...) Possess nothing! Buddha and Christ taught us this, and the Stoics and the Cynics.''[41] But in the last volume he gleefully tells how, after the war, politicals did start to defend themselves against the thieves, and maintains that the politicals were to blame for their own misfortunes for not having done so earlier.[42] On a broader scale, Claude Lefort also points to something very like a contradiction running right throught *Gulag*. He observes that the work contains a sustained criticism of materialism and intermittent but strong adherence to a spiritual outlook. Yet for all this Solzhenitsyn remains acutely aware of conditions in this world, and indeed the bulk of the evidence he has collected is a protest against the appalling abuse of man in his basic material requirements. Lefort notes that Solzhenitsyn's attitude to hunger, for instance, is by no means that of an anti-materialist.[43]

All this is true. Solzhenitsyn does contradict himself, if you choose to read *Gulag* in that way. But to draw conclusions on this basis is perhaps to misunderstand the way in which Solzhenitsyn thinks in general, and certainly the way in which he presents his material in *Gulag*. We remember the remark in which he blesses prison, but we forget its context:

> Lev Tolstoi was right when he *dreamed* of being put in prison. At a certain moment that giant began to dry up. He actually needed prison as a drought needs a shower of rain!
>
> All the writers who wrote about prison but who did not themselves serve time there considered it their duty to express sympathy for prisoners and to curse prison. I...have served enough time there. I nourished my soul there, and I say without hesitation:
>
> *"Bless you prison*, for having been in my life!''
>
> (And from beyond the grave come replies: It is very well for you to say that—when you came out of it alive!)[44]

The movement of this passage reveals something of the characteristic pattern of Solzhenitsyn's thought in *Gulag*. It goes like this: Tolstoi, though never in prison, blessed it; on the other hand most writers who have never been in prison feel they should curse it; but then again I can confirm Tolstoi's insight from experience; yet I know from that same experience that my own remark is only half of the truth. As may be seen, particularly in his plays, the manner in which Solzhenitsyn expresses himself is extremely didactic. Yet, however justified it may be to suggest that this didacticism has a tactical origin as a weapon against established dogma, we now see far more clearly what could only be surmised from *A Candle in the Wind*: the didactic manner hides something which may sometimes be uncertainty, sometimes an unwillingness to judge, and often an internal debate. *Gulag* reveals again and again how alive is Solzhenitsyn's continuing argument with himself. A further instance of this can be seen in the first two chapters of the section entitled "The Soul and Barbed Wire," where he explores the question of the spiritual effects of imprisonment. His first chapter develops the proposition implicit in the quotation above: imprisonment purifies the soul. But his second adopts the opposite view, propounded by Shalamov, that it only corrupts, developing it savagely and convincingly before concluding: "Yes, the camps were calculated and intended to corrupt. But this didn't mean that they succeeded in crushing everyone."[45] Solzhenitsyn's own optimism and faith are built upon nothing more robust than the possibility that a few could resist this corruption. The two views, for and against, are never far from his mind: he does not dismiss Shalamov's so much as resist it.

Much that is liveliest in the style of Gulag arises from the way in which Solzhenitsyn develops the line of his thought dialectically, posing now one side, now the other. His defence of those who collaborated in the war exemplifies this:

> I will go so far as to say that our folk would have been worth nothing at all, a nation of abject slaves, if it had gone through that war without brandishing a rifle at Stalin's government even from afar (. . .) The Germans had their generals' plot—but what did we have? Our generals were (. . .) nonentities, corrupted by Party ideology and greed (. . .) So that those who raised their hands and struck were almost to a man from the lowest levels of society (. . .) If this movement had been allowed to develop unhindered (. . .) it would have been like a second Pugachev rising (. . .) It was not, however, destined to run its course, but to perish ignominiously, stigmatised as "treason to our holy Motherland!" (. . .)
>
> But what of our friendship pact with Ribbentrop and Hitler? (. . .) And then, the staggering incompetence, the unpreparedness, the fumbling (. . .) the armies abandoned (. . .) was this not betrayal of the Motherland? (. . .)
>
> Awkward questions get no answers in our country (. . .) Instead, this is the sort of thing they yell at us: "It's the *principle*! The very principle of the thing! Does any Russian, to achieve his own political

ends, however just they appear to him, have the right to lean on the strong arm of German imperialism?! ... And that at the moment of war to the death?''

True enough this is a crucial question: Ought you, for what seem to you noble ends, to avail yourself of the support of German imperi-ialists at war with Russia? Today, everyone will join in a unanimous cry of ''No!''

What, then, of the sealed German carriage from Switzerland to Sweden (...) calling on the way (...) at Berlin? The whole Russian press, from Mensheviks to the Cadets, also cried ''No!'' but the Bolsheviks explained that it was permissible, that it was indeed ridiculous to reproach them with it.[46]

We see here the same trait which makes for Solzhenitsyn's talent at depicting argument in his novels; the germ, indeed that bred his interest in "polyphony."

This internal dialogue has its genesis in the practical and unintel-lectual nature of Solzhenitsyn's thought. Everything he writes about here is assessed on the basis of personal experience. In his attitude to the thieves, what he is actually offering in the first of the two ear-lier quotations is a pragmatic piece of advice: if you know what is good for you, you will give up your possessions. Yet being Solzheni-tsyn, he dresses this piece of advice up as something more absolute. This is not to suggest that Solzhenitsyn does not hold the view he expresses, merely to point out that if resistance had been practicable he would not have counselled these pathetic victims twice over to surrender their last possession for the sake of their soul. As for his attitude to violent resistance in the last volume, he candidly admits that his view is not justifiable on moral grounds:

Now, as I write this chapter, rows of humane books frown down at me from the walls, the tarnished gilt on their well-worn spines glinting reproachfully like stars through cloud. Nothing in the world should be sought through violence! By taking up the sword, the knife, the rifle, we quickly put ourselves on the level of our tormentors and persecutors. And there will be no end to it...

There will be no end.... Here at my desk, in a warm place, I agree completely.

If you ever get twenty-five years for nothing, if you find yourself wearing four number patches on your clothes, holding your hands permanently behind your back, submitting to searches morning and evening, working until you are utterly exhausted, dragged into the

cooler whenever someone denounces you, trodden deeper and deeper
into the ground—from the hole you're in, the fine words of the great
humanists will sound like the chatter of the well-fed and free.[47]

The deepest lesson Solzhenitsyn has extracted from his camp experience is one which makes him incapable, at least in *Gulag*, of passing
judgment on anyone who has really suffered. He has experienced
the change that it brings in his own life, and watched it in others:

> No one who has not experienced such misfortune (. . .) can be expect-
> ed to understand or sympathize with or perhaps even forgive the
> mood behind bars at that time . . . in those years, 1949-50. (. . .) Only
> by savagely mutilating their lives could you make thousands of
> thousands in cells, in prison vans and prison trains, pray for a dev-
> astating atomic war as their only way out![48]

No wonder the tone of Solzhenitsyn's written output as a whole
seems to hover between didacticism (apparent and real) and an
absolute refusal to judge. The camp experience which has formed
him, and caused him to embark upon this investigation shows up
modern man's apparatus of critical and emotional response as inadequate to cope with the reality of his condition. For Iosif Brodskii,
Gulag ranks with *Das Kapital* and the *Interpretation of Dreams* as
the third of a trilogy which makes up the portrait of modern man.
He sees it as exploring the realm beyond the point charted in the
West by the literature of the absurd.[49] The judgment is apt, for *Gulag*
traces a development in modern history which differs not only quanti-
tatively, in terms of horror, but qualitatively from anything we have
known (with the possible exception of Nazi Germany). It introduces
us to a new order of experience. This is a world where the birth of the
age of perfect rationality gave rise to extraordinary developments.
On the one hand to a phenomenon of mass repression for irrational
reasons; in which "you can be arrested for *nothing*: and it is purpose-
less to try and correct you."[50] On the other to a world in which rational considerations led to torture being outlawed (after primitive experiments with it on Solovki), not as inhuman, but as unnecessary.
Instead, for example, there were good reasons for feeding prisoners
in transit on salt herring and almost no water: the herring kept for
long periods and needed no cooking; the water was rationed because
the less prisoners took in, the less they would need to get rid of.[51]

What need was there of torture, when burying prisoners alive saved the guards the trouble of shooting them and manhandling corpses into a pit?[52] As Solzhenitsyn remarks about the White Sea Canal project, in which a quarter of a million died to execute a futile project (because it turned out too shallow) with mediaeval technology: "That's what our gas execution van consisted of. We didn't have any gas for the gas chamber."[53] What Solzhenitsyn has written is less an indictment of socialism than a demonstration of how ideology can be made to serve the ends of power, to the point where the theory mocks a reality which has travelled full circle from liberation to oppression. After all, the camps themselves derived from a positive socialist move to create a constructive alternative to incarcerating people in prisons.[54] Yet a few years later prisoners were to yearn for the old imperialist prisons where they could sleep their fill, mend their health in idleness, and talk to their fellow prisoners.[55]

For those who have experienced such a reality the only reaction, it would seem, is a gallows laugh. The point is made by the following passage, in which Solzhenitsyn describes prisoners returning to the cell after hearing their sentences:

> Once more the crash of the door. They called another one out and re-admitted the first. We rushed to him. But he was not the same man! The life had gone out of his face. His wide-open eyes were unseeing. His movements were uncertain as he stumbled across the smooth floor of the box. (. . .)
>
> "Well? Well?" we asked him, with sinking hearts. (If he had not in fact just gotten up from the electric chair, he must at the very least have been given a death sentence.) And in the voice of one reporting the end of the universe, the bookkeeper managed to blurt out: "Five . . . years!"
>
> And once more the door crashed. That was how quickly they returned, as if they were only being taken to the toilet to urinate. The second man returned, all aglow. Evidently he was being released.
>
> "Well, well, come on?" We swarmed around him, our hopes rising again. He waved his hand, choking with laughter. "Fifteen years!"
>
> It was just too absurd to be believed.[56]

There is not much humor in Solzhenitsyn's literary writing. But the mood of hilarity in which so much of this fantastical history is narrated is the most powerful comment on an experience which lies beyond tears.

Ten years after *The Lovegirl and the Innocent*, Solzhenitsyn has created a form original enough and free enough from written precedent to grapple with the subject of the Soviet camps. The mistake was to suppose that the chronicle of camp experience could be adequately contained in the form of art at all. Solzhenitsyn has written two of his finest works about this experience. But it is significant that one of these is about "an almost happy day," while the other is about the most privileged circle of that inferno, the scientists. When art has not been struggling to express a religious ideal, it has generally worked within the narrow confines of the plausible. Aristotle with his unities, the 17th century French playwrights with their concepts of the "vraisemblable," were binding themselves to conventions similar to that of realism. We may interpret realism simply as "truth to experience," as does Ian Watt, or conditionally, with Northrop Frye, as "an art of implicit simile."[57] In either case we demand that the prose does not violate our expectations of life too brutally. In *One Day*, which, like *Gulag*, is written from the point of view of Russia without a voice, Solzhenitsyn complies with that demand. It is no wonder that the figure of Ivan occurs so frequently in the pages of *Gulag*, and that Solzhenitsyn initially incorporated into *Gulag* his review of readers' letters, "They Are Reading *One Day*."[58] For *One Day* is intimately related to *Gulag*, as the other side of the same attempt: one represents the distillation of Solzhenitsyn's camp experience, the other an exhaustive elaboration on the reality behind that distillation.

Gulag, the "literary" documentary, can hardly fail to stand as Solzhenitsyn's most original work, as well as his most important. It alone is free of the need to work within a form whose very aesthetic demands are something of a lie in the face of evil and ugliness: "I can tell you the story," as Vasilii Grossman's camp survivor observes, "but stories are words, and what this was about was life, torture, death from starvation."[59]

Notes

1. A. Solzhenitsyn, *ARKHIPELAG GULag*, vol. 2 (pts. III-IV) [Paris: YMCA-Press, 1974], pp. 421-22; English (trans. Thomas P. Whitney): *The Gulag Archipelago Two* (New York: Harper & Row, 1975), pp. 432-33. In some instances, I have preferred to make my own translations of passages from *Gulag*.

2. Roy Medvedev, "On Solzhenitsyn's *The Gulag Archipelago*," *samizdat* article, reprinted in *Index*, vol. 3, No. 2 (Summer 1974), pp. 65-74, and in John B. Dunlop *et al.*, eds., *Aleksandr Solzhenitsyn: Critical Essays and Documentary Materials* 2nd ed. (New York: Collier-Macmillan, 1975), pp. 460-76; Robert Conquest, "Evolution of an Exile: *Gulag Archipelago*," *Saturday Review/World*, 20 April 1974, reprinted in Kathryn Feuer, ed., *Solzhenitsyn. A Collection of Critical Essays* (Englewood Cliffs, N.J.: Prentice-Hall, 1976), pp. 90-95.

3. A. Solzhenitsyn, *ARKHIPELAG GULag*, vol. 1 (pts. I-II) [Paris: YMCA-Press, 1973], p. 605 n. 4; English (trans. Thomas P. Whitney): *The Gulag Archipelago* (New York: Harper & Row, 1974), p. 613, n. 4.

4. Abraham Rothberg points out in *The Heirs of Stalin. Dissidence and the Soviet Regime 1953-70* (Ithaca and London: Cornell University Press, 1972), p. 248, that Pavel Litvinov was one of the few dissidents who so much as hinted at this underlying theme in the sixties. He did so during his trial in October 1968 ostensibly only to back off from the interpretation:

   > The prosecutor says also that we were against the policy of the Party and government but not against the social and state system. Perhaps there are people who consider all our policies and even our political errors as the logical outcome of our state and social system. I do not think so.
   > I do not think that the prosecutor himself would say this, for he would then have to say that all the crimes of the Stalin era resulted from our social and state system.

5. Ch. 61 ("An Uncle from Tver'"), *Vestnik RKhD*, No. 112-113 (2-3, 1974), pp. 160-73.

6. Raymond H. Anderson, "Solzhenitsyn Seeking Chronicles of Russian Emigres' Experiences," *New York Times*, 19 November 1977, p. 14.

7. GULag 2, p. 77. Trans., p. 80.

8. A. Solzhenitsyn, *ARKHIPELAG GULag*, vol. 3 (pts. V-VII) [Paris: YMCA-Press, 1975], p. 580; English (trans. Harry Willetts): *The Gulag Archipelago Three* (New York: Harper & Row, 1978), p. 527.

9. Tom Wolfe and E. W. Johnson, eds., *The New Journalism* (London: Picador, 1975), p. 32.

10. *Unguarded Thoughts*, trans. Manya Harari (London: Collins/Harvill, 1972), p. 40.

11. *New Journalism*, p. 31.

12. Aleksandr Solzhenitsyn, *Sobranie sochinenii*, vol. 6, 2nd ed. (Frankfurt/Main: Posev, 1973), pp. 358-59. English in Leopold Labedz, ed., *Solzhenitsyn. A Documentary Record*, 2nd ed. (Harmondsworth: Penguin, 1974), p. 313.

13. *GULag* 3, pt. V, chs. 7, 10, 11.

14. Mihajlo Mihajlov, *Underground Notes* (London: Routledge & Kegan Paul, 1977), p. 77; Joseph Brodsky, "Geography of Evil," *Partisan Review*, vol. 44 (1977), p. 637.

15. *GULag* 1, p. 17. Trans., p. 3.

16. *Ibid.*, p. 497. Trans., p. 499.

17. *GULag* 2, p. 376. Trans., p. 383.

18. *Ibid.*, p. 378. Trans., p. 385.

19. A. Solzhenitsyn, *Bodalsia telenok s dubom* (Paris: YMCA-Press, 1975), p. 422. Olga Carlisle, whom Solzhenitsyn made responsible for the American publication of *Gulag*, sets out to refute the accusation of mercenary motivation in her *Solzhenitsyn and the Secret Circle* (London: Routledge & Kegan Paul, 1978).

20. See Solzhenitsyn's contribution, "Na vozvrate dykhaniia i soznaniia," in the collection *Iz-pod glyb* (Paris: YMCA-Press, 1974), pp. 7-28. English in *From Under the Rubble* (Boston: Little, Brown, 1974), pp. 3-25.

21. *Telenok*, p. 399. English (trans. Harry Willetts): *The Oak and the Calf* (New York: Harper & Row, 1980), pp. 371-72. (All translations from *Telenok* are my own.)

22. Up to the year 1959. Solzhenitsyn cites Professor Kurganov, *GULag* 2, p. 10; trans., p. 10.

23. For example, Stephen Carter, *The Politics of Solzhenitsyn* (London: Macmillan, 1977), p. 25.

24. *GULag* 3, p. 580. Trans., p. 527.

25. Brodsky, *op. cit.*, p. 639.

26. *GULag* 3, p. 418. Trans., p. 400.

27. *Iz-pod glyb*, p. 8. Trans., p. 4.

28. *GULag* 3, pp. 239-40. Trans., p. 229.

29. *GULag* 1, p. 442, Trans., p. 442.

30. *Ibid.*, pp. 235ff., 421ff., 514ff. Trans., pp. 229ff., 421ff., 517ff.

31. *GULag* 3, p. 373. Trans., p. 356.

32. *Ibid.*, p. 106. Trans., p. 98.

33. *GULag* 1, p. 543. Trans., p. 549.

34. A point developed by Claude Lefort in *Un Homme en Trop. Réflexions sur "L'Archipel du Goulag"* (Paris: Seuil, 1976), pp. 30-45.

35. *GULag* 3, pp. 456-57. Trans., p. 436.

36. *Crowds and Power* (Harmondsworth: Penguin, 1973). The book was first published in 1960.

37. *GULag* 2, p. 311. Trans., p. 317.

38. *Ibid.*, p. 318. Trans., p. 323.

39. For example, Lev Z. Kopelev, "A Lie Is Conquered Only by the Truth," and Sergei Elagin, "Repentance: Its Theory, History and Prescription for Today," both

reprinted in Roy Medvedev, ed., *Samizdat Register 1* (London: Merlin, 1977), pp. 205-38 and 239-68, respectively.

40. *GULag* 2, p. 604. Trans., p. 617.

41. *GULag* 1, p. 512. Trans., pp. 515-16.

42. *GULag* 3, p. 45. Trans., p. 42.

43. Lefort, *op. cit.*, pp. 211-19.

44. *GULag* 2, p. 604. Trans., pp. 616-17.

45. *Ibid.*, p. 614. Trans., p. 627.

46. *GULag* 3, pp. 34-35. Trans., pp. 31-32.

47. *Ibid.*, p. 246. Trans., pp. 234-35.

48. *Ibid.*, p. 413. Trans., p. 394.

49. Brodsky, *op.cit.*, pp. 638-39.

50. *GULag* 2, p. 298. Trans., p. 304.

51. *GULag* 1, p. 494. Trans., p. 494.

52. *GULag* 2, p. 383. Trans., p. 390.

53. *Ibid.*, p. 91. Trans., p. 91.

54. *Ibid.*, p. 21. Trans., pp. 21-22.

55. *GULag* 1, p. 593. Trans., p. 601.

56. *Ibid.*, p. 281. Trans., pp. 275-76.

57. Ian Watt, *The Rise of the Novel* (Harmondsworth: Penguin, 1966), p. 13; Northrop Frye, *Anatomy of Criticism* (Princeton University Press, 1973), p. 125.

58. "Chitaiut 'Ivana Denisovicha'," in *Sobranie sochinenii*, vol. 6 (Frankfurt/Main: Possev, 1971), pp. 243-62.

59. Vasilii Grossman, *Forever Flowing* (London: Andre Deutsch, 1973), p. 151.

The Gulag Archipelago: Alternative to Ideology

JOHN B. DUNLOP

The aim of this paper is to discuss, and if possible to systematize, the "positive" message of *The Gulag Archipelago*. In choosing to focus my attention in this fashion, I am of course aware that the major thrust of *Gulag* is *negative*, that its intention is, in the words of one commentator, to depict "what happens to a man and the world when man and life are *reduced* to ideology."[1] However, while Solzhenitsyn's polemical goals in the book have been elucidated by a number of commentators—to take one example, I might mention Martin Malia's fine essay in the January, 1977 issue of *The Russian Review*—his positive gropings and grapplings have not yet received systematic and sustained attention.

In his seminal *Notes from the Underground*, Dostoevskii examined what the fruits of a logical application of the theories of nineteenth century radical socialists to mankind would be (the work, as is well known, seeks specifically to counter Chernyshevskii's *What Is to Be Done?*). Scrutinizing human nature closely, Dostoevskii showed that Chernyshevskii's "scientific socialism" would result in deforming and tormenting man and that human nature would inevitably revolt against the logics of this monstrous theory. In *The Gulag Archipelago*, Solzhenitsyn continues Dostoevskii's work by showing what happened once Chernyshevskii's theories—plus the refinements of his successors and admirers, such as Lenin—became state policy. Both *Notes from the Underground* and *The Gulag Archipelago* confront human nature with a materialistic view of man which includes a commitment to determinism, a flinty ruthlessness toward those who would obstruct "progress," and a yearning for the social anthill and "Crystal Palace." But there is of course a crucial difference between the two works. Dostoevskii was combatting theory; Solzhenitsyn is at war with *applied* theory.

In *Gulag*, Solzhenitsyn shows the effect on Russia of the rule of ideology. As he demonstrates, twentieth century totalitarianism presses down on the individual with awesome force. To survive physically one is frequently forced to inform on one's neighbors or join the chorus of voices shouting "death! death! death!" as erstwhile colleagues at work are paraded off to execution. In the concentration camps—which, in many ways, represent the purest expression and distillation of ideology—the pressures and incentives to survive at the *expense* of those around one are overwhelming. Surely all must capitulate. But not all do. As Solzhenitsyn interjects in one place: "If corruption was so inevitable, then why did Ol'ga L'vovna Sliozberg not abandon her freezing friend on the forest trail, but stay behind to face almost certain death together with her—and save her?"[2]

Like Dostoevskii during his period of Siberian imprisonment, Solzhenitsyn observed his fellow zeks with the attentive eye of genius. To his own personal observations he added material derived from the accounts of others and, after his release, from memoirs sent to him. With wonder he notes that what is astonishing is not that so many capitulated before a raging neo-barbarism but that more than a few burst the shackles of ideology and successfully remained human beings. It is this revolt by the élite of human nature against the dead hand of ideology that rivets Solzhenitsyn's attention in *The Gulag Archipelago*; he is keenly interested in all its manifestations.

On the lowest and least remarkable level, it is the revulsion felt by Lieutenant Koverchenko, an intrepid parachutist who is simply *bored* with the vapid proclamations of ideology. His revolt—which is not consciously motivated—takes the form of wild, drunken adventures which ultimately earn him a twenty-five-year prison term. (As a footnote, one might observe that this way of opting out of the system is widely utilized in today's Soviet Russia. Vladimir Maksimov's uneven but suggestive novel *Seven Days of Creation* offers insights into this mode of rebellion.)

On a higher level, we are shown the revolt of those who choose physically to combat the regime. Solzhenitsyn's generally favorable attitude toward such persons is moderated and, to some extent, undercut by his deep distrust for what happens to those who take up arms even against unseemly evils. (At one point in *Gulag*, he asserts his belief that corruption is "probably inevitable" for those who resort to violence.[3]) Yet, though theoretically he can countenance only "moral revolution," Solzhenitsyn finds it difficult to condemn those who took up arms against an anti-human totalitarianism. Yes, he admits, all the books of the philosophers warn against the consequences of fighting evil with the sword, but what is one to do when one is being crushed and compressed into nothingness? As the popular adage, which Solzhenitsyn cites approvingly, puts it: "...evil cannot be cast out by good [*blagost'iu likhost' ne izoimesh'*]."[4]

And in the opening chapter of the first volume of *Gulag* Solzhenitsyn wonders:

> What would things have been like if every Security operative, when he went out at night to make an arrest, had been uncertain whether he would return alive and had to say good-bye to his family? Or if, during periods of mass arrests, as for example in Leningrad, when they arrested a quarter of the entire city, people had not simply sat there in their little burrows, paling with terror at every bang of the downstairs door and at every step on the staircase, but had understood that they had nothing to lose and had boldly set up in the downstairs hall an ambush of half a dozen people with axes, hammers, pokers, or whatever else was at hand?... Or what about the Black Maria sitting out there on the street with one lonely chauffeur—what if it had been driven off or had its tires spiked?[5]

He answers his own queries thus:

> The Organs would very quickly have suffered a shortage of officers and transport and, notwithstanding all of Stalin's thirst, the cursed machine would have ground to a halt!... We didn't love freedom enough... We purely and simply *deserved* everything that happened afterward.[6]

Solzhenitsyn's strictures against physical resistance to tyranny would seem to be balanced or at least held in abeyance in such passages. Similarly, in volume two he cites with obvious approval the "rare and shining example" of a front-line soldier who had not lost his courage in camp. In 1947, this former soldier overpowered and disarmed two convoy guards, shot them both and then informed his shocked fellow prisoners that they were free. When they timorously declined his summons to liberty, he set off on his own and succeeded in killing and wounding several of his pursuers before taking his own life. Solzhenitsyn's comment: "The entire Archipelago might well have collapsed if all former front-liners had behaved as he did."[7]

In volume three, Solzhenitsyn's interest in those who chose to rebel physically occupies a considerable portion of the narrative. He writes with respect and affection concerning a fellow camp graduate, Georgii Tenno, whose plan, once he learned he had contracted a mortal disease, was to dispatch a score of murderers, including the honored pensioner Viacheslav Molotov. Rationalizing and justifying Tenno's thought, Solzhenitsyn writes: "This would not be murder, but judicial execution, given that the law of the state protected murderers."[8] Only the rapid progress of cancer, which sapped his strength more swiftly than he had anticipated, kept Tenno from making the attempt. Solzhenitsyn also describes the rebellion in 1948 of a brigade of zeks, led by a former colonel, who chose to march on the city of Vorkuta. His comment: "The hopelessness of this rising as a military operation is obvious. But would you say that dying quietly by inches was more hopeful?"[9] Volume three also makes more explicit than volume one had done Solzhenitsyn's admiration for the Vlasov movement—a new "Pugachevshchina" supported by the broad masses of the populace. And the last volume extols the great Novocherkassk uprising of 1962, the first major rebellion in a Soviet city in forty-one years, "a cry from the soul of a people who could no longer live as they had lived."[10]

As I see it, the purpose of this concluding volume of *The Gulag Archipelago* is not to incite the Soviet populace to turn on its masters but rather to show that, with the waning of ideology in the post-war years and Khrushchev era, human nature began to reassert itself in mass actions. A "cry from the soul" occurs, a spontaneous and collective rebellion against institutionalized death.

Another choice for those who refuse to be deformed by ideology is escape, and *Gulag* devotes not a few of its pages to those adventurous spirits who attempted flight. "Escape!" Solzhenitsyn writes, "What desperate courage it took! Without civilian clothes, without food, with empty hands, to cross the fence under fire and run into the bare, waterless, endless open steppe!"[11] Georgii Tenno, with his twin tatoos of "Liberty!" and "Do or die!" seems to represent for Solzhenitsyn the archetypal escaper. (One should perhaps add that the dividing line between escapers and physical rebels becomes somewhat blurred, since those in flight are sometimes called upon to use violence to ward off their pursuers.)

While Solzhenitsyn has great sympathy for the spontaneous rebellion of bold spirits, he is clearly more at ease with purely *moral* rebellion. Here—in a Russian tradition going back to Saints Boris and Gleb—fulfillment is found in self-immolation. In treating instances of moral rebellion, Solzhenitsyn appears to distinguish between those whose reaction to injustice and institutionalized lies is visceral—one simply stands up and says no!—and those whose defiance is grounded in a world-view. An appropriate example of what I have called "visceral" rebellion would be Anna Petrovna Skripnikova, who is discussed at the end of volume two. For her, survival is "nothing in comparison with common justice."[12] And Solzhenitsyn comments: "...if everyone were even one-quarter as implacable as Anna Skripnikova—the history of Russia would be different."[13] The costs of moral rebellion, as Solzhenitsyn demonstrates at length, are not significantly different from those of choosing physically to oppose the system. In volume one, for example, we are offered the case of a nonpolitical offender named Smelov who went on a hunger strike in a Leningrad prison. He was visited by a prosecutor who asked him: "Why are you torturing yourself?" Smelov replied: "Justice is more precious to me than life." Smelov was ordered to be taken to an insane asylum, where he was told: "We suspect you may be a schizophrenic."[14] Or there is the case, also reported in volume one, of the dissatisfied prisoner who protested against a suspicious weighing of bread rations: "I demand a reweighing..." To the prisoner's visceral objection to injustice the prison authorities have a reflex response:

> 'Which one here spoke out against the Soviet government?... Aha, you're the bastard? You're the one who doesn't like the Soviet government?... You stinking scum! You counterrevolutionary! You ought to be hanged...'[15]

The "rebel" is taken away, and the response to the official's query, "Now who else is dissatisfied?" is, of course, silence.

One mode of protest which might seem almost logical in light of the scale of the suffering is suicide. But this option is vehemently rejected by Solzhenitsyn. "...is suicide," he asks, "really resistance? Isn't it really submission?"[16] And elsewhere he adds: "A suicide is always a bankrupt, always a human being in a blind alley..."[17]

The next step up the ladder from a spontaneous nonacceptance of injustice and lies is to possess a counter-ideology to the prevailing one. In volume one, we are introduced to a Colonel Konstantin Iasevich, a former White officer who grasped the nature of Bolshevism from the beginning and devoted his life to combatting it. Placidly and with a firm spirit the self-disciplined colonel awaits his inevitable execution. "... He had evidently," Solzhenitsyn writes, "a clear and exact view of everything around him...."[18]

At the highest level are those with a "point of view" (*tochka zreniia*).[19] A point of view is the ultimate and perhaps only enemy of ideology, for not only does it provide a reasoned critique of the ideology and the system it spawns but it offers *an alternative worldview* which prompts its adherents to do spiritual battle with the ideology. During the infamous Moscow show trials, Bukharin and his associates, Solzhenitsyn feels, were unable to exhibit independence because they lacked a point of view and, in fact, remained slaves to the ideology which was seeking to take their lives. Those with a point of view possess the necessary artillery to destroy ideology and the firmness to withstand it by electing *not* to "survive at any price."[20]

Let us examine several examples which Solzhenitsyn offers of persons who had a point of view:

> They wanted to drag [the philosopher Nikolai Berdiaev] into an open trial; they arrested him twice...he was subjected to a night interrogation by Dzerzhinsky himself. Kamenev was there too...But Berdiaev did not humiliate himself. He did not beg or plead. He set forth firmly those religious and moral principles which had led him to refuse to accept the political authority established in Russia. And not only did they come to the conclusion that he would be useless for a trial, but they released him.
> The man had a *point of view*![21]

The second example he gives is that of an old woman and religious believer:

> They kept on interrogating her every night. Two years earlier, a former Metropolitan of the Orthodox Church, who had escaped from exile, had spent a night at her home on his way through Moscow....
> At first the interrogators took turns, and then they went after her in groups. They shook their fists in the little old woman's face, and she replied: 'There is nothing you can do with me even if you cut me into pieces....you are afraid of each other, and you are even afraid of

killing me.' (They would lose their main lead.) 'But I am not afraid of anything. I would be glad to be judged by God right this minute.'[22]

It is not accidental that in these instances Solzhenitsyn finds "point of view" related to Christianity. He is not saying, of course, that only Christians can be courageous—he is even willing to attest the courage of the SRs and Trotskiites who were ground to bits by the very machine they helped set in operation. What he appears to be maintaining is that only Christianity offers an effective antidote to Marxism-Leninism, only it can exorcise the demons which have been rending Russia since 1917. Solzhenitsyn's views have understandably not set well with socialists and liberal Marxists. Neo-Marxist dissenter Roy Medvedev, for example, protests vehemently:

> Solzhenitsyn does not even consider it possible for nonreligious people to distinguish between good and bad . . . Solzhenitsyn does not understand that socialist convictions can be the basis for a genuinely humanist set of values and a profoundly human morality. And if up to now the problems of ethics and morals have not yet found satisfactory treatment in Marxist-Leninist theory, this by no means implies that scientific socialism is incapable by its very nature of establishing moral values.[23]

Solzhenitsyn would undoubtedly retort that "scientific socialism" should have pondered "the problems of ethics and morals" a bit more before undertaking to experiment with the lives of millions.

Solzhenitsyn's religious views, which permeate *The Gulag Archipelago* and serve as a bone of contention for many besides Roy Medvedev, seem to have resulted from his close observation of humanity while he was in prison. The analogy to Dostoevskii is again relevant. Their paths to religious belief, however, were different. Dostoevskii, a philosopher and theological anthropologist, deduced laws of human nature which led him to religion; Solzhenitsyn, on the other hand, seems to have concentrated on the question of ethical behavior. A superior ethical stance—rooted in a "point of view"—characterized many of the believers he observed or heard tales of from his fellow zeks. He notes, for example, that during the Kengir camp rebellion the religious believers were "as always the calmest."[24] He frequently lauds Russian women believers for behavior worthy of the Christian martyrs of the first century. And he praises Patriarch Tikhon, first head of the Russian Church after the Revolution, who stated at the Moscow Church Trial of 1922 that he would obey Soviet laws *"to the extent that they do not contradict the rules of piety."*[25] Solzhentisyn's comment: "Oh, if only everyone had answered just that way! Our whole history would have been different."[26]

An important question which directly relates to Solzhenitsyn's "positive" message in *Gulag* concerns how the past is to be righted. What about the millions who succumbed to the threats and blandishments of ideology? And what about the executioners themselves, the legions of Soviet Eichmanns?

Running like a red thread through the book is Solzhenitsyn's belief that the victims of oppression who gave in should not be judged. "Do not be the first to cast a stone at them," he pleads.[27] And elsewhere he explains that the "basic viewpoint" of the book is that all who suffered "ought rather to be vindicated than accused."[28] The pressures on the victims were, after all, enormous, perhaps unprecedented in human history.

But what about the executioners? At times, Solzhenitsyn gives way to an inconsistent but understandable delight that the terror swallowed up many of its children. Roy Medvedev has lectured the writer on this point: "... I was unpleasantly surprised by Solzhenitsyn's words that he had somehow been 'consoled'...by the thought of the degradation to which Krylenko was reduced in Butyrki prison before he was shot, the same Krylenko who had condemned others to similar degradation."[29] Medvedev wonders whether this is "decent," let alone Christian, of Solzhenitsyn, though he neglects to mention his own commitment, as a neo-Leninist, to the necessary bloodshed of revolution (see, for example, his book *Let History Judge*).

Solzhenitsyn's wrath against the agents of the terror is usually tempered in *Gulag* by an awareness that he himself could easily have become one of the executioners. Besides being an indictment of Marxism-Leninism and all its works, the book is also a confession. Were it not for his own resuscitative passage through the inferno of camps, prison, and exile, Solzhenitsyn could, he admits, have become one of the victimizers. "If only," he writes, "it were all so simple! If only there were evil people somewhere insidiously committing evil deeds, and it were necessary only to separate them from the rest of us and destroy them. But the line dividing good and evil cuts through the heart of every human being... Socrates taught us: *Know thyself!*"[30] And in another place he writes:

> 'Know thyself!' There is nothing that so aids and assists the awakening of conscience within us as insistent thoughts about one's own transgressions, errors, mistakes... Whenever I mentioned the heartlessness of our highest-ranking bureaucrats, the cruelty of our executioners, I remember myself in my captain's shoulder boards... and I say: 'So were *we* any better?'[31]

A knowledge of the dark potentials of one's own nature thus serves to moderate any desire for vengeance. Yet Solzhenitsyn believes that it is possible for a human being to pass beyond the state of moral flux common to all men and to cross over a mystical threshold of evil:

> Physics is aware of phenomena which occur only at *threshold* magnitudes... You can cool oxygen to 100 degrees below zero Centigrade and exert as much pressure as you want; it does not yield, but remains a gas. But as soon as minus 183 degrees is reached, it liquifies and begins to flow.
>
> Evidently evildoing also has a threshold magnitude. Yes, a human being hesitates and bobs back and forth between good and evil all his life. He slips, falls back, clambers up, repents, is overtaken once more by darkness. But just so long as the threshold of evildoing is not crossed, the possibility of returning remains....[32]

Solzhenitsyn's strong awareness that he *could* have become a "blue cap" and executioner does not blind him to the depths of evil which can be plumbed by a human being, depths which have been justified and even extolled by twentieth century totalitarianism.

In *Gulag* Solzhenitsyn calls for Nürnberg-type trials of those Soviet citizens guilty of crimes against humanity. Employing the yardstick of the 86,000 Germans brought to trial in their homeland after World War II, he estimates that approximately one-quarter of a million Soviets should be asked to stand in the dock. "... For the sake of our country and our children we have the duty to *seek them all out and bring them all to trial*!"[33] Each should be compelled to state clearly: "Yes, I was an executioner and murderer."[34] The country needs these trials as a rite of purgation to prevent its youth from becoming cynical, but above all the executioners themselves are in need of them. Perhaps, Solzhenitsyn seems to feel, such a stark and unavoidable rendezvous with truth may induce at least some of them to cross back over the threshold of evil.

Solzhenitsyn believes that his own arrest and the dramatic reversal of his personal fortunes had a salutary effect on his life. As Dr. Kornfeld, a Jewish convert to Christianity, tells the future writer shortly before being murdered in the camps: "... I have become convinced that there is no punishment that comes to us on earth which is undeserved....if you go over your life with a fine-tooth comb and ponder it deeply, you will be able to hunt down that transgression of yours for which you have now received this blow."[35] These words of his murdered mentor remain with Solzhenitsyn as "an inheritance"; he comes to realize that "the meaning of earthly existence lies not, as we have grown used to thinking, in prospering, but...in the development of the soul."[36] (Incidentally, it was this encounter with Dr. Kornfeld, reported in volume two of *Gulag*, which seems to have been the spark for Solzhenitsyn's conversion to religious belief.)

The Gulag Archipelago is a profoundly *personalistic* book. Repect for the unique value, even sanctity, of the individual is a cornerstone of its message. Where Marxism-Leninism sees individuals as minute particles of larger and more important entities, such as classes—some of whom it may be necessary to exterminate as "insects"—Solzhenitsyn wants to propagate the infinite worth of each individual human being. *Gulag* is a kind of celebration of personality, a personalistic feast. In prison, Solzhenitsyn is "filled to the brim with the joy of being among them [people]."[37] And elsewhere he writes: "I love that moment when a newcomer is admitted to the cell for the first time... And I myself love to enter a new cell..."[38] Each human being who perished before a raging totalitarianism was a pearl of great price; each name must be rescued from oblivion.

A final point deserves to be mentioned. The act of writing *Gulag* is itself a "model" of behavior which flies in the face of a materialistic ideology which proclaims physical well-being as the highest good. While at work on volume two, Solzhenitsyn reports: "The dragon emerged for one minute, licked up my novel [the reference is to the seizure of a manuscript of *The First Circle*] with his red tongue...and retired behind the curtain for the time. But I can hear his breathing, and I know that his teeth are aimed at my neck... And with devastated soul I gather my strength to complete this investigation, so that it at least may escape the dragon's teeth."[39] *The Gulag Archipelago* was written in the shadow of death, and that should not be forgotten.

Notes

1. Alexander Schmemann, "Reflections on *The Gulag Archipelago*" in John B. Dunlop, Richard Haugh, and Alexis Klimoff, eds., *Aleksandr Solzhenitsyn: Critical Essays and Documentary Materials*, 2nd ed. (New York: Collier Books 1975), p. 523. Italics in original.

2. A. Solzhenitsyn, *ARKHIPELAG GULag*, vol. 2 (pts. III-IV) (Paris: YMCA-Press, 1974), p. 613. English translation: *The Gulag Archipelago Two* (New York: Harper and Row, 1975), p. 627. Here and on a few subsequent occasions I have chosen to tamper with Thomas Whitney's translations.

3. *ARKHIPELAG GULag*, vol. 3 (pts. V-VI-VII) (Paris: YMCA-Press, 1975), p. 293, footnote. Translation: *The Gulag Archipelago Three* (New York: Harper and Row, 1978), p. 278.

4. *Ibid.*, p. 246. Trans., p. 235.

5. *ARKHIPELAG GULag*, vol. 1 (pts. I-II) (Paris: YMCA-Press, 1973), pp. 26-27, footnote 4. Translation: *The Gulag Archipelago* (New York: Harper and Row, 1974), p. 13, footnote 5.

6. *Ibid.* Italics in original.

7. *GULag* 2, p. 391. Trans., p. 399.

8. *GULag* 3, p. 202. Trans., p. 191, footnote 7.

9. *Ibid.*, p. 241. Trans., p. 230.

10. *Ibid.*, p. 557. Trans., p. 507.

11. *Ibid.*, p. 80. Trans., p. 75.

12. *GULag* 2, p. 648. Trans., p. 662.

13. *Ibid.*, p. 650. Trans., p. 664.

14. *GULag* 1, p. 474. Trans., p. 473.

15. *Ibid.*, pp. 506-507. Trans., pp. 509-510.

16. *Ibid.*, p. 473. Trans., p. 472.

17. *GULag* 2, p. 589. Trans., p. 601.

18. *GULag* 1, p. 272. Trans., p. 267.

19. On this, see my article "Solzhenitsyn's *The Gulag Archipelago*: Ideology or 'Point of View'?" *Transactions of the Association of Russian-American Scholars in USA*, VIII (1974), pp. 20-26.

20. *GULag* 2, p. 597. Trans., p. 610.

21. *GULag* 1, p. 139. Trans., pp. 130-131. Italics in original.

22. *Ibid.*, pp. 139-140. Trans., p. 131.

23. Roy Medvedev, "Solzhenitsyn's Gulag: Part Two," *Dissent*, Spring (1976), p. 162. For a collection of Medvedev's articles on Solzhenitsyn, see his *Political Essays* (Nottingham: Spokesman Books, 1976).

24. *GULag* 3, p. 340. Trans., p. 324.

25. *GULag* 1, p. 352. Trans., p. 348. Italics in original.

26. *Ibid.*

27. *Ibid.*, p. 127. Trans., p. 117.

28. *GULag* 2, p. 259. Trans., p. 265.

29. Medvedev, *op. cit.* p. 159.

30. *GULag* 1, pp. 175-176. Trans., p. 168. Italics in original.

31. *GULag* 2, p. 603. Trans., p. 616. Italics in original.

32. *GULag* 1, p. 182. Trans., pp. 174-175. Italics in original.

33. *Ibid.*, pp. 184-185. Trans., p. 177. Italics in original.

34. *Ibid.*, p. 185. Trans., p. 177.

35. *GULag* 2, p. 600. Trans., p. 612.

36. *Ibid.*, p. 601. Trans., p. 613.

37. *GULag* 1, p. 194. Trans., p. 187.

38. *Ibid.*, p. 588. Trans., p. 596.

39. *GULag* 2, p. 210. Trans., p. 214.

Observations on the Narrative Structure of
The Gulag Archipelago

ELISABETH MARKSTEIN

In discussing *The Gulag Archipelago*, George Gibian writes that: "An exclusively technical analysis of a book saturated with suffering and bearing witness to a gigantic historical and national tragedy would be an exercise in callousness."[1] The point is sternly expressed, and rightly so. Yet, inappropriate as it may be for the critic or literary scholar to don the robe of impassivity in tackling *Gulag*, professional integrity dictates that he should scrutinize the way it is written, the notorious "how," regardless of the appalling "what" which constitutes its subject matter. That this "what" can never be brushed aside, goes without saying.[2] The fundamental impossibility of separating form from content is nowhere more evident than in the case of *Gulag*. But this, surely, is the familiar dilemma which confronts the study of literature: any literary investigation or attempt at interpretation must, almost without exception, diminish its subject, for literary criticism, unable and unwilling to compete with literature on the artistic plane, inevitably renders it mundane. With his quotations and analyses, the scholar tears the fabric of art to shreds and invades its sanctum sanctorum by dotting each "i" where the artist himself has deliberately refrained from doing so. (This is particularly clear in the case of lyric poetry: if, as she herself stated, Anna Akhmatova did not like to see her verses in print and could not abide having them read in her presence,[3] we can well imagine what she felt whenever she read an *analysis* of them.) And if there is any justification for this kind of vivisection, and for assuming in the present instance that the reader is already familiar with the factual content of *Gulag*, then that justification is to be found in the most elementary goal of literary criticism and scholarship: to cultivate in readers and students the art of reading.

How do people read *The Gulag Archipelago*? By and large, it is read as an *investigation* ("issledovanie"), as a collection of facts. In its weekly list of bestsellers, the German magazine *Der Spiegel* placed *The Gulag Archipelago* under the rubric *Sachbuch*, suggesting a scholarly, or popular scholarly publication. And many readers have read the book in that vein. So, too, have literary critics. This tendency to treat *Gulag* as a political work was aggravated, soon after the appearance of the Russian and German editions, by the sensational news of Solzhenitsyn's deportation from the Soviet Union. Such criticism treated *Gulag* as an historical work and laboriously sought out historical inaccuracies. At times, it took the author to task on ideological grounds.[4] It singled out specific extra-literary themes in the book, such as the de-glorification of Lenin, a new departure in "exposé literature."[5] It was forever noting Solzhenitsyn's success in capturing the panorama of labor camp life, occasionally dwelling upon his vivid eye for detail, and almost invariably paying due respect to his moral stance.[6] In short, criticism, still shaken by the contents of Solzhenitsyn's "investigation," did not concern itself with the work's *artistry*; indeed, it often seemed blind to the fact that, whatever else it may be, *The Gulag Archipelago* is also a remarkable piece of literature.

Gradually, however, criticism began to address itself to the question of the artistic quality of *Gulag*. Since an exhaustive bibliography lies outside the scope of the present article, I shall confine my attention to two essays, each published in a different American collection: these are Vera Carpovich's "Lexical Peculiarities of Solzhenitsyn's Language,"[7] and George Gibian's "How Solzhenitsyn Returned His Ticket," which has already been cited above. Both of these essays inevitably overlap at certain points with this article. Vera Carpovich examines the lexical features of *Gulag*, noting its variety of lexical registers. To the stylistic levels of colloquial and popular speech, Old Slavisms and criminal slang, which she analyzes, one might wish to add Sovietisms, the official language of the party and of the Soviet press: this Carpovich mentions only in passing, although, as we shall see, it has an important role to play in the composition of *Gulag*. In his most interesting essay, George Gibian treats the narrative aspects of *Gulag*, observing that Solzhenitsyn "steps outside the conventions of detached, descriptive, historical or legal reports of research results."[8] Indeed, for all that *Gulag* is unquestionably (though not exclusively) an historical work, the only style of speech missing from it is the scientific and technical (apart, that is, from the lightly parodied scientific turns of speech in the chapter "Zeks as a Nation," which bears the subtitle "An Ethnographical Essay by Fan Fanych"[9]). However, while speaking of the "many distinguishable kinds of writing" in *Gulag*,[10] Gibian conducts his analysis on the basis of *thematic* distinctions, and in this respect his approach differs substantially from our own.

Our aim, then, is to formulate certain observations on the narrative structure as such, and to endeavor to show how this structure acts to determine the genre of the work.

*   *   *

At the beginning of the 1930s, at the time he was working on his *Youth Returned*, Mikhail Zoshchenko wrote: "(...) I think it is precisely here, in the realm of fact (taking this in the wider sense, to include history, science and memoirs) that new genres are to be discovered. Genres such as we know them are inadequate, and literature can hardly fail to move beyond them."[11] Is not *The Gulag Archipelago* just such a new genre?

In the interview on literary themes which he gave to Nikita Struve in 1976, Solzhenitsyn briefly set forth what he understood by the genre of *artistic investigation*, a term which he had coined: "An artistic investigation draws upon real-life, factual material (untransmuted, that is), but also employs all the resources available to the artist in uniting these individual facts and fragments, such that the overall design emerges with a conclusiveness no wit less complete and compelling than that of a piece of scientific research."[12] The present essay is devoted precisely to these "resources available to the artist," which facilitate, in Tomashevskii's words, "the arousal of other interests [i.e., not scientific or agitational] which are locked up within the literary work itself."[13]

How difficult and relative a matter it is to separate out such elements, can be shown by the example of what might be termed Solzhenitsyn's extreme metaphorization. The very title of the book is a metaphor, and within *The Gulag Archipelago* metaphor carries not only a figurative, but a compositional load. The titles of the chapters are, in themselves, macro-metaphors or, to use Mirskii's term, "mother-metaphors":[14] "The Ships of the Archipelago," "The Ports of the Archipelago," "From Island to Island," "The Archipelago Metastasizes," etc. Yet neither the metaphorization in the book, nor its abundance of rhetorical figures is sufficient to distinguish *The Gulag Archipelago* as a genre, for the same features may be characteristic both of publicistic, and of popular scholarly writing.

As we know, writers' attempts at self-characterization do not always find agreement among literary critics. Even so, let us consider the context in which Aleksandr Solzhenitsyn himself views his work as an artist. "I thought of myself as the chronicler of the Archipelago, I wrote and wrote (. . .),"[15] he declared. Many years later he would reiterate: "I became the accredited chronicler of labor camp life, to whom people brought the whole truth."[16] And on the same occasion, he explained that he "had no way of processing that *vast torrent* of material, other than in the form of a vast work such as this."[17] Evidently, then, this torrent of material forms, as it were, the basis of the *investigation*, while the way in which Solzhenitsyn has processed it constitutes its *artistry*.

At first glance, the material in the book may strike the reader as raw and unpolished, but a second, less superficial glance reveals that this is not the case. Far from concealing the fact that he is working, as an historian, from sources and from the testimony of eyewitnesses, Solzhenitsyn goes out of his way to remind us that this is so: "here is one eyewitness's account (. . .)," "Karpunich recalls (. . .)," "according to the testimony of A. P. K-va (. . .)," "I. A. P-ev reported (. . .)," "according to the accounts of the Military Collegiate of the Supreme Court," etc. He cites authentic letters,[18] complete biographies,[19] makes use of court records.[20] As a result, certain readers, and even the author himself (in his Postscript), have felt the book to be somewhat repetitive. The impression is accurate, but does not detract from the artistic value of the book, for these repetitions bring out the sheer multiplicity of facts, in which is condensed the experience of several generations. The torrent of material is laid bare; revealed for what it is, this material makes up the basis of the book as *chronicle*. Deprived of other possibilities, historiography in the Soviet Union has, in the twentieth century, created the *chronicle*, taking as its subject matter the history of the prisons, camps, and of "freedom," and as its point of reference the October Revolution of 1917. The German critic Walter Benjamin once made an aphoristic distinction between the historian and the chronicler: the historian *writes* history, but the chronicler *narrates* it.[21]

This brings us to the question of how Solzhenitsyn the chronicler *narrates* the history of the Gulag.

Evidently evildoing also has a threshold magnitude. Yes, a human being hesitates and bobs back and forth between good and evil all his life. He slips, falls back, clambers up, repents, things begin to darken again. But just so long as the threshold of evildoing is not crossed, the possibility of returning remains, and he himself is still within reach of our hope. (I, 182; Tr. 175)

Mine was, probably, the easiest imaginable kind of arrest.(...) The brigade commander called me to his headqarters (...). (I, 31; Tr. 18)

In other words, we never did trust the engineers—and from the very first years of the Revolution we saw to it that those lackeys and servants of former capitalist bosses were kept in line by healthy suspicion and surveillance by the workers. (I, 55-56; Tr. 43)

In addition, that same year Stalin trampled underhoof (*pokopytil*) the long-since prostrate Mensheviks. (I, 61; Tr. 49)

Four quotations, four narrative perspectives, four different styles: elevated rhetoric, neutral narrative, the language of the Party and its press, and conversational, colloquial speech. Such examples of stylistic variety may be found even within the confines of a single page, and herein lie the difficulties of translating *Gulag*: the translator involuntarily narrows the stylistic range, at least as regards the peculiarly Soviet language of political agitation. Apologies are due for the abundance of examples which will be offered to the reader in the pages which follow, but, after all, any analysis must proceed by way of the text itself.

As Dmitrii Likhachev writes in his *Poetics of Ancient Russian Literature*: "The artistic image of the chronicler, an invisible presence in any chronicled account, enters the reader's consciousness as that of a contemporary noting down passing events, and not that of a 'scholar and historian' creating collections of chronicles, which is the way he tends to be presented in scholarly studies of the Russian chronicle."[22] Solzhenitsyn, however, as a contemporary author-chronicler, *consciously* constructs this image of a contemporary, of a collective narrator-figure, recounting the history of the Gulag from a present-day standpoint, yet while the tracks are still fresh. And this he does with the aid of a highly complex narrative structure, involving the correlation between his own speech and attitudes as author, and the speech of his characters. Without forgoing the first-person "I" in the narrative passages which form the tie-beams of this "vast work'' (as in the first and second examples cited above), he constantly gives the floor to the dramatis personae of the accumulated material, to those witnesses whose tales, reminiscences and letters helped him to create ''our common collective monument to all those who were tortured and murdered'' (I, 10; Tr. xi).

Interwoven with the voice of the author-narrator are the voices of a multitude of his contemporaries—cell-mates, camp-mates, readers who responded to the appearance of *Ivan Denisovich*. At times, the author hands over the entire narrative function to a personified storyteller, in a form which is explicitly that of *skaz*.[23] More often, the author-narrator limits himself to introducing *another* person's word and *another* person's speech, what Bakhtin describes as ''words, expressions, attributes and epithets infected by the intentions of others.''[24] In fact, any of the author's informants can emerge as a ''potential narrator-figure.''[25] Metaphorically, one might say that the material itself had *begun to speak*. And this is precisely the function of the multiplicity of styles in *Gulag*. To these contemporaries all the stylistic levels of the Russian language, including thieves' cant and Soviet newspaper jargon, come easily, and, conversely, all these levels are comprehensible to the contemporary Russian reader. This, incidentally, explains why Solzhenitsyn often does not bother to explain such examples of thieves' cant as *nasedka* (stool-pigeon), *urka* (professional criminal), *stukach* (squealer), *sharashka* (privileged special prison), *parasha* (latrine bucket; rumor), or *kostyl'* (legal minimum ration).

Practically speaking, monological narration tends to dominate only in passages of an autobiographical nature (as in the second example) and, to some extent, in the generalizing reflections and abstractions of the author himself (the first example). For the rest, the tonality of the narrative is polyphonic, laced with stylistic interruptions, impersonal direct discourse and elements of *skaz*. Consider the following excerpts by way of illustration:

Another person's word (standing out against a neutral narrative background): ''They *swept away* (*zameli*) Karger's archive of the Enisei Ostiaks and banned the alphabet and primer he had devised for them—and this *little nation* (*narodets*) was thereby left without any written language'' (I, 19-20; Tr. 6). ''If the person to be arrested is *vicious*, then it's better to seize him outside his ordinary milieu (. . .)'' (I, 22; Tr. 8). ''Transferred from Corrective Labor Camps to

Special Camps, these *animals* must be aware at once of their strict-
ness and harshness—but obviously someone must first devise a
detailed program!'' (III, 60; Tr. 57).

Impersonal Direct Discourse: ''(...) he (Stalin) did not overlook
the children—the children *whom he loved so well, whose Best Friend
he was, and therefore had his photograph taken with them*'' (II, 435;
Tr. 448). Here the very solecism emphasizes the presence of disparate voices.[26] "Captain Second Class Burkovskii carries the mortar.
Whatever is built is all for the good of the Motherland'' (III, 82;
Tr. 76). In this example we hear the voice of Burkovskii himself
("Motherland" with a capital letter). Again, when the prisoners
have their glasses taken away for the night, not to be returned until
two hours after reveille, we read: ''The same was true of the business
with eyeglasses: *why bother about them at reveille* [warden's voice]?
They'll give them back just before the end of the night shift'' [pris-
oner's voice] (I, 212; Tr. 205). The impersonal direct speech of
another figure is often cited in whole blocks, for which a more appropriate term would be *truncated skaz*.[27] "A convenient world outlook
gives rise to a convenient juridical term: social prophylaxis. It was
introduced and accepted, and it was immediately understood by all.
(...) *And, indeed, when else are unreliable fellow travellers, all
this shaky intellectual rot, to be arrested, if not on the eve of the war
for world revolution? When the big war actually begins, it will be
too late*'' [this is the voice of the *organs*, of the Cheka-KGB] (I, 54;
Tr. 42).

Not only have the raw materials of which *Gulag* is composed
begun to speak, but their subjects even freely exchange temporal,
spatial, and evaluative standpoints. Here, for example, the author-
narrator is recounting what happened after N. Stoliarova was freed
from camp: ''(...) Stoliarova returned to the camp compound, told
the guards some tale about coming to fetch her things (...), and...
went home to her hut!'' And suddenly the eye of an imaginary
camera (and with it our perspective) moves into the barrack itself:
''There never was such happiness! Her friends flocked around,
brought her gruel from the kitchen (oh, how nice it tastes!), they
laugh and listen to her stories about how lost and homeless she was
outside. No, thanks—we're more comfortable here. Roll call. One too
many!...'' (III, 467; Tr. 446). Now we have the perspective of those
doing the arresting: ''Not everyone can be arrested at home, with a
preliminary knock at the door (...)'' (I, 22; Tr. 8). Now the per-

spective of those on the receiving end: "For those left behind after the arrest there is the long tail end of a wrecked and devastated life. And the attempts to go and deliver food parcels. But from all the windows they bark back at you (. . .)" (I, 20; Tr. 6).

The grammatical present interrupts the narrator's retrospective tone. A dialogue between different positions ensues: "They try to tell us that up there on the summit the chief of literature [Gor'kii] made excuses, that he didn't want to publish praise of USLON. [interrupting voices:] But how can that be, Aleksei Maksimovich? With bourgeois Europe looking on? But right now, right at this very moment, which is so dangerous and so complicated!" (II, 61; Tr. 63). As in the ancient Russian chronicle, so too in Solzhenitsyn's chronicle, there is no single point of view, no single narrator.[28]

In the artistic organization of this polyphony a special, dynamic role falls to constructions involving personal pronouns, which identify the voices of the various characters. Let us consider some examples. Solzhenitsyn the author has reserved the first-person "I" for himself. All the autobiographical and memoir elements in the book are organized as an *Ich-Erzählung*, in which the figures of author and narrator coincide and the narrative norm is predominantly neutral. Such is the story of Solzhenitsyn's own arrest, his work in the camp, his exile.

The pronoun "we" represents at once a collective group of prisoners from the camps and prisons ("We never, of course, lost hope that our story would be told. . ." [III, 495; Tr. 471]), and simply "we"—the people, our generation, our country, Russia, concepts which embrace even the executioners. "Over our very cradles the song had resounded: 'All power to the Soviets!'" (I, 244; Tr. 238). "For we honor Great Evildoers. We venerate Great Murderers" (III, 386; Tr. 368). "We ourselves released from every obligation, not merely to his Motherland but to all humanity, the human being whom we drove to gnawing on bats!" (I, 252; Tr. 246). This "we" unifies and, in a sense, defines the popular view of the events described, while at the same time distinguishing between various perspectives. This is the "we" of folklore, of national unity, it is the "we" and "ours" of the ancient Russian chronicles. Only occasionally does the author introduce "we" as a form of politeness: "We insistently urge our readers not to forget the principle of provincial multiplicity" (I, 356; Tr. 352).

"You" stands, as a rule, for the reader, whose close ties to the narrator are vividly illustrated in the line: "And those who, like you and me, dear reader, go there (to the Gulag) to die (. . .)" (I, 17 Tr. 3).

Particularly fruitful in *Gulag* is the pronoun "thou" *(ty)*, understood as a generalized subject of speech, whose voice is incorporated in the form of indirect personal discourse. This "thou" (here rendered as "you") can be the voice of an interrogator: "And if your opponent is so strong that he refuses to give in, all your methods have failed, and you are in a rage? Then don't control your fury!(. . .) After such a storm of fury you feel yourself a real honest-to-God man!" (I, 159; Tr. 150). It may also stand for the "rabbit" at the moment of his arrest: "Since you aren't guilty, then how can they arrest you? It's a mistake! They are already dragging you along by the collar, and you still keep on exclaiming to yourself: 'It's a mistake! They'll set things straight and let me out!' (. . .) as for you, well, you're obviously innocent!" (I, 26; Tr. 12). Or it may stand for the same rabbit after his interrogation: "For a week or a month you had been an abandoned waif, alone among enemies, and you had already said good-bye to reason and to life (. . .) Then all of a sudden you were alive again, and were brought in to your friends (. . .)" (I, 189; Tr. 181). Or, again, it may express a general proposition in personalized form: "And there's another advantage: if you sleep in the daytime, your sentence passes more quickly."

In opposition to the collective "we" of the prisoners and people stand "they"—the "organs," the investigators and guards. "They order us to extol *them* as legendary heroes" (III, 99; Tr. 92. Italics in original). *Their* language is the Newspeak of Orwell's *1984*. It is not *our* human language at all, but one so alien that it requires a translator. "But the interrogator writes down the deposition himself, translating it into *his own* language (. . .)" (I, 130; Tr. 120. Italics in original). "We were always vainly imploring the interrogator not to write 'my repulsive, slanderous fabrications' instead of 'my mistaken statements,' or not to write 'our underground weapons arsenal' instead of 'my rusty Finnish knife'" (I, 132-33; Tr. 123). "Didn't we used to say 'reins,' the way cabmen do? But now we say 'driving straps'! It used to be called 'mutual back-scratching,' but that smells of the stables too. And now it's collective responsibility!" (II, 115; Tr. 116). And if a certain "inducement" crops up in the text, the author has the foresight to explain in a footnote: "An affectionate term for—torture" (I, 155; Tr. 146).

On the lips of the narrator *their* language, Newspeak, is always "made strange" and given a sarcastic ring. *Their* word serves only for parody, and *their* voice is always set against the voices of the author and of the witness-figures who do not belong with them. If the spoken word of these latter characters was biphonic and unidirectional, then that of the "organs," the newspapers and the authorities, is biphonic but, in Bakhtin's terms, multidirectional (*mnogonapravlennyi*).[29] Between Newspeak and *our* language there is a constant dialogue, a constant tension. Newspeak forms the basis of the satiric current in *Gulag*, and for its translators probably the most difficult task has been to convey the sarcasm intact to readers unfamiliar with this international Newspeak. How is one to render, without sacrificing their rich associations, such brilliant and inventive expressions as "the responsible latrinebucket-bearer" (I, 211; Tr. 204), "the historically central issue then became Vigilance" (II, 569; Tr. 583), or the following passage: "The newspapers pointed the finger. The newspapers disclosed. The newspapers also exposed the sallies of the calss enemy—so that he could be hit harder (. . .). And overall the newspapers reflected the flow of camp life (. . .)" (II, 462; Tr. 475).

This process engenders a multiplicity of voices, a polyphonic exposition. Because of its polyphony and shifting perspective, and in spite of differences in thematic scale, it is *One Day in the Life of Ivan Denisovich*, of all Solzhenitsyn's works, that is most closely related to *Gulag*. In *Gulag* the "we" is, of course, much broader, but a common "we," which included both Shukhov and his campmates, was already present in *Ivan Denisovich*, as too was the mingling of the hero's perspective with that of the narrator.[30] *Ivan Denisovich* offers a group portrait of the camp inmates, with their individual voices and points of view. In *Gulag*, the hero is multiplied a hundredfold and more: as a true chronicler, Solzhenitsyn strives to "express the collective feelings, the collective attitude toward what is depicted."[31]

But this does not exhaust the aims of the author-narrator: in addition, he endeavors to "organize" his reader's reactions, to involve him in the narrative process. The author-narrator is forever thinking about his reader, and is aware of his presence. He tries to anticipate his reactions and objections, draws him into the discussion. "But I can already hear angry cries from my compatriots and contemporaries. Stop! Who are these people who you dare to tell us about?'' (III, 12; Tr. 10). The narrator muses: "We could then play the thing down, put all the blame on the Stalin cult again: there were excesses, now they have been corrected. Everything's O.K. But (...)'' (III, 15; Tr. 13). The narrator also allows the arguments of different characters to conflict, leaving it up to the reader to decide whose part he would take in the ensuing dialogue. A good example is the discussion during the hunger strike in camp (III, 277; Tr. 262-63). The narrator himself plays an active role in the dialogue, interrupting his characters, wrangling with them, taking the Public Prosecutor Krylenko to task (in Part 1, chapter 8), and challenging the evidence of the "loyalists" (Part 3, chapter 11). He seizes upon the thoughts of others, argues pro and contra, ruminates, interrupts, forms a mental picture, only to stop short, saying: "No, no, that's still not right!" (I, 368; Tr. 364). It is precisely for the sake of this tense, impassioned dialogue that he "admits" foreign voices into his narration.

The narrator's spirited turn of speech bursts the confines of the written language, constantly spilling over into oral speech: *pravda i to.*.. (that's true, too), *net-net.*.. (now and then), *nebos'.*.. (I dare say), *vót tak.*.. (there's a fine...!), *smeshno skazat'.*.. (ridiculous as it seems), *no vot neudacha.*.. (but how unlucky!), *nu, v samom dele.*.. (Well, in actual fact), *vot i vse.*.. (and that's all there is to it). All such *skaz* elements have the effect of transforming the reader into a listener, and thus draw him closer to the narrator. For the author it is essential that he should thus mobilize his reader, in order that he may eventually move on from exhaustive factual exposition into the area of reflections and conclusions.

The author's reflections form the third construct of the narrative system of *The Gulag Archipelago*. We have seen how the narrator figures as *Ich-Erzähler*, speaking directly in the name of Solzhenitsyn, the army captain, prisoner, camp inmate and exile. Next we saw him elaborating his material, lending a sensitive ear to the voices of his heroes, and freely interspersing his own speech with their voices. He captured and conveyed a great number of such voices, from those of the camp and prison inmates to those of their captors and executioners. Each of his characters had his own history, his own fate, and together they constituted a *torrent of material*. Solzhenitsyn masterfully organized this material, creating, as it were, an "enfilade" of consecutive chambers, or that "collection of smaller but to a certain extent independent units"[32] which is familiar to us from the Russian chronicle. Having done all this, it is time for the narrator to reflect upon his material. For the second time, he changes his function. The resulting tri-unity may be schematically represented as: *Ich-Erzählung*—narrator supported by a multiple and polyphonic hero—narrator as moralist, philosopher and preacher.

There is scarcely a chapter in the three volumes of *Gulag* that does not have a few pages of such generalized reflections: about how a man becomes an executioner and the corrupting effect of leaving such men unpunished, about why there was no opposition and what form it might have taken, and about much else besides. This is the quintessence of all that has been set forth hitherto. From the voices of the contemporaries who have helped to write the book, there springs forth Truth. The Truth about the age we live in. About man himself.

The style of narration changes. The voice begins to flow more smoothly; fragmentary, elliptical constructions are replaced by sustained periods; Old Slavisms come into their own; the past tense gives way to the artistic, timeless present of the sermon (at the beginning and end of Part 1, chapter 4, for instance). This is the passionate word of Truth, and it is no accident that it should be precisely passages such as these which invite comparison with *The Life of the Archpriest Avvakum*. These pages of reflections anchor in our memory all that has gone before, and the preservation of historical memory is, after all, one of the goals of the artistic investigation, *The Gulag Archipelago*. This Truth embraces the entire national experience, and in fixing it, Solzhenitsyn employs a device that is itself popular and folkloristic—the accumulation of proverbs (both authentic, and of his own creation), sayings, aphorisms and maxims in which his reflections abound. Solzhenitsyn directly acknowledges his source: "It would take a long time to describe all this in educated speech, but there's a folk saying about the search which covers the subject: *They're looking for something that was never put there*" (I, 20; Tr. 6); "As the folk saying goes: *If you speak against the wolf, speak for him as well*" (I, 168; Tr. 160); "*A submissive sheep tastes good to a wolf*" (I, 25; Tr. 11); "But—*it takes sense to show mercy*" (I, 276; Tr. 271), etc. This style is further augmented by camp sayings, such as: "*Without 'tukhta' and ammonal, never could we have built the canal*" (II, 164; Tr. 167); and by aphoristic endings of the sort: "And I think this exposition proves that the *Organs* always earned their pay" (I, 103; Tr. 92).

The meditations and reflections bind all the historical material of Solzhenitsyn's chronicle into a single whole, making of it a syncretistic work with cognitive, ethical and esthetic aims (it may seem little short of blasphemous to speak of esthetic matters in connection with the history of Gulag, but herein lies the courage of Solzhenitsyn the artist). This whole dynamic interweaving of voices and perspectives, these elliptical constructions, the *skaz* elements with their transition to oral exposition and folkloristic stylization, all these stylistic interruptions, in which the author is revealed as active partner in a dialogue—all of these features, as we have attempted to show, constitute the complex narrative structure of *The Gulag Archipelago*. In other words, they constitute one of the aspects of the *artistry* of this literary *investigation*.

—*Translated from the Russian by the editors.*

Notes

1. George Gibian, "How Solzhenitsyn Returned His Ticket," in K. Feuer, ed., *Solzhenitsyn: A Collection of Critical Essays* (Englewood Cliffs, N.J., 1976), p. 113.

2. Compare Sidney Monas: "In teaching Solzhenitsyn's novels, we cannot refuse their content," in his "Fourteen Years of Aleksandr Isaevich," *Slavic Review*, vol. 35, No. 3 (1976), p. 526.

3. Lidiia Chukovskaia recalls Akhmatova telling her on 3 March 1940: "If I saw a copy of *Russkaia mysl'* or *Appolon* with some of my poems in it lying on the table, I used to pick it up and hide it. It seemed indecent to me, as if I were to have left a stocking or a bra lying on the table.... And as for anyone reading my poems aloud when I was there, well, that I just couldn't stand." *Zapiski ob Anne Akhmatove*, vol. 1 (Paris, 1976), p. 73.

4. Roy Medvedev, "On Solzhenitsyn's *The Gulag Archipelago*," in John B. Dunlop, Richard Haugh and Alexis Klimoff, eds., *Aleksandr Solzhenitsyn: Critical Essays and Documentary Materials*, 2nd ed. (New York, 1975), pp. 460-76.

5. See, for example, Klaus Mehnert, "Der *Archipel Gulag* als Literatur," *Osteuropa*, No. 4, 1974, pp. 522-33; and Roman Gul', "Lenin i *Arkhipelag GULAG*," *Novyi zhurnal*, No. 115, 1974, pp. 228-50.

6. See, for example, Heinrich Boll, "Die himmlische Bitterkeit des Alexander Solschenizyn," *Frankfurter Allgemeine Zeitung*, 9 February 1974; and Alexander Schmemann, "Reflections on *The Gulag Archipelago*," in Dunlop et al., pp. 515-26.

7. In Dunlop et al., pp. 188-94.

8. Gibian, p. 116.

9. Part 3, chapter 19.

10. Gibian, p. 114.

11. Mikhail Zoshchenko, *Izbrannye proizvedeniia v 2-kh tomakh* (Leningrad, 1968), p. 34.

12. *Vestnik RKhD*, No. 120 (I, 1977), p. 135.

13. Boris Tomashevskii, *Teoriia literatury. Poetika* (Moscow-Leningrad, 1928), p. 5.

14. Dmitrij Mirskij, *Geschichte der russischen Literatur* (Munich, 1964).

15. Aleksandr Solzhenitsyn, *ARKHIPELAG GULag 1918-1956*, vol. 1 (Pts. I-II) [Paris: YMCA-Press, 1973], p. 495. English translation: *The Gulag Archipelago* (New York: Harper & Row, 1974), p. 471. Henceforth all references to this volume of *Gulag* and the two subsequent volumes will be given on-page after the model: (I, 495; Tr. 471). On several occasions changes have been introduced into the English text as published.

16. *Vestnik RKhD* interview, p. 132.

17. *Ibid.*, p. 133. At the risk of incurring Aleksandr Isaevich's displeasure, I repeatedly omit his italics and introduce italics of my own in order to clarify my argument.

18. Pt. 6, ch. 7; Pt. 7, ch. 1.

19. Pt. 2, ch. 4.

20. In the chapters of Pt. 1 concerning the law, and elsewhere.

21. Walter Benjamin, "Der Erzähler," in *Schriften*, II/2 (Frankfurt am Main, 1977), p. 451.

22. Dmitrii Likhachev, *Poetika drevnerusskoi literatury* (Leningrad, 1971), p. 295.

23. For example, in Pt. 5, ch. 7, "The White Kitten."

24. Mikhail Bakhtin, *Voprosy literatury i estetiki*, vol. 3 (Moscow, 1975), p. 129.

25. *Ibid.*

26. Bakhtin writes that: "The syntactic construction of intended hybrids is *fractured* by the two individualized lingual wills." *Ibid.*, p. 173.

27. "(...) truncated *skaz* is a *skaz* narrative which has lost its constructional independence." E. Mushchenko, V. Skobelev and L. Kroichik, *Poetika skaza* (Voronezh, 1978), p. 207.

28. Likhachev, p. 359.

29. Mikhail Bakhtin, *Problemy poetiki Dostoevskogo* (Moscow, 1963), especially ch. 5.

30. Tatiana Vinokur, "O iazyke i stile povesti A. I. Solzhenitsyna 'Odin den' Ivana Denisovicha,'" *Voprosy kul'tury rechi*, No. 6 (1965), pp. 16-32.

31. Likhachev, p. 59.

32. *Ibid.*, p. 316.

The Calf and the Oak: Dichtung and *Wahrheit*

EDWARD J. BROWN

Readers of *The Calf and the Oak* are fascinated and shaken by its account of a lone writer's courageous, unremitting struggle against one of the powers of darkness, with all its police, its armies and navies and its thousands of atomic weapons; though the ''Oak'' still stands at the end we know that our ''Calf,'' head unbowed and ready to engage the enemy again, is the real victor. David has met Goliath—the comparison is suggested by Solzhenitsyn himself—and while he hasn't killed him, has planted a heavy stone in his stupid forehead and exposed the rude creature to scorn and contempt. Many consider this to be the best thing Solzhenitsyn has yet written, and indeed one is tempted to shout, with the late Vladimir Weidle: ''An astonishing, a magnificent book. When reading it you are simply absorbed and cannot tear yourself away. I find no flaws in it. I'm ready to ring out all the bells for it...''[1] And Efim Etkind's comment draws attention to its extraordinary linguistic power: ''Chaque nouveau livre de cet auteur est une découverte du russe.''[2] We shall see that there are some who deny the historical value of *The Calf* and accuse its author of errors, distortions, and worse, but even they offer tribute to it as a work of verbal art.

The Calf provides total aesthetic satisfaction simply because it draws upon the primal eldest archetype: the struggle between good and evil, two forces once seen by Milton ''in dubious battle'' on the plains of heaven. We follow every turn of that dubious, unequal, and shifting battle in the calf's case from his emergence out of the underground (from the deep water, he will say) to deliver that first magnificent volley *One Day in the Life of Ivan Denisovich*, down to the last but not yet final manoeuvre, his expulsion by the minions of evil from the territory of the Soviet Union itself. And of course that territory is always the ground of contention. The story of the struggle in heaven is exactly reversed: here the forces of evil are in control of Russia, which they have turned into a regimented, infernal paradise, and they expel good angels onto foreign territory which they have designated as Hell.

The genre of such a deeply archetypal work is difficult to fix. It bears the subtitle "sketches of literary life," but what is there literary about the life of a writer who must hide what he writes from the police, protect every source and helper from the threat of incarceration, squirrel away a magnum opus from all eyes until "the proper time," outwit, outflank and defeat the enemies of literature, who happen also in the Soviet Union to be its tutors and publishers? Obviously the subtitle "sketches of literary life" is ironic, and Vladimir Lakshin simply misses the point when he complains that Solzhenitsyn talks only about himself and not about "literary life in the Soviet Union."[3] Literary life indeed. That subtitle suggests a hackneyed Soviet genre under the rubric of which a narrator selects "typical" events from some area of Soviet life to describe and comment upon. But the events set forth here break all patterns of "typicality" and this confused even a good and honest Soviet critic.

Solzhenitsyn's novels all lie on that uncertain border between history and literature, a disputed area occupied by historians but sometimes contested by novelists. *The First Circle* and *August 1914* deal directly with historical matters and, like Tolstoi's *War and Peace*, introduce real historical characters into the artist's plotted action. All of his works, in all genres, investigate, analyze, reflect, and represent the reality of Russian experience in the twentieth century and therefore are historical documents of a special kind. *The Calf* too is located in that border area of which I have spoken, but the historically real personages in it figure as agents in a fateful struggle between God and his enemies, a struggle in which Solzhenitsyn is the chosen instrument of the former. The result is that the people, some of them still living, who take part as actors in this mighty drama play out their parts in a way that transcends the literal and the biographically factual. This has led to some misunderstanding.

The book is aglow with a sense of mission and studded with affirmations of faith in that mission. "Many things in my life I did contrary to my own principal purpose, not understanding the true path, but always something set me straight."(126) "And I think that for the first time in my life I saw, I realized that I was making history."(162) "From December to February, ailing though I was and

obliged to tend the fire and cook for myself, I completed the first
version of *Gulag*... But it was not I that did it. My hand was
guided!"(164) "*The Cancer Ward* I never dispatched to the West. It
was proposed that I do so and there were channels, but for some
reason I refused, and without any ulterior plan. But it reached the
West anyway *(sam popal)*, and—well, that means it had to, God's
good time had come."(224) "God saved me from covering myself
with shame..."(230) And there are of course prayerful acknowl-
edgments of the true source of his more-than-human strength: "How
wisely and strongly dost Thou lead me, O Lord!"(231)

Verbal echoes of higher intervention are frequent in *The Calf*.
Could it have been an accident that the typing of *Gulag* took place at
his retreat far from Moscow, a place of peace and of tender green
called Christmas *(Rozhdestvo)* (233), or that Tvardovskii underwent
his harrowing experience of truth, the reading of *The First Circle*,
during "the three days of Easter"? (92) It is true that military meta-
phors and analogies are frequent in *The Calf*, but when he speaks of
the onward march of those "samizdat battalions" there is no doubt
that we have to do here with *Christian* soldiers in a holy struggle.

Indeed it is not easy to pigeon-hole Solzhenitsyn's *Calf* as to
genre, and one is inclined to say of it what Lidiia Chukovskaia says
of Herzen's *Byloe i dumy (My Past and Thoughts);* that it is one of a
kind and belongs to no nameable genre except its own: "Memoirs?
Autobiography? Novel? Collection of political articles and philosophical statements?" There are elements of them all in *The Calf*,
including a kind of profession of faith. I would suggest a close affinity
with another great work of literature, the *Life* of Avvakum written by
his own hand.[4] Numerous passages in that work parallel the affirmations I've selected from *The Calf*; Avvakum's *Life* glows with faith in
the rightness of a cause and as eloquently damns the enemies of that
cause. And like the language of *The Calf*, Avvakum's language is
simple colloquial Russian, replete with proverbs and sayings and
vulgar enough to dispose of an array of sinful and disgusting enemies
of truth.

Whatever its value as history, the fact that *The Calf* is a work of
literary art becomes abundantly clear if we view it in the context of
Solzhenitsyn's novels, since it shares with them essential thematic
and stylistic features. A central theme of *One Day*, *The First Circle*
and *The Cancer Ward* is the transcendence in practical as well as

moral reason of the *zek*, the prisoner, and especially the millions unjustly imprisoned. Professor Chelnov in *The First Circle* offers the speculation that "only the prisoner really has an immortal soul, but the free man may be denied it for his vanity." The *zek* is the center of that novel's world and he enjoys fundamental advantages over the free people, most of whom have never escaped the trap of lies and fear. We think of the highly successful novelist Galakhov (probably modelled on the late Konstantin Simonov) who must choose carefully the topics he will treat and exercise adroit circumspection in the selection of "typical" details, or of Iakonov, whose brilliant position has been achieved at the cost of his self-respect. The prisoners on the other hand are free to think, to entertain other than official ideas, to know a part of the truth and to seek the rest. In *One Day* the news that comes to the prisoners from the "outside," from the free world, tells of a life debased and depressed both materially and culturally. In her letter Shukhov's wife describes the tasteless stencilling of cheap carpets, a profitable village "craft," and her account of life and labor on the collective farm chills the honest soul of Ivan Denisovich. Kostoglotov, the former *zek* in *The Cancer Ward*, has a special fund of human strength that grew in him during a long imprisonment, and how can he not feel scorn and contempt for the well-fed and chauffeured Rusanov? A leitmotif of *The Calf* is precisely the unique human quality of the camp experience. Of Soviet literary men who had never shared this experience he says that all of them, "social novelists, solemn dramatists, and of course all the more the journalists and critics, all have agreed in concert not to tell the main truth, whatever they write about." During his years in the underground the Calf had been convinced that there were many more like himself who knew the truth and could tell it: "The truth consists not only of jails, executions, camps, and exile, but if you avoid those things entirely you cannot write the main truth."(13) And the following marvellously moving passage, difficult if not impossible to convey fully in English, reveals the gulf that separated Solzhenitsyn from Tvardovskii, helps to explain the awkward relationship between them, and effectively answers any charge of "ingratitude" to his publisher:

> Of course I was obliged to Tvardovskii, but only for myself. I had no right to consider just my personal interest or what the opinion of me might be on the *Novyi mir* staff, but must take as my main premise

that I stand not for myself alone, that my destined career in literature
is not just mine but belongs to all those millions who never scratched
and clawed their way out, never told in hoarse whispers the story of
their fate as prisoners, nor revealed the things they discovered too
late in the camps. Just as Troy was not in the least obliged to Schlie-
mann for its existence so also our buried camp culture has left us its
own legacy. And so when I returned from a world which never
returned its dead I dared not swear an oath of loyalty either to *Novyi
mir* or to Tvardovskii, dared not reckon on whether they would see
that my head was not a bit turned by my fame and that I was simply
engaged in occupying a *place d'armes* and doing it with cold calculation. (60)

The sense of a prior debt to the unjustly dead of the labor camps
permeates *The Calf* and colors every moment of the protagonist's
struggle. While writing his Nobel acceptance speech he noted that
it had been customary for laureates to speak of the nature of art, of
beauty and the structures of literature:

...to discuss the nature of literature or its possibilities would be for
me a difficult and boring treatment of what is of secondary importance: what I'm able to do, that I'll do and show; what I can't do I
won't attempt. And if I gave such a lecture, just how would former
prisoners react to it? Why was he given a voice and a platform? Was
he afraid? ... Has he betrayed the dead? (336)

Solzhenitsyn reports that at one time he believed that there could
be nothing worth reading in officially published Soviet literature and
that Russian literature existed only among the outlawed and excluded, those like himself who knew the truth but were hiding their
works "until the proper time":

But then I believed a day would come when all of us together would
emerge from the depths of the sea like the thirty-three bogatyrs. And
then our great literature would be restored, that literature which had
been submerged with us on the bottom of the sea since the time of
the Great Turning Point, and maybe even before that. (14)

He learned later of course that there were only a few heroes like
himself and nothing like the fairy-tale "thirty-three," and he modified
his judgment somewhat of the official literary product, admitting that
there were a few writers above ground and without camp records

who had a vital word to say(14), yet the conviction remains with him that the ex-prisoner who writes is special and important, and he had no patience with Tvardovskii when the latter rejected the poems of the "camp brother" Shalamov.(68)

Just as in *The First Circle*, *The Cancer Ward* and *One Day*, the pivot of movement in *The Calf* is contrast and conflict between the *zek* world and the world of those "others" whether camp guards or free and prosperous citizens. It is important to realize, moreover, that the "others" in this work include the editorial staff of *Novyi mir*. The ex-prisoner from the provinces who still lives in a humble shack is repelled by their ample quarters, which one reached by way of a wide and lordly staircase "suitable for filming in a scene of a grand ball."(25) His honest poverty is insulted by the handsome advance they can offer him: "the advance alone was equal to two years of my salary."(32) Tvardovskii loved him "as a feudal lord loves his best vassal."(64) The protagonist (whom I refer to as the Calf), afraid he will not find time in his life to complete his sacred mission, is always in a hurry, but Tvardovskii's tempos are different: "Now, after our great success [says Tvardovskii] why shouldn't we sit a while, sip a bit of tea with rolls, chew the fat *(pokaliakat')* about big things and little?" And here the Chief offers the example of an establishment writer, Simonov (who might be modelled on Galakhov in *The First Circle!*): "That's what all writers do, take Simonov"—A. T. [Tvardovskii] jokingly offered me him as an example—"They'll sit a bit, have a leisurely smoke. Where are you always hurrying off to?"(64) But the Calf's needs are simple: just to be let alone to do his writing in peace and free of worry about publishers(102), and to hell with all those unwanted and unasked for laudatory reviews by respectable figures like Simonov, reviews which are like "the threads of a spiderweb" threatening to entangle him and impede him from his true purpose, upon which no Simonov or Tvardovskii could ever look with favor.(64) Nor was he impressed by the "slavishly exaggerated" celebration of his talents that filled the sycophantic press immediately after the appearance, with Khrushchev's blessing, of *One Day*.

The former *zek* is not obliged to treat those others as equals and to be open and honest with them could be a fatal mistake. When Tvardovskii managed to get him an interview with Demichev, the head of Agitation and Propaganda, a man whose face showed not a trace of honest human feeling and whose speech was dull and banal, the Calf managed deftly to pull the wool over the bastard's eyes:

"At first he was watchful and suspicious, but in the course of our two-hour interview he warmed up to me and believed everything I said."(105) Similarly in his informal chat with the secretaries of the Writers' Union he quite frankly lied (*vru*) about the writing of his famous letter to the Congress of the Writers' Union, and they believed and nodded.(189) Not even with Tvardovskii could he be open about his plans and strategies: "I hadn't opened myself to him, the full network of my plans, moves, and calculations had been concealed from him...."(113)

Among them all the Calf does make an exception of Tvardovskii, who figures in the book as a kind of tragic hero, his fatal flaw symbolized by the red party booklet he carried in his coat pocket ("next to his heart"); whose conscience is crippled by his commitment to the vile system that rewarded him so well. The Calf tried with some success to reeducate the Chief of *Novyi mir*, and if he never fully succeeded the reason probably was that Tvardovskii had never walked through the purifying fire of the camps:

> My own head had been straightened out by my first years in jail and a similar process had begun with Tvardovskii after Khrushchev's speech at the Twentieth Congress. But, just as in the Party as a whole, the process soon slowed down, then was choked off and even reversed itself. Tvardovskii, like Khrushchev, was in a trancelike (*zakliatom*) state of lifelong captivity to the accepted ideology...(149)

And if Tvardovskii lacked the fortitude to fight when *Novyi mir* was slowly being strangled, the reason was that "[for such a struggle] Tvardovskii needed that fire-resistant hardness which is cultivated only in the Archipelago of the *zeks*."(264)

What separated him from Tvardovskii and from all successful Soviet figures, then, was the camp experience. Only the camp, only isolation and suffering bestowed upon a human being the mark of authenticity. In one of many great scenes the Calf, with an uncanny sense of novelistic structure, reduces the Chief of *Novyi mir* to a drunken stupor in the course of which, visiting upon himself an exquisite poetic justice, he demands to be treated as a *zek*, and asks the Calf to abuse and tongue-lash him like a camp officer. It happened in Solzhenitsyn's house in Riazan' during a visit there of Tvardovskii for the purpose of reading *The First Circle*. The Chief was mesmerized by the book as he read it over a three-day period, swilling

the while heroic quantities of cognac and vodka. Friends of Tvardovskii have expressed understandable outrage at this scene and at
Solzhenitsyn for invading the privacy of an embarrassing alcoholic
episode, but he has replied that no one has a right to withhold the
truth, and he might have added that in the artistic economy of the
book as a whole the scene could not be spared. Here is the scene.
Tvardovskii had been joking drunkenly about the possibility of being
sent to jail himself:

> He kept on joking, but the air of the prison penetrated him more and
> more as he read, and it infected his lungs...
>   The feeling he had that maybe he himself would not escape a
> sentence (or, more likely, a melancholy stirring within him, just as in
> Tolstoi when he was an old man: it's too bad I wasn't jailed, I'm the
> one who really should have been...) showed itself a number of times
> during that visit... He was especially interested in life behind bars
> and he'd question me curiously: "But why do they shave the heads?"
> or "Why don't they allow any glass dishes in?" Apropos of one line
> in the novel he said "If you're going to the stake, then go, but it has
> to be for something." Several times, without any air or feeling of
> amusement, he reiterated his promise to take packages to me in jail,
> but only on condition that I bring things to him if I stayed out.
>   And toward the evening of the second day when it became clear
> as he read that the jailing of Innokentii was inevitable...—and also
> after three tumblers of well-aged vodka—he got terribly drunk and
> insisted that I "play" with him at being an "MGB lieutenant," in
> fact that I shout at him and accuse him of things while he stood at
> stiff attention...
>   I had to help him undress and get to bed. But in a little while we
> were all awakened by a loud noise: A. T. was shouting and carrying
> on a conversation with himself, in a number of different voices, taking
> the part of several speakers. He'd lit all the lamps that there were in
> his room (in fact he liked to have all the lights on he could in a room—
> "it's jollier that way") and he was sitting at the table, no bottle now,
> in just his undershorts. He was saying pathetically: "I'll soon go
> away and die." Then he'd give out a roar: "Silence! On your feet!"
> and he'd leap up at his own command and stand at attention before
> himself. Then again he'd feel very grieved: "Well, no matter, I can
> do no other." (Meaning that he'd made up his mind to go to the
> stake for my fearsome novel.) (87-88)

Thus the Chief who claimed to have "discovered" Solzhenitsyn and who treated him as a "vassal," who had prospered under Stalin and even given his talent to a poetic justification of collectivization, is so shattered by *The First Circle* that he catches at last a momentary glimpse of the prison truth, and is ready, even if only for an alcoholic moment, to accept the stake itself for the sake of that truth. Truly a moving and a pregnant scene, the product of a consummate artist who has himself suffered through to the truth and spares no one in his pursuit of it.

The portrait of Tvardovskii in *The Calf*, though it has offended his friends and his family, is in fact a brilliant literary achievement. The Calf brings to life an immensely attractive and able human being, a good poet and in his deep Russian heart an honest man, who suffers from the afflictions of intellect and conscience that have resulted, as the Calf sees it, from a long compromise with evil. But Tvardovskii is not totally lost, and the account of his dealings with the Calf is also the story of his gradual evolution toward enlightenment. At first he is shown as a typical bloated, brutish Soviet bureaucrat, alien to the streets of Moscow and unable to move about in them except by chauffeured limousine—and he had to have a large limousine, his bulk was uncomfortable in a modest Moskvich; often absorbed in familial creature comforts, the purchase of a new dacha, for instance; a lordly *barin* who hardly spoke to his subordinate editors on the lower floor, and who regarded the *Novyi mir* operation as his own "fief" (140-141); an eminence of power who when he took a train never had to stand in line with other people to get his ticket; a typical Soviet contradiction in terms: a poet decorated with a Stalin prize. In his social position and in his style of life with all its power and privilege *that* Tvardovskii is hardly distinct from the Party bureaucrats, literary hacks and successful writers we meet both in *The Calf* and in the novels. But Tvardovskii is radically different from all of them because he had once allowed himself, as we've seen, a breath of the prison air.

It was Tvardovskii's fatal flaw that he was devoted both to the Party and to Russian literature, and it was impossible to serve at one time those two masters. He served Russian literature well by publishing Solzhenitsyn's works, but only at the cost of persuading himself that "there was nothing in them incompatible with the idea of communism," that, in fact, they were not anti-Soviet works. He even maintained that Solzhenitsyn "took a party position":

"A party position"—that's my novel he was talking about! Very interesting. Nor was that the cynical formulation of an editor determined to "push the novel through." That confusion of my novel with the "party position" was honestly and sincerely the only possible method, otherwise Tvardovskii, a poet and a communist, could not have set himself the goal of publishing my novel. (89)

Clearly the Calf could never open himself fully to his benefactor: "Our orbits were so far apart that we could never meet." (184) He is aware, moreover, that Tvardovskii's false position accounted for his many weaknesses, not least the weakness for alcohol. As he himself is drawn deeper and deeper into the sickening and frustrating struggle with the literary bureaucrats he grows in understanding of Tvardovskii and even sympathizes with that worst fault:

> ...As I prepared to break a lance again [with the various "secretaries"] I felt weary and needed to shed that useless, sterile, and totally unnecessary nervous tension that I felt. But how? Take medicine? But there is one simple remedy: a little vodka early in the evening. Right away all edges softened and I wasn't harassed for an answer or a snappish retort, and I slept soundly. And then I understood another thing about Tvardovskii: for thirty years what had he had except vodka to help him shed that vexing, scalding, shameful and bootless tension? Just cast a stone at him after that! (201)

One of the chief themes of *The Calf* is Tvardovskii's suffering, hesitant movement toward resolution of the inner conflict. Gradually the Calf came to recognize that the Chief possessed qualities he hadn't expected and that did not fit the image of a Soviet bureaucrat. To the Calf's astonishment he warmly approved the famous letter to the Writers' Union on censorship and other things. "No. I hadn't really figured that man out" is his comment. (184) And evidence begins to accumulate that Tvardovskii is changing. (196) After circulating copies of a second letter of complaint to the "secretaries" the Calf, for a moment doubting and disheartened about the course he had taken, shared his doubts with Tvardovskii, but to his great surprise the Chief said he'd done just the right thing: if you start something you should finish it. "Once more he astonished me. What had become of his timidity and all his weary evasions?" And a further reflection in the same context: "How long we'd known one another—and we didn't know one another at all." (199) The deeper into the "plot" we go the more attractive Tvardovskii becomes. The Calf, with his perfect eye for a scene, pictures Tvardovskii as he saw his visitors off from the dacha on a snowy evening:

> A. T. thought he'd like to take a walk and he put on a kind of rough half-length jacket and a cap, took a stick for support—not a very thick one—and in the quiet snow he walked with us to the gate. He looked very like a peasant, maybe a just barely literate one. He took off his cap and snow fell on his bright, huge, balding head, the head of a peasant. But his face was pale and haggard. He was heartsick. I gave him a farewell kiss... The car moved off and he just stood there in the snow, a peasant leaning on a staff. (216)

As Tvardovskii's evolution proceeds and he moves closer to his downfall and death, he not only excites our sympathy as a human being but we see him more and more in his true native context as a peasant from Smolensk, out of place in the lordly quarters of *Novyi mir* among his sycophantic staff, one whose party booklet had been an honest aberration.

Throughout the year 1968 his evolution proceeded apace and we hear of the rapid "broadening and deepening" of views and principles that had seemed fixed forever: "And he was going on fifty-eight! Neither straight nor easy was the path of his growth...but he was moving!" (247) He even got to be interested in western broadcasts: "And what do you know! We were sitting and chatting and suddenly he jumped up, very gracefully considering his bulk, and caught himself up, quite openly: 'Why we've missed three minutes of it. Come on and listen to the BBC!' *Him*?! The BBC?!'" (249) Soon we find Tvardovskii being called by his patronymic alone, Trifonych (263), a measure of rapid progress toward enlightenment, the simple life, and intimacy with the Calf. That "Trifonych" has come a long way from the power-conscious literary bureaucrat we met in the early pages of *The Calf*. I would suggest without any attempt at irony that modern literature offers few examples of "character development" more poignant than this account of Tvardovskii during the last years of his life, and the poignance is sharpened unbearably by the fact that the events of the story are intimately involved with our own history and heavy with our hopes and fears. With overtones

of agony and grief the Calf unfolds the story of Trifonych's gradual
reduction to impotence as editor of *Novyi mir*, his forced resignation
and his death. In a scene which Solzhenitsyn tells us in a footnote is
reminiscent of the defeated and hopeless General Samsonov's
farewell to his troops in the novel *August 1914*, we witness Tvardovskii's last words to his editorial staff, even including those on the
lower floors who had worked faithfully but with little recognition from
Tvardovskii or anyone else. And after the Chief's departure:

> ...the members of the editorial board had some drinks in Lakshin's
> capacious office, sat together for a while, then left. But the small
> fry couldn't bring themselves to break up on that last day. They
> ante'd up a ruble apiece—even some of the authors, the more modest
> ones, contributed—got some wine and refreshments, and it occurred
> to them: why not go up to Tvardovskii's office! It was already dark but
> they lit the lights, set the plates and glasses around and sat down in
> quarters to which they'd seldom been admitted and never all to-
> gether. "We're abandoned now!"
>
> No one sat at Tvardovskii's desk but they poured a glass for him
> and set it down there: "We forgive him his persecution!" (303)

One thing the Calf could not forgive, that he had surrendered spine-
lessly, not even a whimper: "There are many ways of dying. *Novyi
mir* died ignobly, as I see it, with its head bowed."(305)

The Calf's judgment of the *Novyi mir* editorial board, apart from
Tvardovskii, is severe, and his opinion of the journal itself quite low.
"The devotees of *Novyi mir*," he says, "had no standard for judging
it except comparison with the utterly worthless company of the other
Soviet journals, dull and even nauseating as they are in their content
and sickening in their lack of any literary standards."(65) The fatal
flaw in the character of *Novyi mir* itself was its concept of its own role
as a loyal opposition. That made it necessary for them to induce in
themselves the belief, before they could publish him, that Solzhenitsyn too was loyal, in fact one of their own (*nash*).(227) At times the
Calf's wrath against *Novyi mir* seems stronger than against all
those miserable Soviet rags that nobody read because *Novyi mir*
provided a flickering and really false light in the dark and gave many
people hope where there was no hope. Anything that ameliorates or
improves the situation of the enemy impedes the ultimate aim: to
destroy the system itself. And here Solzhenitsyn's position seems to
parallel that of extremist revolutionaries in our own times who

believe that action to relieve the people's lot under capitalism is a betrayal of the cause. The Calf reveals his deep contempt for *Novyi mir*, perhaps inadvertently, when he tells us that he never read it until after it published *One Day*, and then only at the urging of Tvardovskii he got out back numbers and read them from cover to cover. He emerged from the reading with a modicum of respect for the journal, though it still fell far short of the standards he would have set. It could hardly have published a single number had it met them—but then, so be it!(65-66)

Tvardovskii is a tragic figure, but his associates on the editorial board seem a company of evil grotesques. And it is precisely as a *company*, a band of weaklings and compromisers that they appear in *The Calf*. Several pages are devoted to Lakshin individually but as a rule he is coupled with the others and we are invited to feel distaste for the spinelessness or dishonesty of Lakshin-Kondratovich, or Lakshin-Khitrov-Kondratovich, or Zaks-Kondratovich. (Three other members of the board at that time, Mar'iamov, Dorosh, and Vinogradov, are mentioned only occasionally, and with no particular venom.) They are the ones who counsel caution: "Let's not rock the boat," "There's just so far we can go," "Let's not take a chance on wrecking the journal!" and so forth. Their evil effect on Tvardovskii is clearly related to the fact that they are members of the Party. Lakshim forfeited all respect by joining the Party in 1966, the year of Siniavskii and Daniel'(!), an action not forgivable and beyond understanding. Party members they may be, yet their motives for base actions are also base. The Calf blames them for the failure to capitalize on that golden moment right after the twenty-second Congress when Khrushchev's campaign against Stalin reached its apogee and radical departures on the part of *Novyi mir* might have succeeded. And why weren't any undertaken? "Only because the vital forces on the journal were crushed and the camouflaged puppet-show at the top (Zaks-Kondratovich) were quick to sacrifice anything you like just as long as nobody made any waves or rocked their comfortable boats."(66)

Solzhenitsyn has contrived an aesthetically satisfying structure for the editorial operations of *Novyi mir*, one that fits well the overall design of the book. Presiding on the very top floor is a heroic but flawed figure who has been granted a glimpse of the truth but still serves the devil and lies. On the lower floors the work of producing the journal proceeds under the guidance of honest people like Berzer, head of the prose section, and others devoted to literature and to the truth. It is they who welcome the *zek* when he brings them a manuscript and through their crafty intercession succeed in bypassing the editorial board to bring *One Day* directly to the Chief, who immediately understands its virtues and knows he must publish it. Between the people on the lower floor with whom the *zek* identifies and the Chief sits the editorial board, Lakshin-Zaks-Kondratovich-Dement'ev-Khitrov, whose function it is to maintain the journal's comfortable compromise and see to it that the Chief does nothing "foolish." The pattern faintly suggests an old Russian political archetype: the Little Father Tsar' is a benevolent force if you can just get to him; but his officials are deceivers and oppressors.

Lakshin in his answer to *The Calf* contends that this picture is a primitive distortion of the facts, then promptly wrecks his case by ascribing Solzhenitsyn's "mistaken" picture to the lies and gossip of Berzer; a curious lapse on the part of a frequently perceptive literary critic.

So far I have attended to *The Calf* as a structure of basic archetypal themes, but the artistic power of the book is an effect also of its carefully fashioned language, a style that perfectly suits the theme of truth in conflict with lies and evil. In this too *The Calf* invites comparison with Solzhenitsyn's work as a whole. What stunned and delighted readers of *Novyi mir* when they found *One Day* in 1962 was precisely its language, and Tvardovskii in his Introduction was at pains to explain and justify such a radical departure from "normal" publishing practice. To a generation raised on the controlled and labored puristic banality of the Soviet literary journals Solzhenitsyn offered a prose saturated with the reality of a language free from all official norms: the idiom of the *zeks* themselves, who are thus superior to the clean world even in the way they speak. Read against the background of Soviet socialist realism, the uninhibited conversational style of *The Calf* is a sudden free torrent of truth, a speech full of honest scorn at the faces of evil the ex-prisoner sees all around him. In a wonderfully revealing passage the Calf tells us how he "dreamed of a photo album":

> ...some photographer should do an album to be entitled: "Dictatorship of the Proletariat." No commentary, no text at all, just *faces*, two or three hundred self-important, over-fed, sleepy but also violent mugs—getting into their limousines, mounting the speakers' plat-

form, looming over their desks—and no commentary at all, just
"Dictatorship of the Proletariat." (226)

That passage is a key to *The Calf*, which invites us to contemplate
just such a collection of faces, caught at ugly work of various kinds.
These pictures are of course created out of language and supplied
with a commentary where the dominant linguistic figure is the epithet, in the use of which the Calf exhibits impressive range and resources. B. G. Zaks of the editorial board seldom appears without an
epithet: "sterile, somewhat boring"(26), "cowardly"(98), "the
circumspect Zaks"(93). Adzhubei, the editor of *Izvestiia*, is "red-
faced and supercilious" and Satiukov, the editor of *Pravda*, is "worthless and insinuating."(71). And the Calf meets with three secretaries
of the Writers' Union to discuss his famous letter: "K. Voronkov (a
jawbone!), G. Markov (a fox fresh from a meal), S. Sartakov (an ugly
mug but kind of funny)." And when the Calf entered the room:
"Voronkov deferentially swung himself out of his armchair—he had
the build of a heavyset bouncer—and draped a smile over the jawbone. For all you knew it could have been one of his happiest
days."(187) And when all the "secretaries" and their companion
lackeys gather at a meeting to discuss your latest novel they are like
an assemblage of dogs and they bite at your heels.(200) There's the
"poisonous" Chakovskii, editor of the *Literary Gazette*, and the
"fierce" Gribachev, a poet who writes lyrics about the unity of party
and people.(201) "Cheats and swindlers" (*zhigany*—202), all of
them. The repugnant gallery of grotesques includes the face of the
venerable and long established novelist, Fedin, member of the
editorial board of *Novyi mir*, and Chairman, no less, of the Union of
Writers. His long life has left the ugly marks of all his baseness and
many betrayals (Siniavskii and Daniel', Pasternak): "In the case of
Dorian Gray all of it accumulated on the picture, but Fedin managed
to show it all on his face."(204) Pozdniaev, editor of *Literaturnaia
Rossiia*, is "bald, shameless, slippery, and cautious." Not only their
faces, but their names also, by some happy poetic accident, are
grotesque. At the Sheremet'evo customs office he meets one "Zhi-
zhin" and he asks, "But what has become of the Russian people? We
know where they went—they were sucked down into the Gulag. And
look what's come up to the surface: these Zhizhins, Chechevs,
Shkaevs."(234) The name of Ovcharenko appropriately suggests a
police dog. And the whole crew collectively are nothing but *"pliu-*

gavtsy,'' a vulgar epithet of contempt palely translated by some such English paraphrase as "scummy bastards."(248)

The Calf is loaded with vulgar epithets, studded with popular proverbs and sayings (in fact the Calf refers explicitly to the proverbial riches upon which he draws [129, 133, 134]) and colloquial in its syntax and sentence structure. Its sentences, though not short, tend to be loosely structured. Syntactic inversion, occasional anacoluthon and casual ellipsis are elements in the structure of an oral discourse so charged with emotion that sometimes it forgets the "rules" of syntactic clarity. A better vehicle could hardly have been contrived for conveying the Calf's high anger at the very sight of the moral lepers, who, he maintains, dominate Soviet society. In fact that photo album he visualized is this book itself, *The Calf.*

Epilogue: "Who Steals My Purse Steals Trash"

There is already a formidable set of essays that sharply challenge the historical value of *The Calf* and even call in question the honesty and humanity of its author. Nor is it surprising that some of the living people who figure among the gargoyles displayed in it have spoken up in their own defense. The historian Roy Medvedev, who receives brief but harsh treatment for his mistaken views (397), has answered with an essay in defense of Tvardovskii accusing Solzhenitsyn of ingratitude to a number of people "who in fact contributed a great deal to his literary career."[5] Medvedev enters a number of corrections into the picture of Tvardovskii and presents convincing evidence both of character and courage in the editor of *Novyi mir.* He touches the nub of the matter in trying to make a distinction between Tvardovskii and other card-carrying characters such as Sofronov and Kochetov:

> ...Yes, Tvardovskii was a member of the party. But the main lines in the struggle of the 1960's ran precisely between various currents of *socialist* thought and between different tendencies within the party...[6]

Da ist der Hund begraben! As I've suggested above, the Calf viewed all those card-carriers from a galactic distance; in his perspective they merge into a single mass whose disputes over the correct "socialist" path are pointless quibbling far astray from the principal business of humanity. I've also tried to show that he singles out Tvardovskii alone and presents him as a beautiful human being torn by a tragic contradiction between "ideology" and his best impulses. In my opinion Solzhenitsyn in that portrait does not break faith with essential historical truth. The friends of Tvardovskii who object to the dark colors in the portrait betray, I think, an expectation that someone they admired and revered will be presented to history as a kind of saint, an icon worthy to hang on the wall beside Belinskii, Tolstoi, the "sainted" Pushkin, and even, perhaps, Lenin. In other words, the shape taken by this dispute betrays its Soviet provenance, as I will try to show.

Tvardovskii's daughter, Valentina Aleksandrovna, composed an outraged open letter to Solzhenitsyn which bitterly accuses him of injustice to the memory of her father, who was responsible for his, Solzhenitsyn's, literary career.[7] She makes in a briefer compass some of the same points made by Lakshin: 1) that Tvardovskii did indeed discover and push through his works to publication against heavy odds, and that the treatment of him in *The Calf* is evidence of base ingratitude; 2) that Solzhenitsyn arrogates to himself a special, privileged knowledge of what's true and right; 3) that he rejects absolutely Soviet life and any "democratic" organization in favor of a return to some earlier "patriarchal" form of social organization. The latter two charges are undoubtedly just, as Solzhenitsyn's later writings make perfectly clear, but what about the Calf's ingratitude? Both Lakshin and Valentina Aleksandrovna insist on standards of "gratitude" more suitable to a feudal society or a modern analogue of feudalism than to a society based on intercourse between free and equal men. Solzhenitsyn acknowledges no fealty to Tvardovskii as his lord, master and protector, and why should he? He was obligated only to give Tvardovskii works of high literary quality and to treat him with respect; having done that his debt is fully discharged. Nor did "fealty" oblige him to soften the contours or touch up the rough spots (of which there are many) in his portrait of Tvardovskii. As a matter of fact the reactions to *The Calf* of Lakshin, Medvedev, V. A. Tvardovskaia and many others betray in the most innocent and unsuspecting manner the effect of Soviet conditioning, of the attitude that the lone individual, having no assured rights in law or custom, has a special need for and owes a sacred debt to his patron and benefactor. It is an attitude not unknown outside the Soviet Union, in the Mafia for instance, or in certain modern American political or business organizations where the one thing you must have is "loyalty to the man who put you in your job." But obviously the accusation of ingratitude contributes nothing to an understanding of *The Calf*, or of Tvardovskii, though one must sympathize with Valentina Aleksandrovna's feeling that her father has not been presented in the most favorable light, and with Lakshin's urge to defend the staff of *Novyi mir*, a journal which published, after all, some of the most important contemporary writers: Vladimov, Nekrasov, Siniavskii, Belov, Bondarev, Erenburg (his memoirs), and of course Solzhenitsyn.

There is one important piece of evidence that the Calf does less than justice to Lakshin. We recall the many pages given to Tvardovskii's alcoholic episodes and the Calf's final judgment that the strain of his false position in dealing every day with brutish apparatchiks was responsible for his excesses and "who should cast a stone at him?" But there is no suggestion anywhere that Lakshin or other members of the staff ever felt disgust or strain or sought relief from them in vodka, an omission which I think falsifies history in the interest of literary effect. In the structure of *The Calf* there could be only one tragic hero, Tvardovskii, supported by humble editors on the lower floor—and one lone *zek*.

The Calf itself, together with the polemical literature which has grown up around it, is, as I have suggested, a peculiarly Russian and Soviet cultural phenomenon. I have already mentioned Avvakum's *Life* as an early example of a literary work having certain stylistic features in common with *The Calf*. A striking historical precedent not only for *The Calf* but also for Solzhenitsyn's views as to the weakness and worthlessness of the West is provided by Aleksandr Herzen. In his *My Past and Thoughts* Herzen creates a great literary work out of the materials of his own life, a literary work, moreover, deeply involved with the fate of Russia and her suffering under a dreary and immoral gendarmerie. Herzen, like the Calf, often adopts a system of emphasis and omission that lends to real events an artistic form. Figures on the side of evil, beginning with Nicholas himself and including officers, landowners, noblemen, gendarmes, and even some of Herzen's comrades at the University, are stigmatized and belabored with great verbal skill and without fear of action for libel.

Some commentators have noted a resemblance to Lenin in Solzhenitsyn's dogmatic style of thought, his scornful intolerance of opposition, and his inability to see nuances in the spectrum of that opposition: who can forget Lenin on "the *renegade* Kautsky"? And the Calf attacks such western left-wing activists as Bertrand Russell and Jean-Paul Sartre with about equal venom. (167) Devoted and religious in serving his own concept of the world, he needs simplification, and certainty that the struggle of good with evil is between a sharply defined evil and a clear good. And when Valentina Aleksandrovna mockingly quotes the Calf: "I know better. I see farther. I decided," and then adds, "These words from your book sum you up totally for me, Aleksandr Isaevich," she is using, apparently unconsciously, a description often applied to Lenin himself by former collaborators. And the style of Lenin's thinking and writing as Solzhenitsyn brilliantly mimics it in *Lenin in Zurich*[8] bears a distinct resemblance to the style of *The Calf*, as witness many passages from the former, taken at random:

> Piss-poor, slobbering pseudo-socialists with the petit bourgeois worm in them would try to capture the masses by jabbering away "for peace" and even "against annexations." And everybody would find it quite natural: against war means "for peace," doesn't it?... They must be hit first and hit hard. (29)
> Talk peace with the menshevik scum! (19)
> There were so many of them everywhere, these pseudo-socialist muddlers... Was Trotskii any better though, with his pious fatuities—"neither victors nor vanquished"? What nonsense. (86)[9]

It would be misleading to suggest that these similarities are any more than superficial; certainly Lenin could never have fashioned great works of art such as *Lenin in Zurich* and *The Calf*.

And the mark of contemporary Soviet ways of life is also upon the polemic which at the present writing is in full swing.[10] *The Calf* impugns the motives and the behavior of a number of people still living in the Soviet Union and exposes them to obloquy and also ridicule, but because those people live in the Soviet Union they cannot enter an adequate defense, and the attacks would therefore seem unfair by our standards. Yet such a procedure is normal Soviet practice: those attacked in the Soviet press never have a chance to reply. The pattern was broken when Lakshin, who suffered grievously at the hands of the Calf, found an outlet for an answer in an émigré journal *The Twentieth Century (Dvadtsatyi vek)* edited in London by Roy Medvedev. His answer when it appeared in Russian impugned the motives of Solzhenitsyn, questioned his character and his veracity, and, while granting him the title "great writer" exposed him otherwise to obloquy. Up to that point nothing had happened that went beyond the usual bounds of a Soviet polemic, but when Lakshin's article was translated into English and submitted for publication (along with two others intended to set the *Novyi mir* record straight) to the Cambridge University Press in London, problems arose, and the Press withdrew the book from its publication list until changes could be considered. Soon after that *The Calf* was translated into English and published by Harper and Row in New York, and Lakshin's answer has appeared in book form under the imprint of the MIT Press.[11] The polemic has thus been removed from its original Soviet ambience and set down within the jurisdiction of a democratic legal system. It will be interesting to observe what follows.

Notes

I am grateful to Michael Nicholson and John B. Dunlop for bibliographical assistance that was most helpful. This essay is a somewhat modified version of a chapter in my *Russian Literature Since the Revolution*, Revised and Enlarged Edition (Harvard University Press, 1982), and appears here by permission of the publisher.

1. "Vo ves' kolokol," *Russkaia mysl'*, 10 April, 1975.

2. *Le Monde*, 11 April, 1975.

3. V. Lakshin, "Solzhenitsyn, Tvardovskii, i *Novyi mir*," *Dvadtsatyi vek*, 2, London, 1977, p. 161.

   All references to *The Calf and the Oak* that follow are to the pages in the Russian language edition: *Bodalsia telenok s dubom* (Paris: YMCA-Press, 1975). The translations are my own.

4. Lidiia Chukovskaia, *"Byloe i dumy" Gertsena* (Moscow: Khudozh. lit., 1966), p. 140. Lakshin also suggests a comparison with Avvakum: *op. cit.*, p. 205.

5. Roy A. Medvedev, "Solzhenitsyn and Tvardovsky," in *Political Essays: European Socialist Thought Series No. 8* (Nottingham, England: Spokesman Books, 1976), pp. 110-119.

6. *Ibid.*, p. 114.

7. The letter has been translated into Italian and published in *L'Unità*, 27 June 1975.

8. Professor Donald Fanger has called my attention to two articles on dissident literature in *Sintaksis*, No. 2, 1978, which throw special light on the problem of language and on other formal problems faced by the dissident writer at the moment he breaks through to the surface and ends his enforced silence. Georges Nivat in his "Vyzov i provokatsiia kak esteticheskaia kategoriia dissidentstva" (pp. 91-111) uses Solzhenitsyn as his prime example: "So as to discover once more some meaning in human speech he was obliged, first of all, to look in the dark for the lost *intonation*." (102) And again: "Having emerged from his aphasia the dissident writer discovers a new manner of speech, one which leads him back to life again, sobbing and wringing his hands."(106) Siniavskii's article is "Iskusstvo i deistvitel'nost'" (pp. 111-119).

9. Page references are to the translation of *Lenin in Zurich* by Harry Willetts (New York: Farrar, Straus and Giroux, 1976).

10. Solzhenitsyn published in Paris (YMCA-Press) in 1979 part of a "Sixth Supplement" to *The Calf and the Oak* under the title *Skvoz' chad* [*Through the Smoke*]. In it he deals with the latest attempt of the KGB to answer his attacks, a book published in Moscow in 1978 by "Progress" under the title: *Spiral' izmeny Solzhenitsyna* [*The Twists and Turns of Solzhenitsyn's Betrayal*]. The author on the title page is one Tomáš Řezáč, a Czech who emigrated in 1968 only to return soon after to work for the new Czech government. The points made by Řezáč, who claims to have known Solzhenitsyn well, are the following: his grandfather was a local tyrant who disappeared mysteriously, his father was a White Guardist, executed by the Reds, his uncle was a bandit, he suffered from epilepsy, he is a coward, a thief, a roué, and a treacherous writer, he deliberately and cleverly contrived his own arrest near the end of the war in order to escape the front, he tried to get his friends sentenced as well, he was an informer in the prison camp, and, among many other things, he is mentally ill. The last charge, Solzhenitsyn points out, would have been more effective had it been made earlier (*Skvoz' chad*, p. 18). That's the best the KGB can offer.

11. *The Oak and the Calf; Sketches of Literary Life in the Soviet Union.* Translated from the Russian by Harry Willetts (New York: Harper and Row, 1980); Vladimir Lakshin, *Solzhenitsyn, Tvardovsky, and* Novyi Mir. Translated and edited by Michael Glenny (Cambridge, Mass.: MIT Press, 1980).

Solzhenitsyn's Different *Circles*:
An Interpretive Essay

GEORGES NIVAT

Solzhenitsyn is reluctant to talk about himself. Like most survivors of the confined world of camp or prison, he in his turn cuts himself off from the world at large behind a wall of silence, seclusion and noncompliance. In so doing, he seems to fear that the outside world has aggressive designs upon that inner "self" which he learned to defend so vigorously in the world of captivity. This abhorrence of self-disclosure (whether freely given or extorted) makes him a "classical," an altogether pre-Freudian, writer. There is an "external" quality to his works, in the sense that the inner world seems to have but a limited part to play in them. Instead, man is defined by his own gestures and actions, by his own history. Even *The Oak and the Calf*, which would appear to be a "memoir," is in reality a thoroughly exogenous work, a combat manual, a handbook of tactics and ballistics. In it Solzhenitsyn makes plain his distaste for self-disclosure and for such a "flaccid genre" as memoirs. Thus, even though almost all of his work has an autobiographical basis, we would be unwise to expect from this author any intimate revelations about himself. This return to the classicism of the "detestable self" is no mere literary pose; it is the product of an intense inner struggle. Others, no doubt, will in due course subject it to analysis and psychoanalysis. When they do, they will have no literary dreams to analyze, for there would appear to be none in Solzhenitsyn's works, with the exception of Rusanov's self-denunciatory dream in *Cancer Ward*.

Perhaps this refusal to confide in others, this preoccupation with protecting one's individuality, one's innermost being, against outside pressures—perhaps this indicates a secret trauma, a difficulty in coping with life, or at least a problem of identity? The rereading of *The First Circle* which we are able to undertake today may yield some new answers. *The First Circle* is not merely the account of one specific experience in captivity, and its title is not just another of

those innumerable instances where Solzhenitsyn points an analogy
between the civilized world of ancient times and the concentration-
camp world of today. It is, over and above this, a "defense," a
bulwark—the first line of defense for the Gulag victim's vulnerable
"self" against aggression or suspicion. The very structure of the text
is defensive. It bristles with ironies, and at the heart of this unremitting irony lies a relationship between the captive, or "carceral"
nucleus of society and its outer, "pericarceral" ring. The construction of the entire novel is based upon the relationship between this
nucleus and its surrounding ring: there is the Ark of the "Zeks"
and the false Ark of the Non-Zeks (the banquet at the home of prosecutor Makarygin). To this spatial relationship is added an historical
one. The time of the Gulag is the nucleus toward which pre-Gulag
time, with its own practitioners of violence, gravitates: the wives of
the zeks and the wives of the Decembrists, the Stalin trials and the
"Lay of Prince Igor," etc. . . .

Some characters originate in the outer ring and penetrate to the
nucleus: the "free" engineers (Roitman, Iakonov), the women secretaries and engineers (Simochka, Klara); and a tiny fragment of the
nucleus may even be propelled momentarily back toward the outer
ring (such is the visit of the zek Gerasimovich to the minister Abakumov and his proud refusal to *collaborate*). In this last episode, Gerasimovich "notifies" Abakumov that it is in effect he, Abakumov, who
belongs to the "carceral" cosmos, and not the other way about. As
for the carceral nucleus of the "sharashka," it too is arranged in
circles, with elements orbiting at a greater or lesser distance from a
central triad: Sologdin-Nerzhin-Rubin. Although we learn who
Sologdin and Rubin are, Nerzhin remains a mystery, for he is the
"soul" of the nucleus. In his quest for the truth, he moves between
his two comrades, facing now one "double," now the other—and this
in addition to his symmetrical explorations of the people (Spiridon)
and of art (Kondrashev). It is he who pilots this Ark of the Just, this
Rosicrucean pinnace, on which sail, in a Stoic intemporality won
through the wisdom of the Gulag, the flower of all the knights of the
sharashka.

This, Solzhenitsyn's first and masterful *grande oeuvre*, is thus a
well-conceived fortification. At its center is the "eternal soul of the
zek," and orbiting around it are the different virtues to be won in
the Gulag—laconicism, irony, a keen perception of the world in its
most humble aspects, a sort of beatification of everyday life. And

orbiting around these virtues are the zek's ruses, the code of conduct, of language and of gesture which he elaborates, and which permits the "immortal souls of zeks" to *recognize* one another. (This same code operates in each one of Solzhenitsyn's works.) Around these "Stoics" are the impure, the intimidated, the evil-doers and the hounds, at which point we pass from the carceral nucleus to the pericarceral ring. This circularity is evident in the text itself: Volodin (a candidate for the Ark) appears in the first and last chapters, while in the middle of the novel is formed a nucleus of key-chapters, to which "The Castle of the Holy Grail" and "The Ark" incontestably belong (chapters 42 and 48 in the familiar version, chapters 46 and 53 in the new). Nerzhin is the "soul" of both these chapters; he is at once the knight of the Grail, pensively poised at the brink of the abyss in mystic contemplation of Perfection, and the mathematician-sage, who has set sail on the Ark of Detachment, Asceticism, and Intellect, the imponderable and impalpable Ark on which the Ancients dreamed of reaching the shore of archetypal bliss.

The new element in our reading of Solzhenitsyn's masterpiece is the availability since December 1978 of two different redactions. We were already aware that prior to *Circle 87* (the 87-chapter edition) there had been a *Circle 96* (a version with 96 chapters). Solzhenitsyn states as much in *The Oak and the Calf*. Moreover, he had published four "suppressed" chapters, three in *Vestnik RKhD* (chapters 44, 61 and 90) and one in the journal *Kontinent* (chapter 88). But Solzhenitsyn's preface[1] reveals a somewhat more complicated state of affairs. Begun during the Kok-Terek exile, the novel was completed in Mil'tsevo, at the home of Matrena, in 1957. At that time there appear still to have been no chapter divisions: the work was an unbroken, homogeneous narrative. In 1958, at his wife's apartment in Riazan', Solzhenitsyn took it up again and produced a second and a third redaction. These three versions were later to be destroyed for reasons of security. In 1962, when *One Day in the Life of Ivan Denisovich* was under discussion at *Novyi mir*, the fourth, definitive, redaction was composed. In the meantime, Solzhenitsyn was passing from "underground" status to that of a published author. With the possibility of eventually publishing *The First Circle* in mind, he corrected and pruned the text. This text represents the *lightened*, in some measure self-censored, version of 1964, which is divided into short chapters, each forming a kind of lyric whole. It was this variant of the text, reworked in order to "sharpen" it, which was sent to the

West and published through the offices of Olga Carlisle.[2] During the summer of 1968, at the height of his struggle with the Soviet authorities, Solzhenitsyn set about restoring the former 96-chapter redaction. Finally, in 1978, he introduced some new retouching before the text was set in print for inclusion in his *Complete Works* (prepared on an IBM Composer at his home in Cavendish and published by the YMCA-Press in Paris).

This complex textual history, which extends over a full twenty-three years, demonstrates the fundamental importance which *The First Circle* has for Solzhenitsyn. It has its own history; it occupied his thoughts through all the most crucial years of his life as a writer. We can attempt an interpretation of this textual history by comparing the YMCA-Press edition of 1969 with the Vermont-YMCA edition of 1978. The 1978 edition is *Circle 96,* composed between 1955 and 1958, restored in 1968, and emended in 1978. This is a clandestine "first redaction," which was subsequently retouched, and it is appropriate that we should take account of these "touches," even if we are obliged at times to fall back upon conjecture. The 1969 edition is *Circle 87,* the self-censored version of 1963, "resharpened" in 1964 (as hope of its publication in the USSR faded). Thus the second *Circle (Circle 96),* which has only recently appeared, represents a revised first version, whereas the first *Circle* to appear (*Circle 87*) is, broadly speaking, the second (actually it is the fifth redaction, according to a note in the 1978 book edition), albeit the second revised in a spirit of greater acrimony.

*   *   *

Circle 96 is distinguished from *Circle 87* by an obvious modification in the plot. The Volodin we formerly knew, inspired by the friendship he bore for his family doctor, warned the latter on the eve of his meeting with fellow-doctors from abroad that, if he were to hand over a specimen of his latest pharmaceutical discovery, he would fall into a trap set by the secret police. This variant was inspired by the "Doctors' Plot." But now we meet a Volodin moved by active hatred of the communist regime, who warns the American embassy that American scientists are about to betray the secret of the hydrogen bomb and pass it on to Soviet agents. This is a variant inspired by the Rosenberg affair. The plot-mutation involved is a considerable one. The first redaction (*Circle 96*) is "harder"—Volodin actually "betrays" the regime which he "represents," and an important part of the book is devoted to the ethics of "treason": should one or should one not betray a regime if that regime is perverse (this is rather reminiscent of medieval disputations on the legitimacy of tyrannicide). Moreover, since the recent appearance of an interview with Lev Kopelev (*New York Times*, 16 August 1979), and especially since the prepublication of a chapter from Kopelev's memoirs dealing with the "sharashka" (entitled *Assuage My Pain*),[3] we know that Kopelev, the prototype of Rubin in the novel, actually was assigned the task of identifying the voice of a man who had warned the Amercans. The fact that Solzhenitsyn proceeds from reality is thus confirmed yet again.

There is a sharp change in tonality from one plot to another. The very significance of Volodin's gesture is different. In 1958 it is hatred, in 1964—pity. In 1958 Rubin has no moral dilemma to resolve—deciphering the voice of a traitor does not trouble his conscience at all. In 1964 the helper of military counterespionage becomes a helper of the ordinary police. *Circle 96* presents a sharp contrast in positions: it is the Solzhenitsyn of hatred who is reincarnated in Volodin, and who guides him to the home of his old uncle to take lessons in "tyrannicide." In 1964, in *Circle 87*, the positions are less sharply contrasted. Is this a result of "toning down" the book for publication, of self-censorship, or is there, among these various reasons, another, more profound explanation: that the author himself evolved from a position of hatred toward the oppressor to a position of pity, a position where hatred has been sublimated by intellect? It is just such a sublimation that we find in *Cancer Ward*, in the remorseful nightmare of Rusanov, which restores in our eyes his link with the world of the living, whereas the Shikins of *The First Circle* are utterly dead. ... And perhaps this is a sublimation that has become alien once more to the writer of 1978, as he puts the finishing touches to the restored "hard" version of the novel?

Twenty-one chapters of *Circle 96* are either "new" or altered in comparison with *Circle 87*, to say nothing of the numerous stylistic modifications found in the remaining chapters. The chapters which are entirely new fall into two groups, those devoted to Volodin and those devoted to Stalin. Elaborate care has been taken with the new distribution of chapters: as in the edition published in 1969, the titles are listed without page numbers to form a kind of musical overture which establishes the leitmotifs of the work.[4] The central nucleus of chapters (43-53) now stands out even more clearly, and we can see how it is intersected by all the major themes of the book and, too, by the water line of that elaborately rigged vessel—the Ark chapter. In this central nucleus, only one chapter, chapter 44, is completely new, but it is of paramount importance for the poetic texture of the book as a whole. Its title "Na prostore" is difficult to translate, and means something like "Out in the Open," "In the Open Air," or "In the Wide Open Spaces."

This chapter 44 forms perhaps the very heart of the work. Klara, who, in the preceding chapter, had recalled "the woman who washed the stairs"—that slave of the Gulag whose ghost still haunts the sumptuous residence of prosecutor Makarygin—has accepted an invitation from her brother-in-law, Innokentii Volodin, to go for a walk in the country. Innokentii is a bright and energetic Soviet diplomat, who would not have a care in the world if something had not snapped within him. Newly aware of the "double thinking" required of him and inwardly at odds with the regime he serves, Innokentii, who has spent too much time abroad, now yearns for Russia, for the Russian countryside. This country walk with Klara affords him a vision of the Expanse of Russia, a space at once mystical and defiled, which nevertheless stands for spiritual freedom. "Listen, sister," he says. "What a good thing that we came here instead of going to the forest. This is just what's been missing in my life: a clear view on all sides. And being able to breathe easily like this!"[5]

Klara and Innokentii walk into a landscape of such immensity that its undulations are scarcely perceptible, and come to an old cemetery, abandoned and without a fence. Looking at Innokentii, Klara is reminded of Esenin upon his return from Europe: an unhappy prodigal son of the Russian soil, a *déraciné*... "Their raincoats seemed to fall to the ground of their own accord, and somehow they found themselves seated, facing this Expanse. From this shaded spot they had a clear view out into the sunlight."[6]

This magic circle of Russian Space, the center of which seems to be the bell tower of the Church of the Nativity (an abandoned, desecrated church which they will discover a little further on), is the Russian circle, the magic "visual reservoir" (*okoem*)[7] of Russian space. It is defiled by thundering tractors and by sacrilegious hands, but it is wide open, free of deceit. Indeed, the very guilelessness of this naked immensity is its best possible protection: in the name of this Russia, Russia the protectress, one is justified in "betraying" her tyrant masters. Soon, though he does not yet know it, Volodin will find himself inside the carceral circle, where the Ark of the free awaits him.

> He looked at her, his eyes those of a sick man. He seized a broken twig to write with and traced a circle on the damp earth. "Do you see this circle? It is the fatherland. It's the first circle. And here is the second." He drew a larger one. "That's humanity. And do you think the first one fits inside the second? Not a bit of it! There are walls of prejudice here. Even barbed wire and machine guns. It's almost impossible to get through, either in body or in spirit. So, in fact, there's no such thing as humanity—only fatherlands and more fatherlands, each one different from the rest..."[8]

Carceral circle, circle of the fatherland... Each of them (and they are all analogous) can enclose or liberate. The circle of Russian space liberates those who are able to discover spiritual freedom within it. The circle of incarcerated space liberates the zek who attains to freedom of the soul. (There is the same circular representation of Russian space bordered by forest in "Matrena's Home," and the same circular refuge for the Russian survivors of the Prussian forests in *August 1914*.)

However, Volodin, as he moves toward the carceral circle, does not cease to be alone. Another theme emerges as we read this key chapter: fear of self-disclosure, the self's defensive refusal to allow another individual ultimate access to it. Klara would like to console her brother-in-law, to tell him that on those fundamental issues which separate him from his wife, his colleagues, and the regime that he serves, she is on his side. But the circle that protects also forbids free disclosure: "What causes this membrane to be drawn between one person and another, when you can almost see and feel how you might help each other. But it was not to be. It could not be."[9]

Thanks to this "new" chapter we arrive at the very source of the carceral circle, wherein the eternal souls of the zeks find refuge. Here is suffering and security: for women only frustration, it would seem; but for these men, unshackled and delivered from everyday cares, here is liberation in the profoundest sense—an apparent submission to the most niggardly constraints, which is, in reality, an emancipation from the material, the historical, and from the temporal itself. Everything here is transparent; lightened and sublimated, the

Rosicrucean Knight sails within a circle of intemporality known only
to certain ancient sages, and perhaps to Parsifal at the moment when
his hands touched the mystic Grail.

May we venture to suggest that this new variant (*Circle 96*)
brings out even more clearly the bond between Platonism and the
"sharashka," between the archetypal world of Perfection and this
circular Prison-City, which is a "u-topia" for him who accepts the
asceticism of incarceration, for those knights of the intellect, incor-
ruptible and beyond the reach of their guardians, who of themselves
transform the sharp-spiked circle of the prison stockade into a
mystical circle of space and abstract freedom? In *One Day* we witness
a comparable sublimation: the labor of Ivan Denisovich, the convict,
is transformed into the liberation of Ivan Denisovich, the man. We
may recall the narrator of *Notes from the House of the Dead*, who so
often walks the length of that high stockade, burnished by the rain,
which encloses him; if he notes the boredom and brutality which it
engenders, does he not also conclude that it is within this circle that
the strongest and richest energies of his fatherland are confined?
From Dostoevskii through to Solzhenitsyn, the analogous circles of
the Russian *ostrog* ("jail") and the Russian horizon stand as images
of a potential Perfection...

Chapter 61, which is devoted to Volodin's visit to his "uncle in
Tver'," establishes in a sense his psychological genealogy. His
mother, the favorite sister of the "uncle in Tver'," had been a young
noblewoman, infatuated with justice and poetry. Her private notebooks reveal to Innokentii a hitherto unsuspected moral and poetical
culture. His father had been a Bolshevik sailor, one of those who in
January 1918 took part in the violent dispersal of the Russian Consti-
tuent Assembly. As for the uncle from Tver', he was one of the few
people to demonstrate against the dissolution of this, the only "free"
parliament which Russia had known in modern times. With the
miserly cunning of an Harpagon, this uncle hoards the newspapers,
yellowed with age, which so inflame Innokentii as he reads them; and
it is he who teaches his nephew that Stalin's power has been built
upon nothing but violence and deceit. And, above all, he instills in
his nephew a determination to serve this iniquitous regime no longer,
a moral obligation to "betray," just as Herzen "betrayed" the tsar'.
"Herzen raises the question (...) of *the limits of patriotism*. Why
must the love we feel for our fatherland be extended to every govern-

ment which rules it, even when this means collaborating in the ruin of our people?"[10]

This new group of problems in the book, what one might call the question of the legitimacy of "treason," makes it easier to understand the debate which animates the knights of the sharashka and, in particular, the "phonoscopy" section. Chapter 47, which follows immediately upon the vision of the Grail, is devoted precisely to a discussion of "collaboration" with the regime ("'Top Secret' Conversation"). In the new version, the issue is: whether it is right or wrong to collaborate with Soviet Russia. The logic of Nerzhin's refusal is impeccable. He wants to live "hic et nunc" and, for him, the radiant communist future holds as little attraction as does the Christian hereafter... Unbeknown to Nerzhin and Volodin, they are both united in a kinship of revolt. Nerzhin tells the communist Rubin: "Give me space! Give us space!" (that same Space which Volodin came to seek in the semi-deserted village of the Nativity). This is a revolt grounded in hatred, hatred as a moral obligation, an unsullied hatred, which is first and foremost an active moral refusal to sustain evil.

This "Herzenian" stage of Solzhenitsyn's development is not yet Christian. It rests upon a morality inspired by Stoicism and love of the humble Russian expanse, which figures so often in Herzen's writing. Herzen was frequently obliged to defend himself against the charge of having *wronged* Russia (the "Act of Accusation," for example). In *Circle 96*, Solzhenitsyn justifies himself using the example of Herzen. All the analogies between the zeks of the sharashka and the Rosicruceans or Stoics of old reveal to us that what matters most to Solzhenitsyn is how to overcome the autonomy of the individual; he is engaged, in short, in a redefinition of *honor*. These men have to reinvent honor in a perverse society where honor has become a "class category," in other words, an object of ridicule. Nerzhin and Volodin act in accordance with *honor*, but elaborate no theoretical basis for this conduct; at least, they disclose none to us. So it is that the discussion between Nerzhin and Rubin in the "new" chapter 47 turns on whether or not one should refuse to "collaborate." Nerzhin, in rejecting Rubin's dialectical defense of socialism, has no other support than this single, frail notion of honor: the theft of the hydrogen bomb, even on behalf of socialism, remains a theft, a vile and base act. See what the fatherland of socialism has been reduced to! Whatever else one may say about them, Volodin, Gerasimovich, Nerzhin, Sologdin, and Rubin as well, are united by this notion of honor: there are certain things which they will not allow themselves to do.

The difference between *Circle 96* and *Circle 87* is a matter of the extent of this refusal, and its field of application. In the 87-chapter version, the refusal is applied to interpersonal relations; in the 96-chapter version, it is extended to relations between the individual and the State.

There is a correlation between this change and the heavier burden borne, in *Circle 96*, by the portrait of the man who embodies the State—by the Tyrant, Stalin. A comparison of the five "Stalin" chapters in *Circle 96* with the four in *Circle 87* demonstrates conclusively that what we have here is not the substitution of one plot for another, but that the published text of 1968 actually is a contracted version of the text of *Circle 96*. Although the retained passages are aired in a different way, there are, in *Circle 87*, no innovations. The difference is one of quantity: in the lightened version the aging despot's monologue is abridged, excessively curtailed, and the "Stalin" pole is weakened as a result. In *Circle 96*, this pole is of paramount importance, as the voluntary prisoner of the Kremlin bunker serves in some measure to exorcize the carceral evil endured by the prisoners of Marfino.[11] For if the true captives gain release from the circle of evil through dialogue and through a sublimation wrought by the intellect, then the Tyrant himself shuts himself away, without intending to, in a prison that almost nothing from the world outside can penetrate, save for the obsequious scratchings of his secretary Poskrebyshev at the heavy padded door. The "new" Stalin dreads and abhors the light of the sun:

> Most intolerable of all for Stalin was the morning and noontime: While the sun climbed in the sky, frolicked, and approached its zenith, Stalin slept in the dark, shut and locked away, enshrouded in heavy blinds. He awoke when the sun was already beginning to set, to abate, to hasten toward the end of its short diurnal life.[12]

This theme is in obvious contrast to the mystical theme of the naissant morning which comes to baptize the prisoners of Marfino with a second, quasi-"Pasternakian" birth. The newborn light of day (*svetalo*) bathes the Church of the Martyr Nicetas (in Iakonov's anguished reminiscences), and the blue eyes of Sologdin open wide before this increate light. "And his soul knew an unshakeable peace. His eyes sparkled like those of a young man. His chest, exposed to the biting cold, swelled with the fullness of being."[13]

In Stalin, hatred of the sun symbolizes the denial of Space. In Stalin is catalyzed that morbid attachment to the closed universe of the prison, from which the convict inmates of Marfino ought to have suffered. He is their ghostly antithesis—an executioner enslaved to a closed *circle*—while they, the victims, communicate with space through every breath they take. "What he [Stalin] liked about this night-time office was that there was no space in it."[14]

Stalin's claustrophilia is felt even in his language: these chapters form a single slow, mumbling monologue in which the Tyrant encloses himself within his own closed discourse (whereas the prisoners of Marfino practice the freest, most Platonic of dialogues). It is as if history, and the history of the Party in particular, were being mulled over in this monologue and recast in the simplistic mold of "Stalinism." The entire universe, rendered infantile in the mind of the great Guide, comes to snuggle meekly beneath his paternal wing. Lenin himself is "put in his place" and reprimanded for his whims and fancies ("A cook's a cook, and that's all; it's her job to cook dinner."[15]). This is the paternal dream of a retarded world, where children never grow up and time stands still, a grandfatherly vision of a society in which all these little Bukharins scheme in vain. This masterly portrait, in which a cloak of senility seems to petrify the movement of history, is at once a great piece of writing and an excellent study of Tyranny: the Tyrant imagines himself an effective and absolute father of his people and dreams of a universe confined as in ancient times within the quietude of one *familia*.

The most striking feature of this biography is that Solzhenitsyn adopts the theory that Stalin was an agent of the tsarist Okhrana, portraying the old dictator as preoccupied even to his last years with removing any trace of the archives of the tsarist secret police. It is this same stain on his past which the maniac of the 1937 show trials projects onto his victims, making them all confess to a crime of duplicity which is, in reality, his own.

In the way they are written, the Stalin chapters in *Circle 96* are themselves not without a certain "duplicity." In fact, there is an obvious *double-jeu* between the ruminations of the Tyrant and the way Solzhenitsyn, the author, uses this character to settle old scores:

Lenin's role is diminished, "October" is reduced to a happy fluke which could as easily have gone wrong, and ought to have done, while all the Bolshevik leaders, viewed from the perspective of Stalin's implacable "realism," seem puerile. Solzhenitsyn uses the same method once again in *Lenin in Zurich*, but with perhaps less success than here. The whole art of these chapters lies in the authenticity of such "ruminations": not for an instant does the former seminarian, half-cynical, half-superstitious, believe these prattling "ideologists." Here we see him thinking about Trotskii:

> Only a complete ass could believe there was going to be a revolution in Europe. They'd lived there long enough, but they hadn't grasped a thing, while he, Stalin, had only needed to make one trip and he'd taken it all in. We ought to be thanking heaven that our *own* revolution succeeded.[16]

One could note many changes in point of detail: the allusions to the writers Virta and Vishnevskii have disappeared in *Circle 96*, while, on the other hand, Pil'niak makes an appearance. There is, however, no explicit mention of his "Tale of the Unextinguished Moon" (which tells of the murder of Frunze by Stalin's surgeons): the senile despot is capable of grasping only the general outline; details do not interest him.

In chaper 46 ("The Castle of the Holy Grail") another significant detail occurs: in the final revision of the text, Lenin's name disappears from the list of "fiery souls" which Nerzhin and the painter Kondrashev draw up—fiery souls who created that indomitable, violent Russia, so unlike the false and affected stereotype imposed by Levitan and other painters... After listing the Old Believers, Zheliabov, and the terrorists of the "People's Will" movement, Nerzhin had added Lenin. The Solzhenitsyn of 1978 deletes him—not, to be sure, from vengeance, but because the image of Lenin is in his eyes irremediably *sullied*. Lenin is no longer even the main culprit. Behind him, in *Lenin in Zurich*, looms the revolutionary speculator and Jew, Parvus. And before him stretches the treachery of Miliukov and all those other "liberals."[17] Again and again, the Lenin of *Circle 96* is seen—through the "belittling" eyes of Stalin—as no longer playing any major role. A cynic himself, he is judged and surpassed by another cynic, one who manipulates men as effortlessly as a child plays with its toys.

Of all the characters in *The First-Circle*, it is Sologdin who is modified and "retouched" in the most interesting way. In chapter 26 ("Sawing Wood"), Nerzhin reminds Sologdin of their first meeting, a meeting of which Sologdin's prototype, Dimitrii Panin,[18] has given us his own version. This encounter is of the utmost importance, for it is clear to anyone who has studied Solzhenitsyn's life and work that Panin-Sologdin may well have played a decisive role in the moral and intellectual development of the zek Solzhenitsyn-Nerzhin. The present rift between the two men is simply a further complication in the history of this relationship. Panin's *Solzhenitsyn and Reality* (*Solzhenitsyn i deistvitel'nost'*. Paris: author's edn., 1976) is a kind of anti-Solzhenitsynian catechism in which he systematically criticizes every position adopted by Solzhenitsyn the publicist. The book makes it quite evident that their relationship was initially that of a mentor toward his pupil, or a father toward his son. In other words, when Solzhenitsyn arrived at the "sharashka," still a naive zek, it was Panin who instructed him in his revolt against, and even his hatred of, the regime. The subsequent history of this relationship traces the emancipation of the pupil from his teacher. Hence the tensions, the rancor, the insinuations, and especially the retouching of portraits, which characterize the present relationship between Nerzhin and Sologdin. Solzhenitsyn emended his portrait of Sologdin. Panin revised his memoirs of Solzhenitsyn. In 1973, Panin wrote: "After we got out of prison, we rarely saw one another and our opinions diverged" (*Notebooks of Sologdin*). In 1976, he commented: "I gave full due to his talent as a writer, but was harshly critical of his errors" (*Solzhenitsyn and Reality*). Ever since he has been in the West, Solzhenitsyn has felt at his back the accusing shadow of the "master" whom he once adored and who today cruelly condemns him. Whatever position he takes, he must always anticipate, at least mentally, Panin's relentless one-upmanship. His every attitude is judged "weak," his anti-Soviet belligerence is deemed insufficient, his every offensive derisory. Moreover, Solzhenitsyn is suspected of wishing to perpetuate the reign of evil in Russia so that he can preserve his own position as "preceptor" in the eyes of the West. This rather unexpected (and evidently impassioned) diagnosis was prompted by Solzhenitsyn's opposition to emigration. "Where," writes Panin, "did Solzhenitsyn get this spitefulness, this hatred, and this failure to comprehend even the most elementary things?"

One could point to many other symptoms of this curious mutual animosity and recrimination between the two men, a state of affairs which (in our view) was declared by Panin and tacitly maintained by Solzhenitsyn. Naturally, each of these men has had a very different impact. Panin is a passionate but limited publicist, locked up within his own, incommunicable gnoseological system, while Solzhenitsyn is a writer of world stature, who is able to communicate with men of today. Nevertheless, the Nerzhin-Sologdin relationship would seem to be fundamental for the genesis of Solzhenitsyn himself, and it is possible to detect certain stages of this relationship even in the textual history of *The First Circle*. The Sologdin of *Circle 87* is above all slightly "touched," an eccentric, loved for his eccentricity, his purity and his talent. But let us not forget that he is completely preoccupied with saving himself, and himself alone, through the invention of the Absolute Encoder. Sologdin believes only in individual prowess. He battles alone against the Hydra, and he expects to prevail alone. The Sologdin of *Circle 96* is the same, but to these familiar traits others have been added. The initial meeting between Nerzhin and Sologdin is astonishing. Listen to Nerzhin's confession, or rather his profession of love:

> "It was morning. I went down [to wash], whistling something softly. You were busy drying yourself, and you lifted your face from the towel in the semi-darkness. And I . . . I was dumbfounded! It seemed like the Holy Face on an icon. Later, when I'd had time to get a closer look, I realized that you were far from being a saint—I won't flatter you . . ." Sologdin burst out laughing.
> "... Your face isn't soft at all, but it's extraordinary . . . And I immediately felt I could trust you; five minutes later I was already telling you everything . . ." "Yes, I was amazed at your precipitancy."[19]

Not only does Sologdin have the face of an icon, an "archeiropoetic"[20] face, but he embodies a hard and triumphant Christianity, à la Greco. He speaks like the Grand Master of Santiago:

> But imperturbable was the blue of Dmitrii Sologdin's eyes. Arms crossed imposingly on his breast—a pose that particularly suited him—he declaimed in rising tones:
> "My friend! Only those who wish the ruin of Christianity would compel it to become the faith of eunuchs. No, Christianity is the faith of the strong in spirit. We must have the courage to see the evil in

the world and eradicate it. Be patient, you too will find your way to God. Your 'I don't believe in anything' gives no sustenance to a thinking man; it is mere spiritual impoverishment.''[21]

As we can see, the Sologdin of *Circle 96* has a completely different stature. A new Christ or new Grand Inquisitor, he dominates Nerzhin, bending him almost instantly to his will. Now, Nerzhin has come to consult with him on a point of morality that is of fundamental importance in the Gulag universe (it occupies a central place in the play *The Lovegirl and the Innocent*, and is taken up once more in *The Gulag Archipelago*): to wit, how is one to behave toward the professional criminals (*urki*) who terrorize the "politicals," with the active complicity of the guards? Must one answer violence with violence? Sologdin does not hesitate: one must extirpate the evil, one must kill. The author himself refers us, in a symbolic allusion, to—the Karamazovs. ("That same day, after hearing all your evangelical revelations, I threw a small question at you..." "...A Karamazovian one."[22]) Of the two "Russian boys" who meet here to debate questions of good and evil, it is clear that Sologdin is the elder, that he is Ivan, but an Ivan identified even more closely with the Inquisitor, an Ivan freed from doubt, a "crusader" in the struggle against Evil. Nerzhin, disquieted and undecided, comes to consult with him and receives a lesson in "virile," even militant, Christianity (he himself is still at the "Stoic" stage, still engrossed in the wisdom of antiquity). Man must struggle, he must wage war (Sologdin is further likened to the warrior-saint Aleksandr Nevskii), he must achieve perfect mastery of the self, cost what it may. (Like Alesha, Nerzhin runs from one person to another soliciting advice.)

This chapter 26 (which, together with chapter 27, corresponds to chapter 24 of *Circle 87*) sheds a great deal of light on the first, so to speak initiatory, relationship between Nerzhin and Sologdin—a relationship that implicitly acknowledges the weakness, nay, the inferiority of the initiate Nerzhin-Solzhenitsyn. For in succumbing so promptly to the icon-like *aura* of Sologdin, Nerzhin was at once right and wrong. He was right in that Sologdin was an authentic master; wrong in that what this master taught was precisely defiance, authority and secrecy. The submission of pupil to master had been "precipitate." Sologdin has mastered his inner self, he has organized it into successive defenses and fortifications. There are nine *spheres* in the Sologdinian "self," just as there are nine circles in Dante's

Inferno. "Don't forget that we live with vizors down. Our whole life through with vizors down. We've been given no choice. And in any case, quite apart from this, men are generally more complicated than novelists would have us believe."[23] In other words, Nerzhin is at fault even in his precipitate declaration of allegiance. He justifies himself, it is true, by reminding his master that it is a law of prison life that one must be able to discern *at first glance* the true nature of anyone entering the cell. But Nerzhin the disciple is by definition both innocent and guilty. The very doctrine of the master ruled out any such rapid submission. The lesson which Sologdin administers is twofold. On the one hand, it is the lesson of an accomplished zek, a citizen of the convict world: one must fortify one's own self and never surrender it to anyone. On the other hand, it is the lesson of a Solzhenitsynian alter ego, sitting in judgement of the author: no one can do without an inviolable reserve, a secrecy of the "self."

This lesson, "played out" so well in chapter 26, leads us back to the problems raised at the beginning of this article. Solzhenitsyn, ex-convict and former victim of the concentration-camp world, could not have failed to suffer a profound emotional trauma. To the spontaneous expression of the quest for communication with others— embodied in Nerzhin—Solzhenitsyn the writer opposes that fortification of the "self," that obstinate refusal to bare one's soul, which belongs in the arsenal of the zek Sologdin.

The textual history of *The First Circle*, such as it can be read in the texts published to date, and such as we infer its intermediate stages (probably never to be revealed by the author) to have been, allows us to perceive a significant evolution in the character of Sologdin. Initially, he is a Christ-like figure, a master of all thoughts, and a merciless one at that, since he even condemns the "precipitous" submission of his pupil. Subsequently, he is reduced to the level of a champion of individualism, amiable but "peculiar." When the final touches have been added to the 1978 edition, Sologdin reappears newly enhanced and at the same time humbled by the moral superiority which Nerzhin shows in refusing to "collaborate" and abandoning the comfort of the first circle for the wretched life of the eighth or ninth circle. To Sologdin, who proposes that Nerzhin join his research group and "give it [his] best shot" (*vkalyvat'*), Nerzhin responds in the new version: "But if you do give it your best shot, when do you find time for your own inner development?"[24]

On this occasion Nerzhin the pupil has conquered his master

Sologdin. It is he who leaves to "fortify" his own "self," and it is Sologdin who "collaborates," thus weakening his fortifications. We recall how, at the end of this chapter 95 (chapter 86 in *Circle 87*), Nerzhin takes the hands of his warring friends, Rubin and Sologdin, wishing to reconcile them before descending further into the Inferno. This chivalrous scene masks what could possibly be the most profound line of development in the book: Nerzhin's progressive emancipation vis-à-vis Sologdin. At the "round table" of the new knights there has been an elder, a "master." But when the cycle of *The First Circle* is complete, this *primus inter pares* is no longer Sologdin, but Nerzhin himself.

In any event, we cannot expect to receive from Solzhenitsyn himself the secret keys to his book. This entrancing book, this cathedral of all the writer's leitmotifs, this *chanson de geste* of the knights of Gulag, has a profound soteriological mission. It is therapeutic for its creator, and it plays an equally salutary role for us: it releases and liberates us from secret, deep-rooted, voluntary and painful submission to totalitarian ideology. It is a sublimation of the state of enslaved will (in Luther's terms) through the re-establishment of dialogue and exchange between *equals*. This is why it reunites Platonic dialogues with the medieval songs of the Grail cycle: like them, it is a mystic and euphoric moment of human fraternity.

—*Translated from the French by the editors.*

Notes

1. Aleksandr Solzhenitsyn, *Sobranie sochinenii*, vols. I and II (*V kruge pervom*) [Vermont-Paris: YMCA-Press, 1978]. See the foreword to volume I and the history of the text at the end of volume II. Solzhenitsyn explicitly compares the fate of *The First Circle* with that of Bulgakov's *Master and Margarita*.

2. The history of the publication of *The First Circle* is recounted by Olga Carlisle in her book *Solzhenitsyn and the Secret Circle* (New York: Routledge & Kegan Paul, 1978). This version is violently contested by Solzhenitsyn in a comment appended to the American edition of his book *The Oak and the Calf*.

3. *Vremia i my* (Tel-Aviv), No. 40, 1979, pp. 178-205.

4. In the 1969 edition, this "musical" prologue even had a curious typographical arrangement, one insisted on by the author himself: the title-leitmotifs were graphically located in the middle of the page, symmetrically disposed about a central axis.

5. *Sobranie sochinenii*, I, p. 336.

6. *Ibid.*, p. 339.

7. Solzhenitsyn revives the old Russian word *okoem* (horizon), which went out of use in the nineteenth century. In Russian, the word has a kind of plasticity, a semantic connotation superior to that of the current loanword, *gorizont*. This one word epitomizes Solzhenitsyn's poetics.

8. *Sobranie sochinenii*, I, pp. 348-49.

9. *Ibid.*, p. 348.

10. *Ibid.*, II, p. 83.

11. The "new" redaction restores the authentic name of the "sharashka"—Marfino—which had been changed to Mavrino in *Circle 87*. The official designation of the "Marfino sharashka" was "Special Prison No. 16."

12. *Sobranie sochinenii*, I, p. 121.

13. *Ibid.*, p. 194.

14. *Ibid.*, p. 175.

15. *Ibid.*, p. 122.

16. *Ibid.*, p. 133.

17. Cf. the prepublication of certain chapters from *October 1916*, as well as his interview with Janis Sapiets of February 1979.

18. Panin now lives in Paris. He is the author of *Notebooks of Sologdin*, *The Oscillating World*, and several apologetical brochures published in Brussels by the Russian Roman Catholic publishers, "La vie avec Dieu."

19. *Sobranie sochinenii*, I, p. 200.

20. This word occurred in a suppressed variant of the novel. It reappears in *August 1914* in a passage about Samsonov, "the seven-pood lamb."

21. *Sobranie sochinenii*, I, pp. 200-201.

22. *Ibid.*, p. 200.

23. *Ibid.*, p. 199.

24. *Ibid.*, II, p. 382.

Prussian Nights: A Poetic Parable for Our Time

KENNETH N. BROSTROM

Poetry composed by Aleksandr Solzhenitsyn must be, at least initially, an object of curiosity for those who know him as a prosaist of genius. Certainly the special role accorded to verse in his more familiar works would seem to guarantee high aspiration: he often associates poetry and poetic motifs with the most vital movements in his characters' spiritual lives and with their moral dilemmas.[1] For a number of years we have known of the existence of Solzhenitsyn's verse, at least 12,000 lines of which were composed and committed to memory in the camps. (A fascinating and chilling description of the dangers attending this creative labor can be found in *The Gulag Archipelago*.[2]) But only 69 lines, apparently from this corpus, had appeared in print prior to the writer's exile in 1974. Thus, the approximately 1,400 lines of *Prussian Nights* published in that same year[3] were an important addition to his work; together with other short poems and poetic fragments presently in the public domain[4] they provide a rather substantial basis for study of Solzhenitsyn as a poet.

We know nothing and will not speculate about revisions this poem may have undergone after 1950 (the date it bears), nor about possible reasons for its sudden publication soon after its author's exile. Nor will we attempt a definitive judgment of this poetry's ultimate value. Suffice it to say that Solzhenitsyn is an accomplished poet, and that, beyond its verbal artistry, his poetry exhibits strengths we recognize in his prose. A profound moral awareness informs his powerful depiction of men caught up in events too often terrible and largely beyond their control; the elaboration of their ethical quandaries is accompanied by subtly orchestrated patterns of action, meditation, and imagery which together generate the integrity of an authentic work of art.

The narrative material for *Prussian Nights* is drawn from Solzhenitsyn's own wartime experience, and its narrator is a man much like he presumably then was. A former university student—polite, sensitive, reserved, but exhibiting a youthful lack of moral assurance and marked by a degree of callous indifference born of war's barbarity—the narrator enters East Prussia with the Soviet armies during the winter of 1944-45 in command of an artillery battery. He is swept along in the rapid, unhindered advance and witnesses the orgy of devil-may-care drunkenness, wanton destruction, looting, murder, arson, and rape visited upon German civilians and towns. Unable finally to resist the repellent seductions of this dance of death, he commits a genteel rape and is overcome with self-loathing.

The narrator's irresolute oscillation between the behavior and values of his past and the reckless nihilism of the present determines the general movement of his verse narration, a complex series of shifts between action and meditative withdrawal from action. It also governs Solzhenitsyn's use of extremes in style, from the substandard crudities of rampaging bumpkins to the refined and precise verbal elegance of the intellectual. He is generally successful in fitting either extreme to the trochaic tetrameter line in which the poem is written (with but a single passage in dactyls). But there is no sharp division between the narrator's standard Russian and the substandard reported speech of his troops. Rather the narrator's language encompasses the entire verbal spectrum between these extremes, and his style at any moment registers his dissonant, ambivalent attitude toward himself and his lawless countrymen. For example, rollicking licentiousness, memories of a literary stereotype, and ironic self-mockery conjoin in the following passage addressed to a column of Cossacks and marked by the rhythms and diction of the vernacular:

> V nashei zhizni bespokoinoi—
> Nynche zhiv, gliadi—ubit,—
> Mil mne, bratsy, vash razboinyi
> Ne k dobru veselyi vid.
> Vybirali my ne sami,
> Ne po vole etot put',
> No teper' za poiasami
> Est' chem po nebu pal'nut'!... (p. 29)

> Our lives don't see much relaxation.
> Alive? Watch out or you'll be dead!
> By your cheerful brigand faces

—so sinister—I'm comforted.
This road was not our own decision.
No one asked us if or why.
But now under our belts we've something
Worth a salvo in the sky! (Conquest, p. 45)

And so the narrator celebrates in this discordant song his acquisition
of writing materials, gentlemanly plunder removed from an abandoned post office soon to be burned.

These eight lines form two quatrains with alternating feminine
and masculine rhymes, but they are printed without stanza breaks.
Although *Prussian Nights* is not rigorous stanzaic poetry, its lines
nevertheless coalesce into rhymed clusters ranging from couplets
and triplets to pentastichs and several hexastichs; two related rhyme
patterns predominate in quatrains and pentastichs (aBaB [as in the
passage above] and aBaaB). However, the generally irregular rhyme
scheme and the unbroken printed text tend to accentuate, not the
poetic texture of particular passages, but the developing narrative.
That integral narrative is our first concern, for it presents us with
more than a young, slightly jaded idealist's pilgrimage into hell. It
is a parable for our time, for a century populated more than any
before by people of humane predisposition and good intention who
have too often stoked the fires of that hell.

We are accustomed to thinking of Nazi Germany in these terms.
And no Russian reader of *Prussian Nights* is likely to forget the
barbarism which emerged from the world of brick homes and tiled
roofs, paved roads, solidly built barns, and well-preserved Gothic
churches described in the poem's early pages. But if Nazi atrocities
committed in Russia provoke in part the events depicted there, they
are not allowed to provide a moral rationalization. Solzhenitsyn refers
to past acts of the German army only by implication, while in the
present not a single heroic, or even terrible, military engagement
is portrayed. He allows no ambiguity to infiltrate his ethical position:
Germans, all civilians, women of all ages, the elderly, even an infant,
are helpless and pathetic victims of Russian aggression. Repeatedly
the narrator echoes Moscow's demand for Old Testament "justice":
"Blood for blood! Tooth for tooth!" But replies in kind never rise
above the initial wrong. The Russians merely mimic their hated foe
by acting upon the barbarous principle that might makes right.

This evocation of Jehovah's wrathful visage figures significantly in Solzhenitsyn's effort to explode all spurious justifications and embellishments of the hideous, the ideological included. In Neidenburg the Russians are met by a longsuffering German Communist, who with solemn joy greets his proletarian brethren with bread and salt, the ancient Russian gesture of humble hospitality. But this "bastard" (*gad*), this "spy," this "vermin" (*chumnoi*), is swiftly arrested and sent off to SMERSH (the police organ for counterespionage), to a certain Solov'ev, who bears, probably ironically, the name of Russia's greatest religious philosopher. Meanwhile, a gang rape has left the German's daughter dead and his dying wife pleading for the deathblow (pp. 22-26). Similarly, "class allies," an elderly and ill German farmer and his wife, are nonchalantly shot after feeding their guests from the East, while their grandson, perhaps wounded, makes good a hair-raising escape through window and snow into the forest (pp. 43-44). The "liberation of Eastern Europe," the "inevitable historical collapse of Fascism," the "international brotherhood of the toiling masses," these and other shibboleths grounded in ideology and endlessly propounded in the immense Soviet war literature, collapse here under the accumulating weight of criminal violence.

Despite the callous gaiety, effectively rendered in diction and rhythm, which characteristically attends such crimes, Solzhenitsyn makes of these soldiers something more than obstreperous, vengeful cutthroats. They too are victims of power, first of all the power of ancient fears and prejudices associated with "the German" which are now endorsed by Moscow. Fascist Italians, for example, pass the Russian columns untouched, while Poles, allies but old targets for Russian discrimination, suffer verbal abuse, and their young women are raped while desperately crying out their nationality (pp. 32, 46). Solzhenitsyn's Nobel Speech, his fiction, and his polemical works witness fully to his conviction that values and beliefs impressed by enculturation and individual experience have the power to enslave men's minds. This certainly does not free these Russians from guilt. But their mindless response to old prejudice, their habitual and benighted acquiescence to Moscow's dictates, their brutalization in war, all cause them to view every German categorically as *enemy*, as a noxious, loathsome thing and not a human being. Suddenly they find themselves in a universe where the principle "all is permitted" is a supreme virtue. The enormity of this ethical error is ironically underscored by their ignorance of

Dostoevskii, who has at least been read by many of their German victims (p. 45). (The connotative richness of this reference to Dostoevskii should be apparent, and need not be pursued in detail here.)

The Russian soldiers are victims of power in a more literal sense. They resemble their own leaders, for whom the maxim "all is permitted" has always been a guiding principle of government, especially in dealing with internal "enemies," whom they regard as a species of vermin. The only sustained break in this poem's metrical scheme occurs in a somber description of an endless column of such "enemies," Russian prisoners of war returning to their own "savage land," to its camps for the living dead. The shift from trochees to dactyls, resulting in a longer line, together with the imagery surrounding these men "needed by no one," creates a mood both ominous and funereal (p. 47). Moscow has termed them *Enemy*! and they have ceased to exist as human beings for their fellows. As it turns out, there *is* one unforgivable sin in this permissive universe: having been a POW.

Solzhenitsyn shares with Dostoevskii a conviction that the human enactment of evil may be conditioned by environment, but that evil itself is rooted more deeply in man's nature. It resides in our impulse to deify the isolated self at the expense of the other, to follow the easy path of self-interest, eschewing the difficult path of self-transcendence on behalf of the other. The gratuitous violence in *Prussian Nights* is reminiscent of a symbolic event described near the conclusion of *Cancer Ward*: an "evil man" blinds a Macaque Rhesus monkey by throwing tobacco into its eyes, "just for the hell of it" (*Prosto tak*!). The principle implicit in this act, in all its infinite permutations and combinations, leads implacably to the law of the jungle between men and between nations—that is, to destruction and chaos.

Creation of a chaotic hell on earth is the perception which shapes the imagery associated with the Russian invasion. A fiery holocaust, an implacable surge of molten "lava" (p. 8), advances over the winter landscape during the first half of the poem; everything falls to the torch. Fire seems to fill the firmament as natural phenomena— dawn, dust, stars, and wind (pp. 7-8)—are transformed into a metaphorical description of this all-consuming inferno: "Chto zh, gori, dymi, pylai,/Trudoliubnyi gordyi krai" (p. 15). Serpentlike flames (p. 8) of "just" punishment engulf entire towns and villages as these Russian surrogates for Satan's demons enact a Last Judgment decreed in Moscow ("Otomshchaem my vragu!" p. 7). But certain targets are emphasized: a school, homes and barns, a church. And a piano is destroyed in a street. That is, emblems of a peaceful, ordered existence, of productive labor, culture, the life of the family and of the spirit, are incinerated in an orgy of blasphemous hilarity ("Pir i vlast'! Likuet khaos!" p. 10).

Especially important here are the interrelated motifs of private life and domestic life: the dignity of the individual is repeatedly violated by rape, while homes, grounded in loving sexuality, are invaded and looted, and an infant is apparently murdered (p. 42). The ethical nihilism and impulse toward chaos inherent in human evil make war here, not only on persons but on any conviction that life, the life of the individual and of the community in its most fundamental expression, is inherently orderly and valuable. Such nihilism is inevitably life-denying, not life-affirming. So despite their vitality, the Russian troops are agents of hell and hellfire, that is, of death. For them sexuality, perhaps the most basic motif in *Prussian Nights*, is no longer the mysterious source of new life; it is merely a source for nihilistic, aggressive self-pleasure. The victim becomes a thing, and rape becomes the moral equivalent of murder, which transforms the victim into a thing literally. The equation of rape and murder is evident in the sexual undercurrent of the poem's rollicking opening lines; there cannons, death-dealing weapons, acquire their predictable connotations, while Germany is described in feminine terms, as an "evil witch" who now must "open" her "gates."[5]

> Rasstupis', zemlia chuzhaia!
> Rastvoriai svoi vorota!
> Eto nasha udalaia
> Edet russkaia pekhota!
> Kholmik, pad', mostok i kholmik—
> Stoi! Skhodi! Po karte—tut.
> Budet zlaia ved'ma pomnit'
> V nebe zimnem nash saliut! (p. 5)

> Open up, you alien country!
> Wide open let your gates be thrown!
> For, approaching, see how boldly
> Russia's battle line rolls on!
> Hillock, dip, small bridge, and hillock—
> Halt! Check on the map—we're there.

Dismount! The foul witch shall remember
Our salvo in the wintry air! (Conquest, p. 2)

This equation has its most powerful expression in the episode preceding the narrator's own rape of a German woman. A magnificent and proud young German woman is stopped by two Russians, one of them, Baturin, a seasoned cutthroat. We anticipate, in company with the narrator, that another rape will ensue. Instead she is shot, riddled by both her captors with automatic weapon fire.

All of this suggests why the narrator's own crime committed in the poem's final episode is the apotheosis of his pilgrimage, a journey of the spirit which takes him from confused and passive, uncertain collaboration in evil (he experiences both revulsion and exhilaration) to active participation in the dance of death. The spiritual pilgrimage is obviously an important structural principle in much of Solzhenitsyn's work, as it often has been in the works of the Russian classics. During the modern period generally, such literary pilgrimages are rather often depicted as unsuccessful. In the present instance, we might compare this narrator to Kostoglotov in *Cancer Ward*, who exits from that novel having failed a critical test but with an anguished awareness of his moral failure. And in that anguish there is some affirmation.

Of course one might view the narrator's crime as the result of his progressive contamination by the world. In a sense he is no stranger to East Prussia, for as a schoolboy he studies Russian military defeats in that area during World War I. The "circles, dots, and arrows" (p. 17) on maps signifying military operations had become familiar and meaningful to him. He begins his own journey-pilgrimage there with preconceptions of a calculated, a *teleological*, march toward Berlin. Instead he is swept along in a series of discontinuous, chaotic, disorienting movements which are perfectly in harmony with his troops' aimless violence.[6] His moral sense is eroded by the persistent perception that he moves through a disordered and therefore meaningless world in which morality is irrelevant. His faltering commitment to ethical behavior is reflected in a tawdry refrain from the nineteenth-century Spanish composer and violinist Sarasate, "Oh, what heart could withstand?!" which at intervals haunts and tantalizes him. Like Babel's intellectual protagonist Liutov (*Red Cavalry*), this young man is caught in the moral quagmire which opens up in terrible times between what is and what we dream ought to be. But his dilemma loses every trace of moral heroism or tragedy when he *chooses* to rape. At the very least we can say this: in doing so, he chooses for himself and thus for chaos, and against humanity.

Unlike Babel', however, Solzhenitsyn never allows us to question where the good lies, even as he admits the inevitable impact of events on moral choice. Earlier, when the atrocities in Allenstein culminate in a soldier's intention to murder an infant, a lone voice cries out, "You're King Herod, your priest's a beast!" ("Sam ty Irod, pop tvoi zver'," p. 42). The narrator's problem is not so much his uncertain knowledge of the good, but his deftness in rationalizing the bad. An instructive example involves the Sarasate leitmotif noted above. It is linked to another by the same composer, even more tawdry: "This fan of black, a fan so precious." The cheap romanticism of these phrases, their philistine vulgarity, is precisely what discredits them: behind their tinsel passion lurks the worm of greedy lust in all its moral insignificance. The fan is certainly related to fire imagery and probably to woman as the object of sensuality; it opens for the first time prior to the final rape, not to cool but to "waft the searing heat of life" toward the narrator (p. 56). In the same passage he invites the "stings of serpents," and he alludes to the Medusa, who recalls, together with the black fan and the heat, the "evil witch" in the poem's opening lines. Hell is undoubtedly present in his temptation, but he embellishes it with literary, traditional religious, and musical references to camouflage the ugliness of its spiritual mediocrity— until it is too late for anything but remorse.

Such "civilized" camouflage is not without parallel elsewhere in *Prussian Nights*. Earlier in Allenstein the narrator encounters an old acquaintance, a former university lecturer specializing in the literature of the French Enlightenment. They are akin in their literary interests and their war experiences. Their conversation is excited, even breathless; they recall the past, they discuss the eighteenth century's pride in man, in reason and progress, they ponder the questions (Rus', the Mongols, Europe) which have tormented and entranced generations of Russian intellectuals (pp. 32-40). But all the while this "civilized" man forces a German railroad dispatcher at gunpoint to accept unsuspecting trains into the Allenstein terminal. There they are met by Cossacks, the passengers are robbed, often raped and sometimes shot, while most are marched to assembly points for transport to the Russian camps. Humanity aside, this treacherous ambush serves no rational military purpose. So this intense discussion of the past and its values, which causes "living life" ("'zhivaia zhizn'"") to shine in the previously drunken eyes of this officer, is nothing more than an escape: those values have no bearing on the present. As the narrator leaves the terminal, he notices a "civilized," elderly Russian general limping squeamishly among German corpses, a human vulture indicating to his aides which valuables he wishes to plunder. Similarly, the narrator later walks among a group of German wives, indicating to a master-sergeant which one will share his bed (pp. 58-60).

Any such escape is illusory here—these actions betray the past and its values. It will not suffice to say that chaotic, violent events in an alien German environment sever these Russians psychologically from a dear and distant, unreachable past. They themselves are eager enough to apply the past to the present when it suits them: "We won't forget! We won't forgive!" The narrator's first, venial sin—appropriating writing materials—reflects his love of repose and reflection, in such contrast to the rape and pillage around. Still, he hesitates, then justifies his action by referring to his own past suffering over the wretched quality of pens, pencils, and paper during his schooldays. There is humor, but also self-mockery in this episode (pp. 26-29), precisely because he senses that his moral rationalization is akin to that of his troops in their policy of revenge through rape.

The narrator plays a third game with the past in order to rationalize present desires and pleasures: we have been and are helpless pawns in the paws of fate, of events beyond our control, but now we've had a bit of luck, so grab it! (See the passage cited above: "V nashei zhizni bespokoinoi...") If the narrator escapes into the comfortable dimensions of the past, he does not hold the gun pointed at the railroad dispatcher; if he uses the past as moral rationalization for his appropriation of writing materials, he refuses any active role in vengeful destruction by fire (p. 15). His tendency to be passive is apparent in his gravitation toward this third principle, and it is to it that he appeals during a lengthy tirade on ethics prior to launching his own rape:

Carpe diem!—gedonisty
Nas uchili—DEN' LOVI!
Dni osypiatsia, kak list'ia,
Zagusteet tok krovi. (p. 55.)

Carpe diem! The hedonists, they

Always taught us—*Seize the day*!
But the days like leaves are falling,
The current of the blood runs thicker. (Conquest, p. 89)

That he is plunged into remorse after the fact is predictable insofar as his passivity reflects his innate moral sense. *Carpe diem* reduces life to the pursuit of hedonistic pleasure, to the flesh alone. If his reason can support this principle in the context of chaos, his conscience knows better.

The source of that final remorse is not betrayal of the past and its values, but calculated betrayal of another human being. In so doing, the cultivated narrator, apparently out of place in a world gone mad, suddenly proves capable of ugly disorder himself. Solzhenitsyn's awareness of man's capacity for moral dereliction is nowhere more clearly expressed; the entire poem moves toward this merger of the passive, restrained commander with the active barbarism of his subordinates.

The initial step in this direction is the narrator's appropriation of writing materials; it is important precisely because he is rather ashamed even though no person is betrayed. This episode is bracketed by two others involving rape. The first is the betrayal of the German Communist and murderous rape of his wife and daughter. In the second (pp. 29-32) a woman, dressed and coiffed like a German but speaking fluent vernacular Russian, emerges from a house and disdainfully defies the soldier banging at her door with his rifle ("P'ianyi, griaznyi, t'fu kakov!"). But others join him, and this "servant" (so she claims) or Hausfrau suddenly becomes ingratiating, and leads them to a neighboring house filled, she promises, with German virgins ("Nemok-tselok polon dom," p. 31). The betrayal of one's neighbor continues in the next episode, in which the German dispatcher sends his fellow countrymen to their doom to save his own skin.

This is an important motive for the narrator's ambivalent passivity as well. He indicates that his restraint is not an unambiguous response to a moral imperative by referring to himself as "Pilate" (p. 15), who collaborated with evil by passively withdrawing, by washing his hands to maintain the appearance of civilized decency. Like Pilate the narrator is a *man in command*, but he issues few orders and none to protect helpless civilians, chiefly women.[7] Is he powerless or fearful of consequences? If primarily the latter, his restrained behavior is less good than evil: it reflects self-interest at the expense of others, it is a betrayal.

Thus, the venial self-interest evident in the seizure of writing materials escalates during the succeeding atrocities, even though the narrator never dirties his own hands. His imitation of Pilate continues in his own assault on a woman, which he arranges to keep secret. He prefaces that episode with the tirade on ethics noted above, in which he criticizes official writers (Shaginian, Surkov, Gorbatov, Erenburg) for "varnishing" reality. But he immediately mimics them by recalling Sarasate and by rejecting the moral relevance of philosophy and religion in a rather arcane reference to the legendary Indian philosopher Charvaki.[8] Having varnished his own greedy, aggressive desire for his share of the women, he embarks upon a refined rape by proclaiming the ethically relativistic, ultimately nihilistic, fatuous slogan, "Everyone acts like this!"

Solzhenitsyn frequently creates multiple thematic resonances through significant juxtaposition of episodes. The moral equivalence of murder and rape is the fundamental bond between the poem's last two episodes, the shooting of the beautiful German and the narrator's rape of Anna. Both episodes begin with the narrator hedonistically preoccupied with his own snug comfort. In the former he is sucking candy and nestled in the soft, upholstered seat of a captured German Opelblitz. So he is rather indifferent to a photograph of a German officer taken from the woman and thrust at him by the vengeful soldier Somin. The officer is her husband, and his insignia *may* be that of the SS. The narrator's almost inadvertent, dismissive wave of the hand seals her fate, and he shouts "Hey, lads!" too late (p. 53). Initially there is only mild regret: "How fresh" her beauty had been!

But that beauty is not forgotten: after the nihilistic meditation on morality which links these episodes, the narrator enters a lowly room packed with five husbandless German families busy with domestic chores. But *"such a one* I could not find" (*"Takoi* ne nakhozhu," p. 59). He arrives from other, far more comfortable quarters nearby, where he has dined and was enjoying an after-dinner smoke and reverie until he learned of the women's presence. For the first time he abandons his passivity. He commits his crime not amid fires nor during the frantic, chaotic advance toward Berlin; his crime arises during repose and from prior moral contemplation.

If premeditation magnifies the narrator's guilt, so does recognition of his victim's humanity—the only instance of such recognition in the poem. Although he enters the room of German women looking for a well-favored female, his first, faltering question of Anna is "Wie heissen Sie?" Certainly he is aware of Anna's lack of flesh, but he also notices her timidity and the almost imperceptible motion which straightens her kerchief as she looks up from a washtub. She is to be brought by a solicitous master-sergeant to a vacant wing of the premises, where he waits in "ambush" (*zasada*, p. 62, probably an echo of the ambush set earlier for unsuspecting civilian trains in Allenstein). Anna is told she must milk cows for the Russians, and the narrator watches her approach through a window in the wing. He notices she is "somehow touchingly quiet," and that sadness is in her expression, and meekness in her glance, as the sergeant orders her to enter the wing rather than the cowshed. A surprised tremor distorts her mouth as she sees the narrator beyond the door, and he suddenly loses his ability to speak German. He remembers her apologetic smile then, as she realizes her agitation may imply suspicion. Her shawl has slipped from her shoulders in the cold, and the confused narrator, "for some reason," delicately wraps it about her again. This is an exquisite, simple gesture of concern, but he swiftly betrays it and Anna when she backs uncertainly toward the threshold. He slams the door and beckons without looking at her: "Komm!" That gesture ("pomanil") recalls the dismissive one ("makhnul rukoi," p. 52), which led to the German bride's murder. Standing with his back to the "beggars' bed" he has prepared, the narrator awaits Anna's word that she is "ready" (p. 63). And we remember that earlier the bride fell to the ground with a scream, then lay motionless in the cold snow, in a curled, fetal ball, ready for the fatal bullets. Anna pleads after the rape, "Doch erschiessen Sie mich nicht!" With anguish the narrator recognizes in the final two lines that the two women are now bound together by his own, personal crimes: "Akh, don't be afraid... Ah-h-h/ On my soul there's a soul..."

Perhaps shame causes the narrator to avoid bringing Anna to his own comfortable quarters. Instead he "squeamishly" tosses a greasy mattress and bedraggled pillow on an old bedstead which he finds in the deserted, cold, trash-filled wing. These hurried "domestic" arrangements recall the violated homes behind the advancing Russian army; they are in harmony with the obsessive lines by Sarasate, which parody genuine feeling. The German women, to the contrary, are performing necessary domestic chores, and Anna's hands still steam slightly from laundry (p. 63). This is the warmth of genuine life, not the violent fire of destruction. The narrator had expected but did not find in himself the "blaze" of passion or a "molten, joyous ringing in the muscles" (recall the "lava" of the Russian advance). An abandoned home, trash, cold—the chill of moral death—provide an appropriate environment for this criminal parody of private love between a man and a woman.

And this is how civilized, good men can create an immoral parody of genuine life as they act and react amidst the inevitably amoral movements of history. This parable aims to show that they must—we must—rise above passive distress over barbarism, we must rise to anguish over our passive, and sometimes active, collaboration with it. Morality for Solzhenitsyn resides in what we do and fail to do—not in what we feel.

Notes

1. See Laszlo M. Tikos, "Poetry in Solzhenitsyn's Works," *Art International*, vol. 17, No. 7 (Sept. 1973), p. 65.

2. Aleksandr Solzhenitsyn, *Arkhipelag Gulag, 1918-1956: opyt khudozhestvennogo issledovaniia, V, VI, VII* (Paris: YMCA-Press, 1975), pp. 106-107; in English: *The Gulag Archipelago, 1918-1956: An Experiment in Literary Investigation, V-VII*, trans. Harry Willetts (New York: Harper and Row, 1976), pp. 98-109.

3. *Prusskie nochi: poema* (Paris: YMCA-Press, 1974); also found, together with an English translation by Robert Conquest, in *Prussian Nights: A Poem* (New York: Farrar, Straus and Giroux, 1977). All page references are to the YMCA text; unless otherwise indicated, translations are my own. With that original text Solzhenitsyn also released his own reading of the poem, recorded in the Soviet Union in 1969.

4. For a very useful bibliographical discussion of Solzhenitsyn's poetry, see Michael Nicholson, "Solzhenitsyn in 1976: A Bibliographical Reorientation," *Russian Literature Triquarterly*, no. 14 (Winter 1976), pp. 462-82.

5. The first line of the poem also carries these connotations: "Rasstupis' zemlia chuzhaia!" literally "Make way, alien land!" The verb *rasstupit'sia* is used in the folk language with sexual implications, specifically with regard to the earth, ploughing, and planting: "Rasstupis' ty, mat' syra zemlia!" meaning, "Open up, damp Mother Earth!"

6. Important here is the repetitious verb *katit'* ("Katim, katim po Evrope"); or note the passage on pp. 42-43.

7. After the shooting of the beautiful German, the narrator recalls a similar murder of an old man committed by Somin, one of the killers here; he admits that a single word of command would have stopped that crime, and then he rationalizes his failure to do so.

8. Pp. 54-56; there is here, perhaps, a deliberate and blasphemous reference to Christ, when the narrator speaks of the goblet (*kubok*) brought by life, the bitter contents of which must be drained. Cf. Matt. 26:39.

Solzhenitsyn's Intellectual Antecedents

DONALD W. TREADGOLD

I

The late Max Hayward, in his fine short introduction to the English translation[1] of *Iz-pod glyb* [*From Under the Rubble*], accurately identifies the antecedents of that volume as *Vekhi* [*Landmarks*—perhaps better, *Milestones*—1909] and *Iz glubiny* [*De Profundis* or *From the Depths*, 1921].[2] The authors of the essays collected in *Iz-pod glyb* intend acknowledgment of that lineage, as shown in the title itself of the volume. Hayward terms it a "phonetic echo" of *Iz glubiny*; it is a form of word play in Russian. *Iz glubiny* is specifically referred to only once in the book, by F. Korsakov, but *Vekhi* is mentioned several times, by Korsakov, "A.B." (pseudonymous initials), and Solzhenitsyn himself, who discusses the symposium at length in his essay "The Smatterers."[3] Clearly the contributors are seeking to continue, or, better, restore a link with the pre-revolutionary tradition.

Solzhenitsyn is best understood as the chief figure in the contemporary generation of the continuing if sometimes interrupted effort to recover the Russian national tradition within a context of cosmopolitan reflection and acceptance of many aspects of Western culture.[4] Such a persistent effort may be traced to its beginnings independently of whether toilers in that vineyard know who first planted the grapes, that is to say, who or what their own intellectual antecedents were. We do not know exactly what Solzhenitsyn and his fellow authors of *From Under the Rubble* know about Russian intellectual and cultural history. It is no secret that under the Soviet regime, even since the death of Stalin, it is only an ideologically sanitized version of such topics which can be written and published. But it is not only the Communist cultural dictators who are responsible for the failure of young Russians to learn about their own past.

Old Russian culture was a religious culture, based on Eastern Orthodox Christianity. Or, more precisely, the high culture was predominantly religious, from the eleventh century on, and in its inception derivative from Byzantium. The phenomenon of *dvoeverie* ["double faith"], or persistence of remnants of paganism alongside Christianity, was significant, but it was as prominent in Ireland as in Russia, and it was characteristic to some degree of every converted people throughout Christian history; there were many aspects of the folk culture not clearly related to any kind of religion that continued without embarrassment to believers. Neither the problem of survivals of pagan religion nor that of extrareligious folk culture is peculiar to Russia, and neither phenomenon is prominent enough in Russia's cultural tradition to explain any special features in it. For several centuries Russian literature developed in a manner that was characterized by the prominence of religious themes—as in saints' lives, homilies, and quotations from Byzantine ecclesiastics—or secular problems approached from religious premises—as in Byzantine law or indigenous chronicles. The virtual non-existence of any knowledge of Greek among Russian churchmen, let alone Latin, deprived Russians of any opportunity to learn from Plato or Aristotle, the pre-Christian Greek poets and playwrights, or (with modest exceptions) the Byzantine theologians and philosophers.

For the barbarians throughout Europe, Christianity was the path to civilization (and ethical improvement and statehood in the style of the eleventh and twelfth centuries); but to those converted from Rome, it brought Latin with it. To those converted from Constantinople, it did not necessarily bring Greek; Church Slavonic, based on a Macedonian vernacular, meant a readier comprehension of church services for the illiterate, impoverishment of education for actually or potentially literate churchmen. There was much that was creative and uplifting in old Russian culture, pursuing its own values and genius, but there was little to prepare it for encounters with cultures boasting higher philosophical and scientific attainments.

The encounter with the West began in the fifteenth century. While Western Europe expanded and matured in the High Middle Ages, Russia wrestled with the effects of the Mongol conquest and the partial reorientation eastward that it produced. In the eleventh century Kiev was as advanced as any newly converted barbarian state of Europe; in the fifteenth century Muscovy was a cultural backwater.

Quasi-religious arguments riffled the stagnant surface, borrowing on occasional writings brought in from the West. Muscovy was occupied with conquest of her neighboring states and defense against the Tatars beyond Russian habitation to the southeast. As the Reformation and Counterreformation shook Poland and the triumphant Roman Catholics drove eastward into Moscow during the Time of Troubles, Muscovites mobilized to repel them militarily but also had learned that they were in no position to withstand Polish intellectual and religious challenge. And so in the seventeenth century their clerics who aspired to leadership began to attend Jesuit schools in Poland, often undergoing casual conversion to the Roman church before and reconversion to Orthodoxy after the experience. As the century wore on there appeared in consequence learned Russians who had had good Polish educations: Simeon of Polotsk, who survived the religious battles in which the Russian Church lost, or drove, the "Old Believers" into schism and then became tutor to the Tsar Alexis's children; Stefan Iavorskii, Peter I's chief assistant for religious matters; Feodosii Ianovskii, who replaced him; Feofan Prokopovich, who edged out Feodosii in the same capacity.

Feodosii and then Feofan, who reacted to their Roman educations by hostility to Rome, supported Peter I in his radical attempts to westernize in a manner borrowing heavily from Protestantism, his successful subjection of the Russian church to state control, and his creation of a new system of clerical education based on the use of Latin. The consequences for literature and culture in general were as far-reaching as those for religion. Eighteenth-century literature in Russia is nearly a wasteland. Even Russia's first university, Moscow, used Latin as the language of instruction for many years after it was established in 1755. The nobility began to learn French; many German scholars were imported to staff the new Academy of Sciences; the use of Russian was often scorned, and it was only given a form in which modern literature could develop by Karamzin at the turn of the century. German philosophy was introduced into the Russian universities—more were added by Alexander I to the lone institution in Moscow—by clergymen who had studied at the Orthodox seminaries created by Peter I. Orthodoxy was partly westernized, Russian belles lettres were composed in the Western manner, the nobility spoke Western languages. At least they could converse with Napoleon's soldiers when they penetrated all the way to Moscow.

And the officers who pursued him all the way to Paris as he withdrew returned with the newest French, and English and German, ideas to their homeland.

Two great discontinuities resulted from the Petrine reforms. One was the gulf that opened between the westernized educated classes and the common people, mainly the peasantry, who either remained Orthodox or—as was true of a substantial minority—had become Old Believers. The Old Believers had at the time of their break with the official church (1667) boasted notables with an education to equal that of anyone on the other side. By the nineteenth century they constituted a fragment of Old Russian culture of an earlier era, lacking leadership though clinging to their faith, cut off from the processes of westernization by choice and by circumstance.

The other discontinuity related to the past. Time and again some innovator in Russian history perished and was forgotten because no receptivity, of a cultural or technical kind, could be found among those whom he wished to influence. Such was the case with Maksim the Greek, who died in 1556 after more than thirty years of being immured in a monastery as punishment for his views and whose very identity (he was born Michael Trivolis) was forgotten. There was Juraj Križanić, the lonely Croatian cleric who originated Pan-Slavism and was rewarded for his love for Russia by fifteen years of Siberian exile (though he was released and permitted to leave the country in 1676), and thereafter was forgotten and rediscovered much later. The decades of Roman Catholic education of Russian and Ukrainian churchmen were blotted out, so that Petr Chaadaev in his scandalous *Philosophical Letter* could write in 1829, "the syllogism of the West is unknown to us" though the syllogism had been meat and drink for such luminaries as Iavorskii, and, more broadly, scholasticism was taught several generations of clerics. Those instances were not the only ones. Russians' discoveries of radio and the electric light were not (unlike other cases) the retrospective products of the imagination of Stalin's flunkeys but were real. However, there had been no one who knew what to do with them.

Thus the task posed by the first men in the nineteenth century to seek the roots of their own traditions, to search after the basis of the national feelings that were stirring within themselves, was one of rediscovery. The fundamental break had followed the innovations of Peter the Great. A century or more had intervened in which the Orthodox tradition had been distorted in the Protestant-leaning seminaries, confined to the clergy when many nobles were receiving the rudiments or more of a Western-oriented education, and stunted in its growth. At the same time Russian popular culture came to be despised or ignored by the new westernized elite. The icons were left to be covered with smoke and dirt or metal fittings; the ancient churches were no longer admired and new construction was on ugly Western-influenced lines; folk costume and song were thought to be the province of the hopelessly backward *narod*.

The task was taken up first by the Slavophiles. The facile juxtaposition of this group of men with the so-called Westerners, as if Slavophiles were mindlessly reactionary xenophobes as against the rationally progressive Westerners, became the mode in Western analyses of the two "circles" and in the consciousness of Russian intellectuals themselves. Moreover, the notion was ready to hand that present-day Russian intellectuals, or at any rate "dissidents," may be similarly grouped into two neat categories, one of which is composed of people who like the West, as all good persons should, and therefore deserve the sympathy of all, as contrasted with repulsive types who like Russia. Indeed, a number of accounts have been written touching on Russian intellectual history which are based on assumptions not much more sophisticated than those.

In fact the term "Westerner" seems to have been used retrospectively much more often than during the early 1840s, the period when the two circles are supposed to have flourished, and can with only grave difficulty be made to identify any "circle" at all. It may be best understood as a term which was used to refer to what most if not all right-thinking, decently educated people thought for generations before the 1840s as well as after, and the people who continued to think that way despite the appearance of the Slavophiles with their jarring and discordant ideas.

As for the Slavophiles, they were a fairly heterogeneous lot, and the differences among them have been neglected.[5] But they shared a common desire to develop national feeling, largely on the basis of exploration of the Russian cultural past, in the area of both high culture and low culture. They did so, admittedly, as a result of acquaintanceship with the ideas set forth by Herder and other Germans about the value of all peoples and specifically in pursuit of philosophical propositions advanced by Schelling and Hegel. They also may have known something about how other peoples of Eastern Europe—Czechs, Slovaks, Croats, Serbs, and others—who had not enjoyed statehood in modern times, as well as the Poles who had had a state for centuries before its remnants disappeared in 1795, had been busying themselves in philological and folkloristic studies with a similar purpose. It is curious that such efforts among small stateless peoples seemed to evoke Western admiration, but not when they occurred among Russians.

National feeling might, to be sure, become a mania; those who argued the worth of their own people might end by asserting its superiority to all others and its natural right to oppress minorities within state boundaries or neighbors beyond them. The leading Slavophile, Aleksei Khomiakov, upheld all sorts of merits in the Russian tradition and sought to renew and revivify its links with the Eastern Orthodox tradition, which had become feeble in the consciousness of his generation. But he rejected contentions that Russians were superior to other peoples. To be sure, he wrote all sorts of historical rubbish, imposing grandiose "principles" of interpretations on history in the style of his German masters, but they were not designed to show that Russia was always right. Ivan Aksakov, in contrast, carried nationalism to a point of hostility to foreigners, and he was not alone. The Slavophiles developed a kind of quasi-anarchist and therefore utopian attitude toward the state, suffered from a number of sentimental illusions about the future of Russian society which they borrowed from Western Romanticism, and unjustifiably idealized certain moments from the past, especially the pre-Petrine period. But these failings, which may be duplicated in the history of national feeling in many countries in the nineteenth and twentieth century, must be weighed against the sound and healthy determination to discover what in the past warranted pride and what in the future could benefit a people whose heritage had long been submerged.

In the 1860s Fedor Dostoevskii, emerging from a period of imprisonment, exile, and intellectual crisis, came to wrestle with some of the same problems. Working with Apollon Grigor'ev and N. N. Strakhov, he and the so-called *pochvenniki* aimed at closer understanding of the "soil" of Russia and what it meant for the Russian people.[6] Dostoevskii addressed himself to the problem of evil, rooted in human nature and not confined to any group; he strove for reconciliation between Slavophiles and Westerners, the intelligentsia and the common people. But the violence of the revolutionaries alarmed him; many of their attitudes he knew well because he had shared

them in the 1840s. Especially in *Besy (The Possessed)*, his critique
of those who wished to destroy existing society in blind confidence
that they could replace it by an earthly paradise offended many
contemporaries and made him unpopular, even anathema, for a
time among the intelligentsia.

In the 1870s Dostoevskii became fascinated with Vladimir
Solov'ev, the brilliant and precocious man who had the best claim to
date to be considered a Russian philosopher. After Dostoevskii died
in 1881 Solov'ev concerned himself with theocracy—the problem of
Christianizing the secular order—but he put aside the dream of a
Europe in which the Pope would head the church and Alexander III
the state. (It was not the only fantasy that occupied Solov'ev during
his lifetime.) He turned to political liberalism, but his life ended in an
apocalyptic mood, in 1900.

By the end of the century the ascendancy of the materialists and
positivists in philosophy, the socialists and secularists in politics, had
been shaken. In certain respects the reception of Marxism, during the
1890s, marked the apogee of such views (Marxists rejected posi-
tivism but still shared some of its attitudes) and at the same time an
opening to a diversity of cultural currents. The chief figures of the
beginning of Marxism in Russia were noteworthy: Petr Struve,
Nikolai Berdiaev, Sergei Bulgakov, and others. Vladimir Ulianov
(Lenin) stood in their shadow, though not for long. Except for Lenin,
these figures passed through Marxism as a school rather than
adopted it as a cause or a secular religion. They were soon leaving
Marxism behind for neo-Kantian idealism, as shown in their symposium *Problemy idealizma*, 1902; *Vekhi*, 1909; and finally *Iz glubiny*,
1921.

The esthetic revival which also created a stir in the 1890s had
begun earlier. In the later 1870s a circle interested in old Russian
art formed at Abramtsevo, near Moscow, and in 1882 built a church in
the style of medieval Novgorod. The painting of historical themes and
imitation or variations on traditional artistic styles were stimulated,
but at the same time there was lively interest in the newest West
European art. Juxtaposition of passion for the kinds of beauty that
were old in Russia and the kinds that were new in the West continued
in the startling innovations of the *Mir Iskusstva* [*The World of Art*]
group beginning in 1898. In the meantime esthetic values *per se* were
defended and exemplified in literature, especially poetry, starting
with the symbolists after 1894, continuing with the Acmeists and

Futurists. The work of the Acmeists Anna Akhmatova and the younger Osip Mandel'shtam, both Christians, extends well into the Soviet period. The symbolists acknowledged the influence of Vladimir Solov'ev, as well as Dostoevskii and that poet of the first rank now neglected in both the USSR and the West, Fedor Tiutchev.

By the early years of the century many young Russians were devouring the new painting and poetry and admiring the rediscovery of old icons and architecture in Russia, while also following new trends in the contemporary West with close attention. Chekhov, the Ballet Russe, Stravinskii were exported to Paris with great success. The rediscovery of the Russian tradition was popular in both Russia and the West. It continued up to World War I. In the years immediately previous to the war a series of Religio-Philosophical Meetings and Assemblies in the two capitals and elsewhere brought together clerics and secular intellectuals, with the result of short-run puzzlement and incomprehension, long-run prospects for narrowing or even closing the widest cultural gap produced in Russia by the period of the Empire. Time was needed to regain the lost link with the past; it was one thing to declare icons and *bijou* churches worthy of attention as art or architecture (not only as adjuncts to worship), and another to clean, restore, and study them thoroughly. It was not until the Moscow exhibition of 1913 that the icons could be said to have been fully recovered. Continuation or renewal of the techniques concerned remained to be achieved. The Soviets kept the village of Palekh working on Byzantine-derived types of painting, though the product was not icons but fairy-tale scenes on cigarette boxes.

The Revolution made possible some folkloristic exploration and analysis, and Soviet specialists—some of them very highly skilled—were allowed, sometimes encouraged and supported, to restore icons and churches. But great quantities of icons were sold or lost and thousands of churches permitted to fall into ruin or simply destroyed outright. The entire religious component of the Russian tradition was relegated to the garbage heap; ecclesiastical institutions could be studied from the economic or sociological viewpoint, not as spiritual forces, and great caution was therefore required in approaching the subject at all. The icons were to be treated as folk art, not images of the eternal, the churches and liturgical music as products of the common people who, oppressed by superstition, had no chance to display their talents in the proper humanist pursuits. During the era of Stalin the risks of handling such topics in other than the prescribed fashion greatly increased. And yet somehow, when the Stalinist miasma lifted somewhat from the arts, traces of the Silver Age, that great flowering of Russian creativity during the reign of Nicholas II, were still visible. Christian writers survived, or returned, here and there: Anna Akhmatova, Osip Mandel'shtam, Boris Pasternak, Marina Tsvetaeva, Valerii Tarsis.[7] But during the post-Stalin years they died or were sent abroad. There was a substantial revival of interest in the Russian past beginning in the 1960s. Some of its manifestations were officially permitted or even encouraged; others were banned and punished.

II

What Solzhenitsyn knows of such developments, above summarized in simplified form, is not clear from his published work. But they are antecedents of his (and of his fellow contributors to *From Under the Rubble*), whether he knows it or not. Father Alexander Schmemann's analysis of him as a Christian writer evoked from Solzhenitsyn the response, puzzling or even ridiculous to a certain sort of critic: "You have explained me to myself." But there was every reason for him to react in such a manner; his formal education could not have touched on the essentials of a Christian outlook or many other features of the Russian cultural tradition; nevertheless, in the discourse, the prose and poetry, and the life of the Russian people much of it survived. In *1984*, Orwell depicts the survival of the ditty "Oranges and Lemons" even though everyone has forgotten what it means. Russians are in a far more enviable condition in such respects, but the principle is similar. Solzhenitsyn may indeed need to have elements and aspects of the tradition to which he belongs described and explained. And there is every reason why Western students of Russia should be able to do what few if any Soviets (whether pro-Communist or not) are capable of doing by way of giving an account of that tradition.

It may be worth pausing a moment to grasp what Soviet scholars have *not* done, could not do, but under another sort of government would certainly have done in the half century during which only foreigners could study the Russian tradition in all its fullness and objectivity. During those years some books, serials, and manuscripts were destroyed in Russia. Some (how many?) have been preserved but their use denied to many scholars. In what attics, monastery libraries, or other dusty corners of the USSR may not quantities of precious sources—and art objects—still survive? In China in 1980 one will hear mention of the "ten lost years" from 1966 to 1976—lost in terms of the closure of educational institutions and the suspension of almost all intellectual and artistic labors. In Russia educational institutions never closed in any remotely comparable manner; nevertheless, the black-out on fundamental aspects of the national tradition has lasted over fifty years. The clergy themselves have been forced to connive in the black-out. Western scholars, reared in a tradition wherein religion played a less prominent role[8] (though some omissions scarcely forgivable on such grounds might be mentioned, Westerners have at least made their choices of topics for study freely), have rarely pointed to the magnitude of the great blank space in contemporary understanding of the Russian past.

Two methods of tracing the antecedents of Solzhenitsyn may be used. One is to study his published works in chronological sequence, the other is to study his spiritual journey year by year. It might seem that the latter is the only defensible way. However, the story of his influence and the reception of his writings and ideas depends on the former, both in the USSR and abroad. He could not and did not tell us all about his own path of discovery in the course of publishing his books. Partly the reason may have been danger—if not of bodily harm or confinement, of loss of the chance to continue publishing, or peril to others who had played a part. Partly, without doubt, his attention was less on himself than on his work, his success in literary creation, in conveying his message. (The word "message" will trouble some critics, but it is the right one, if understood as a term covering not merely a given philosophical or moral proposition or several propositions but also, or rather, a way of looking at reality and human life.)

To begin with, then, the novels give us only scattered hints of indebtedness. An especially interesting one appears in *August 1914*, published in 1971. (It was also the year in which Solzhenitsyn made his Christianity public, as discussed below.) The lines refer to "Sania Lazhenitsyn," and one may easily deduce that his own father is meant, Isaakii Solzhenitsyn; but his own father died a few months before he was born, and it is doubtful that he was able to discover what Isaakii had read as a young man. More probably what is at issue is ancestry not of blood but of ideas. Here is the passage.

He regarded himself as a Tolstoyan. But then he was given Lavrov and Mikhailovskii to read and—how true they seemed to be. Then he read Plekhanov, and there was the truth again—and so beautifully consistent. Kropotkin also went straight to his heart and was no less true. But when he came to read *Vekhi*, he shuddered—it was the complete reverse of all he had read before, yet true, piercingly true![9]

Exegesis of such a passage may verge on the hazardous. Was there a period when Solzhenitsyn regarded himself as a follower of Tolstoi's ideas? *August 1914* has occasioned a temptation to comparison with *War and Peace* in the minds of everyone who has opened its pages. It also deals with a war crucial to Russian history in which the central character(s) is or are witness to decisive events, and in both cases the author deals with the last major Russian war previous to the one in which he himself fought. But it soon becomes clear to any serious reader that *August 1914* is, if anything, an anti-*War and Peace*, a repudiation of Tolstoi's entire conception of history, a depiction of events in which individuals made a difference—despite the deeply rooted causes of Russian military failure, at least in the first great battles of World War I, causes which Solzhenitsyn does not gloss over. However, the casting of the first volume of what was conceived as a great cycle in the form of a challenge to Tolstoi may suggest that Solzhenitsyn once lay under his spell—not only of his superb style and literary craftsmanship, but of his ideas.

Lavrov and Mikhailovskii were non-Marxian socialists, Plekhanov a Marxist, Kropotkin an anarchist; they all were heroes of the intelligentsia and revolutionaries in one way or other. *Vekhi* was the "complete reverse" of what they wrote, in the sense that the essays questioned the governing assumptions of the four individuals mentioned and, moreover, of fifty years and more of Russian radicalism. "Complete reverse" plainly did not mean coming to love Nicholas II and his regime; it meant a sharp challenge to the conviction that getting rid of them overnight would necessarily inaugurate the millennium or at any rate a new era of freedom and prosperity, and to the assumptions of historical sociology and philosophical materialism which held that a set of bad institutions need only be swept away without a need to try to change man's level of spiritual culture and inner psychological make-up. (It may as well be noted here that nothing was as well calculated to infuriate people who held such views as to have it asserted, on the morrow of the Revolution, that in this respect *Vekhi* had been proven right.) Lazhenitsyn is not said to have come to believe that the writings of the four radicals were false instead of true. What the passage says is that *Vekhi* came to supersede them with the "piercingly true" analysis it contained.

Probably only Russianists paused over the passage just discussed or bothered to try to find out what it meant. But in *From Under the Rubble* that was impossible. One either came to grips with *Vekhi* or did not understand the book. *Vekhi* is Solzhenitsyn's point of departure and the basis for his crucial essay, "The Smatterers." (The term is the translators'; the original is *obrazovanshchina*, a neologism which combines with the usual word for "education," *obrazovanie*, the suffix *-shchina*, often rendered as "the wicked deeds of" whatever precedes it. The word "dilettantes" would probably improve on "smatterers" but still may lack the element of moral opprobrium present in the original.)

The essay begins with a comparison of the evaluation of the intelligentsia found in *Vekhi* with Solzhenitsyn's own, reminding the reader that 65 years have elapsed. There are four headings. The first, "faults of the old intelligentsia," includes sectarian clannishness, consistent opposition to the state, subordination of truth to the presumed welfare of the masses, passionate atheism, faith in science and human omnipotence. Most of these are said to have passed away, sometimes to have been replaced by exactly opposite qualities—some of which the author treats ambiguously. The second, "virtues of the pre-revolutionary intelligentsia," Solzhenitsyn admits was not so labeled by the authors of *Vekhi*, but he does not hesitate to list as such: search for a world view and for faith (though not a religious one), a wish to serve that faith at the sacrifice of self. These qualities are said to have been mainly reversed, and here Solzhenitsyn regards the reversal as calamitous. Third is the category "faults at the time" which now appear almost as virtues: readiness to submerge individual needs to seek universal equality, readiness for suffering and martyrdom, dedication to struggle to destroy society in its existing form. (Obviously the second and third headings are related and overlap somewhat.) Fourth come "faults inherited in the present day"— though Solzhenitsyn has just said that some of the faults-that-appear-virtues are also inherited. These include lack of serious interest in the history of Russia or history as a reality, preference for abstractions, spiritual arrogance. It is noteworthy that he ends by throwing a "dash" of Dostoevskii into this category: faintheartedness and a

tendency to jump to pessimistic conclusions. Thus he links Dostoevskii with *Vekhi* in his own intellectual pedigree.

But the old intelligentsia has passed away and has been replaced
by another. The latter is easy to define; it means in the USSR today
simply anyone who has passed beyond the seventh grade in school-
ing. It is this group as a whole to which Solzhenitsyn specifically
applies the title term of his essay. But he retains the old definition
of the old intelligentsia as a "new, religionless, humanist order"—
some said, a quasi-monastic order—from which Dostoevskii, Tolstoi
(in part), Vladimir Solov'ev, and other great thinkers were excluded,
he thinks justifiably. All this is then used as a springboard to challenge the writers of a series of rather ephemeral articles which present rather insipid and unconvincing—even to themselves—programs for the resuscitation of a real intelligentsia out of the mass of
dilettantes, self-serving, prudent, explaining that their children's
welfare does not permit them to speak the truth or protest. Some of
them declare that the situation is so bad that even the "people,"
that is, the Russian peasantry, is dead or moribund, with only a dim
memory of its own former traditions and virtues. Solzhenitsyn views
all this realistically, and admits truth in the bleak portrayal of his
countrymen in the essays he quotes. But he retorts: "the masses, the
smatterers—they all consist of *human beings*, and there is no way in
which the future can be closed to human beings…it is never too late
to take a turn for the good and the better" (p. 29). And his modest
proposal (genuinely modest, unlike Swift's) is: do not lie. To the
Westerner, at least one not familiar with Soviet society, it is almost
beyond comprehension that such a restrained precept could if followed destroy careers in large numbers and shake a whole system.

Much of Solzhenitsyn's comparison of the old and new intel-
ligentsias in Russia, to be sure, requires for fairness a comparison
of the old and new systems—the government of Nicholas II with the
government of Brezhnev, tsars with commissars. (He has elsewhere
made some remarks on that subject, but he does not in *From Under
the Rubble*.) Passionate atheism in a state headed by a Christian
monarch has quite different causes and effects from the same thing
in a Communist state. Spiritual arrogance is apt to be roughed up by
an October Revolution. Who is ready for martyrdom when millions
are being done to death under Stalin for no offense at all, when even
their own families would never know when or where or even whether
they were martyred? Remember the anecdote in which the Soviet

guard asks a prisoner for what crime he is serving twenty-five years; the reply is, "for nothing"; the guard retorts, "nonsense; for nothing you get only ten years." The Soviet state is bound to yield responses different from those produced by the relative freedom of the later Romanovs.

Certain themes of *Vekhi* are not repeated in *From Under the Rubble*, and certain details are different in an interesting way. In his essay, "The Intelligentsia and Revolution," Petr Struve examines the question—perennially fascinating to educated Russians, as Solzhenitsyn notes—of the definition of "intelligentsia." But he excludes Novikov, Radishchev, and Chaadaev, "people verily enraptured by God," as well as the great writers Solzhenitsyn excludes, and then comments perceptively on Herzen, whom Solzhenitsyn does not mention, declaring that though Herzen "sometimes wears the uniform" of the *intelligent* he is "actually a different spiritual type" for all his socialism and atheism. Back of the mid-nineteenth century Solzhenitsyn is not prepared to go; but then Struve does not go back of the late eighteenth century, when writing 65 years earlier. Neither one wishes to unscramble all of Russian cultural history, or indeed even to make a pass at doing so. Moreover, neither one wishes to plumb the question of where the intelligentsia came from—to trace its social links with the village clergy, the intellectual links with the early nineteenth-century seminaries, in which German Protestant influences prepared the way for a reception of Kant and his philosophical successors which antedated their introduction into the universities, which in turn was appropriately accomplished by seminarians who became professors. This is not to demand what would be unreasonable of Struve or Solzhenitsyn. Neither was writing a scholarly cultural history; both were writing in a tradition of publicistics intended to convince or at any rate offer persuasive assertions for discussion; both had much to say that was plausible as far as it went.

Themes of *Vekhi* absent in *From Under the Rubble* include the passionate plea for legal consciousness made by Kistiakovskii, which could be offered in the knowledge that a beginning had been made in developing just such ideas; he writes that *Pravo*, the only weekly devoted to the improvement of formal law, is "only ten years old." In the USSR no expression of that aim as such is even possible today, for it would be regarded as bourgeois rubbish. Izgoev's remarkable critique of Russia's students is scarcely applicable. To be sure, it begins with a brief account of a Russian revolutionary and atheist family in Paris whose son becomes a Christian convert, which if its locale were transferred to *Moscow* would have much pertinence today. But it goes on to argue that the intelligentsia have no family in the proper sense, offers then shocking (not today!) details about the sexual promiscuity among their children; he declares that Russian students do very little reading and seldom take notes at lectures, that they make revolutionary atheism into a compulsory orthodoxy, deviation from which is punished by ostracism and boycott of both fellow students and professors, steal and cheat, but justify their own actions by commitment to an "ideal." Perhaps an overlapping indictment of present-day Soviet students could be mounted, but it sounds much more like a list of charges made against American students of the 1960s.

The first three essays in *Vekhi*, however, are very close in spirit to *From Under the Rubble*. The first two are by Christians. They are Berdiaev's "Philosophic Truth and the Moral Truth of the Intelligentsia," which uses the neologism *intelligentshchina*, comparable to Solzhenitsyn's *obrazovanshchina*; and Bulgakov's "Heroism and Asceticism: Reflections on the Religious Nature of the Russian Intelligentsia," which carries further thoughts he expressed in a previous essay on "The Intelligentsia and Religion" and concludes by finding among the *intelligenty* both a bad, indeed demonic side and a positive one in a "higher religious potential. . . [an] intense search for the City of God." The third is Gerzhenzon's "Creative Self-Cognition," a non-Christian's critique of the alienation from the people on the part of the intelligentsia similar to that to be found in Berdiaev and Bulgakov—and in Solzhenitsyn's "The Smatterers."

In *From Under the Rubble* are to be found topics which could not yet be discussed in 1909. No socialist state existed. In 1974 Communism had ruled for over fifty years in Russia, twenty-five years in China's central government, about that in Eastern Europe. Against that background Shafarevich indicts socialism from the time of Sargon of Akkad through the empire of the Incas to Babeuf to Nazism and Soviet Communism. (The question of whether the despotism of the Orient and modern Communism are fundamentally similar need not be explored here; Shafarevich thinks they are, and makes a case—though one really based not on institutional analysis but certain common features and practices.) Mikhail Agurskii compares totalitarianism—especially Soviet—and Western democracies, and sketches some features of what he sees, and hopes for, as the future society.

Shafarevich returns to analyze the question of nationalities in the USSR—a theme absent from *Vekhi*, which confined its attention to the Russian tradition. He repudiates nationalism of any kind, points out how Russians have suffered as minority nationalities have from Soviet rule, and proposes reconciliation of the ethnic groups concerned. The same question is addressed in another essay of Solzhenitsyn's, "Repentance and Self-Limitation in the Life of Nations." It contains a remarkable passage in which Aleksandr Isaevich plunges into the midst of one of the most bitter, if not the very bitterest, ethnic antagonisms which affect Russians, that between them and the Poles; he catalogues the crimes of each against the other, and declares that only "mutual repentance" (confessing that he "writes for posterity" and expects nothing of the sort very soon) can heal the wounds. His central message here is that Russia needs to "withdraw into itself for a time" to heal its soul, educate its children, put its own house in order. Nothing comparable to these essays appears in *Vekhi;* decades of bitter experience have made nationalism and socialism pressing issues in a new form. As the authors of *From Under the Rubble* see it, the two "-isms" have caused infinite suffering to Russians and to the minority peoples of the USSR, not to mention the rest of the world.

The remedy? In a series of four essays, "A.B." (a pseudonym), F. Korsakov, Evgenii Barabanov, and Vadim Borisov offer a Christian perspective. "A.B." invokes Bulgakov's and Frank's essays in *Vekhi* as predecessors of his in arguing that only "heroic spiritual striving" can lead man and society to freedom. But Frank does not mention Christianity, but only "religious humanism," whereas the thrust of Bulgakov's essay is a tracing of the intelligentsia's Christian origins, by action and reaction, and though he adds a call for a return to Christian belief he points to no hopeful signs of such a development. In the later volume, however, "A.B." asserts that there is a "rebirth" of Christianity in Russia despite the "general decline in faith and religious feeling" in the "rest of the world."

Korsakov declares that *Vekhi*[10] "exhausted the subject" of the ills of the intelligentsia. He takes up the question of the church—the Russian Orthodox Church specifically—but assumes rather more than argues its divine mission and the obligation of the Christian to take part in it, and the apocalypticism of Father Pavel Florenskii hovers over the entire piece. Barabanov, despite some dubious discussion of the ecclesiastical history of Byzantium and Russia—again, how could he have learned better?—summons the Orthodox Church to transform the world; he is to be sure thinking in long-range terms and does not discount the difficulties. Borisov discusses the individual and the nation within the Christian framework, terming both "universalism" and "nationalism" "atheist ideologies" of significance both to world history and to the history of Russia. "Nationalism," writes Borisov, "must not be identified with national feeling...the latter is its tool, no more"; nationalism yields "the doctrine of [the] superiority [of a given nation or ethnic group] to all others," and typically ends in a "cult of force" for one's own state. In contrast, Christianity "regards mankind as single in nature, but plural in personality, with every personality [that is, both individual and national] having an absolute value."

The final essay in *From Under the Rubble* is Shafarevich's: "Does Russia Have a Future?" The title is taken from, or provoked by, Amal'rik's *Will the Soviet Union Survive Until 1984?* Amal'rik's answer is pessimistic, ultimately negative; Russia has no future. Shafarevich declares that resurrection is possible; that Russia "has passed through death and may hear the voice of God." It is not certain, but in his view it is possible, and the essay and indeed the whole book are a call for that resurrection. Shafarevich writes, "God makes history through men," and he is asking for human action.

Solzhenitsyn is one man, and he has his personal characteristics and peculiarities, as a writer and thinker. But he is more; he clearly belongs to a group of like-minded contemporaries, doubtless more numerous than those ready or willing to contribute to such a symposium as *From Under the Rubble*, under their own names or pseudonyms, probably to be found scattered in several Russian cities and towns. Finally, he and his group belong to a tradition. The tradition concerned is the one which honors and values old Russian culture and the history of Russia. (If the group does not sufficiently clearly distinguish between the oppressive institutions of Muscovy and the Empire on the one hand and the culture on the other, that need not detain us here.) It stands as the end of the line of persons and groups who challenged the received wisdom of the 1820s (and earlier and later), namely, that Russia's hope lay in ceasing to be Russian and becoming Western.

The challengers were chiefly the Slavophiles, Dostoevskii, Solov'ev, and several different groups of the Silver Age, whose spokesmen in thought were the authors of *Vekhi* and *Iz glubiny*. In Dostoevskii but even more explicitly in the later writers concerned, assertion of Russian national feeling was made not in opposition to Western themes but alongside and in tandem with them. Not universalism—which eliminates all categories between the individual and mankind itself—and not nationalism—which claims superiority for one's own nation, but Christian *agape* among all men, with due attention to their real and valid associations in family, fellow-workers, nation, and state; that is the message of *From Under the Rubble*, in which Solzhenitsyn plays the leading role. "From under the rubble" will come not necessarily—or rather simply not—any earthly paradise, but renewal and hope for Russia. In contrast to what? Destruction, as predicted by the Westernizer Amal'rik. Why? Because of vital strength within the Russian people of today, their inheritance from yesterday. Not just the "Left Leninist-Communists" and "Left Westernizers" postulated by Andrei Sakharov's essay of 1968 (which is the point of departure of whole book *From Under the Rubble*) as the only hopeful elements in Russian society, but the Matrenas and the Vorotyntsevs and the Nerzhins, the decent men and women, with all their weaknesses, perhaps without any ideology at all. Strength within the present as contrasted to what? Zero, as depicted by the early Westernizer Chaadaev; as, some would say, Peter the Great assumed to be the case from the way he treated his people in practice.

III

Solzhenitsyn, like his great brother dissident, Sakharov, was first a Marxist. In some ways the parallel of the two pairs, Solzhenitsyn and Sakharov with Khomiakov and Herzen, may be tempting, though one should never expect such parallels to be complete and across more than a century the comparison is obviously not without its defects. Khomiakov did not perceive how rapidly national feeling could be converted into nationalism or how brutal and un-Christian the conversion could be. Herzen may or may not have said, "some day Genghis Khan will return with the telegraph," but he certainly did say, "Communism will sweep across the world in a violent tempest—dreadful, bloody, unjust, swift"; nevertheless, he did not resolve the problem of how to retain his assumptions and yet avoid

the tempest. Solzhenitsyn and Sakharov had much bitter experience
to draw upon that men of the 1840s did not have. Closer to our time
was the intellectual pilgrimage of the authors of *Vekhi*; most of them
began as Marxists.

One may read several of Solzhenitsyn's works and suspect that
he was never a serious Marxist. Knowing at least in a vague way that
the whole Soviet educational system is based on Marxism, many
Westerners—even specialists on the USSR—may be misled into
dismissing the consequences of that fact, especially because "no one
believes it any more," as some Soviet émigrés may put it in an assertion American pragmatists are all too ready to credit. It is true that
we do not have an autobiography (not that such an account is ever
a full and final story of a life); *The Oak and the Calf* tells only the story
of Solzhenitsyn's relations with the Soviet literary authorities beginning, after an introduction of few pages, with 1961. We may or may
not ever have a full account of when and how he moved from Marxism
to Christianity. But it may be the most interesting question of all
regarding his intellectual and spiritual development.

But in *The Gulag Archipelago*, that remarkable work of his, unlike
anything else he or others have written, some hints are to be found.[11]
He tells us that at an early stage of his sentence, in prison in 1945, he
was still siding with Marxists in the kind of argument that is endemic
among Europeans and especially Russians. There he encountered an
old revolutionary named Fastenko who had known Lenin and therefore was to be taken with especial seriousness; Fastenko told him to
question *everything* (*Gulag* I, 190-196). Obviously that injunction
remained at the back of his mind, doing its work over a period of time.
In 1946 an Orthodox clergyman named Divnich who had spent much
time in Europe condemned Marxism, "declaring that no one in
Europe had taken it seriously for a long while—and I [Solzhenitsyn]
defended it, because after all I was a Marxist" (I, 602). A certain
young man named Boris Gammerov asked him why he ridiculed a
public prayer of the late Franklin D. Roosevelt's as hypocritical.
"Why do you not admit the possibility that a political leader might
sincerely believe in God?" asked Gammerov (I, 611-614). Solzhenitsyn evidently then was forced to consider just that possibility, and
put the direct question to Gammerov, did he believe in God? The
reply was affirmative. Later Gammerov talked to him about the ideas
of Vladimir Solov'ev, whose works he had never read (II, 194). Finally, he acknowledged the influence of Boris Kornfeld, a convert from

Judaism to Christianity, who on his deathbed taught Solzhenitsyn that not material prosperity but "the development of the soul" constituted the purpose of life (II, 612-613). And he wrote a poem tracing his pilgrimage from childhood religious upbringing to rejection of religion to his return:

> God of the Universe! I believe again!
> Though I renounced You, You were with me! (II, 615)

Western correspondents have had ample opportunity to ask him about his intellectual and spiritual evolution; few have even tried. Georges Suffert, editor of *Le Point* (Paris), a far from sympathetic interlocutor, put to him a few disjointed questions on the subject in an interview published in *Encounter* (April 1976). Solzhenitsyn told Suffert that he was attracted to Marxism by its "aspirations to justice" (though the choice of words was the interviewer's), declared that he would have returned to Christianity with or without the experience of the camps, and reported that the "ideology [of Communism] disappears completely" and is stripped bare by camp life; "first comes the fight for survival, then the discovery of life, then God." In response to a quite unprovoked question about whether Solzhenitsyn wanted a world war, he declared that only Suffert's "cock-eyed" conception of history could have prompted such a question and that "inner purpose is more important than politics" of any kind. Evidently nothing has annoyed Solzhenitsyn more than Western journalists' efforts to locate him somewhere on a left-right political spectrum.

Ericson points out that Solzhenitsyn made his Christianity public only in 1972 in his open letter to Patriarch Pimen of the Russian Orthodox Church, apparently composed shortly after he joined the church (or rejoined it).[12] This was followed next year by his open letter to Soviet leaders, which, Ericson contends, "did more damage to Solzhenitsyn's reputation in the West than did all the rest of his writings put together." He was called a "nationalist," "elitist," a "not-very-thinly disguised Tsarist," a "political romantic," and much else. It would be tempting to assemble parallel passages from the torrent of hostile criticism that greeted *Vekhi* in 1909 and from the attacks on Solzhenitsyn in 1973. One might conclude that there could have been no Russian Revolution and no half-century of Soviet rule in Russia in the meantime, and that Western liberals refused to learn anything from those events. (It is amusing to note that when environmentalists or an aspiring Californian politician declare that industrial cities have their drawbacks, that is progressive, whereas when Solzhenitsyn says so that is reactionary.) But only one retort—private and not public—of his need be quoted here. He bitterly attacked the *New York Times* to Olga Carlisle for accusing him of nationalism "when, on the contrary, I want Russia to return all her acquired dominions, such as the Ukraine and Estonia, to their people. They [the *Times*] don't know what they are talking about!"[13]

Solzhenitsyn suggests that Russia was less ready for democracy in 1973 than it was in 1917. No serious historian could easily disagree with that contention. In 1917 Russia had several decades of experience with a respectable system of courts and local self-government, and for twelve years had had a more freely elected parliament than any since then. In 1973 nothing of the sort was preserved in the living memory of any Russian. But we must add that in 1973, the Russian intelligentsia was more definitely cut off from its own tradition, by dint of Soviet education for those in the USSR, of isolation from Russian life for those abroad, or some combination of both, than it was in 1917—or 1909, when *Vekhi* was published. Solzhenitsyn and his fellow contributors to *From Under the Rubble* inveigh with reason against those who have distorted and stifled the Russian tradition, for they themselves, along with other Russians, suffer from the consequences. Their knowledge and perspective regarding Russian history may not be unexceptionable, their own temptation to distort in the process of correcting distortions may be difficult to avoid. Instead of gentle, sympathetic efforts to assist them in their noble task, the West has responded with suspicious reprimands. Among the milder examples was Rosalynn Carter's advice to Solzhenitsyn, after the Harvard commencement speech, that he contemplate Boy Scouts helping old people to cross the street, a remark her husband may well have had the chance to veto if he wished. Anyone who had been subjected to serious intellectual discipline of any kind might have been tempted to react to all this by loud laughter. What might Boris Gammerov have said?

The final point to make is that Struve and the other authors of *Vekhi* have something in common with Solzhenitsyn and his friends who wrote *From Under the Rubble* that needs emphasis. In both cases most of the writers concerned had a prolonged and intensive exposure to Marxism, and underwent an intellectual and spiritual migration to Christianity. The *vekhovtsy* had been the foremost thinkers of Russian Marxism in their time (Bolshevik hagiography to the contrary; the West should not allow the story of Russian Marxism to be corrupted any more than the story of Russian Christianity). Solzhenitsyn and his friends could not claim such title in their own day—but perhaps no others could either; the days when the Bukharins and the Riazanovs could still use Marxism as an instrument for analysis rather than merely as a stick to beat enemies or critics of the state were long past. And yet it bears remembering that Solzhenitsyn, in the early stages of his incarceration at the hands of the Stalin regime, remained a Marxist. Certainly there were many, many like him in that respect; and despite his sweeping statement that camp life dissolved Communist beliefs, some kept their Marxism through years of imprisonment or exile to the time when they were released.

In one sense Russian intellectuals today—those who would earnestly avoid being dilettantes, at any rate—are philosophically back in the early 1900s. They have passed through Marxism, retaining its determination to ask fundamental questions and to study systematically and thoroughly the story of mankind, as well as its passion to communicate knowledge and truth to all people, including the humblest and most deprived. Several, at least, have returned to Christianity, endeavoring to combine its everlasting truths with understanding of human events, notably including those cataclysms of the twentieth century in Russia which have affected to some degree the whole human race. They may not have done so with complete success, and perhaps there are even some areas of failure. But their conviction is, with Christ, that the truth shall make men free, and they labor in a vineyard as old as Hilarion of Kiev, who discussed "law and grace," the message of both Testaments, in the eleventh century.

Notes

1. Alexander Solzhenitsyn and others, *From Under the Rubble*, trans. by five persons under the direction of Michael Scammell (Boston, Toronto: Little, Brown and Company, 1974).

2. *Vekhi* has been translated into English twice, first in six installments in *Canadian Slavic Studies*, 1968-71, second in book form as *Landmarks* (New York: Karz Howard, 1977). Hayward's introduction accurately states that *Iz glubiny* was "printed" in 1918 but does not mention that it was not released until 1921, and then in very few copies. A "second edition" with new introductions was published by the YMCA-Press, Paris, 1967.

3. A possible source of confusion in this intellectual genealogy is *Smena Vekh* [*Change of Landmarks*, 1921], any connection with which Solzhenitsyn disavows in this essay, declaring that the title of *Vekhi* was in that volume "exploited by another group of writers with narrowly political interests and low standards." None of the authors of the essays in *Vekhi* in fact contributed to *Smena Vekh*. The *smenovekhovtsy* were arguing the need to accept the Bolshevik regime. In the present-day United States they might have been sued for violation of copyright.

4. In *The West in Russia and China*, 2 vols. (New York: Cambridge University Press, 1973), I used the term "syncretism" for this type of combination of an attempt to recover the indigenous cultural tradition with acceptance of the West in relation to both Russia and China. Some friendly reviewers took exception to the term, perhaps because it has been used to refer to mindless eclecticism and specifically the combination of dubiously compatible elements of different religions—in a word, to intellectual or religious hash of a low order. I take the point, but know of no better term without venturing into the realm of grotesque neologism. Few others have adopted the *term*, which is the affair of those concerned; lamentable, however, is the fact that no others I know have discussed the *phenomenon*. Evidently the categories of "nationalism" and "internationalism" have become so popular that persons and groups who exhibit traits of both together, or of neither one, cannot expect fair treatment or understanding.

5. I have an essay awaiting publication on the subject, but the unresolved problems of the volume concerned make it unwise to offer a citation.

6. Wayne Dowler in his article, "Echoes of *Pochvennichestvo* in Solzhenitsyn's *August 1914*," in *Slavic Review*, vol. 34 (March 1975), pp. 109-122, studies this influence, and may attribute too much to it, but has useful things to say.

7. Mandel'shtam and Pasternak were converted Jews. Despite the popular and often official anti-Semitism of the later Imperial period (before Catherine II there were almost no Jews and little anti-Semitism in Russia), Jews—converts to Christianity, adherents of Judaism, or simply non-religious persons—make a substantial contribution to all cultural currents, from revolutionary to anti-revolutionary ones.

8. It is worth a reminder that in the Western Middle Ages scarcely a single contributor to cultural life is to be found who was not a clergyman, as distinguished from Byzantium, in which laymen played significant roles, but Westerners may not always make allowances for cultures in which religion lasted longer. And it is noteworthy that in this respect, at least, Russia was more like the West than like Byzantium.

9. A. Solzhenitsyn, *Avgust chetyrnadtsatogo*, 2nd ed. (Paris: YMCA-Press, 1971), p. 25. See the comment on this passage by Gleb Struve, "Behind the Front Lines: On Some Neglected Chapters in *August 1914*" in John B. Dunlop, et al., eds., *Aleksandr Solzhenitsyn: Critical Essays and Documentary Materials*, 2nd ed. (New York: Collier Books, 1975), pp. 442-444. As the son of the chief figure behind all three symposia earlier referred to, Petr Struve, he is especially alert to the issue of parentage of various kinds—not to imply any less sensitivity on his part to other

issues in cultural history—and specifically to a parentage of ideas to Petr Struve which he shared with Solzhenitsyn.

10. The translator renders the title as "the journal *Vekhi*"—of course it was not a journal but a single symposium, and Korsakov makes no such mistake, which would prove he had not read it.

11. Edward E. Ericson in *Solzhenitsyn: The Moral Vision* (Grand Rapids, Michigan: Wm. E. Eerdmans Publishing Company, published in late 1980) has identified some crucial passages relating to the issue. The three volumes of the English translation of *Gulag* were published by Harper and Row, New York, in 1973, 1975, and 1978.

12. *Ibid.*, p. 181.

13. Olga Carlisle, *Solzhenitsyn and the Secret Circle* (New York: Holt, Rinehart and Winston, 1978), p. 198.

Continuities in Solzhenitsyn's Ethical Thought

DAVID M. HALPERIN

When Aleksandr Solzhenitsyn made his involuntary journey to the West in the early part of 1974, his admirers on the leftward side of the political spectrum in Europe and America found themselves embarrassed and discredited by his first public utterances.[1] The banished writer proved on closer acquaintance to be anything but a *sympathisant* of those who had claimed him as a champion of parliamentary democracy or a spokesman for Western liberal ideas—much less a Leninist critic of the Soviet Union's bourgeois compromises and Stalinist deviations. Even more scandalous than Solzhenitsyn's manifest Slavophile tendencies were his deeply held religious convictions, at which many in the West professed themselves appalled. And yet, Solzhenitsyn's religious ardor was hardly the result of a sudden spiritual awakening prompted by the experience of exile. Quite the contrary: in Part IV of *The Gulag Archipelago* Solzhenitsyn recalls that his conversion, already some time in preparation, took place while he was recovering from surgery during his seventh year of imprisonment (in 1952) and he cites a poem composed at that moment which concludes with an invocation of God and a confession of faith.[2] The religious dimension of Solzhenitsyn's artistic personality had been apparent to perceptive critics from the tenor of his earliest published writings, as Hélène Zamoyska's 1963 essay on *One Day in the Life of Ivan Denisovich*, "Matrena's Home," and "Incident at Krechetovka Station" illustrates.[3] Solzhenitsyn merely revealed upon arrival in the West—more fully, to be sure—the attitudes and beliefs which had already enlivened his previous work. They need not have occasioned astonishment.

In fact, Solzhenitsyn's readership in the Soviet Union and abroad had been gradually apprised of the writer's authentic personal philosophy, even before his forcible expatriation, by the dissemination of *August 1914* and "A Lenten Letter to Pimen, Patriarch of All

Russia." "I was received with 'hurrahs,'" Solzhenitsyn recalls in his memoir of this period, "as long as I appeared to be against Stalinist abuses only (...). In my first works I was concealing my features from the police censorship—but, by the same token, from the public at large. With each subsequent step I inevitably revealed more and more of myself: the time had come to speak more precisely, to go even deeper."[4] Although it has not passed without challenge in the scholarly literature,[5] Solzhenitsyn's claim to have preserved throughout his development a consistent point of view both as a writer and as a private individual can be borne out, I believe, by an examination of his work. In that large oeuvre, certain recurring clusters of themes and images, uniting Solzhenitsyn's ideology with his artistic intuition, argue a sustained continuity of thought and feeling. The following paragraphs propose to identify the major conceptual and figurative elements, common to the early novels and to *Gulag* alike, that support the edifice of Solzhenitsyn's intellectual "system" and serve to express his moral outlook. It will be shown that Solzhenitsyn's position on matters of ethics has remained essentially unchanged throughout his literary career.

About one quarter of the way through *The First Circle*,[6] Anton Nikolaevich Iakonov (an engineer who is the scientific director of the Mavrino technical institute-prison) is threatened and humiliated by Minister of State Security Abakumov. Confronted with the prospect of demotion and arrest, Iakonov embarks on a long nocturnal stroll which turns out to be a kind of interior journey into the past: Iakonov reviews the events of his life which have led, in some sense or other, to his present predicament. Chief among these is the failure of his romance with Agniia, a former fiancée, who seems to represent all the values Iakonov has abandoned in the course of his long climb to prosperity. Agniia is one of Solzhenitsyn's "astral" women, whose feet barely touch the ground;[7] she is frail—almost lifeless—and animated only by a passionate spirituality. Even her name suggests "chaste," "pure," "holy," derived as it appears to be from the Greek *hagnos* or *hagios*. She appeals to Iakonov with the redemptive feminine attraction exercised by Dostoevskii's meek heroines. Agniia even manages to "inspire" Iakonov, already in youth a convinced cynic and hedonist, to belittle the physical component in human relations. In response to her fears of sex, "Iakonov answered excitedly [*s voodushevleniem*], 'But that's not the main thing at all! Not at all! It's only something that goes along with our spiritual union'"

(XXIII, 149). Iakonov's uncharacteristic enthusiasm for spirituality has its effect: Agniia's lips respond "weakly" to his for the first time and she makes a tentative confession of love. Iakonov's willingness to subordinate material to spiritual desires transforms his own perceptions as well; it enables him to understand for the first time the ecstasy of the anonymous Orthodox hymnographer who wrote a long litany in praise of the Mother of God for the Feast of her Nativity and who had been moved, Iakonov senses, "not by a man's passing lust for a woman's body but by that higher rapture a woman can draw from us" (XXIII, 154).

But Iakonov is not equal to such a rarified form of romance; he is too deeply attached to his physical nature. Agniia provokes in him a crisis of desire. He had always been attracted to her by "something other than her body," and in order to remain interested in her he must pretend to himself that the attraction he feels also has an erotic dimension which will grow (XXIII, 149). His self-delusion becomes evident to him during a discussion with Agniia about the Soviet persecution of the Orthodox Church. Iakonov remarks:

> "You've been attracted to the church because it sanctifies your indifference to life. Be careful.[8] Once and for all you must wake up and force yourself to be interested in something—if only in the life process itself."
>
> Agniia hung her head, and her hand, wearing Iakonov's gold ring, drooped listlessly. Her childlike body seemed bony and terribly thin.
>
> "Yes, yes," she acknowledged in a sinking voice. "I fully realize that it's sometimes very hard for me to live—I don't want to at all. The world doesn't need people like me..."
>
> He felt himself breaking up inside. She was doing everything to kill her attraction for him! The courage to carry out his promise and marry Agniia was weakening.
>
> She glanced up at him with a look of curiosity, unsmiling.
>
> "She *is* plain," Iakonov thought.
>
> "Surely fame and success await you, and lasting prosperity," she said sadly. "But will you be *happy*, Anton?... Be careful yourself. By interesting ourselves in the *process* of life, we lose...we lose... But how can I tell you?..." (XXIII, 153-154)

Agniia implies that the "life process" or "process of living" (*protsess zhizni*) excludes something equally significant and valuable. Iakonov laments Agniia's indifference to life and urges her to "wake up" (*vstriakhnut'sia*), to leave off contemplation and lose herself in the emotional and material distractions of daily living. He fails to perceive, however, that it is her very detachment from the "life process" which makes possible the compensatory richness of her inner life as well as the precious insights issuing from it. In fact, Agniia's warning to Iakonov is borne out by events: many years later, in his anxiety over Abakumov's threats, Iakonov loses all interest in the "life process" itself and prefers to wander alone through the night rather than return to the comfort of his beloved family.

According to one account, Solzhenitsyn modelled the character of Anton Iakonov on that of Anton Vasil'ev, the actual head of the Marfino Institute (where Solzhenitsyn was imprisoned), who later died of cancer and requested in his will to be given a full religious burial by the Russian Orthodox Church, complete with prayers for the repose of his soul.[9] The tragedy of a spiritual decline arrested only in its latter stages, of a conscience stifled but at times still painfully active, is suggested by Solzhenitsyn's portrait of Iakonov—a portrait designed to illustrate the irreversible impact of specific moral choices on the course of an individual's subsequent development. As E. M. Forster once wrote, "It seems to me that here and there in life we meet with a person or incident that is symbolical. It's nothing in itself, yet for the moment it stands for some eternal principle.... But if we are frightened and reject it, the moment, so to speak, passes; the symbol is never offered again."[10] Agniia is symbolical for Iakonov in just this sense. Iakonov's crisis of desire—his alternating allegiance to nature and to spirit—dramatizes Solzhenitsyn's central ethical preoccupation. The tension Solzhenitsyn perceives between an unreflecting immersion in the process of daily life and a contemplative detachment which allows for the possibility of attaining to higher truths is basic to his thought and has continued to inform his writing.[11]

The polarities of natural life and spiritual knowledge are embodied symbolically in the two women with whom Oleg Kostoglotov, the protagonist of *Cancer Ward*, is in love. For Solzhenitsyn as for Dostoevskii, multiple attraction is a symptom of internal division, and Kostoglotov (no less than Myshkin, Stavrogin, or Dmitrii Karamazov) finds his personal conflicts externalized in his relations with women. Zoia appeals to everything in Kostoglotov that is passionately awaiting a return to the living of life, the life which his prison term and disease have prevented for so long. Her very name signifies life—it derives from the Greek word for life: *zoē*. She is fully aware of its meaning and explains it proudly to Kostoglotov, who associates the word (unflatteringly) with "zoo-" (XII, 168).[12] Zoia is countered by another "astral" woman, Vera Gangart. *Vera* means "faith" in Russian; indeed, Vera's attraction lies in her purity and constancy, as befits her astral nickname Vega (the name of a star important in navigation). Kostoglotov's experience thus recapitulates in greater detail Iakonov's crisis of desire and exemplifies the conflict "between 'irrefutable materialism' and spiritual values or ideal aspirations" which constitutes one of the novel's major themes.[13] Both Zoia and Vera are portrayed sympathetically, but Solzhenitsyn—reversing the priorities of Pasternak's great masterpiece—leaves us in no doubt as to which figure ranks higher in his own allegorical scheme: Life is only a nurse; Faith is a doctor.

Solzhenitsyn explicitly revealed the identity of the mutually exclusive alternatives open to man in a prose poem entitled "A Reflection in Water," which is reproduced here in its entirety.

> On the surface of swift-running water [*potok*] you cannot make out the reflections of objects near or distant. Even if it is not muddy, even if it is free of foam, reflections in the ceaselessly wavering ripples, the boisterously shifting race are deceptive, vague, incomprehensible.
>
> Only when, from stream to stream, the current [*potok*] has reached a placid estuary, or in still backwaters, or in small lakes with never a tremulous wave can we see in the mirror-smooth surface the smallest leaf of a tree on the bank, every fibre of a fine-combed cloud, and the intense blue depths of the sky.
>
> So it is with you and me. If, try as we may, we never have and never shall be able to see, to reflect the truth in all its eternal fresh-minted clarity, is it not simply because we are still in motion, still living?...[14]

At first this seems little more than a gloss on a famous passage of St. Paul: "For now we see through a glass, darkly; but then face to face: now I know in part; but then I shall know even as also I am known" (I *Cor.* 13:12). But for Solzhenitsyn it is not so much the mere fact of being alive that is a hindrance to knowledge as the condition of being in rapid motion—and such motion is an inevitable consequence of living in the modern world amid a welter of "back-firing motor-cycles, howling radiograms, crackling loudspeakers."[15] We must choose between moving and seeing.

Solzhenitsyn's dualism, as it emerges from the preceding passages, is epistemological rather than moral in emphasis. It is concerned less with the conditions of goodness than with the conditions of knowledge. Solzhenitsyn is not obsessed with purity; he would never argue that Dmitrii Sologdin in *The First Circle* is morally superior to Dr. Liudmila Dontsova in *Cancer Ward* simply because the former is a contemplative whereas the latter is immersed in the details of her daily life and professional duties. But Solzhenitsyn would claim that Sologdin has managed to achieve a number of moral insights which are denied Dontsova by the very nature of her busy routine. Solzhenitsyn's favored characters share a tendency to detach themselves from the "life process," or at least to welcome such detachment when it occurs.

In *The First Circle* Gleb Nerzhin seems to owe his moral penetration to an ingrained reluctance to participate in the "life process": "From his youth on, Gleb had dreaded more than anything else wallowing in daily living [*povsednevnaia zhizn'*]. As the proverb says: '*It's not the sea that drowns you, it's the puddle*'" (XXVII, 186). (Solzhenitsyn elsewhere applies this proverb directly to himself.)[16] The conflicting claims of living and knowing are brought to bear on Nerzhin when he is offered the possibility of earning an early release from prison by working on an arduous cryptography project: "Was he, then, to surrender to the tentacles of cryptography?... Fourteen hours a day, no time off even for breaks, his head crammed with theories of probability, theories of numbers, theories of error, a dead brain, a dried-out soul? What would he have left for contemplation? What would be left for learning about life?" Nerzhin reminds himself that the benefits of doing cryptography work include the material comforts of the special prison for intellectuals and the likelihood of avoiding a new term in the labor camps—perhaps the difference between surviving and perishing. He then asks himself, "But why live a whole life? Just to be living? Just to keep the body flourishing? Fine sort of flourishing! What do we need it for if there's nothing else?" (IX, 55). Nerzhin's decision appears to recapitulate a discovery Solzhenitsyn describes himself as having made in prison when he was offered a similar opportunity: "But I had begun to sense a truth inside myself: if in order to live it is necessary *not to live*, then what's it all for?''[17] Nerzhin, who admittedly has "attained that stage of development where the worse begins to appear the better," even goes so far as to suggest that "when Lev Tolstoi dreamed of being put in prison, he was reasoning like a truly perceptive person with a healthy spiritual life" (VIII, 46).

The logic behind this bizarre declaration is not difficult to infer. According to the author of "A Reflection in Water," it is impossible to glimpse the truth while one is still in motion, still alive. (And under Stalin, any independent attempt to glimpse the truth is likely to catapult you out of motion into the beyond anyway: as the police put it, "After all, you only live once. Why *think about things?*'')[18] But there are certain states of being so close to death that one can actually be said to have ceased to move even while remaining alive. In such a condition, one may be granted a privileged insight without the interposition of the "glass"—and one has little to lose by looking. Sickness unto death is one of these states: what should keep a man, Kostoglotov asks in *Cancer Ward*, from thinking "about the meaning of life, when he himself is on the borderline between life and death?" (XI, 138). Such proximity to death seems to provide a variety of characters in *Cancer Ward*, who have not been accustomed to scrutinize the quality of their existence, with the opportunity and incentive for sustained introspection. As Helen Muchnic has observed, "Set in the context of imminent death, *Cancer Ward* is a drama of mortality, a race with time, not for life but for an understanding of life. . . .''[19]

A different but similarly privileged perspective is afforded by the condition of exile. Solzhenitsyn quotes approvingly a letter from Kutuzov to the banished Radishchev:

> It grieves me to tell you this, my friend, but. . .your position has its advantages. Cut off from all men, remote from all the objects that dazzle us—you can all the more profitably voyage within yourself; you can gaze upon yourself dispassionately, and consequently form less biased judgments about things at which you previously looked through a veil of ambition and worldly cares. Many things will perhaps appear to you in a completely new aspect.[20]

And Solzhenitsyn adds, ". . .because I cherished the purer vision it gave me, I was fully conscious that exile was a blessing to me."[21]

He speaks elsewhere of his *ssylka prozrachnaia*,[22] evoking by this image of lucidity and transparency the visionary alternative of stillness held out by "A Reflection in Water."

But what resembles a living death more closely than any mortal illness, exile, or other possible condition is the experience of incarceration. "Descriptions of prisons have always stressed their horrors. Yet isn't it even more appalling[23] when there are no horrors? When the horror lies in the gray methodology of years? [...] One has to live through it; it cannot be imagined. [...] Only endless, uninterrupted *years* can bring to fruition the true experience of prison" (*The First Circle*: XXXIV, 237-238). In order to convey this experience as best he can, Solzhenitsyn likens prison most frequently to a living death, an unearthly state of disembodiment. He compares the meeting between a prisoner and a free relative to the scene depicted on ancient Greek funerary steles:

> The living look fondly at the dead person, who looks toward Hades, neither merry nor sad, with a clear [*prozrachnyi*] and all too knowing gaze. [...] Visiting relatives were not supposed to know where their living corpses dwelt. [...] They saw only well-fed, well-dressed people with white hands who had lost their former talkativeness and smiled sadly and assured them that they had everything and needed nothing (*The First Circle*: XXXIV, 236).

At the end of the First Part of *Gulag* Solzhenitsyn describes the process whereby a prisoner acquires this unique, unearthly quality; the imagery he uses is distinctly reminiscent of "A Reflection in Water."

> Torn from the hustle-bustle of everyday life [*zhiznennaia sueta*] in so absolute a degree that even counting the passing minutes puts him intimately in touch with the Universe, the lonely prisoner has to have been purged[24] of every imperfection, of everything that has stirred and troubled him in his former life, that has prevented him from settling into transparency [*otstoiat'sia do prozrachnosti*].[25]

The startling image in the final clause is redolent of the peculiar vocabulary current in the Soviet labor camps. The word "transparent" (*prozrachnyi*), which regularly appears (as we have seen) in a variety of related contexts, pertains to prisoners and to other similarly attenuated spirits almost in the maner of a stock epithet. It is featured in the colorful phrase *tonkii, zvonkii i prozrachnyi* ("thin, ringing and transparent") which Solzhenitsyn reserves for dignifying an "authentic" (*nastoiashchii*) prisoner in contrast to one whose responses are slow and out of practice.[26] He also applies it to the "risen" Kostoglotov at the end of *Cancer Ward*: "...there emerged from the clinic some new Kostoglotov, 'thin, ringing and transparent,' as they used to say in the camp...." (XXXV, 460).[27] Detachment from life makes you ghostly, lucid, transparent.

Many of these themes and images come together in Chapter 48 of *The First Circle* in which Solzhenitsyn describes the state of mind characteristic of the prisoners at the Mavrino *sharashka* during their weekly rest period. The title of this chapter, "The Ark," refers to the dormitory where the prisoners have been hermetically enclosed for the duration of their free evening.

> Those who floated in the ark were weightless [*nevesomy*] and had weightless thoughts. They were neither hungry nor satiated. They had no happiness and so felt no anxiety about losing it. Their heads were not filled with petty official calculations, intrigues, promotions, and their shoulders were not burdened with concerns about housing, fuel, bread, and clothes for their children. Love, which from time immemorial has been the delight and the torment of humanity, was powerless to communicate to them its thrill or its agony. Their prison terms were so long that no one even thought of the time when he would go out into freedom. [...]
>
> The light of bright bulbs reflected from the white ceilings, from the whitewashed walls, flooded their lucid minds with its thousands of rays.
>
> From here, from the ark, confidently plowing its way through the darkness, they could easily survey[28] at a glance the whole tortuous, wayward flow [*potok*] of accursed History, as from an enormous height, and yet in detail—down to a pebble on the river bed—as if they had dived into the stream.
>
> In these Sunday evening hours solid matter and flesh no longer reminded people of themselves. [...]
>
> Perhaps this was, indeed, that bliss [*blazhenstvo*] which all the philosophers of antiquity tried in vain to define and teach to others (XLVIII, 344).

The language of this extraordinary passage contains a constellation of images and associations which are beginning to become familiar. First of all, there is the image of the stream, here called History, an emblem of the course of human existence as a whole. Related to the image of the stream is the vocabulary of immersion and transparency, joined to the notions of height and depth, near and distant views. But Solzhenitsyn's language for communicating the experience of imprisonment includes other sets of recurring terms: floating, weightless, incorporeal. The prisoners' bodies appear to be dissolved as if in death and their souls set free, their minds receptive to the light of truth. By its very horror, "the gray methodology of years," prison purifies man of his grosser attachments—whether material or emotional—and weans his soul away from participation in bodily existence. Earlier in the novel Nerzhin provides a vivid and highly personal account of the philosophic bliss that attends on such purification: "I have a heart-to-heart conversation or I read an honest page and I'm on the crest of a wave. I haven't had any real life for many years, but I've forgotten about that. I'm weightless [*nevesom*], suspended [*vzveshen*], disembodied [*nematerialen*]!! I lie there by myself on my upper bunk and stare at the ceiling. It is very close, it's bare, the plasterwork is bad—and I tremble with the utter joy of existence! I fall asleep in perfect bliss" (*blazhenstvo*: VIII, 45).

What Nerzhin describes is the reward of his successful abstraction from the "life process"; the familiar terminology for expressing that withdrawal predictably recurs. Almost twenty years after the start of his work on *The First Circle*, we find Solzhenitsyn continuing to use identical language to communicate his own sense of detachment and transition in the face of imminent rearrest: "weightlessly suspended (*nevesomo vzveshennyi*) yet still on earth."[29] Elsewhere, the metaphor of incorporeality is associated with a special clarity of insight, as in the passage from "The Ark": in Part II of *Gulag* Solzhenitsyn playfully addresses a prisoner who is being transported *incognito* on a train, alone, but surrounded by free passengers.

> To you the true measure of things in the Universe is so clear! The measure of all weaknesses and all passions! And these sinners aren't fated to perceive it. The only one there who is alive, truly alive, is incorporeal you, and all these others are simply mistaken in thinking themselves alive.
>
> And an unbridgeable chasm divides you! You cannot cry out to

them, nor weep over them, nor shake them by the shoulder: after all, you are a [disembodied] spirit, you are a ghost, and they are material bodies.[30]

The refining, purgative experience of prison finally culminates in "that glimmering light which, in time, the soul of the lonely prisoner begins to emit, like the halo of a saint."[31]

Solzhenitsyn therefore appears to endorse the teaching of his character, Dmitrii Sologdin, that prison can be considered not only a curse but also a blessing (*blagoslovenie*: XXIV, 163).[32] Sologdin particularly stresses the intellectual and contemplative advantages of incarceration; after exhorting Nerzhin "to find out where you are spiritually, understand the correlation of good and evil in human life," Sologdin adds: "There's no better place to do it than prison" (XXIV, 162-163).[33] Nerzhin comes to agree, and when his wife discerns in the course of their brief interview how well imprisonment seems to suit him, he acknowledges the truth of her insight:

> Sometimes he was not at all sorry to have spent five years in prison. These years had come to mean something in themselves.
> Where could one learn about people better than here?
> And what better place to reflect about oneself?
> How many youthful hesitations, how many wrong starts, had he been saved from by the iron path of prison? (XLII, 296)[34]

Nerzhin takes advantage of the positive opportunities prison affords him. He has an "insatiable desire to resolve in prison everything he had not been able to figure out in freedom" (LXII, 453) and his desire is rewarded, just as Innokentii Volodin is able to comprehend in prison the significance of a maxim of Epicurus which had been "unrefuted and difficult to grasp yesterday in freedom" (LXXXIV, 635).[35] Thus, when Nerzhin is in a good mood,

> his thirty-year-old life [appears...] full of meaning in both big and small things; a life striding from one bold success to another, in which the most unexpected steps toward his goal were his departure for the war and his arrest.... Seen from the outside it appeared an unhappy one, but Nerzhin was secretly happy in that unhappiness. He drank it down like spring water. Here he got to know people and events about which he could learn nowhere else on earth, certainly

not in the quiet, well-fed seclusion of the domestic hearth (XXVII, 186).

Nerzhin's preference for knowledge over participation in the "life process" explains his positive outlook on imprisonment: "Thank God for prison [*blagoslovenie tiur'me*]!! It gave me the chance to think" (VIII, 44). This exclamation coincides with a remark by Alex, the protagonist of Solzhenitsyn's play *Candle in the Wind*: "There are moments when I say, 'God bless you, prison.'"[36] Solzhenitsyn closes his chapter on spiritual "ascent" through suffering in Part IV of *Gulag* with an identical declaration:

> And that is why I turn back to the years of my imprisonment and say, sometimes to the astonishment of those about me: "BLESS YOU, PRISON [*BLAGOSLOVENIE TEBE, TIUR'MA*]!"
> Lev Tolstoi was right when he *dreamed* of being put in prison. [...]
> All the writers who wrote about prison but who did not themselves serve time there considered it their duty to express sympathy for prisoners and to curse prison. I...have served enough time there. I nourished my soul there, and I say without hesitation: "BLESS YOU, PRISON, for having been in my life!"[37]

Solzhenitsyn is not a blithe optimist nor, despite occasional insinuations to the contrary by George Steiner and other Western commentators, is he a masochist; he never underestimates the human cost of imprisonment. As one critic has emphasized, "the paradoxical notion of an invaluable freedom which only prisoners can enjoy never lapses into a sentimentality...which might seem to threaten it: namely, a view of tyranny as a power which, to adapt Goethe's words, wills forever evil yet does forever good...Solzhenitsyn *never kisses the rod.*"[38] While Solzhenitsyn does believe that every punishment (no matter how unfair) can be justified to oneself and accepted as commensurate to the guilt for which each individual stands indicted by his or her own conscience,[39] he refuses to convert this belief into "a universal law of life. [...] One can get all tangled up that way. One would have to admit that on that basis those who had been punished even more cruelly than with prison—those shot, burned at the stake—were some sort of super-evildoers. (And yet... the innocent are those who get punished most zealously of all.)" Solzhenitsyn escapes from this muddle by concluding "that the

meaning of earthly existence lies not, as we have grown used to
thinking, in prospering, but...in the development of the soul.''[40]
True punishment consists in drowning in the "life process" itself and
thereby forfeiting the opportunity for spiritual growth. Prisoners are
uniquely fortunate in that they alone, according to a popular prison
notion, are "certain to have an immortal soul; *free* people are often
denied one because of the vain lives they lead [*za suetoiu*]."[41] A life
in freedom and a knowledge of truth are directly opposed in normal
circumstances: "How can one preserve one's life and at the same
time arrive at the truth?" Solzhenitsyn asks.[42] (It is a rhetorical
question!) For Solzhenitsyn, as for the Socrates of Plato's *Phaedo*,
philosophy is the art of practising dying and prison is the ideal place
to practise it.

> Nerzhin felt compelled to work swiftly so that, having performed
> his assigned work he could disengage himself for a longer time[43] from
> all motion. He had once said to Simochka, "I am active because I hate
> all activity." "And what do you like?" she had asked shyly. "Con-
> templation," he had replied. And indeed when the squall of work
> passed, he would sit for hours hardly changing his position. The skin
> of his face would turn gray and old and the wrinkles would appear
> (VI, 37).

Nerzhin is a representative of the tradition against which Yeats re-
volted when he dreamt of a place "where the body is not bruised to
pleasure soul." But in Solzhenitsyn's universe, developing the soul
demands abstraction, separation, all the "useless purities" which
could have saved the autobiographical narrator of *Prussian Nights*
from his final act of abomination.[44] The animal logic of life must be
interrupted, must be broken, in order for the spirit to take flight.

*   *   *

A number of the passages under discussion here were examined
and interpreted differently by Francis Barker in a recent attempt to
demonstrate "the degeneration [in Solzhenitsyn's literary career] of a
radical opposition to the Soviet bureaucratic regime into an authoritarian moralising."[45] Barker begins by taking as "a paradigm of the
more general changes in Solzhenitsyn's work...the mutation of a
single recurrent idea," namely, "the notion that...some aspects of

prison life...are beneficial." For example, Nerzhin's meditation on the advantages accruing to him from "the iron path of prison" represents, according to Barker, "a limited statement of a limited benefit" and "tells us more about Nerzhin than it does about prison," whereas in *The Gulag Archipelago* "it is no longer the voice of a realistically limited character who perceives that, owing to the peculiarities of his unique personal history, he has derived certain unexpected advantages from prison, but the voice of a seeming omniscience which has begun to make larger, mystifying claims for the abstract and unspecific 'prisoner' who is thus canonised." Barker does admit that such "prison mysticism...is foreshadowed more strongly" in Chapter 48 of *The First Circle* ("The Ark"), which "threatens to overstep the [empirical] limits" normally placed by Solzhenitsyn in his early work on "the ultimate significance" of specific details or incidents, "but this remains a threat [merely]."[46] Later on in his study Barker allows that a "universal ethics" can be seen as the "covert contents" of the early novels, if only in the form of "a system of judgements buried deep in the text," but he insists that "the ethical scheme is active only as the unexplicit margin between the negativity of the protagonist and the positive ideologies which his negativity admits but holds at a distance."[47]

While Barker's investigation into the form of Solzhenitsyn's writings is often admirable, his argument underrates the rigorous demands deliberately placed by their author on the reader's moral sense. The content of Solzhenitsyn's ethical thought remains deeply buried in these texts only so long as one declines to seek for it. It pervades and shapes his early plays and novels no less than his literary memoirs and *Gulag*. The differences in authorial voice among these works, their varying degrees of directness, can be accounted for satisfactorily by the requirements of genre and narrative point of view. The professional ideologues of the Soviet Writers' Union, at any rate, with their enhanced sensitivity to nuances of doctrinal impurity, were not fooled by the "unexplicit margin" harboring Solzhenitsyn's ethical scheme in his early works; they recognized in him neither an advocate of "pure Leninism" nor a radical critic of bureaucracy but a resolute opponent of all materialist philosophy.[48] And, as everyone knows, they never make mistakes!

Notes

1. On Solzhenitsyn's first public statements, see J. B. Dunlop, "Solzhenitsyn in Exile," *Survey*, vol. 21, No. 3 (Summer, 1975), pp. 133-154. See also the essays on Solzhenitsyn's reception in the West elsewhere in this volume.

2. *ARKHIPELAG GULag* (pt. IV, ch. 1), vol. 2 (Paris: YMCA-Press, 1974), pp. 601-602; *The Gulag Archipelago Two*, trans. T. P. Whitney (New York: Harper and Row, 1975), pp. 614-615.

3. Hélène Zamoyska, "Soljenitsyne et la grande tradition," *La Table Ronde*, vol. 185 (1963), pp. 61-81.

4. Aleksandr I. Solzhenitsyn, *The Oak and the Calf: Sketches of Literary Life in the Soviet Union*, trans. H. Willetts (New York: Harper and Row, 1980), p. 327 (in a Supplement dated "December 1973").

5. Francis Barker, *Solzhenitsyn: Politics and Form* (London: Macmillan, 1977), p. 102, n. 9, attempts to distinguish Solzhenitsyn's personal views from the ideology of his fiction, maintaining (for example) that although Solzhenitsyn "abandoned ['purified Leninism'] as a personal viewpoint in 1946[,] it only disappears from his fiction in the mid-sixties." I shall have more to say about Barker's interpretation at the conclusion of this essay.

6. References within the body of the essay are to chapter and page number of *V kruge pervom* (Paris: YMCA-Press, 1969). I have preferred to cite from this, the 87-chapter version of *The First Circle*, and to borrow selectively from its English-language translation by Thomas P. Whitney (New York: Harper & Row, 1968). I have, however, checked the text against the restored and revised 96-chapter version, published by Solzhenitsyn as vols. I and II of his *Sobranie sochinenii* (Vermont and Paris: YMCA-Press, 1978) and have noted discrepancies where they occur. On the two versions of the novel, see Georges Nivat's essay in the present volume. I concur with Solzhenitsyn's own judgment (*The Oak and the Calf*, p. 11) that the artistic quality of his work often benefitted from being "lightened" (*i.e.*, toned down) for the purpose of publication in the Soviet Union.

7. On Agniia and Solzhenitsyn's "astral" women in general, see John B. Dunlop, *Solženicyn's "The First Circle,"* Ph. D. dissertation, Yale University, 1973, pp. 228-239.

8. The injunction *osteregis'* is inserted at this point in the 96-chapter version and seems to be required by the context.

9. Testimony by Perets Herzenberg (one of Solzhenitsyn's prototypes for the character of Rus'ka Doronin) in an interview published in the magazine section of the Tel Aviv evening newspaper *Maariv*, 15 March 1974. (I would like to thank Dina Crockett for drawing my attention to this interview and for translating it.)

10. *The Longest Journey*, Part I, chapter 14.

11. Cf. Helen Muchnic, *Russian Writers: Notes and Essays* (New York: Random House, 1971), p. 424 (on this theme as it pertains to Gleb Nerzhin) and p. 443 (on the symbolism of the squirrel and mountain goat Kostoglotov sees at the zoo).

12. Chapter and page numbers refer to the most recent text (Vermont and Paris: YMCA-Press, 1979), the fourth volume of Solzhenitsyn's authorized *Sobranie sochinenii*. The translation is that of Bethell and Burg (New York: Farrar, Straus and Giroux, 1969), adapted where necessary.

13. Helen Muchnic, "*Cancer Ward*: Of Fate and Guilt," in Dunlop, et al. eds., *Aleksandr Solzhenitsyn: Critical Essays and Documentary Materials*, 2nd ed. (New York: Collier Books, 1975: hereafter abbreviated "Dunlop"), p. 285.

14. A. Solzhenitsyn, "Otrazhen'e v vode," *Sobranie sochinenii*, 3 (Vermont and Paris: YMCA-Press, 1978), p. 170; trans. H. Willetts, *Encounter*, vol. 24, No. 3 (March 1965), p. 5.

15. A. Solzhenitsyn, "Dykhanie," *Sobr. soch.*, 3, p. 163; trans. H. Willetts, *Encounter*, vol. 24, No. 3 (March 1965), p. 3. Cf. J. B. Dunlop, "Solzhenitsyn's Sketches," *Transactions of the Association of Russian-American Scholars in the U.S.A.*, vol. 6 (1972), p. 23 (repr. Dunlop, p. 319): "Modern man...is unable to penetrate the essence of things because he, like a swift-moving stream, is in frantic motion."

16. A. Solzhenitsyn, *Bodalsia telenok s dubom* (Paris: YMCA-Press, 1975), p. 364; *Oak and Calf*, p. 338.

17. *ARKHIPELAG GULag* (pt. I, ch. 7), vol. 1 (Paris: YMCA-Press, 1973), p. 287; English: *The Gulag Archipelago*, trans. T. P. Whitney (New York: Harper & Row, 1974), p. 280.

18. *GULag* 3 (pt. III, ch. 10), p. 311; trans. p. 317.

19. Muchnic (see Note 13), p. 279.

20. *ARKHIPELAG GULag* (pt. VI, ch. 6), vol. 3 (Paris: YMCA-Press, 1975), pp. 461-462; *The Gulag Archipelago Three*, trans. H. Willetts, p. 441.

21. *GULag* 3 (pt. VI, ch. 6), p. 462: "I dorozhe etoi ochishchennoi tochkoi zreniia, ia vpolne osoznanno dorozhil svoeiu ssylkoi"; trans, p. 441.

22. *GULag* 3 (pt. VI, ch. 6), p. 464; Willetts translates it effectively (p. 443) as "crystalline exile," although the literal meaning is closer to "transparent."

23. Where the 1969 edition has *strashnee*, the 1978 edition reads *uzhasnee*, and in the following sentence *nedel'* ("of weeks": 1978) is found in place of *let* ("of years": 1969).

24. The word is *ochistit'sia*; compare the phrase *ochishchennaia tochka zreniia*, used to characterize an exile (Note 21).

25. *GULag* 1 (pt. I, ch. 12), p. 483; cf. Whitney, p. 483, who makes the image more explicit by writing "prevented his muddied waters from settling...." The extended metaphor is not found in the Russian text.

26. *Bodalsia telenok*, p. 474; cf. *Oak and Calf*, p. 446.

27. V. V. Carpovich, *Solzhenitsyn's Peculiar Vocabulary: Russian-English Glossary* (New York: Technical Dictionaries Co., 1976), p. 298. (I would like to thank Alexis Klimoff for help in uncovering the provenance of this expression.)

28. The 1969 edition reads *ozariat'sia*; the 1978 edition *ozirat'sia*.

29. *Bodalsia telenok*, p. 427; *Oak and Calf*, p. 399 (in a Supplement dated "June 1974").

30. *GULag* 1 (pt. II, ch. 4), p. 583; trans., p. 591.

31. *GULag* 1 (pt. I, ch. 12), p. 483; trans., p. 483.

32. This chapter shows substantial variations in the 1978 edition.

33. The last sentence is omitted in the 1978 edition.

34. The 1978 edition is more positive and emphatic: "Po suti vovse ne zhal' piati prosizhennykh let.... Nerzhin uzhe priznal ikh dlia sebia svoerodnymi, neobkho-dimymi dlia ego zhizni" (XLVI, 363). There are also other alterations of a political nature in the 1978 edition.

35. The 1978 edition simply reads *vchera poniat' ne mog* (XCIII, 367).

36. A. Solzhenitsyn, *Candle in the Wind*, trans. K. Armes and A. Hudgins (Minneapolis: U. of Minnesota Press, 1973), p. 24.

37. *GULag* 2 (pt. IV, ch. 1), p. 604; trans., pp. 616-617.

38. D. Jacobson, "The Example of Solzhenitsyn," *Commentary*, vol. 47, No. 5 (1969), p. 83.

39. *GULag* 2 (pt. IV, ch. 1), pp. 601-603; trans., pp. 613-616. In his writings since *Gulag*, Solzhenitsyn has spoken with greater assurance about the positive purpose behind his own misfortunes, "that bright meaning beyond and above my self and my wishes," for example, or "the higher and hidden meaning of that suffering...." (*Oak and Calf*, pp. 111 and 146).

40. *GULag* 2 (pt. IV, ch. 1), pp. 600-601; trans., p. 613. Cf. the statement ascribed to Solzhenitsyn by a hostile critic, Jeri Laber, "The Real Solzhenitsyn," *Commentary*, vol. 57, No. 5 (May 1974), p. 33: "'The cultivation of one's soul is more important than the well-being of countless generations.'"

41. *The First Circle* (XXIX, 202). Cf. Solzhenitsyn's description, later in the same novel, of the prevailing attitude among prisoners: "Those who were free lacked the immortal soul the zeks had earned in their endless prison terms. They made stupid and greedy use of the freedom they were allowed to enjoy. They besmirched themselves with petty schemes, idle pursuits" (LXXIX, 575).

42. *GULag* 2 (pt. III, ch. 6), p. 191; trans., p. 194.

43. At this point the 1978 edition alone has the word *nadol'she* (VII, 45).

44. A. Solzhenitsyn, *Prussian Nights*, trans. R. Conquest (New York: Farrar, Straus and Giroux, 1977), pp. 88-89.

45. Barker, *Solzhenitsyn: Politics and Form*, p. 1.

46. *Ibid.*, pp. 10-13.

47. *Ibid.*, pp. 35-43.

48. See, for example, the transcript of the Meeting of the Secretariat of the Union of Soviet Writers on 22 September 1967 which is included among the documents accompanying *The Oak and the Calf*, pp. 463-480, esp. pp. 473-476.

PART THREE
Documentary Materials

Solzhenitsyn at Peredelkino

LIDIIA CHUKOVSKAIA *

...At that time [January 1974], Solzhenitsyn was living in one of the rooms on the lower floor of the dacha (we were keeping the upper floor sacrosanct and had already turned it into a kind of museum). He had first moved to Peredelkino at my father's invitation in the summer of 1965, when I still hardly knew him. Since that time, both before and after father's death, the two of us had more than once chanced to live under the same roof, either in the city, or out at the dacha. Sometimes he would stay with us for several days in a row, sometimes for a week or even a month; then he would disappear for a long time, only to reappear again as suddenly. Here he could always find shelter; for years he kept a set of keys to our apartment. Circumstances might change, but he could move in with us at a moment's

* Lidiia Chukovskaia (b. 1907) is the daughter of Kornei Ivanovich Chukovskii (1882-1969), literary critic, translator, and celebrated writer of comic verse for children. Chukovskaia, whom Solzhenitsyn has described as "an essayist of whom Russia can be proud," shares her father's keen interest in the use of language, but has focused particularly on the esthetic and ethical consequences of its *ab*use. Her long experience as an editor yielded a book, *In the Editor's Laboratory*, published in the Soviet Union in 1960. Better known in the West are her two fictional works, *The Deserted House* (*Opustelyi dom*) [first published in 1965], and *Going Under* (*Spusk pod vodu*) [1972], both devoted to the moral pressures and ambiguities of life in Stalinist Russia, and neither deemed publishable in her homeland. Chukovskaia was a close friend of the poet Anna Akhmatova, and her most recent publication in the West is the two-volume *Notes on Anna Akhmatova* (*Zapiski ob Anne Akhmatovoi*) [YMCA-Press, Paris]. In the last years of his life, Kornei Chukovskii had become one of Solzhenitsyn's most illustrious supporters, offering him the shelter of his dacha in the privileged community of Peredelkino. Chukovskaia, who is in ill health and is almost blind, resides in Moscow. Her many essays and statements over the years in defense of Siniavskii, Daniel', Solzhenitsyn, Sakharov, and others eventually proved intolerable to the authorities, and in January 1974 she was expelled from the Soviet Writers' Union. The excerpt which follows is drawn from her account of that period of her life, *A Process of Expulsion* (*Protsess iskliucheniia*) [Paris: YMCA-Press, 1979], pp. 132-44, translated from the Russian by the editors and published by kind permission of Professor Efim Etkind.

notice, regardless of the circumstances: it made no difference to us whether they were singing his praises or baying at his heels.

He would move into our city apartment or to the dacha, and we would be close—right next to each other—yet each of us would continue to live his own life, pursuing his own routine, his own life's work. Wherever Solzhenitsyn happened to dwell and wherever fate cast him, he never for a moment ceased to be the absolute master of his own life. At the same time, I have never seen anyone so skilled at protecting the even tenor of other peoples' lives from disruption, however foreign they might be to his own. Wherever he found himself, he always had his own rigid and indisputable schedule for the day—broken down not just into hours, but into minutes. I, too, have my own routine, one frequently disrupted by illness, and never so minutely plotted out as his—but my own, for all that.

Aleksandr Isaevich would go to bed early, for he was an early riser. One night, around midnight, I was seeing off some guests in the hallway near to the door of the room where Solzhenitsyn was then living. Afraid that I might wake him up, I began to speak in a half-whisper. But Aleksandr Isaevich had overheard my efforts. "If my presence is going to inhibit you in your relations with other people," he told me next morning, "then it will be imposssible for me to go on spending the night here." With fierce inflexibility, he rebuffed our every attempt to spare him the cares of everyday life. While he was staying at our dacha, he did everything for himself: cooking, washing up, cleaning his room.

During his last three months in Russia, Solzhenitsyn lived almost the whole time in Peredelkino, making short trips into the city to see his family. We lived in adjacent rooms, with his door next to mine and only a wall between us, but never did we enter each other's rooms unless there was an urgent reason. We saw each other rarely, meeting only in the "neutral zone"—the living room, corridor, or kitchen—and when we did meet, there were no long conversations between us. A long chat (except about work, or the creative process) would have been relaxation, idleness—and Solzhenitsyn and idleness are two quite incompatible things. It was as if, at a certain moment (I do not know why or when), he had sentenced himself to imprisonment in some strict regime camp, and was now rigidly enforcing that regime. He was convict and guard rolled into one, and his own surveillance of himself was, perhaps, more relentless than that of the KGB. This heroic task called for broad shoulders, for an entire lifetime of toil with never a day off. And the main instrument of his labor was complete and well-fortified solitude. The perpetual haste which came over Solzhenitsyn in the company of others (and which so bewildered and annoyed his acquaintances) was, in reality, an urgent, even violent drive to achieve concentration and depth, and thus to absolve his task. He allowed himself no indulgences, and set to work even before first light.

Sometimes, I would find a short note on the refrigerator in the kitchen: "If you are free by nine, let's listen to the radio together." This meant that he would finish his task earlier than usual that day and would grant himself an unexpected twenty-minute furlough: time to listen, talk a while, ask questions, tell something of his own experiences. (Sometimes, when he noticed that I was getting ready to go to the cemetery, Aleksandr Isaevich would walk with me to the grave, and afterwards, as we were coming back down the path between the fences, where it is too narrow to walk side by side, I would be amazed at his vigilance and solicitude. Closely examining the slippery path, he would anticipate where I might stumble. Then, without interrupting our conversation, he would alert me, sometimes by a word of warning, or a touch of his hand, sometimes lending me his shoulder for support at just the right moment.) But such walks together were few and far between. Every day, without fail, the camp-guard would lead the convict out for his regulation two or three hours of exercise, whatever the weather, but I doubt that he freed him from his labor even during those walks. Whether he was laying a new ski-trail in the deep snow of our garden, or breaking a path from fence to fence, as he strode the length of the grounds—Solzhenitsyn continued his work, frost or no frost. And, I dare say, continued it not just in his mind, but on paper, despite the freezing weather. He would thread the tiny pearls of his letters from one edge of the paper to the other on lines drawn tight as bow-strings. He avoided walking in the streets of the writers' village, except to go to the train station, and preferred to take his walks on our land, among the giant pine trees. "Don't you get tired of walking back and forth, from one fence to the other?" I once asked him. "No," he replied, "I got used to it in the sharashka."

Even the time he spent at breakfast, lunch and dinner did not go to waste. He would regularly tune in to the radio at mealtimes, listening intently and jotting down notes. He ate a long way from my room, out in the kitchen, so that the radio would not interfere with my work. When he was leaving for the city, he would not come into my room to say goodbye—once again, lest he should inadvertently tear me away from my work. But in case I should be alarmed at his sudden disappearance (these were troubled times, and there was no knowing what might happen to him from one moment to the next), he would leave a note on the refrigerator: "I've gone"—then the time and date. He would return suddenly, without warning, sometimes without so much as a sound: I would go out into the hallway and all at once I would come across his sheepskin or jacket hanging there. And a feeling of relief would come over me. Each time, I would catch myself thinking: Solzhenitsyn is here, he is working, he is here with us—so we've really no cause for complaint, everything is still all right.

Sometimes, meeting me in the corridor or the living-room, Solzhenitsyn would fire a question at me in passing, a question which seemed to be haphazard, but which actually followed on from a conversation we had had some time before, or from a thought which had been secretly nagging at his mind.

Once, as he came into the house from the yard after a long walk— engulfing me, through the wide open door, first in the chill of the forest air, then in the chill of his sheepskin, mittens, boots and beard—he quickly asked, right there in the entrance where he had found me: "Tell me, do you like Pasternak's long poem 'Lieutenant Schmidt'?" He took off his cap, then pulled off his sheepskin and hung it up. "Yes, I do," I replied. "A lot?" he asked again almost sternly, knitting his brows above eyes which, after the frost, showed brilliant blue against his ruddy complexion. "A lot." He looked at me once again, as if to make sure I was telling the truth, then went off to his room.

Another time, Aleksandr Isaevich suddenly appeared in front of me in the kitchen as I was watching a pan of milk to make sure it did not boil over.

"Excuse me, but could Akhmatova have left Russia in the twenties? Did she have the opportunity? Was it that she herself didn't want to go, or wouldn't they let her?"

"It was her own wish not to leave. All her closest friends went, but she didn't want to."

"Are you quite sure?"

"Absolutely. After all, you can even tell from her poetry:

Not with them am I, who left their land
To be dismembered by its foes.''

"Only from her poetry?"

"No, I heard it directly, too. She told me so herself back in the 1930s when she was describing how it had been in the twenties."

Again, once he had obtained the information he needed, he did not pursue the conversation, but left immediately.

He placed an extraordinarily high value on his time. ("I'm a ferocious time-keeper," he once said to me.) To me there was nothing irritating about his passion for economizing each hour, minute, and second of the day, his loathing for any waste of time. Quite the contrary, I admired and envied this trait:

> Sleep not, sleep not, o artist.
> Surrender not to sleep.
> You hostage of eternity,
> And prisoner of time. (Pasternak, "The Pilot")

A frivolous life is that same sleep, to which no artist dare surrender once he has conceived of his life as a "commission" (to use Baratynskii's term). (It is worse, even, than sleep, for sleep at least invigorates us.) Speaking about the executions under Stalin, Akhmatova once said: "Our late Alighieri would have created a tenth circle of Hell out of this." That is the kind of "commission," among many others, which Solzhenitsyn took upon himself. In the last years of his life in Russia, he was for me not only the writer who had brought us the living word from the nether regions, not only the author of *Ivan Denisovich*, "Matrena's Home," "The Right Hand," *Cancer Ward*, and *The First Circle*—in my eyes he was already Dante Alighieri, the creator of *The Gulag Archipelago*. "A workshop for human resurrection"—that is how I would describe his desk, his room, his task. In *Gulag*, one is struck by the abundance of facts and thoughts, by the fullness of the artistic word. For in the degree to which each word is charged with meaning and nuance *Gulag* may only be compared with such masterpieces as Pushkin's "Queen of Spades," Tolstoi's "Khadzhi Murat," and Chekhov's "The Bishop."

In *Gulag*, we are struck by the diversity of the factual material, even by how scattered it seems, and yet, at the same time, we recognize the unity, rigor, and precision with which the whole edifice is constructed. Would that I could live to see the appearance of a literary critic equal to the task of probing the essence of this work's unprecedented power: its verbal capaciousness and the resilience of its unruly syntax. Solzhenitsyn leads the reader through all the circles of Hell, lowers him down into the gloom of the nether world, and, through the power of his lyrical epos (or should we say "epical lyric"?), forces us, who are bereft of memory to relive with him the fate of hundreds, even thousands of individuals. And, more importantly, he forces us to make sense of all that was endured by them... and by us.

"He's always in a hurry..." "He's always looking at his watch ..." his disgruntled acquaintances would say. Or even: "He only ever has time for his own affairs, for *himself!*" This about a man who took upon himself a task which we had shirked! About a man who gave voice (and what a voice! the voice of an artist!) to those thousands whom he had resurrected from the dead. And behind the voice of these thousands, echoed the voice of millions more. But around Solzhenitsyn the air was thick with whispers: "He only ever has time for *himself.*"

For himself!

And you, idle chatterers, have you ever tried to descend each day anew into the depths of the underworld, and to return to earth once more, bearing your terrible spoils? Have you ever attempted to dredge up the experiences of the past, thought by thought, fate by fate, camp by camp—and to raise this colossal sculpture, this majestic monument on a communal grave beyond the Arctic Circle? With the seven parts of his book, Solzhenitsyn founded and cast—a new literary form, new not only for Russian literature, but—I venture to think—for world literature as well. Literary criticism has yet to come up with a precise definition for it, just as we are struck, to the present day, by the innovative qualities of *Dead Souls*, *Notes from the House of the Dead*, and *My Past and Thoughts*, and can find no precise definition of their form... No, never, in the whole nine years of my acquaintance with Solzhenitsyn—both before I knew about *Gulag* and afterwards—was I ever surprised at his "haste." How could he fail to hurry? After all, for him even *Gulag* is not the end of his commissioned task, but a digression before his main, impending work. Not from vain caprice did he don the ascetic's chains; no mere affectation caused him to glance at his watch when conversing with friends, or even with grand and portly editors; not for nothing did he, persecuted and oppressed as he was, force himself to roam the length and breadth of the land in order to seek out one more eyewitness, listen to one more account, verify one more detail. Filled to overflowing with the fates of other men—now so intimately his own!—he would hurry back to his desk once more, back to the workshop of human resurrection. In inviting Solzhenitsyn to live with us in Peredelkino in November 1973, we, of course, realized that it was not in our power to preserve him from his foes, but we gave our word, to him and to ourselves, that we would protect his work, his "haste," his routine, from the intrusions of the idly curious—and even from ourselves.

It is my proud hope that we kept our word.

"He's always in a hurry." Yet, on that evening of January 9th, 1974, when I arrived at the dacha after being expelled from the Writers' Union, Aleksandr Isaevich did not hurry anywhere. He helped me off with my things, and then we sat down at the table in the living room across from one another. I took out the stack of papers from my briefcase. "Let's shut ourselves off from Kataev," he said, jumping up, and vigorously shut both halves of the blinds over the large picture window which covers one whole wall. "We'll shut ourselves off from Kataev," he repeated. (The window of our living room looks out directly onto the writer Kataev's fence, shed and dacha.) Aleksandr Isaevich sat down again and looked at me expectantly. It is not a wide table, and I could see his face clearly. The scar, intersecting the forehead, emphasized the straightness of his features. A straight nose, straight hair, a straight forehead—a face which seems to have been straightened out from within solely by an effort of will. Concentration deepened the scar, and the more deeply that line cut into his forehead, the more distinctly the basic structure of his face showed through. It seemed almost to bare itself, sharply and nakedly delineated. There was nothing superfluous. Only the foundation.

Several days before I was expelled, and without saying a word to me, Solzhenitsyn had taken special measures: he had written a letter to his former colleagues in the Writers' Union. I did not learn about this until much later. Here is the full text of his letter:

6 January 1974

Dear Sarra Emmanuilovna,

The question I would like to put—not to you personally, but perhaps through your good offices—is this: how much longer will writers go on behaving like chickens, obediently awaiting the slaughter, and blithely doing nothing to prevent the slaughter of others?

What is a "community" like that worth? What can writers such as these teach the people? Why do they even bother to write books at all? Everyone knows about the forthcoming expulsion of Lidiia Chukovskaia and Vladimir Voinovich, but will it actually take place unhindered, without *opposition* (and I mean active countermeasures, not empty protests after the event)? If so, then the worthy community of writers is no less contemptible than the bureaucrats who run it. Which ever way you look at it, the rank and file still constitute a majority.

Should you choose to discuss this matter with anyone, feel free to refer to me and to show them this letter.

Yours,

A. Solzhenitsyn

Unaware at the time that any such letter existed, I was momentarily surprised by the persistence of Aleksandr Isaevich's questions: how many people had been in the vestibule, how many had gone up to the second floor with me to Room No. 8 (all of them!), and how many had tried to get inside... "But how could they get in?" I asked, astonished at his question. There had been a guard at the door. They requested and demanded to be let in, they sent notes. But Narovchatov did not allow anyone to come in with me—not even Sarra Emmanuilovna Babenysheva, who had asked permission to accompany me because of my half-blindness.

"But, surely, with so many of your friends there, all of them together could have forced open the door?"

"How could they? The door was locked from the inside, and there was a guard outside."

"Still, they should have burst their way in!"

"But that would only have meant that the session would not have taken place. The chairman would have had the wit to postpone it. And the next time, they wouldn't have had just one guard at the door, but a whole detachment of militia."

The scar grew deeper. Solzhenitsyn did not ask any more questions, but waited to hear my story. I tried to give a blow-by-blow account, rummaging around among my notes. But I could not manage it. I could see the boldly written page numbers clearly enough, but the notes themselves, which I had made standing up, were difficult to decipher. And so, setting aside my pile of notes (which had so irritated and frightened my recent interlocutors), I began to describe what happened, not from notes but from memory. As I recalled the moments which had been so painful for me, he listened with an attention so tangibly intense that it gripped my words like the iron hoops round a keg. I tried to convey the Pharisaism of Agniia Barto, who even stooped so low as to invoke the shade of my late father in her moment of vengeance on me, and the brazen way she spoke of goodness while doing evil. I tried to depict Iurii Iakovlev's inept, premeditated show of emotion; the cunning lies of that un-venerable, inveterate liar Lesiuchevskii; the blasphemous tongue of Zhukov, recalling our victory in World War II to comfort poor suffering Lesiuchevskii; the boorish coarseness of Mednikov, Samsonii and Rekemchuk; the brutishness of Gribachev; the courteous treachery of Strekhnin, who obliged them by misrepresenting my text; the refined hatred of Kataev...

The scar listened. "What is it that gives this man such strength?" I thought, involuntarily looking at the living lineaments across from me, as I told my tale. "It must be his ability to concentrate himself, his entire being—not just a part, but the whole of that which we call 'I'—to collect and concentrate himself, his individual 'I,' on the 'I' of another." Now he was completely concentrated upon me and upon my suffering. Fully. Totally. It is as if there were a lever somewhere within him: he pulls the lever, throws a switch, and turns on the whole of his attention; then he switches it off again, when he so desires. If he had not discovered this ability—to respond to another person's pain with the very essence and foundation of his being—how could he ever have created Matrena, not to mention the entire population of the Gulag Archipelago? Thanks to the piercing intensity of his attention and his memory, hundreds upon hundreds of individual fates have been grasped and assimilated, absorbed and memorized, returned to life and—whether we like it or not—presented, as a gift, to us.

"Kataev? Talking about decency!" he interrupted me when I got as far as Kataev. Actually, he did not really interrupt; the words seemed to resound somewhere within him. "Of course! How could it be otherwise! The man with the least spark of decency has to be the one to raise the question of decency. Although, it's hard to say which one of them has the least spark..."

I went on with my story. Solzhenitsyn listened. When his working concentration deepened, so did his scar, while his face grew straighter and straighter, underlining and sharpening his features...

From the heights of his compassion, I looked back on the past day. Well, it hadn't been easy. Even now, it wasn't easy. For minutes on end, the feeling of humiliation would leave me, only to return again. I went on: "You're a pathetic person," Samsonii had yelled at me, lounging in his chair, "You think you're really somebody, but you're just pathetic."

"And, in fact, Aleksandr Isaevich, I did turn out to be rather pathetic. After Lesiuchevskii told one of his lies, for instance, and I couldn't think of anything to say, or later on, when I was making my final statement: they all started shouting. I dropped my papers on the floor and spent a long time fumbling around on the floor before I somehow gathered them together."

"And nobody helped you?"

He stood up. Perhaps even jumped up.

"Nobody. No, of course they didn't."

"Not a single person?"

The scar cut into his forehead so deeply that each feature beneath it was transformed into a blade. It was no longer a face, but a knife.

"Not one."

"I am now going to cry," he said.

(Even now, it seems to me that I must have misheard him. But I was not mistaken. That is what he said.)

We sat across from one another, downcast.

Neither of us started crying, of course. On the contrary, we were so relieved that my tale was over, that the tension dissipated, and we even laughed a bit. "Kolia! My friend! Take care of yourself..." [one of my interlocutors had shouted solicitously].

"Did they really go so far as to recall the taking of Berlin just to comfort Lesiuchevskii?"

"Yes, Aleksandr Isaevich, they really did."

He burst into loud, merry laughter. His face, previously so sharp and knife-like, now became round, rustic, even, I would say, somewhat simple. Such faces are very common in Russia. When Solzhenitsyn's face is not concentrated, it is like that of a fitter or mechanic, not long out of the peasantry. Even the scar seemed to have smoothed itself out and vanished. Without trace.

I joined in his laughter.

Solzhenitsyn stood up. (His attention had been turned off. Without this power to control the switch, where would he ever have found the time to transform all that he had assimilated into a lyrically sublimated whole, into those books which we all read?) The lever had worked unerringly. It was time for the convict to return to his barracks for evening rollcall. It was high time, for otherwise the following morning would be lost for work.

Solzhenitsyn looked at his watch.

"Take care of these notes!" he said rapidly, passing me the neatly piled sheets.

This was no longer the same man—no longer an attentive listener, but a man hurrying by.

He threw another quick glance at his watch and said goodbye.

It was time, time for him to go to his room, although the hands of his watch could scarcely have shown the author of *Gulag* how little time he had left to live and work in Russia—just one month and three days.

The ticking watch could scarcely have been spelling out to Aleksandr Solzhenitsyn Akhmatova's famous line:

"On the threshold stands—Fate."

An Interview on Literary Themes with
Nikita Struve, March 1976*

ALEKSANDR SOLZHENITSYN

Aleksandr Isaevich, ever since the speeches you gave in America and England, you are constantly being referred to as a political figure, whereas in fact those speeches were more of a hindrance to your creative work, were they not?

Yes indeed. It's quite striking how, for some reason, everyone who talks to me tries to draw me into politics: it's always my political views that they particularly want to hear. It upsets me very much, but that's the way it is. One reason is, of course, that Russian literature as a whole has traditionally been highly sensitive to social issues...

After all, your vocation from the outset, from childhood almost, was to become a writer...

I spend the bulk of my time and energy working on my books. All these sessions with the press are of limited duration and come about almost by chance. Yes, it is true, oddly enough: ever since the age of eight or nine I have had a notion that I must become a writer, even though I had no idea at that time how this might come about.

And how did you become a writer?

In a serious way—not until I was in prison. I tried my hand at writing even before the war; as a student, I really made an effort and did produce things. But this was not serious writing. I simply did not have the necessary experience. During my years in prison, I began to write in earnest. It had to be done in a truly conspiratorial fashion: the very last thing I could afford to do was to let them find out I was

*From *Vestnik R.Kh.D.*, 120 (1977), pp. 130-158. Published by kind permission of Nikita Struve. ©1976 Vestnik RKhD.

writing! I used to memorize things, learn them by heart—first poetry, then, later, prose as well.

That was in prison, but in the camp your writing became more ambitious...

Well, prison and camp—they're more or less the same thing...

It was in the camps, though, that your long narrative poem really took shape...

In effect, I kept working away at it throughout my years in the camps, then I went on to plays. I couldn't just drift along without trying to get something done. The years were passing by. But the novel, my big novel, the epic which I had thought up as early as 1936—that I could not begin to write in the camp. It was out of the question. All I could do was gather material, think things over, question eyewitnesses. In this sense, camp existence swung me around. On the one hand, it seemed to be leading me away from the central theme I wanted to work on—the history of our revolution. On the other hand, it turned out to be God's wish, as they say, for the camp experience was the ideal preparation for that other theme, which really *was* the main one. Although the camps were a distraction in terms of wasted years and wasted strength, and although they could easily have resulted in my death, it was the camps that steered me into the main stream of the theme which had come to me as a schoolboy.

You postponed working on this project, and began writing novels during your exile in Kazakhstan.

That's not quite right: I *never* postponed it. For me the greatest, most intensely interesting aspect of camp life was the opportunity it gave me to question people who knew something about the revolution. So I kept accumulating material, even though I had no opportunity to make notes. I had never imagined what vast resources the human memory has. I simply could not believe that we people have such powers—far greater than we think. I could jot nothing down, yet even without notes it is amazing how much fits in one's memory, such a mass of material. So I spent all those years memorizing facts and details, then I was set free. But by "freedom" I mean internal exile—practically the same thing as prison—and there, too, it was impossible to do any writing, for I was under surveillance and could expect my quarters to be searched at any minute.

But, even so . . .

The problem was how to keep my material safe . . . I had to invent a way of preserving it and find somewhere to hide it. When I went off to teach, there was only one small lock to keep my tiny house secure. Anyone who wanted to could go right in and find whatever he was after . . . But the prison theme was pressing so hard on me that I just had to work on it. And then I came down with cancer. This fatal disease and the book *Cancer Ward* also demanded their share of my time and energy. And that's how I finished up putting off my main subject for thirty years, and working instead on the prison and camp themes. I wrote about the sharashka, about the cancer ward. I just couldn't fight my way through to my own theme. Then came *Gulag*. The publication of *Ivan Denisovich* put me in an extraordinary position. Hundreds of people sent me their personal recollections of life in the camps. I had to listen to them, assemble all this material, and rework it. That is when I began putting *Gulag* together.

You became a "writer of the people."

I became the accredited chronicler of labor camp life, one to whom people brought the whole truth. And these distractions continued until 1969, so that for thirty-three years I had been living my theme without ever being able to do any real work on it. Not till 1969 could I give myself fully to this, my main project.

But you came to the novel as a form while you were still in exile in the fifties. How did this happen?

To begin with, I think that every writer has his own preferences, in architectural terms, for miniatures, or for huge edifices. But, in addition, life exerts its own pressures: the material that comes our way demands that we write about it, and dictates the appropriate form. Thus, it took a combination of personal inclinations and the exigencies of the material itself, and in the case of *Gulag* the material combined with my predilection for large forms. However, my novels are not exactly examples of the small form, either: *The First Circle* and *Cancer Ward* are both a fair size.

They certainly are . . .

The funniest thing was back in . . . now what year was it? My memory fails me. Yes, in 1963. There was an international symposium in Leningrad devoted to the fate of the novel. They were all saying that the "novel" was already dead. And I had *The First Circle* already written and was working on *Cancer Ward*. I was really tempted to attend, but, after all, I couldn't have even mentioned that I had those two things written. *Gulag* was a different matter: I never planned to write any such thing. I had no way of processing that vast torrent of material, other than in the form of a vast work such as this.

Yes, but Gulag *is, in effect a part of that same story, its culmination.*

Yet the forms I had to choose were almost entirely different. This was an artistic investigation. And then there was the tactical problem of how to work up the material, these letters which had arrived out of the blue—this was all absolutely unplanned and unorganized material. Someone would come and tell me what he wanted to say, not what I happened to need. I had to break it all down into frag-ments, then work out where everything should go.

Isn't that rather like the way cathedrals and mosaics are built?

Well, perhaps like a mosaic. And my novel-epic—I do not call it a novel, but an epopee, a cycle of "knots"—it too is subject to essen-tially the same law: all the surviving material (and precious little *has* survived) must be incorporated, regardless of whether it seems suitable or not, and a place must be found for each item. In the camps, one of my jobs was breaking up iron, heavy cast-iron objects, into pieces. They were then thrown into a furnace, mixed with metal of inferior quality, and what came out was an iron with quite different properties. I sometimes jokingly refer to my materials as lumps of iron—very high-quality iron. I lower it into the smelter, and out it comes, transformed.

But this case is quite different from The Gulag Archipelago, *because you already have the whole plan of the epopee in front of you. You know precisely when it will be completed, and what will go into it...*

Yes, but even *Gulag* could never have been written without a plan. Even as I was assembling *Gulag*, I was aware that it, too, had to be built up out of separate, thematic parts.

Three parts...

No, seven. And there are other factors at work, below the surface—a chronological principle, for instance.

What is particularly striking about your long novels, Cancer Ward *and* The First Circle, *is the extraordinary way in which time and space are condensed [sgushchennyi]: everything is concentrated into a few days and takes place within a confined setting. How did that happen? Was it deliberate, or unconscious?*

Well, it certainly was not a result of any theoretical adherence to the classical unities! No, the confined setting is more likely a result of my own biography. I have spent the greater part of my life in closed premises. But this condensation [*uplotnenie*] is certainly no accident. Let me explain. I regard compactness or density [*plotnost'*] as the primary characteristic of any work of literature—artistic density, density of content, thought and emotion. Any work, large or small, is always dependent upon the question of how compact it is. In other words, how well does it answer its purpose? Even a tiny micro-story can be too long (half a page is all that's needed, and you've already written a full page). While a book of two thousand pages need not be too long at all, as long as it is compact and you don't feel any slackness in it. Of course, to a large extent, the form, compactness, texture and composition of a given work are determined by the material and the purpose of the work. It's no use at all (and probably a very bad habit) to tell yourself: what about trying something new? Maybe I should think up a new form? God forbid! The material itself will dictate the necessary form, just as the material of *Gulag* did to me, without my having to think about what form an artistic investigation should take. An artistic investigation draws upon real-life, factual material (untransmuted, that is), but also employs all the resources available to the artist in uniting these individual facts and fragments, such that the overall design emerges with a conclusiveness no wit less complete and compelling than that of a piece of scientific research.

When you began to write your first long novels, did certain images from Russian literature pass before you or did this [their literary echoes] come about completely spontaneously? What was the guiding force, the material or the tradition?

I am guided by tradition in the sense that I read Russian literature intensively in my childhood and it left its trace in my soul. But that is as far as it goes. While you're working, you don't think about traditions at all, and you don't think about whether you are supposed to be continuing this or that line. It simply does not occur to you. You are carried away by a new project. Take my *First Circle*, for example. It took hold of me. Now, how was I to describe something like this? I had lived there for three years. Was I to describe those three years? But that would have had no edge to it; it had to be condensed. This passion for condensation is obviously a personal thing, not simply inherent in the material. So I condensed it. Some people have written that the novel spans four days, or even five. No such thing! There are less than four days in it, not even three and a half; in fact, there are scarcely more than three days. I do not feel comfortable when I have too much space. Perhaps that is a habit which comes from living in a cell. I cannot cope with a novel if the material is arranged too freely. I only divided *Cancer Ward* into two parts because I felt that a disease which develops the way cancer does cannot possibly be shown in just three days. To depict the disease properly required at least five or six weeks, yet the narrative itself was crying out to be compressed. The whole point of the division into two parts was so that I could fit everything in the first part into a few days, three in all, while drawing out the second part, as I was forced to do—not in order to achieve a smooth narrative flow, but because the course of the disease demanded a plausible period of treatment, five or six weeks in fact.

One never senses a smoothly flowing narrative in your works. You always want to condense, to dynamize everything static.

I just think that this compactness enables us to reveal ourselves most effectively. As in a pithy conversation, for example. But if your interlocutor is vague and boring, it makes you feel almost ill. You sense that he is talking nonsense, and your own remarks start to become dull-witted, so the whole conversation falls flat and nothing comes of it.

Does your concept of compactness operate at the lexical level, too?

Yes, down to the last phrase and the last word. It has been noted that in the late Lermontov there is not a single extraneous, fortuitous word. I am not speaking of rhyme, for rhyme dictates its own requirements, but there is not a single extraneous word in the line. That is a general phenomenon, in prose as well as poetry. Yes, compactness must extend to the individual word and phrase.

Your syntax is amazingly elliptical; you make the word dynamic.

These days, I try to throw out every superfluous word. If there's any way I can do without a word, I throw it out.

But isn't there a certain danger that one might stretch the strings of the language too tight?

I don't think so. Look at Anna Akhmatova. Before her death, she said that an eight-line poem was too long for her; four lines were all that was needed. How often do you hear something like that? In Russian classical poetry, even a twenty-line poem was never considered to be long. But Akhmatova came to the same conclusion [as I have]—it's like sculpturing from stone, constantly trimming everything down. Twelve lines is too long, eight is too long, but four lines . . .

Yes, the comparison with sculpturing from stone is an attractive one, but, at the same time, there is a surprising amount of movement in your writing. How do you manage to combine this sculptured quality with such extraordinary dynamism?

Well, that's not really the kind of thing I can assess. I work with my material, and all I have in mind is how to give expression to that material.

Are you sometimes dissatisfied with what you have written?

When I am, I rewrite it over and over again, always trying to condense. Take *One Day in the Life of Ivan Denisovich*, for example. How was it born? It was just another day in the camps, the work was hard—I was teamed with another fellow, hauling hand-barrows—and it occurred to me that the best way to describe the whole camp world would be through a single day. Of course, you could describe your own ten years in the camp, the whole history of the camps—but it was sufficient to collect everything that happened in one day, like piecing together little fragments. It was enough to describe a single day, as experienced by an average, quite unremarkable man, from morning through to evening. And that would be all. That's how my idea was born in 1952.

In the camp?

In the camp. Of course, at that time it was insane to think about writing it. And then the years passed. I wrote a novel, fell ill, was dying of cancer for a while. But then, one day in—I'm sorry, what was the year?—in 1959, I thought that now I might perhaps be able to do something with this idea. It had simply lain there for seven years. Well, I thought, let's try writing about one day in the life of one zek. I sat down and the story simply poured out! The strain was terrible! Because there are so many of those days all concentrated within you at the same time. And you have to make sure that nothing is left out. I completed *One Day in the Life of Ivan Denisovich* incredibly quickly and then hid it for a long time. When I went to *Novyi mir*, they asked me: "How long did it take you to write it?" It was impossible to admit that I had written it in little over a month, because their next question would have been: "And what, pray, have you been writing for the rest of the time?" I had to keep hiding the truth and dodging their questions, but in actual fact it took me little more than a month.

Is that the way you usually work: years of gestation and then a rapid first draft?

You know, come to think of it, I suppose the moment *is* sudden. Once, after I had been released from the dispensary, I was walking about Tashkent, going to the commandant's office, when suddenly almost the whole of *Cancer Ward* came to me in a flash.

A primary intuition, as it were...

Well, at least as far as the Kostoglotov line goes; that came to me almost complete. But I heard about Rusanov from my neighbors in the ward. I never shared a ward with him myself, and his story-line comes from what they had to say about him. It occurred to me at the time that this might make a story. But once the idea had formed it just lay dormant: for all that came of it, it might as well never have been. But in 1963, when my works had already begun to be published, I wondered what kind of thing I could write, that I could submit openly to *Novyi mir*. And that is how I came to write *Cancer Ward*. I might as easily not have done so; it could have gone on lying there. And if something had distracted me, I might never have written *Ivan Denisovich* either.

Or was it perhaps something that you would eventually have needed to write?

No. I have plots which have never been written up. There is just the initial concept, a few words jotted down, and that is as far as it will go.

So they will never be written?

I'm afraid not, because my main theme is driving me on, and there is little enough time left in my life as it is.

And you don't see yourself deviating from this main theme in the future, if only to give your pen a rest? There are those who would like you to go back to writing in a smaller form occasionally, to return to short stories.

I am aware of how much can be packed into the short form, and working on it is a great delight for any artist. Because there is real pleasure to be had from honing and polishing such a work.

*   *   *

I should like to raise a rather broad question concerning the correlation between reality and imagination. You have been criticized in some quarters for allowing reality to preponderate over imagination. It would be interesting to know how your images are born, and how they are related to their prototypes. For example, you have mentioned Ivan Denisovich. Many people might think that there is an autobiographical element here, but in reality this is a composite image, is it not?

It can't be helped, I really cannot envisage any higher task than to serve reality—i.e., to recreate a reality which has been crushed, trampled and maligned. And I do not consider imagination *(vymysel)* to be my task or goal. I have not the slightest desire to dazzle the reader with my imaginative powers. Imagination is simply a means by which the artist can concentrate reality. It helps to concentrate reality—and that is its only role.

Reality being so rich . . .

All that was needed was to recreate everything as it was. Well, not absolutely identically, for then—this is the familiar principle of art concentrating reality—for then it would not be art at all; it would be too long, and no man can relive the lives of thousands of others. You spoke about Ivan Denisovich. When I hit on the idea of describing a day in the life of one zek, it was, of course, clear that he would have to be one of the most lowly rank-and-file members of the army of Gulag. I made a mental note of the project, but it evolved no further, and when I undertook to write it in 1959, the question was—whom should I pick? I had rubbed shoulders with very many prisoners in my time; I could recall dozens and dozens whom I had known very well, hundreds even. For some reason, the figure of Ivan Denisovich suddenly, and quite unexpectedly, began to take shape. First the surname—Shukhov—came to me quite by chance. I did not choose it; in fact it was the name of one of the soldiers in my battery during the war. Then, together with the surname, came his face and a few real-life details—the area he was from, and the way he spoke. And all at once, this private from a battery in the Soviet-German war began to take his place in the story *(povest')*, even though he had never been imprisoned. Of course, there was a similarity, in that he, too, was just one of the rank and file, only in different circumstances. But Ivan Denisovich's biography—how he ended up in the camp, and how he behaved when he was there—was drawn from people I met in the camp. I didn't get that from the real Shukhov, who, after all, was never inside.

But you were especially close to him?

Not at all! That's just it, I wasn't at all. No, I was much closer to other soldiers. When I was arrested, he stayed on as a soldier in our battery. I've no reason to suppose that he did time later. He was a good fellow, just a nice, elderly soldier. But I never thought that I would write about him. And suddenly he entered the story of his own accord, with a camp biography and a way of behaving that were composite, based on a number of prisoners I knew. Incidentally, there is an autobiographical element here, too, of course—autobiographical in the sense that I could could not have described him if I hadn't served as a simple bricklayer in the camp. It is difficult to pick up any real understanding of a particular kind of work just from hearsay. I am describing a peasant—with his peasant know-how and his zek's grasp of things—but it is inevitable that something of my own experience should go into the picture, too. And the same is true of any fictional character. I describe Rusanov—a man who is my complete opposite in every respect—yet that revulsion and fear which he experiences as he enters the cancer clinic, for example, that, of course, contains an autobiographical element, in fact, an element common to all men. And this is precisely what the potential of art consists in: a man can unerringly intuit and recreate all kinds of other people on the basis of his own experience.

Might it not be more correct to speak of experience than "autobiographical" factors?

Yes, indeed, experience...personal experience.

Do you always spread yourself around like this among the bulk of your characters?

Yes, I would say so. Because without personal experience, of life or of human psychology, it is impossible to write at all. Why is it that young people cannot instantly become writers? Because experience is precisely what they lack. If I set out to describe you, then my task is to enter into you as deeply as I can, and to communicate you to others. But that is impossible if I haven't yet gained any practical experience of human psychology.

Several commentators have remarked that you seem to invest even Lenin with a part of yourself. Is that your feeling, too?

...Lenin is one of the central figures in my epopee, and the central figure in modern history. I have been thinking about him from the very first moment that I conceived the epopee—that's forty years already—and I have been collecting everything I could find about him, one crumb, one fragment at a time—absolutely everything.

But you used to see and understand him in a different light?

I have gradually come to understand him over the course of the years. I have even compiled catalogues listing individual incidents in his life according to the character traits they reveal. Whatever I learned about him, read in his works and in memoirs, I itemized, noting that these events indicated such-and-such a feature, while those events showed another. I do not use the index while I am writing, but it has all taken shape and been systematized in my head. Now that I feel I have matured to the point where I can describe Lenin, I am writing about specific years in his life, the years in Zurich. And, naturally, events from his party work and personal life fit in retrospectively. My sole task is to create the living Lenin, just as he was, ignoring all the official haloes and official legends. But to say that I am drawing on myself in creating Lenin is an utterly superficial assertion. I am drawing exclusively upon *him* himself. At the same time, I could not describe him, just as I could not have described Rusanov, Shukhov, or any other character—Iakonov in *The First Circle*, for instance, or Podduev in *Cancer Ward*—without myself having attained to a certain level of psychological and every-day experience, which enables me to comprehend another person in his own environment and with his own objectives. That is the way it is.

As you walked around Zurich, I imagine you were trying...

That's right, Zurich helped me a lot. After all, I had written the chapters about Lenin in Zurich while I was still in Moscow—one for the first "knot" [*August 1914*], and one for the second. But when I came to Zurich, there was the city itself; then there were people who had known Lenin, and all these libraries, and material about the Swiss Social-Democrats, in whose midst he had lived—material that was impossible to come by in the Soviet Union. And in Zurich, for example, I was helped by the son of that very same Platten who transported Lenin through Germany. They gave me so much material that it was soon swelling to bursting point. Incidentally, that's the best sign that the writing is going as it should: if the material accumulates by itself and expands beyond your expectation, then you can rest assured that the end result will be highly compact. It's quite hopeless to start off by creating a general framework and then to try and fill it with material. It will turn out to be a flabby failure.

But you first wrote Lenin in Zurich *in Moscow. So you were able to form an intuitive picture of Zurich while you were still in Moscow? Unfortunately, we have not read that first draft...*

I think I more or less had the measure of Lenin at that time. I had already been thinking about him for many years. But a great many factual details were revealed to me in Zurich, and I have been able to re-read Lenin's works of the Zurich period in the light of those details. They give the works new meaning; they flesh them out. I thought that I had read this same Lenin back in Moscow, yet I couldn't then understand him from his books as well as I came to understand him once I had assimilated the Zurich materials.

So it not only broadened the work, but also modified its tonality?

Well, it gave it more flesh, and threw things into somewhat sharper relief: I was able to bring out the psychological nuances more precisely. But this didn't affect the general tone of the portrait—that I already understood. Still, it sharpened the contours and increased the density of the work.

So it was a question of absorbing Lenin into yourself, rather than projecting him from out of yourself?

But I simply cannot imagine how I would dare to create an historical character "out of myself." No, I created him from himself. From his whole life, all his qualities, all the episodes and events he experienced—from himself. Only, in so doing, I did not, of course, cease to be the author. It was my task to make him alive, the way he actually was, but, inasmuch as I am the author, my understanding of his psychology, of his party psychology, is naturally based on the fact that I have studied the whole history of the Party, that I have lived in that country, and that I know communism.

The fact that you have, in a sense, rejected the short form seems to indicate a certain tendency to synthesize—to synthesize the experience of Russian history, but also (am I correct?) to achieve a formal synthesis by combining various literary devices.

It is not that I have rejected the short form. It would give me a lot of satisfaction—artistic satisfaction—to have a rest and go back to the short form.

But you cannot permit yourself to do so?

No. Unhappily, the course of Russian history has been such, that in the sixty years which have elapsed since the events I am describing, not one substantial, coherent *literary* account has been written, nor a documentary one, for that matter. The last eyewitnesses are dying off, but it is still possible to question some of the living. The whole fabric of life as it existed before and up to the revolution has been destroyed, and my generation may well be the last which can still treat this material as something other than history, which can write about it not purely in the form of a historical narrative, but drawing upon the vestiges of living memory. In any case, my own childhood memory has preserved the post-revolutionary atmosphere very well. In the twenties, the population of Russia was still almost prerevolutionary in the way it lived. The breath of those times still comes to me. It helps me process the material.

So it is not altogether an historical novel; it is a link between epochs.

I think that this is the last chance for my generation to write, while for the next generation the task will already be a purely historical one.

More retrospective...

Entirely so. Which is why I simply must complete this work. And since its main dramatis persona is Russia as a whole, it is a vast narrative. No matter how much I compress it—and even if God grants me another twenty years of life—I shall still only just succeed in finishing it.

There will be no main hero as in a normal novel?

Absolutely not! This is a principle of mine: a single man, with his personal viewpoint and attitudes, cannot convey the whole course of events and their significance. It is essential that even the main, leading characters, the author's favorites, should run into dozens, with a cast of hundreds in all. But the true protagonist is Russia herself. There can only be one solution to this problem, a solution which I hit upon some time ago: it is wrong to present the whole course of history in sequence. That would turn out to be very long and unreadable. I thought of a way of concentrating the narration, by creating *knots*—another way of increasing the density of the work. Dotted along this historical curve (in the mathematical sense of a curved line of history) are a number of critical points—a mathematician would call them "specific" points. I take all these nodal points and convey them, in the form of "knots," as densely as possible: this means narrating the events of, say, ten or twenty days without interruption. I generally select points which seem to determine the course of events—not necessarily external events, but internal ones, decisive events, historical turning-points. And I give a dense and detailed account of those ten or twenty days. Then comes an interval before the next "knot" begins. That is how the idea of the "knots" came about.

But isn't it hard to correlate the family scenes in the novel with its historical dimension? In August 1914, *the military epopee rather tended to force out the novelistic part.*

This is how I conceived the first "knot." I could not show the whole First World War (even though its history has yet to be written in our country). So I decided to choose one single event—a battle—and to show the entire war through this event. I made that choice when I was nineteen years old, in 1937. I studied the history of the war and realized, even then, that I could not describe its whole course, still less that of the revolution and civil war. That was when I chose the Samsonov catastrophe, and in 1937 I began to write the first chapters—as early as that. Those were my first chapters. And it is typical that when I returned to the project many years later, in 1969, I left this sequence of chapters the way I had composed them—straight out of the year 1937. That is, only the texture and style of the writing were changed; the images were now more polished, since I was already an adult. But this idea of showing the whole war through the Samsonov catastrophe was there from the outset.

I allowed myself to make one "knot" an entirely military one, not because I wanted to write a military history, but because it had to be representative of the war as a whole. So far, very little of the plot has concerned the family, the personal side. And, in fact, they never will occupy the foreground.

They'll never...

No, they will never be in the foreground, because my main goal is to show the course of events in Russia. As for the personal fates of individuals, they always seem very full to the characters themselves, but they do not always have much influence on the course of history.

The culmination of August 1914 is the personal tragedy of Samsonov. Are there to be other such Shakespearian moments in the following "knots"?

That wasn't the way I planned it, you know. It just happened that way. All I had planned to have was the Samsonov catastrophe, but when I began to describe it, the figure of Samsonov began to grow on its own—his own personal tragedy, that is. It was never planned, so I cannot say whether there will be such moments later on. But it is obvious that each "knot" will have its principal actors. They will have their critical moments, and, if I manage to convey it, then, yes, it will always be from that point of view.

You are having to think more carefully about the forms you use to diversify the narrative. You vary the typographical layout, and present the narrative in different ways.

You'll appreciate that (and this is always the case) an artist must not concoct a form, unless the material dictates it to him. The question was: what to do about the form in the case of an enormous narrative like this? If one were to take the usual approach, the work would be too long and anything but compact. It might be pleasant to read, but to read twenty such "knots" in succession would be almost impossible. The events themselves are very concentrated, and they absolutely demand some variation in the narrative *genres* (*vidy*), so to speak. I now have as many as eight such genres in all.

Rather more than in August 1914?

Yes. And I did not invent any of them in order to show off my formal virtuosity, or just for the sake of creating a new form. Far from it! All I am concerned with each time is how to get the material across. Take the idea of a television screen, for instance. I never go seeking out new problems. I never think: how about trying out a TV screen?

You have been criticized for reproducing Dos Passos's method.

Now, Dos Passos... I got to know his writing in a rather original setting—the Lubianka prison. While I was in the Lubianka, they brought in his *1919*. At the time I was more concerned with my prison experiences, but I read it and I was struck by how near it was to what was needed.

Certainly, I learned from Dos Passos, but in a specific sense. I learned two things, if you will—his newspaper montages and his so-called camera-eye—that's his own term for it. However, I think that Dos Passos... I do not really know what goal he had in mind— was he trying to experiment, or was it in order to express his material better? Anyway, I saw that, in their present form, these two techniques were not applicable to my project, but that they might indeed be applicable if they were modified. Take the camera-eye, for example. His camera-eye is not the same as a scenario. If you look at Dos Passos you'll find that you cannot film with his camera-eye. So, why did he call it that? These are more like lyrical fragments...

Yes, that's right.

Lyrical fragments...but I tackle it as if the episode were actually being filmed. I had already had the experience of writing a scenario, *Tanks Know the Truth*. There wasn't a hope that it would ever be filmed during my lifetime. I had to invent a form that would allow the reader to see the film, even as he was reading the scenario. The film might never be made, but it didn't matter—the reader would have already seen it. And I devised a lay-out which would make it easier, not harder, for the reader to distinguish the soundtrack, what was in the frame, the dialogue, and the shooting directions. This is the form that I took up later, in my little cinema-screen episodes.

In the epopee?

Yes. There they are quite small. But there comes a moment in the narration when you suddenly want to do without dialogue, when I, the author, start blocking my readers' view of events, and it is time for him to see them directly. For example, the flight of Blagoveshchenskii's corps. To me it seems impossible to convey the retreat of Blagoveshchenskii's corps other than visually—let the reader actually see the panic. Later, in similar situations, there will be street-scenes and scenes from the revolution—street-scenes in Petrograd, railroad scenes as the deserters journey back to the rear. There comes a moment when the narrator gets in the way; he becomes a wall between the reader and the material. It is better to put a scene like that in front of the reader straight away, so that he can see it all with his own eyes.

These are mass scenes, very rapid and dynamic.

Very dynamic and, yes, basically mass scenes—you're quite right. There aren't even any individual actors left anymore, just representatives of the masses. But all this has to be visual, so that you feel like filming it. But even without filming it, the reader should see the scene immediately; it shouldn't need a movie.

And is the symbolic moment heightened in such scenes?

For the most part it isn't even a question of symbolism, but sometimes they do offer a very convenient place in which to stress the symbolical moment.

For example, that very vivid scene in August 1914, *when the image of the wheel stands out.*

Yes, there is a symbolical image there. I later read critics who saw these fragments as prose-poems. I never conceived of them that way. But because of my desire to influence my reader's visual perception, they are evidently so intensely emotional that they do, indeed, finish up by taking on that additional resonance. This hadn't even occurred to me. Since you mention Dos Passos, I should say that I have used his second innovation, too. But here, once again, I used it the other way round, so to speak. Dos Passos thought up those newspaper montages. With him, they have a functional role: he wants to convey the incoherence of a flood of newsprint which has no actual relation to life. True life is not reflected in this torrent of newspapers, and that's what his montage is meant to show. But with me, it's the opposite, thanks to the peculiarities of Russian life. In the West, it may well be that the torrent of newsprint neither reflects life, nor carries it along in its wake. This may be due to freedom of the press and to the very abundance of publications. In the early history of the Soviet Union—and its later history, as well—newspapers had a completely different significance. Our newspapers were bursts of machine-gun fire, their phrases—firing squads. Our papers made things happen.

When I create a newspaper montage, it is much stricter and tighter, it is composed much more with the plot in mind, because the course of history itself is reflected in these newspaper montages of mine. So their function is completely the reverse, quite dissimilar.

Well, they sometimes have an ironical character.

Sometimes, and sometimes they convey the march of history. It is also a way of economizing resources. Because I use it to capture, briefly and succinctly, a certain historical moment. However, it is essential to apply many other forms of narration, so as to save the reader time, and to keep down the number of pages. Inevitably, this involves introducing certain folkloric elements, especially during the

Civil War period. Just one song, like "Hey, little apple! Where are you rolling?" can, if presented the right way, evoke the spirit of an epoch very succinctly. It can produce a complete psychological shift in just four lines.

So in the following "knots" the folkloric element will be strengthened?

It's not that it will be strengthened, but it will be present the whole time. First there will be genuine folklore, then official folklore.

Then there are the proverbs that I sometimes bring in: they have been misinterpreted by literary critics as pointing a "moral," as if I wanted to sum up, to add a moral conclusion of my own.

As in fables . . .

Yes, and that's precisely what I am not doing. Again, I use this device in a different way. These proverbs, of which there are a few in each "knot"—five, seven, even nine—these proverbs express, as it were, the voice of the people. I have a mental picture: among my readers I see a certain peasant—he may even be illiterate but he listens and listens to what's in the story, then out he comes with his proverb, just rattles it off. It's never simply a conclusion, but always supplements the narrative in a certain sense, and always in a popular form. Perhaps my readers—let us say the intellectuals among them—see one stratum, but the people sees another, and that is the one . . .

A way of revealing the meaning . . .

A new way of revealing the meaning, through the eyes of the people . . .

And finally, the more dynamic future events are—the February Revolution, for instance—the more they will require a dynamic rendering of the text. It is impossible to write narrative chapters smoothly when events are happening hour by hour, minute by minute, and when in the space of three days the country can change beyond all recognition. In these circumstances, it is obvious that one has to present small fragments, to piece events together out of fragments, as in a mosaic. Either of these extremes is dangerous: the whole thing could be written in fragments, but that, too, might weary the reader; he could not stand this succession of flickering images . . .

If there are too many . . .

The thing to do is to try and strike a balance between flowing narrative chapters, which reflect the lives of individual characters, and these fragmentary montages, with their rapid succession of events and very broad canvas.

And will all the strata of society be represented in the subsequent "knots"?

That has always been my aim. I've always wanted to give a full vertical section of society, if possible—as much of it as I can.

Without the participation of the masses and the lower classes there is no history, and there can be no historical novel—that's to say, no historical narrative.

But in the course of an epopee as long as this, you are bound to re-examine even the finished parts. You have finished August 1914, *for instance, and now comes a certain interval before the appearance of the next "knots." Doesn't this compel you to draw the "knots" closer together?*

Of course, when you write a series of books, then connecting them one to another is obviously the correct procedure. At the beginning—the very beginning—I did think of not publishing so much as a single "knot" until the whole work was finished, in other words, I would complete my twenty years or twenty-five years of work, and then publish it. Perhaps that would have been the right way to do it, but who can resist trying to influence the thinking of his contemporaries?

That would be impossible.

You see? I didn't *have* to publish it, but there's always this urge to exert an influence, to present something—if only fragments of history—as it becomes ready.

You need to have a certain contact with your reader through...

Yes, because, if my long years of work have given me any insight into the true course of events, then I would simply like my contemporaries to learn of it.

But the correct thing for me to do would seem to be not to publish any particular "knot" until two others, or at least one, are ready. That way they wouldn't come straight out of the frying pan, but would appear gradually, and readers would be waiting for the next one. That allows a smoother transition and keeps the reader more in touch with the plot.

But the reader is involved in the actual creation of this epopee, just as he was in the creation of Gulag *in Russia. You've had a response from former eyewitnesses now living in the West.*

That's right. I needed *August* as a way to make contact with participants in those events, people who still had something to tell me. I have just recently issued an appeal to émigré readers. It would have been extremely valuable if I could have made such an appeal when I was still living in the Soviet Union. But while I was there I usually travelled about secretly to visit the scene of this or that event, since they were always trying to prevent me from seeing anything, and it was very difficult to interview eyewitnesses. I was in Tambov province and visited the area where the peasant uprising took place. Some witnesses are still alive, but they were all afraid to talk to strangers, and, for my part, I was wary of asking questions, lest the authorities cut short my expedition. It was very difficult for me to gather material there. On the other hand, people have helped me greatly by bringing or sending from various places books which have been systematically destroyed in the Soviet Union. Certain Cheka [secret police] publications, for example. They were all supposed to have been burnt, but somewhere a copy or two has been preserved. People know about my work and bring them to me. I have been greatly helped by persons unknown to me, who sent their accounts, materials, memoirs and books.

In spite of all the difficulties, you are still writing your epopee with the support of the Russian people, with your readers taking an active part?

The whole time. Just as I collaborated with former zeks when I wrote *Gulag*, so I am writing this epopee at a time when participants are still alive and able to give me material. Unfortunately, my expulsion from the Soviet Union has deprived me of the possibility of traveling to the sites of events, but I have already seen a fair amount—including Petersburg, Moscow, Tambov and the Don. I've seen enough—I grew up on the Don and I'm quite at home in the cities of Rostov and Novocherkassk.

Critics have more than once observed that August 1914 *has a rather slow and deliberate beginning. Did you intend to have such a slow-moving story-line? Will it be repeated, or does it eventually disappear?*

I have just told you that during the course of revolutionary events even narrating a series of dynamic actions strikes me as too slow-moving. At the beginning of *August*, on the other hand, the pace is consciously retarded. You know, it's a bit like taking a panoramic photograph: in order to make the individual shots intersect and fit together, you have to let each one slightly overlap the next. The beginning of *August 1914* is done this way in order to show the rather leisurely pace of life in pre-war Russia. It is done for purposes of identification, since not even a scrap of that life can ever come again. Things will never move at that tempo any more. In the future, people will not pay so much attention to family problems, because the pace and dynamics of life will by then be entirely different.

An image of pre-revolutionary Russia, so to speak?

No, not an image. It's there just to acquaint the reader with several chapters depicting the slow tempo of life as it was. The Tomchak family does not have any special significance for the whole of Russia. It represents only one layer of society (one, incidentally, which has been given little exposure), a layer of dynamic, upwardly mobile peasants. But this is not the important thing. It's the slow tempo that matters: this is how it once was, but now it has gone forever.

So it will never return? This serves, then, as a general introduction to the whole epopee?

Yes, it shows a pace of life which has vanished for good.

You have just said that upwardly mobile, dynamic peasants, in fact, the peasantry in general is reflected more broadly in your work. Ivan Denisovich and Blagodarev occupy an important place in your writing. It has even been suggested that you have over-idealized the Russian peasant and shown him without any failings.

The peasantry did, after all, make up more than eighty percent of the Russian population, and if I want the work to be representative, then it's clear that there must be a lot of peasants—and so there will be. As for the question of idealization, well, I would put it differently: people in the West tend to speak about the former Russia as something essentially bad, because all their information about Russia comes from the hands of revolutionaries who hated the country. Therefore, any evidence to the contrary is taken as idealization. Later on, of course, when the peasants are tempted by slogans such as "Throw down your rifles," "Seize the land," and "Steal from the plunderers"—then, of course, the peasant soul will take an abrupt turn towards the dark side.

But Blagodarev will not be tempted?

Well, you know, there are already some hints in *August* as to what he will become, but I don't want to spell it out prematurely. And then the working class . . .

Up to now you have shown practically nothing of it, even though it did already exist in 1914.

It had no place in *August 1914* because that "knot" dealt with a single battle. From the second "knot" on, I begin to pay considerable attention to depicting the working class. There is a legend in the Soviet Union to the effect that the working class made the revolution and was, how shall I put it, its moving force and authority. Actually, the working class was one of the worst victims, one of the most deceived of all our social groups. And perhaps the greatest deception of all was that phantom of a "dictatorship of the proletariat," something which never for a moment existed. Yes, beginning with the second "knot," the figures of workers and whole chapters on the working class will be a constant feature of the narrative.

And will the Communist Party be shown? Will its leaders, apart from Lenin, figure in the text?

Not only the Communist Party, but socialist parties of other varieties, as well. And the Communist Party has its own official list of legendary names, while other names have been liquidated and destroyed.

Take Shliapnikov, for example. I was very tempted. I do mention him in *Lenin in Zurich*, but only through Lenin's eyes. Lenin did not understand Shliapnikov and did not appreciate his worth, whereas in fact Shliapnikov played a role second to no one in the whole party before the revolution. I have a chapter on Shliapnikov in Petersburg in October of 1916, which I finished a long time ago. However, when I made the selection for *Lenin in Zurich*, it wasn't appropriate to include it, much as the book would have benefitted from it. The contrast with Shliapnikov would have helped readers to understand the figure of Lenin. For Shliapnikov was the one communist who was a genuine worker and always tried to remain one, who had genuine connections with the underground and the working class, and who was a genuine historical activist. He met his doom in the very first years of the revolution, when his defense of the workers' interests set him in opposition to Lenin. This spelt his ruin, and with it vilification and oblivion.

Was this because he was a man of the people, or were there some other attendant circumstances?

It was due to one happy circumstance. Though a professional revolutionary, he never ceased to be an excellent turner and a splendid worker. He was proud of the fact that, of all the leaders of the so-called workers' party, he was the only one who worked the whole time.

The others were more intellectuals, or would-be intellectuals.

They were incapable even of earning their bread except by journalism. But Shliapnikov went to the lathe and worked: he fed himself, and Lenin, and others, too...

And these intellectuals will also figure in the work...

They most certainly will—each in a critical moment, as he takes an historic step. Yes, indeed.

Readers have remarked on the very strong satirical strain in certain of your works, particularly Gulag. *Will this be a feature of the "knots," as well?*

No. You know, the reason the satirical side is strong in *Gulag* is because the whole time I was up against a vast unwieldy mass of propagandistic lies. And I was incapable of countering them in a limited space, other than through satire. The satirical touch can get rid of them by the ton. But here, I have to describe history, history in progress, and that does not call for the satirical approach.

Then you are not a satirist by vocation?

No. Not at all.

Some people have said that you are.

No. They're quite wrong.

They claim that you would have been a satirical writer whatever had happened...

You know, that just isn't so. You have to experience our crude Soviet propaganda to realize that there is no way of responding other than through satire; it takes the sharp thrust of satire to shift this ton of lies.

Would you have been a writer under any circumstances? Have you ever thought about what you might have become under normal circumstances—if you hadn't been imprisoned, that is?

I can't even begin to imagine *normal* circumstances, but under Soviet conditions, I must say that there were great spiritual dangers confronting me if I had not been arrested at the end of the war. For, if I had become a writer in the mainstream of Soviet literature, then of course, I would not have been myself and would have lost God. It's not easy to imagine what I might have turned out to be, with all those literary projects of mine. But, luckily, fate led me through the Archipelago: the path seemed long at the time, but actually it could not have been shorter.

What about your personal attitude toward your own works? Do you ever re-read them? Is there any work you like best of all? Or do you lose interest in them and just forge ahead?

Recently, I have begun to re-read some of them. Naturally, when you re-read your old things after a gap of ten years or so, you see changes you would like to make. But the work already exists and has already been around for a long time, so does the author have the right to make changes? The writer himself has changed; he's become a different person. The personal attitude of a writer is always the same: you have a passion for the thing you are writing today, but then it breaks off from you and lives its own separate life.

And you no longer think of it as your own property?

No, not as property. You respond to it as a complete outsider; sometimes it even takes you by surprise. You're standing back from it, and it seems unexpectedly new. There may be paragraphs there that you have forgotten. The work you are writing today fills your whole life.

For the work which you are writing at present, you would need a whole research institute, with so many events and so many layers of society figuring in it. How can you cope with this huge mass of disparate material?

Only by an inordinate amount of work—my own and that of my helpers, people close to me who are helping me.

But it takes a talent for organization, if one is not to be overwhelmed...

Under our terrible conditions, a writer has to be a conspirator, a strategist, and also capable of organizing his material, because there's no hope of setting up an institute, and the material keeps flowing in, vast quantities of it. The work is excessive, very demanding; I don't know whether I will manage to complete the whole project—it will take many days of my life to complete it. A great many, a great many.

*   *   *

I am now going to put a question to you which may be a bit naive. Which figure in Russian literature—which writer—serves as your guiding star? Which writer do you feel closest to?

I think that for all of us, and for more than a century now, the guiding star is Pushkin. In fact, the further we move away from him, the more we realize how much we have lost in him, and how much of what he did needs to be continued. Pushkin is an incomparable star, in that he created our language and literature (not out of nothing, of course)—in this respect he has never had an equal. But, of course, in one way or another we have been brought up on the entire tradition of the nineteenth century. Tolstoi and Dostoevskii have always been an influence, on each and every one of us.

But at one time Tolstoi was a moral authority for you?

Rather to the contrary. I read *War and Peace* when I was ten years old.

Ten?

Yes... I did not understand the personal side of the plot at all, needless to say, but I was completely caught up by the overall composition and the historical scenes. I think that novel had a strong effect on me and on my desire to write an historical novel. But if we are talking about when I was older and already concerned with moral questions, then Dostoevskii poses such questions more sharply, profoundly and prophetically, and with greater relevance to the modern world.

You did not go through the experience of Tolstoianism?

Never... In the novel I talk about it because it was fashionable at that time. I try to show how it eventually led to the revolution.

So this is more an imaginative than an autobiographical element?

Yes, as far as I myself am concerned, because I do not figure in the text. My father did pass through Tolstoianism at one time, and that's why I give him this feature. But, you know, speaking of the present day, I consider that for us writers of the twentieth century—and that includes me as well—there are definite models to be found in the prose of Zamiatin and Tsvetaeva. (Tsvetaeva's prose is altogether concentrated in an unbelievably powerful way.) Hers is a prose for writers, not for readers, and it would have to be diluted ten times over in order for ordinary people to be able to read it.

You are attracted by this verbal compactness...

A verbal compactness with such dynamic twists and turns, and explosions. But there is much about Zamiatin, too, that is striking. Chiefly his syntax. If I regard anyone as my predecessor in syntax, it is Zamiatin. And then there is the unbelievable vividness and power of his portraits. Sometimes he describes a whole face in just one or two words. He did much more than Chekhov in this regard. Chekhov was already trying to avoid describing the kind of eyes, mouth or nose a character had, and instead described by means of a comparison...

An image...

No, not even an image; he would use a comparison to convey the whole face. Zamiatin goes much further; sometimes with a single word, he catches a portrait as expressive as one done by a painter. I don't think that anyone has achieved such heights of laconic portraiture as Zamiatin—it's truly striking.

And you have read a lot by him...

You can't read a lot of him, because he didn't write much. His life took such an unhappy turn that he had no time for writing. There is that well-known prerevolutionary story of his that was banned, about the army, the peacetime army of those days, in a garrison in the rear. And then there was his brilliant *We*. And his stories from the early Soviet period. During the twenties, Zamiatin was virtually the doyen of Russian prose.

Yes, he was the leading figure . . .

That's right, although Gor'kii or someone else was officially regarded as the leading figure. In fact, Zamiatin was unquestionably the one. And in the twenties his was a magisterial voice; he spoke as dean of Soviet letters—and quite rightly, he had every justification—and it was he who wrote annual surveys of literature in 1926-1927.

But then it all ended unhappily, and he was suppressed. They allowed him to leave the country, and, for some baffling reason, here in the West he became completely lost. After all, he was well-versed in the ways of the West. He had lived here. He was a first-rate engineer; he had worked as a marine engineer here, in England, during the prerevolutionary years. There are those "English stories" he wrote. I can't understand why he went into such an utter decline in the West. Perhaps he had given his word that he would keep quiet.

Well, perhaps he did not manage to make the necessary change?

Maybe he was hampered by illness, I don't know. The fate of émigré writers is, in general, a very bitter one. See: the older ones wrote about the past, while the younger ones, like Nabokov, decided to choose English literature.

. . . decided simply to leave . . .

To leave. I consider that fatal for the direction of Russian literature.

Well, that will not happen with you . . .

I am already closer to the older writers than to the younger ones. It is difficult, of course . . .

You got to know Tsvetaeva's works later?

Yes, comparatively recently. It was almost impossible to get hold of her. And Zamiatin wasn't easy to find, either; every little volume was difficult to come by. But now I have a small Zamiatin library of my own. There is no complete edition of his works.

Do you ever re-read Pushkin? When you want to have a rest, from yourself and your works, and you reach for a book—who are you drawn to?

Pushkin is an inexhaustible source for all of us, and, although everyone has always recognized that we grew out of Pushkin, for some reason his prose has been little imitated—his dynamic, surprisingly condensed prose, with its meager attributes and its absence of ornamentation. The late Tolstoi in such stories as "Khadzhi Murat" and "Prisoner of the Caucasus" perhaps came closest of all. But Tolstoi constructed his major novels in a consciously different way; there is no similarity.

There was no one to continue Pushkin's line: he immediately attained such perfection.

Such simplicity... Lermontov derived from Pushkin in some measure. But this rapierlike prose of his had something of a Western hue.

He softened it.

And who knows how it would have developed later. They all died so young—what can one say about what might have happened to Lermontov's prose, or Pushkin's?

So you see your prose, in part, as a return to Pushkinian laconism?

I always avoid the word "return." I'm very wary of it... for what kind of return can there be? We are always going forward, always going somewhere. I dream of the greatest possible laconism. But in the contemporary world, so overloaded with abstract concepts, what can one do to achieve that laconism without impoverishing the content—that is the question.

—Translated from the Russian by the editors.

An Exchange with Boris Souvarine on
Lenin in Zurich

ALEKSANDR SOLZHENITSYN

*The texts which follow form part of a vigorous exchange of views between Solzheni-
tsyn and Boris Souvarine. Before his break with the communist movement, Souvarine
(b. 1895) had been a founding member of the French Communist Party, a leading
figure in the Comintern, and a personal acquaintance of Lenin and other prominent
revolutionaries. Since then, he has acquired a reputation as a distinguished historian,
author of a pioneering biography of Stalin (1935). In 1958, Souvarine founded the review, Le Contrat Social in Paris. He was also the chief contributor of the bulletin Est et
Ouest. In 1976, one complete sixteen-page issue of Est et Ouest (No. 570, 1-15 April
1976) was taken up by the essay "Soljénitsyne et Lénine," Souvarine's appraisal of
Lenin in Zurich. This essay—perhaps the most serious challenge to Solzhenitsyn's historical method which has yet appeared—is already accessible to the English-speaking
reader, albeit in somewhat abridged from, in Dissent, Summer 1977, pp. 324-36. In it
Souvarine expressed his admiration for Solzhenitsyn as a literary and moral figure, but
took him to task in point of historical detail. Many of the issues raised recur in the ensuing exchange. In the main, Souvarine's strictures concern: Solzhenitsyn's comparative
ignorance of historical research on Lenin published in the West; his unwitting vulner-
ability to ideologically warped Soviet historiography; his tendency to mould the facts to
suit his own interpretation of the revolution (as something essentially alien and antagonistic to Russia); and his recourse to improbable fictional episodes. The essay went
unanswered until 1980, when Solzhenitsyn replied in an open letter which is translated
below (from the Russian text in Russkaia mysl', No. 3304, 17 April 1980, p. 5). At about
the same time it appeared in French translation in the journal l'Histoire (No. 22, April
1980, pp. 70-71).*

Document 1

Dear Mr. Souvarine,

Due to my lack of knowledge of French, it is only now that I have
been able to acquaint myself with the full text of your article, "Solzhenitsyn and Lenin," in which you raise certain charges against my
book *Lenin in Zurich* and against my method of work. Since I have no
reason to suppose that you had any personal motive in writing the
article, and since it appears to contain no serious or substantial

objections, I can only explain it in terms of the political predilections of your early years as a communist. But this is all the more reason for not leaving it unanswered.

First of all, you completely ignore the fact that *Lenin in Zurich* is a literary work (at one point you dignify it with the title "novelized fiction"), and thus your criticism is tantamount to draining an aquarium in order to study the life of the fish in it. I am surprised that, among all your other reproaches, you did not ask how Parvus could possibly have squeezed into a traveling case! This is a literary work, yet I tried my utmost to make my presentation of the historical facts irreproachably accurate, even down to the last day and the last hour: and you, for all your counter-efforts, have been unable to find any factual distortions. But what my book is devoted to first and foremost, the theme by which it stands or falls, is Lenin as a psychological type, his character, his inner life and day-to-day behavior. You, however, do not even comment on whether or not I have portrayed this type of mentality faithfully. Instead, you air your own opinions with all the assurance of the last man on earth entitled to pass judgment upon Lenin. Only the fact that you ignore the literary nature of my book could have led you to ask such questions as: Why, when using Lenin's own expressions, does Solzhenitsyn draw only upon the volumes [of the Collected Works] which relate to the period in Zurich, and not upon all fifty-five volumes, covering his whole life? Or, why is Solzhenitsyn content to use only eight out of the one hundred documents published by Werner Hahlweg?

And what method of research do you propose instead? A purely arbitrary one. "One has to know how to read archives," you lecture me, yet you yourself select only those documents which accord with your own notions. Even a documented admission by the German Minister of Foreign Affairs to the effect that Germany gave large sums of money to *Pravda* in 1917—even this you effortlessly brush aside as false. Indeed, you dismiss in the most contemptuous terms the entire Russian press of 1917, together with the written testimony of dozens of Russians, and even such historians as Sergei Mel'gunov and George Katkov. To say nothing of the ridicule you pour upon my attempts to gather evidence from the surviving Russian eyewitnesses to the events of that time. You, on the other hand, regard as superior the evidence of foreigners then living in Russia, and among the most reliable you single out Angelica Balabanova, who herself took Lenin's route through Germany (Balabanova still awaits her historian:

Burtsev began the work of clarifying her connections in *Obshchee delo* of October 1917). Although your article is extremely long, you cannot even find room in it for a serious analysis of the main theses of my book. "The reader would find such a refutation unnecessarily wearisome"—how very convenient! It is not me you are arguing with, but an opponent of your own invention.

You are chiefly concerned with two issues:

1. Whether Lenin made use of German money "before April 1917, at least." (The qualification you add is eloquent in itself.)

2. Whether the railroad car in which Lenin made his trip through Germany was sealed or armored.

On the first point, you are forced to admit that I think precisely as you do: up to the beginning of 1917, Lenin conspicuously did not make use of German money (Party funds were still sustained by what was left of the money looted from the Russian treasury).

As for the second point, you repeat yourself with particular persistence. Eleven times you use the word "sealed," yet in the entire course of my book it is used *not once*. (On one occasion, p. 210 of the Russian edition, I describe the railroad car as "extraterritorial," but you come to the same conclusion!) So why do battle with phantoms? The "sealed" car has entered into folklore, but I do not refer to it, so what are we arguing about?

However, in the course of this noisy dispute, you characteristically reveal your own position. You cite [Balabanova]: "This arrangement implied no compromise or favor on the part of any government." Really? In time of war, one side grants free passage through its territory to a group of subversive political activists from the opposing state, and this does not constitute a "favor"? This was a form of support more valuable by far than gold! You refer to a "completely legal journey by 300-400 people." But what do you understand by "legal," and how does this differ from the traditional attitude of the Comintern? Not only for Russia, but in the eyes of France and England as well, the only way to describe such safe-conduct was "treachery." (The concept of "fatherland" is not treated in your article, but you digress at some length on how a man's origins do not constitute a bond with his homeland. This denial of any moral link with the country of one's fathers, so characteristic of the Comintern, makes itself felt in your evaluation of Lenin's journey.)

It is especially noteworthy, among the specific points raised in your article, that you can bring yourself to deny, even today, that

Hanecki was Lenin's secret agent and special confidant, and to suggest that Lenin "recommended caution" in dealing with Karl Moor (an example of Lenin's customary use of camouflage: he himself made extensive use of Moor's services). But the main question embodied in your article is whether Lenin did or did not take German money *after April 1917*. My book does not cover that period, but your impassioned tone compels me to reply.

Fritz Platten the Younger has demonstrated that during Lenin's passage through Sweden there was a day which has remained secret—a day purloined by Soviet historians—and this subterfuge would have been pointless had it not been necessary to conceal a meeting which Lenin had with Parvus in some remote part of Sweden. And it was after this that the "independent businessman," Hanecki, set up the "Foreign Bureau of the Central Committee" in Stockholm, through which German money poured in to expand the activities of the Bolshevik Party. For all that the Bolsheviks were few in number, their publishing enterprises began a period of furious activity: *Pravda*, with its circulation running into millions, together with hundreds of local publications, completely inundated their socialist rivals, all of whom, for some reason, were short of funds. You write that "money had nothing to do with it," yet editions like these are not created free of charge. The Petrograd counter-intelligence services duly established that the Bolsheviks were engineering "mass" demonstrations by paying participants between five and ten roubles a day; that Kozlovskii, a member of the Central Committee (!) of the Bolshevik Party, was conducting largescale banking transactions with money received from Scandinavia, while Lenin's agent, Evgeniia Sumenson, received a steady and substantial flow of money from the same source. Sumenson exchanged telegrams with Hanecki which can only be interpreted as accompanying large monetary remittances. The arrest of Sumenson revealed that she was not engaged in any of the commercial activities referred to in the telegrams, and there was no merchandise to be found. Only their bodyguard of sailors kept the more important Bolsheviks out of the authorities' hands. All the information about the Bolsheviks that could be obtained at the time was promptly published in the Russian press. But for some reason, and despite the farcically weakened state of the Provisional Government and judicial system, Lenin chose not to come forward and give a dignified rebuttal of these charges (wouldn't that have been splendid—sixty years before you did it!).

Instead, he disguised himself and went into hiding (but what for a mere mortal signals cowardice and irrefutable proof of his guilt, is for the great Lenin but a tactical maneuver).

And now, sixty years on, we hear from you that "money had nothing to do with it," that all this had no influence upon the course of history, and that, although genuine receipts were found, none were signed by Lenin himself (but by other people)—as if there can be no high treason without receipts! With the authority almost of a direct participant in these events, and at a time when their terrible and bloody significance is known to all, you try once again to instill into the reader that primitive Bolshevik interpretation of the October revolution, which has Lenin "simply seizing power with the aid of the good soldiers" of the Petrograd garrison (a fighting unit fit for the operetta stage). You can scarcely conceal your admiration for this great Villain. Several times you let slip such expressions as "Lenin's denigrators," "Lenin-haters," "slanderers"—but only Virtue can be slandered or denigrated. And how can anyone blacken Lenin's name more than he himself did by ordering the execution of peasants for failing to clear away snow, or by giving instructions aimed at the destruction of the Church—using the collection of Church valuables to aid the starving as a squalid pretext for stifling the Church (since the famine itself was the work of the Bolsheviks)? What can anyone say about Lenin and Trotskii (whom you coyly leave aside) that would be worse than simply recalling how they created the first and greatest totalitarianism the world has seen, and how they devised the methods of mass terror, including the technique of drowning people imprisoned in barges (thus anticipating the gas chambers)? Your article is morally dangerous in that it seeks to whitewash the crimes of this pair—and with them the communist system itself—while laying the whole blame on their faithful Disciple [Stalin].

In 1921-1923, when you occupied a leading position in the Comintern—during the years when mass peasant uprisings were being crushed, the years of the first iniquitous trials and the first staging of the "people's wrath" in Moscow under the direction of Trotskii (June 1922)—it may be that your youth prevented you from grasping what was happening. But today, when the truth about Lenin's regime has shown its fangs in almost every corner of the world, it is morally inadmissible to go on sowing the same old seeds in new generations, and to regard Lenin's Terror as "historically justified." How can anyone fail to acknowledge in this day and age that the Comintern

trampled on the backs of the unfortunate peoples of Russia, forcing
them to toil and perish for a chimerical world revolution?

Boris Souvarine replied in l'Histoire, *No. 25 (July-August 1980),
pp. 110-111, under the title "Soljénitsyne: le roman et l'histoire":*

Document 2

To summarize, of the 136 published German documents, not one
compromises Lenin, and a single one mentions *Pravda* as the benefi-
ciary of funds transmitted "through various channels and under
different labels," and therefore without the knowledge of the recip-
ients. Solzhenitsyn sets great store by this message, which [Minister
for Foreign Affairs] von Kühlmann sent to the Kaiser, yet it is as
vague as it is belated (having been written in December 1917). Moreover, it was written by a minor secretary (Bergen) and is a routine
document, typical of an official who tended to make unsupported
claims about unverifiable services he had rendered. Now *Pravda* had
ceased publication in July 1917. Von Kühlmann did not know this, nor
did the Kaiser, and still less Solzhenitsyn.
     In 1915 Parvus received one million roubles from the Wilhelm-
strasse, which he claimed to have sent to Petrograd (and, conse-
quently, not to Lenin, who was then living in Switzerland). As I have
explained, Parvus, in fact, made off with the cash. And Solzhenitsyn
admits that subsequently Parvus did not touch a pfennig. Well then?
     Then again, Parvus's biography, upon which Solzhenitsyn draws
extensively, completely exonerates Lenin and his supporters (p. 181).
Shliapnikov's memoirs do the same. Leonard Schapiro, a reliable
historian, has counted some forty Bolshevik newspapers (not hundreds, as Solzhenitsyn rashly asserts), and these were ephemeral
little news-sheets of between two and four pages, many of which only
ran to a few issues. In this regard, the socialist patriots of all hues
published a hundred times more.
     Contrary to what Solzhenitsyn tells us, Lenin's opponents had
enormous sums of money at their disposal. I have already referred
to Olivier Radkey's book, which gives precise figures: Katerina
Breshko-Breshkovskaia, the "grandmother of the revolution," could

draw upon considerable funds in subsidizing the anti-Bolshevik press.

All that Solzhenitsyn writes about Lenin's thirty-two-hour stay in Sweden is pure invention. Parvus turned up at the hotel in full view of everyone, but Lenin refused to see him and had his companions tell Parvus to go to hell. It was a full session of the Bolshevik "fraction" which set up the foreign information bureau in Stockholm, entrusted to the care of a troika: Vorovskii, Hanecki and Radek. Everything Solzhenitsyn says about it is inaccurate. The bureau operated entirely above ground, and published a small bulletin, which was typed out by the wives of Hanecki and Radek. And that was all.

Nowhere in his public writings does Lenin have one good word to say for Parvus. I provided quotations [in my original article]. This rules out any relationship between them, even if a novelist happens to see fit to attribute imaginary conversations to them.

Forgetting to re-read his own book, Solzhenitsyn denies having written about the famous railroad car. In fact, he did so on pages 181, 184, 185, and 188 of the French translation (Editions du Seuil, 1975), and more specifically on page 186 ("sealed railroad car") and page 191 ("locked compartments").

It is not true that Angelica Balabanova accompanied Lenin on his trip.* She was in the second batch of 240 people—the same ones who had reproached Lenin for leaving too soon. Everything that Solzhenitsyn asserts so peremptorily is inaccurate, except when he blames me for regarding as legal this journey by some 400 Russians hurrying back to their homeland. I do indeed find nothing illegal in their return: the exiles used the only route then possible, and did so without the least prejudice to their rights and obligations.

And I, in my turn, blame those who blame them. And I think it scandalous that people should turn Lenin into a kind of "film star," utterly disregarding those 400 or so others, who have been so neglected, even though in March 1917 Lenin was just one socialist among many.

This leaves the question of the twenty-nine telegrams, not written in code and chiefly concerned with the commercial dealings already exposed by Michael Futrell in his book, *Northern Underground.* Evgeniia Sumenson, at whom Solzhenitsyn points an accusing finger,

---

* This error was introduced by the French translator—Eds.

was a representative of the celebrated Swiss firm of Nestlé, among others. As a result of the din raised by the entire Russian press (which scarcely existed, if Solzhenitsyn is to be believed), judicial proceedings were instigated... but simply fizzled out.

And that, I suppose, is the way Solzhenitsyn's diatribe against historical truth in the name of artistic licence should end.

In fact, this text was a considerably condensed version of Souvarine's detailed "Reply to Solzhenitsyn," published belatedly in Russian in two instalments: Russkaia mysl', *No. 3334 (13 November 1980), p. 12; and No. 3335 (20 November 1980), p. 13. By then, however, Solzhenitsyn had already responded to the version printed in* l'Histoire, *without being aware of the fuller reply. His letter, dated 18 June 1980, appeared in Russian in* Russkaia mysl', *No. 3339 (18 December 1980), p. 7, under the title "O fragmentakh Borisa Suvarina." The full text is as follows:*

Document 3

On the Fragments by Boris Souvarine

I am hard put to it to find another term for the genre chosen by Mr. Souvarine in responding to the open letter which I addressed to him in *l'Histoire.* Just as he avoided the central issues in his original, lengthy article criticizing my *Lenin in Zurich*, so, once again, he avoids them in his reply to my letter, and instead of formulating his objections systematically, he presents them as disconnected fragments which vary greatly in significance.

In what sense was it "legal," as he insists even now, for Russian socialists (and only those bent on withdrawing Russia from the war) to journey across hostile German territory? "Legal" by what laws? Does Mr. Souvarine now acknowledge that according to the laws of all the allied states at that time this was an act of high treason and not just a question of 400 revolutionaries "hurrying home"? He frankly admits that he considers them irreproachable, which must mean according to the laws of the Comintern. It is this relic of the past which makes it impossible for Mr. Souvarine and me to find a common language: for Russia the Comintern was a vampire, sucking its blood and vitality. "Early" Soviet power was just as sordid and brutal as was its "later" counterpart.

There is something paradoxical about Souvarine's indignation over the fact that, "for some reason," Lenin has been singled out from the other 400 "like a film star." No, he stood out by himself, thanks to his boundless cynicism, hypocrisy and practical cunning. Not as a "star"—that comparison is well wide of the mark, but as the greatest villain in Russian and world history. It was none other than Lenin (together with Trotskii) who headed the vicious October coup against a defenceless Russian democracy, and who went on to establish mass terror. How can Mr. Souvarine use the word "exculpate" with reference to this murderer of millions, whose orders to take hostage and execute innocent people are proudly printed in his collected works? Never, throughout the course of human history, will Lenin (or Trotskii) be "exculpated."

Fortunately, Mr. Souvarine does not deny the authenticity of the 136 documents published by Zeman. But what he makes of them is nothing short of astounding: neither Lenin, nor the newspaper *Pravda*, nor, it would seem, any of the Bolsheviks at all was in any way compromised! They simply "did not know" who these millions were coming from! But to the average, impartial reader, it is evident from these documents (and how many more, crucial personal contacts are not recorded here?) that Germany intervened decisively in the Russian revolution by providing material support for the Bolsheviks, and that this aid was accepted with avid delight. Nor does Souvarine repudiate the twenty-nine scandalous Bolshevik financial telegrams of 1917, but he defends himself by noting that "the judicial proceedings fizzled out." So they did, thanks to the ineffable feebleness and indecision of the Provisional Government, but that certainly does not make innocent lambs of the Bolsheviks! Souvarine's explanation of the Foreign Bureau of the Central Committee in Stockholm is quite hilarious: three first-rate Bolshevik functionaries and political intriguers are left in Stockholm just so that the wives of two of them can put out one typewritten bulletin. In fact, it was via this Stockholm center that the Bolsheviks were able to implement their connections (some involving Parvus, some not) with the German financial sources sustaining them (and according to E. Bernstein, the sum in question was fifty million marks in gold). This money enabled the Bolsheviks to stand on their own two feet, and to publish hundreds of newspapers and pamphlets in editions large enough to demoralize an army of ten million men in the space of three months—which is just what was supposed to happen. Even after the October coup, this German aid to the Bolsheviks continued for months—right up to the assassination of [the German Ambassador] Mirbach. (In the last month, a further forty million marks was earmarked for the German Embassy in Moscow.)

The fact (denied by Souvarine) that Parvus met secretly with Lenin in Bern is even corroborated in the early Soviet press (*Bakinskii rabochii*, 1 February 1924). Fritz Platten the Younger shows how the dating of Lenin's movements within Sweden was, for some reason, falsified (in a series of articles in *Volksrecht*, April 1967). Not only did the new meeting with Parvus or contacts made through Hanecki and Radek have to be kept secret, but even the very existence of Parvus: where once Soviet courses in marxism had paid detailed attention to him as a prominent socialist, he was now an unperson and was discarded altogether (nor does he figure in the second edition of the *Large Soviet Encyclopedia*).

Since Mr. Souvarine has the advantage of knowing Russian, he could have confirmed at first hand that the word "sealed" [*zaplombirovannyi*] is used *not once* in the Russian edition of *Lenin in Zurich*, and thus spared me this allegation. And in no language in the world does the statement that Balabanova "took Lenin's route through Germany" mean that she had to be with him in the same railroad car.

Thus, one might have hoped that Mr. Souvarine would gradually come to realize that I am not simply a belletristic writer, but that in all my books I place myself in the service of historical truth.

—Translated by the editors.

PART FOUR

Bibliography

A Select Bibliography of Books
About Solzhenitsyn

This bibliography is intended to follow on from the select bibliography—covering the period from 1962 to mid-1974—which appeared in Dunlop, Haugh and Klimoff, eds., *Aleksandr Solzhenitsyn: Critical Essays and Documentary Materials* (1973, 1975). Included here are expanded editions and English translations of works already noted in the previous listing. In addition, several omissions have been rectified. No account is taken of works by Solzhenitsyn himself, since they are the subject of a separate bibliography in the present volume.

So vast and generally uncharted is the body of secondary literature devoted to Solzhenitsyn that we decided to confine our attention to books (including pamphlets and complete issues of journals). All the titles chosen were published in Russian, English, French or German, with the exception of a single important item which chanced to appear in Danish.

Only one new book-length bibliography has appeared during the period in question:

1. Martin, Werner. *Alexander Solschenizyn: Eine Bibliographie seiner Werke*. Hildesheim/New York: Georg Olms, 1977.

> Not exhaustive, but a methodically presented listing of Solzhenitsyn's works in various languages. Treatment of the publicistic works is much weaker than that of the fiction. Secondary literature is almost entirely excluded.

I. SOURCES FOR THE "SOLZHENITSYN AFFAIR"

The nature of Solzhenitsyn's more recent writings, together with the continuing politicization of his reception in the West, make it difficult to sustain the distinction between this category and works of criticism in the more literary sense. That said, we may note:

A. *Collections of Documentary Materials:*

2. Labedz, Leopold. Ed. *Solzhenitsyn: A Documentary Record.* 2nd ed. Harmondsworth: Penguin, 1974.

> This is the fullest of the various English-language editions, and is more up to date than any edition published in the USA.

3. *Zhit' ne po lzhi: Sbornik materialov, avgust 1973-fevral' 1974 [Live Not by Lies: A Collection of Materials from August 1973 to February 1974].* Moscow: Samizdat, 1974; Paris: YMCA-Press, 1975.

> A useful documentation of the period culminating in Solzhenitsyn's exile from the Soviet Union.

B. *Collections of Responses to Solzhenitsyn's Public Statements:*

4. Berman, Ronald. Ed. *Solzhenitsyn at Harvard. The Address, Twelve Early Responses, and Six Later Reflections.* Washington, D.C.: Ethics and Public Policy Center, 1980.

> The "later reflections" are by the editor, Richard Pipes, Sidney Hook, Harold J. Berman, William H. McNeill, and Michael Novak. They include several serious attempts to grapple with the implications of the address, rather than merely to "react."

5. *Detente: Prospects for Democracy and Dictatorship.* New Brunswick, N. J.: Transaction Books, 1976.

> Contains the texts of Solzhenitsyn's two AFL-CIO addresses of 1975, together with responses from seven commentators, most of them virulently hostile to the writer's perceived "cold war" message. Richard Loewenthal's thoughtful essay stands out in this mediocre company.

C. *Biographical Materials:*

6. Gorlov, A. M. *Sluchai na dache [Incident at the Dacha].* Paris: YMCA-Press, 1977.

An account of how the regime persecuted and harassed the author, a friend and helper of Solzhenitsyn.

7. Panin, Dimitri. *The Notebooks of Sologdin*. New York: Harcourt Brace Jovanovich, 1976; London: Hutchinson, 1976.

English version of the 1973 *Zapiski Sologdina* (Frankfurt/ Main: Posev) by a man who shared Solzhenitsyn's experiences at the Marfino *sharashka*.

D. *Solzhenitsyn, "J'accuse!"*:

There is a growing body of works by persons dissatisfied with Solzhenitsyn in a more personal vein. They range from reasoned reproach to KGB-inspired denunciation.

8. Bosquet, Alain. *Pas d'accord, Soljénitsyne*. Paris: Filipacchi, 1974.

An early, rather squeaky, philippic.

9. Carlisle, Olga. *Solzhenitsyn and the Secret Circle*. New York: Holt, Rinehart and Winston, 1978; London: Routledge and Kegan Paul, 1978.

Carlisle was for seven years an intermediary between Solzhenitsyn and his publishers in the West before their relationship deteriorated. Here she gives her side of the story.

10. Flegon, A. *Vokrug Solzhenitsyna* [*Around Solzhenitsyn*]. 2 vols. London: Flegon Press, 1981.

A garrulous hotchpotch of fact, fantasy, innuendo and adolescent smut, intended to "unmask" Solzhenitsyn. The reader who makes this thousand-page Odyssey may, at least, learn something about Mr. Flegon.

11. Hall, Gus. *The Sakharov-Solzhenitsyn Fraud: What's Behind the Hue and Cry for "Intellectual Freedom."* New York: New Outlook Publishers, 1973.

"Solzhenitsyn is in the stagnant swamp because his forces

of decadent reaction cannot win the minds of the people..."
etc., etc.

12. Lakshin, Vladimir. *Solzhenitsyn, Tvardovsky, and* Novy Mir. Cambridge, Mass.: MIT Press, 1980.

Lakshin, a former member of the editorial board of *Novyi mir*, challenges the view of Aleksandr Tvardovskii and his journal conveyed in Solzhenitsyn's literary memoir *The Oak and the Calf.*

13. Panin, Dimitrii. *Solzhenitsyn i deistvitel'nost'* [*Solzhenitsyn and Reality*]. Paris: author's edition, 1975.

Panin takes sharp exception to the position taken by Solzhenitsyn in his "Letter to Soviet Leaders."

14. Reshetovskaia, N. *V spore so vremenem* [*At Odds with the Age*]. Moscow: Novosti, 1975. An English version appeared as Natalya A. Reshetovskaya. *Sanya: My Life with Aleksandr Solzhenitsyn*. Indianapolis: Bobbs-Merrill, 1975; London: Hart-Davis, McGibbon, 1977.

Ostensibly the memoirs of Solzhenitsyn's first wife, but co-authored by the Novosti Press Agency, which dramatically reduces their usefulness as a source.

15. Rzhezach, Tomash [Řezáč, Tomáš]. *Spiral' izmeny Solzhenitsyna* [*The Spiral of Solzhenitsyn's Treachery*]. Moscow: Progress, 1978.

A "ghost" edition, circulated highly selectively and apparently in tiny numbers. A vigorous and unscrupulous piece of official character assassination, to which Solzhenitsyn responds in *Skvoz' chad.*

16. Simonjan, Kirill Samjonovitsj. *Hvem er Solsjenitsyn?* [*Who Is Solzhenitsyn?*] Skaerbaek, Denmark: Melbyhus, 1976.

Apparently a team effort by Solzhenitsyn's childhood friend and the Novosti Press Agency, developing many of the scurrilous motifs found in Reshetovskaia's memoirs. Solzhenitsyn responds in *Skvoz' chad.*

17. Zil'berberg, Il'ia. *Neobkhodimyi razgovor s Solzhenitsynym*

[An Unavoidable Conversation with Solzhenitsyn]. England: author's edition, 1976.

It was from Zil'berberg's apartment that the KGB confiscated Solzhenitsyn's literary archive in 1965. Here he defends himself against what he sees as his unjust treatment at Solzhenitsyn's hands.

II. DICTIONARIES OF SOLZHENITSYN'S LANGUAGE

18. Carpovich, Vera V. *Solzhenitsyn's Peculiar Vocabulary: A Russian-English Glossary*. New York: Technical Dictionaries, 1976.

A valuable aid to anyone wrestling with Solzhenitsyn's archaisms and neologisms.

19. Flegon, A. *Za predelami russkogo iazyka [Beyond the Limits of the Russian Language]*. London: Flegon Press, 1973.

A lexicographically eccentric compilation which does, however, draw on the works of Solzhenitsyn.

20. Galler, Meyer. *Soviet Prison Camp Speech: A Survivor's Glossary. Supplement*. Hayward, Cal.: Soviet Studies, 1977.

A supplement to the 1972 dictionary which Galler edited together with Harlan E. Marquess, and which was subtitled *A Survivor's Glossary, Supplemented by Terms from the Works of A. I. Solzhenitsyn*.

III. CRITICISM OF SOLZHENITSYN'S FICTION, AND GENERAL WORKS

21. Allaback, Steven. *Alexander Solzhenitsyn*. New York: Taplinger, 1978.

A sensible reading of the major works of fiction, with a strong emphasis upon character and plot. The author does not read Russian and his book is of more interest to the non-specialist.

22. Barker, Francis. *Solzhenitsyn: Politics and Form*. London: Macmillan, 1977; New York: Barnes and Noble, 1977.

An intelligent, provocative essay, which sets out to demonstrate, from marxist positions, Solzhenitsyn's political and artistic "degeneration."

23. Carter, Stephen. *The Politics of Solzhenitsyn*. London: Macmillan, 1977; New York: Holmes and Meier, 1977.

Sets out to "elucidate the content of Solzhenitsyn's political thought" through textual analysis of both fictional and nonfictional writings.

24. Chaix-Ruy, J. A. *Soljénitsyne ou la descente aux enfers*. Paris: del Duca, 1970.

25. Clément, Olivier. *L'Esprit de Soljénitsyne*. Paris: Stock, 1974. English as *The Spirit of Solzhenitsyn*. London: Search Press, 1976; New York: Harper and Row, Barnes and Noble, 1977.

Pays particular attention to religious symbolism and implications in the major fiction before 1974. The English-language edition is expanded to take account of *Gulag* and *Lenin in Zurich*.

26. Ericson, Edward E., Jr. *Solzhenitsyn: The Moral Vision*. Grand Rapids: William B. Eerdmans, 1980.

A readable, albeit familiar, exposition of the major works which pays particular attention to Solzhenitsyn's Christianity.

27. Falkenstein, Henning. *Alexander Solschenizyn*. Berlin: Colloquium, 1975.

A brief "life and works."

28. Feuer, Kathryn. Ed. *Solzhenitsyn: A Collection of Critical Essays*. Englewood Cliffs, N. J.: Prentice-Hall, 1976.

A most useful and well-edited volume containing new essays by Patricia Blake, George Gibian, Robert Louis Jackson, and Walter Kaufmann, as well as translations and reprints of pieces by Michel Aucouturier, Robert Conquest, Victor

Erlich, Wolfgang Kasack, Alexis Klimoff, Roy Medvedev, Georges Nivat, and Nikita Struve.

29. Gul', R. *Solzhenitsyn: Stat'i.* New York: Most, 1976.

A collection of Gul's essays previously published individually in *Novyi zhurnal.*

30. Kodjak, Andrej. *Alexander Solzhenitsyn.* Boston: Twayne Publishers, G. K. Hall, 1978.

Described by the author as a "modest introduction" to the period before Solzhenitsyn's deportation, the book contains pages of lively and sensitive exposition, but is all too often marred by inadequate scholarship.

31. Krasnov, Vladislav. *Solzhenitsyn and Dostoevsky: A Study in the Polyphonic Novel.* Athens: University of Georgia Press, 1980.

It is good to see stated with such enthusiasm the case for Solzhenitsyn's affinity with Dostoevskii rather than Tolstoi (even if it is over-stated) and for Solzhenitsyn as polyphonist *à la* Bakhtin (even though he is not one).

32. Lefort, Claude. *Un homme en trop: Réflexions sur "l'Archi-pel du Goulag."* Paris: Seuil, 1976.

33. Lopukhina-Rodzianko, T. *Dukhovnye osnovy tvorchestva Solzhenitsyna* [*The Spiritual Foundations of Solzhenitsyn's Works*]. Frankfurt/Main: Posev, 1974.

Includes chapters on the figure of the "righteous man," on conscience, and on the concept of justice.

34. Marion, Corinne. *Qui a peur de Soljénitsyne?* Paris: Fayard, 1980.

In a sense, a "sequel" to Olivier Clément's *The Spirit of Solzhenitsyn*, concentrating upon the religious aspect of *Gulag, The Oak and the Calf* and other more recent literary and publicistic writings.

35. Martin, André. *Soljénitsyne le croyant.* Paris: Albatros, 1973.

An anthology of Solzhenitsyn's religious pronouncements, together with extensive background information and editorial comment.

36. Medvedev, Roy. *Political Essays*. Nottingham: Spokesman Books, 1976; Short Hills, N. J.: Enslow, 1977.

Includes Medvedev's published essays on: *The Gulag Archipelago*, "Letter to the Soviet Leaders," and *The Oak and the Calf*.

37. Myers, Allen. *Solzhenitsyn in Exile: A Marxist Analysis*. New York: Pathfinder Press, 1974.

A short pamphlet responding to the *Letter to Soviet Leaders*, and reproaching Solzhenitsyn for his retreat from marxism into "the dead end of mysticism and a romanticized past."

38. *Modern Fiction Studies*, 23, No. 1 (Spring 1977).

A special Solzhenitsyn issue, containing nine essays and a bibliography.

39. Moody, Christopher. *Solzhenitsyn*. 2nd revised ed. New York: Barnes and Noble/Harper and Row, 1975; Edinburgh: Oliver and Boyd, 1976.

Expands the original 1973 edition to take account of *The Gulag Archipelago*.

40. Nielsen, Niels C. *Solzhenitsyn's Religion*. Nashville: Nelson, 1975; London: Mowbray, 1976.

Well-intentioned, but poorly executed.

41. Neumann-Hoditz, Reinhold. *Alexander Solschenizyn in Selbstzeugnissen und Bilddokumenten*. Reinbek bei Hamburg: Rowohlt, 1974.

An interesting, competent and lavishly illustrated general introduction, with main emphasis upon the biographical.

42. Nivat, Georges. *Soljénitsyne*. Paris: Seuil, 1980.

Easily the best brief introduction to Solzhenitsyn's life and works yet to appear in any language, and one from which specialists can profit, as well as general readers. It is richly illustrated and includes a detailed biographical chronology.

43. Nivat, Georges. *Sur Soljénitsyne: Essais.* Lausanne: l'Age d'Homme, 1974.

A valuable collection of published essays by one of the most consistently stimulating students of Solzhenitsyn's works.

44. Nowikowa, Irene. Ed. *Seminarbeiträge zum Werk Aleksandr Solženicyns.* Hamburger Beiträge für Russischlehrer, vol. 3. Hamburg: Buske, 1972.

An early and neglected volume, which focuses upon the literary, rather than the political, dimension of Solzhenitsyn's works. It contains a bibliography and fourteen brief contributions on Solzhenitsyn's use of genres, his "polyphony," lexis, treatment of dialogue, and many other topics.

45. Rzhevsky, Leonid D. *Solzhenitsyn: Creator and Heroic Deed.* University of Alabama Press, 1978.

An English version of his *Tvorets i podvig*, first published in 1972 (Frankfurt/Main: Posev).

46. Shmeman, Aleksandr. *O Solzhenitsyne.* Montreal Orthodox Cathedral, 1974.

Contains five essays previously published in *Vestnik RKhD* (Paris).

47. *Soljénitsyne: Colloque de Cerisy.* Paris: Union Générale d'Editions, 1974.

The proceedings of a colloquium on Solzhenitsyn held at the Centre Culturel International in Cerisy-la-Salle in 1973. Speakers include Michel Aucouturier, Olivier Clément, Georges Nivat, Marc Slonim and others. The quality of the presentations, and particularly of the subsequent discussion, is uneven.

48. Vilner, Joseph. *Solzhenitsyn and the Future.* Hicksville, N.Y.: Exposition Press, 1975.

Strong criticism of the *Letter to Soviet Leaders* from a basically sympathetic commentator.

49. Weerakoon, R. *Alexander Solzhenitsyn: Soldier, Prisoner, Writer.* Colombo, Ceylon: International Publishers, 1972.

Sympathetic life-and-works appraisal by a Ceylonese of the Trotskyite Left, who believes Solzhenitsyn to be a Leninist reformist.

Solzhenitsyn in 1981:
A Bibliographical Reorientation

MICHAEL NICHOLSON

The present bibliography summarizes changes in, and new information about the canon of Solzhenitsyn's works, which have come to light during the period from 1973 to early 1981.* Readers who require details of the publication history of established works and editions are referred to:

A. Artemova, "Bibliografiia," in Aleksandr Solzhenitsyn, *Sobranie sochinenii*, VI, 2nd ed. (Frankfurt/Main: Posev, 1973), pp. 555-655;

Donald M. Fiene, compiler, *Alexander Solzhenitsyn: An International Bibliography of Writings by and about Him* (Ann Arbor: Ardis, 1973); and

Werner Martin, ed., *Alexander Solschenizyn. Eine Bibliographie seiner Werke* (Hildesheim, New York: Ulms, 1977).

The volume of evidence bearing upon the textual history of Solzhenitsyn's writings has increased markedly in the latter half of the 1970s, and account is taken here of questions of dating, textual authenticity, censorship and self-censorship. Solzhenitsyn's own efforts to set his literary house in order are embodied most vividly in the new edition of his collected works: Aleksandr Solzhenitsyn, *Sobranie sochinenii* (Vermont, Paris: YMCA-Press, 1978-). There have been some changes in the scheduled contents of the collection since it was first announced, but by the time Volume IX had appeared, in Summer 1981, the disposition of the first eighteen volumes was as follows:

I-II	*The First Circle*
III	Short Stories
IV	*Cancer Ward*

---

* It emends and considerably expands my "Solzhenitsyn in 1976: A Bibliographical Reorientation," *Russian Literature Triquarterly*, No. 14 (Winter 1976), pp. 462-82.

V-VII	*The Gulag Archipelago*
VIII	Plays and Film Scenarios
IX	Essays and Speeches
X	Shorter publicistic writings
XI-XII	*August 1914*
XIII-XIV	*October 1916*
XV-XVIII	*March 1917*

In his preface to the collected works, Solzhenitsyn indicates its unique features:

> But now, on the eve of my sixtieth year, the time has come to sort out those texts which have attained their final form, and that is the purpose of the present collection. My wife is studying and check-ing all the texts, drawing upon my surviving literary archives; together, we are going through them with greater care than would be possible if we were dealing with some distant publishing house. Thus, the very process of typesetting has become a daily stage in the final editing of the texts, and modern technology enables us to set them up ourselves in the seclusion of our own home—a kind of *samizdat* in exile. (Vol. I, p. 3)

Apart from the fact that this new collection contains previously unpublished works and variants, Solzhenitsyn appends notes on the provenance of the texts. Wherever possible, this information has been incorporated into the appropriate entries in the bibliography.

The following abbreviations are used:

CR	*Congressional Record*
FAZ	*Frankfurter Allgemeine Zeitung*
Gulag I, etc.	*The Gulag Archipelago*, Vol. I, etc. Arabic fig-ures indicate the page number in the Russian edition (YMCA-Press, 1973-); italicized Arabic figures refer to the corresponding page of the English translation. For details of editions, see item 26.
IHT	*International Herald Tribune*
NRS	*Novoe russkoe slovo*
NYT	*New York Times*
NZZ	*Neue Zürcher Zeitung*

Oak, The	*The Oak and the Calf.* Arabic figures indicate the page number in the Russian edition; italicized Arabic figures refer to the English translation. For details of editions, see item 133.
Posev *Rasskazy* (1976)	A. I. Solzhenitsyn, *Rasskazy* (Frankfurt/Main: Posev, 1976). An early authorized edition of the short prose.
RM	*Russkaia mysl'*
Skvoz' chad	A separately published fragment of the Sixth Supplement to *The Oak and the Calf* (q.v.).
Udgaard	Interview with N. M. Udgaard (see item 112).
[*V Spore*]	N. Reshetovskaia, *V spore so vremenem* (Moscow: Novosti, 1975), the memoirs of Solzhenitsyn's first wife, prepared for publication with the active participation of the Novosti Press Agency. The asterisk and brackets indicate the unreliability of this source. It appeared in English as Natalya A. Reshetovskaya, *Sanya; My Life with Aleksandr Solzhenitsyn* (New York: Bobbs-Merrill, 1975).
[*Veche*]	Two earlier chapters of Reshetovskaia's memoirs, included in the *samizdat* journal *Veche*, No. 5 (25 May 1972).
Vermont Sobr. soch. I, etc.	Aleksandr Solzhenitsyn, *Sobranie sochinenii* (Vermont, Paris: YMCA-Press, 1978-), Vol. I, etc.
Vestnik RSKhD	*Vestnik Russkogo Studencheskogo Khristianskogo Dvizheniia.*
Vestnik RKhD	*Vestnik Russkogo Khristianskogo Dvizheniia*
Zil'berberg	Il'ia Zil'berberg, *Neobkhodimyi razgovor s Solzhenitsynym* (England, author's edition, 1976).

In preparing this bibliography I have received generous assistance from Martin Dewhirst, Alexis Klimoff, Patricia Blake, and Michael Scammell.

*   *   *

Items in the bibliography are arranged according to the following plan:

I. BELLES–LETTRES

BEFORE 1948

Juvenilia:

Wartime writing:

1948 AND AFTER

A. Prose

Published in the Soviet Union:

Published outside the Soviet Union:

B. Poetry

C. Drama

D. Film Scenarios

E. Miscellaneous

II. NON-BELLETRISTIC WRITINGS AND STATEMENTS

A. Before 1974

B. 1974 and After

Index of Titles

*   *   *

I. BELLES–LETTRES

BEFORE 1948

Juvenilia:

In an autobiographical note to the Nobel Foundation, Solzhenitsyn dismisses his earliest literary endeavors as "the usual youthful nonsense," and dates the beginning of his serious writing from the late 1940s, the period of his imprisonment. Apart from references to his work on what would eventually become *The Red Wheel* (item 24), Solzhenitsyn has little to say about his efforts in prose before the war. In *Skvoz' chad*, however, he does recall the school literary journal of which he was co-editor as well as one particular literary venture of those years:

1. "A novel by three madmen" ("roman trekh sumasshed-shikh"): "You [Kirill Simonian], Lidiia [Ezherets] and I churned out our 'novel by three madmen,' taking it in turns to write a chapter each, without agreeing in advance on the fate of the characters—the next one could just disentangle himself as he saw fit" (pp. 42-43).

On the same occasion, Solzhenitsyn speaks of accumulating "one exercise book after another" full of adolescent compositions, some of which were sent to literary luminaries. (Leonid Timofeev is named as one who gave a discouraging appraisal of his efforts in verse.) [*Reshetovskaia lists three titles, apparently of unpublished short stories, which she describes as belonging to this period. They are:

2. * "Mission Abroad" ("Zagranichnaia komandirovka");

3. * "The River Pointsmen" ("Rechnye strelochniki"); and

4. * "The Nikolaevskiis" ("Nikolaevskie") (*V spore*, 32 & 45).

If Reshetovskaia is correct, Solzhenitsyn submitted these stories to Lavrenev and Fedin shortly before the war.]

Wartime writing:

This subheading refers to projects on which Solzhenitsyn is known to have been engaged during the war years, rather than to later works which drew upon his wartime experiences. His attitude towards his plans of this period is suggested in a scene from *The Gulag Archipelago*, where he describes overhearing a conversation about the war while under escort in 1946. His first impulse is to join in, but then he realizes that: "After two years *here*, two years in the Archipelago, the roads I travelled at the front have faded, my frontline comradeship, too—everything has faded. One wedge drives out the other" (*Gulag I*, 586, 594).

5. *War Diary* (*Voennyi dnevnik*). Thus Solzhenitsyn describes a number of notebooks, confiscated upon his arrest and eventually consigned to "the hellish maw of the Lubianka furnace." In them he recorded what he saw during the war, as well as the stories and opinions of those he met. They were evidently intended to serve as the basis for a novel: "These diaries constituted my claim to becoming a writer (...) one more novel that has perished in Russia..." (*Gulag*, 144-45, *136*). Some of the "stories" contained in the diary were about contemporary life in the kolkhoz village, and were narrated by Solzhenitsyn's friend, Ovsiannikov (*Gulag I*, 177, *169-70*). It is, of course, entirely possible that the materials in the *War Diary* were related to some or all of the remaining projects in this section.

6. "Love the Revolution" ("'Liubi revoliutsiiu"). In the collection of photographs entitled *Solzhenitsyn: A Pictorial Record* (Paris: Seuil; London: Bodly Head; New York: Farrar, Straus and Giroux, 1974) the caption to a picture of Solzhenitsyn on p. 17 read: "On the Khopër River, early in 1942. Solzhenitsyn was serving as a military transport driver in a Cossack unit (...) Solzhenitsyn's impressions of this winter are recorded in an unfinished (and unpublished) story called 'Love the Revolution.'" This *Pictorial Record* is an authorized publication. [*Reshetovskaia associates the same title with *The Red Wheel* (item 24).]

7. [*The Sixth Course* (*Shestoi kurs*). Reshetovskaia refers to a long work ("bol'shaia povest'") of this name about a former student who takes part in the Orel-Kursk battles (*V spore*, 20, 40, 42, 45, 72). Solzhenitsyn himself saw action in the Orel area, and Reshetovskaia's remarks suggest that the work would have contained a substantial autobiographical element. In the *Veche* chapters she ascribes to Solzhenitsyn a comparison of his *povest'* with V. Nekrasov's *In the Trenches of Stalingrad*. At one point she states that: "Never again (after his arrest—MN) would he express any desire to resurrect the chapters of *The Sixth Course*, over which at one time he had worked the whole night through" (*V spore*, 72). On the other hand, a passage which she cites in *Veche* would seem to indicate that Solzhenitsyn had not entirely abandoned his plans for the work even as late as April 1947.]

8. [*Reshetovskaia mentions a story, "In the Town of M" ("V gorode M"), which Solzhenitsyn was reportedly working on in

mid-1943. She describes it as based in part on the Bronevitskii couple, their neighbors in Morozovsk in 1941, and in part upon Solzhenitsyn's own impressions of life in towns liberated during the Russian counter-offensive (*V spore*, 32 & 35). According to Reshetovskaia, Lavrenev read the story and offered his critical opinion of it (*ibid.*, 45). This item is treated separately here because, without mentioning a story of this name, Solzhenitsyn has himself discussed at some length the "collaborator" Bronevitskii. Solzhenitsyn's attitude towards him and others like him changed drastically in the postwar years (*Gulag III*, 22-28, *20-25*).]

[*In addition, Reshetovskaia cites four titles, allegedly designating unpublished stories on which Solzhenitsyn worked during the war years. They are (with page references to *V spore*):

  9. *"The Lieutenant" ("Leitenant"), 28, 29, 35;

  10. * "Letter No. 254" ("Pis'mo No. 254"), 35;

  11. * "The Fruit Orchard" ("Fruktovyi sad"), 41, 114;

  12. * "A Woman's Tale" ("Zhenskaia povest'"), 41.]

In 1956, the KGB investigator handling Solzhenitsyn's rehabilitation read the stories which he had written at the front and which were on his file as "incriminating evidence." The investigator found nothing anti-Soviet in them, praised them, and suggested that Solzhenitsyn take them and try to have them published. For conspiratorial reasons he had to decline (*Gulag III*, 464-65, *444*).

1948 AND AFTER

A. Prose

Published in the Soviet Union:

13. *One Day in the Life of Ivan Denisovich* (*Odin den' Ivana Denisovicha*). *Vermont Sobr. soch.* III, with a brief glossary of labor camp jargon. Solzhenitsyn regards it as a short story (*rasskaz*), rather than a *povest'*, as it was designated in Soviet editions (*The Oak*, 31,

24 fn.). A typewritten copy from Solzhenitsyn's archive confiscated in 1965 bore the pseudonym and title: Stepan Khlynov, *Shch-854* (*Zil'berberg*, 75). In *Vermont Sobr. soch.* III, he speaks of his own title as *Shch-854* (*A Zek's Day*) [*Shch-854* (*Odin den' odnogo zeka*)]. The story was given its final title by Aleksandr Tvardovskii, editor-in-chief of *Novyi mir*. *Ivan Denisovich* was conceived in Ekibastuz labor camp in the winter of 1950-1951 (1952, according to the 1976 interview with N. A. Struve), and written in less than two months during 1959. In 1961 Solzhenitsyn prepared a politically toned-down version which was eventually published in the Soviet Union under celebrated circumstances. He refers to widespread *samizdat* circulation of the story during 1962 (*The Oak*, 416, *388*). Three editions eventually appeared in the Soviet Union, each representing a slightly different text:

   i. *Novyi mir*, 1962, No. 11.
  ii. *Roman-gazeta*, 1963, No. 1.
 iii. "Sovetskii pisatel'," Moscow (book edition), February 1963.

In addition there was a 1963 Braille edition by "Uchpedgiz," Moscow in two volumes, each of 250 copies. On 14 February 1974, one day after Solzhenitsyn's expulsion from the Soviet Union, the Head of the Main Board for the Preservation of State Secrets in the Press directed that all these editions, together with issues of *Novyi mir* containing other stories by Solzhenitsyn, be removed from libraries and from the book trade, thus formalizing a process already underway for some years (see the directive reproduced in *Khronika tekushchikh sobytii*, No. 34 (31 December 1974), pp. 88-89; English ed., pp. 91-92. A text bearing Solzhenitsyn's authorization, dated April 1968, was published by YMCA-Press, Paris in 1973, and is included in the 1976 Posev *Rasskazy* and *Vermont Sobr. soch.* III. This version is not yet available in English. The quasi-censoring of the story is described in the early part of *The Oak*. Variants revealed by a comparison of the four versions published to date are numerous, often interesting and occasionally substantial. They do not, however, suggest the need for a thorough-going reappraisal of the work: see Gary Kern, "Solženicyn's Self-Censorship: The Canonical Text of *Odin den' Ivana Denisoviča*," *Slavic and East European Journal*, Vol. 20, No. 4 (1976), pp. 421-36; and two much slighter pieces— Thomas Weiss, "How the Censors Changed 'Ivan Denisovich' and 'Matrena's Home,'" *Radio Liberty Research*, RL 96/75 (7 March 1975); and A. Artemova, "Novoe izdanie rasskazov A. I. Solzhenitsyna," *Posev*, 1976, No. 4, pp. 60-61). In a kind of sequel to the story Solzhenitsyn allows Ivan Denisovich to take up the narrative for a few pages of *The Gulag Archipelago* (II, 214-16, *218-21* & 218-21, *223-26*).

14. "Matrena's Home" ("Matrenin dvor"). *Vermont Sobr. soch.* III, with a textual note according to which: "The story is completely autobiographical and authentic. The life and death of Matrena Vasil'evna Zakharova are reproduced as they happened. The real name of the village is Mil'tsevo, Kurlovsk Region, Vladimir District." The text in *Vermont Sobr. soch.* is dated 1959, but the YMCA and Posev authorized editions (see below) give "1959-1960, Ak-Mechet'—Riazan'." Tvardovskii changed the title from Solzhenitsyn's original "The Village Cannot Stand without a Righteous Man" ("Ne stoit selo bez pravednika"). An anonymous typescript under that title, with photographs attached to five of its pages, was confiscated with Solzhenitsyn's literary archive in 1965 (*Zil'berberg*, 76). The version published in *Novyi mir*, 1963, No. 1, had been softened by the author and subsequently underwent pre-censorship modifications in consultation with *Novyi mir*, as described in the early sections of *The Oak*. The most significant change was the adjustment of the date of the action from 1956 to 1953 in order to disassociate Khrushchev from the gloomy picture of rural life which the story presents. The YMCA-Press (Paris) published an authorized edition in 1973 in the same volume as *Ivan Denisovich*, and this version is included in the 1976 Posev *Rasskazy*, as well as in *Vermont Sobr. soch.* III. Some 35 differences between the *Novyi mir* and YMCA texts are discussed in Vera Carpovich, "*Matrenin dvor* A. I. Solzhenitsyna," *NRS*, 19 February 1974, p. 5. Existing English translations are based on the *Novyi mir* edition.

15. "Incident at Kochetovka Station" ("Sluchai na stantsii Kochetovka"). *Vermont Sobr. soch.* III. [*Reshetovskaia claims in *Veche* that Tvardovskii rejected the original title, "The Green Cap" ("Zelenaia furazhka").] The story was written in November 1962, based on real events which occurred in 1941, and it was first published in *Novyi mir*, 1963, No. 1 (although excerpts had previously appeared in *Pravda*, 23 December 1962, p. 4). In these publications the real place-name "Kochetovka" was changed to "Krechetovka," lest it be construed as an attack on Vsevolod Kochetov, editor of the rival journal *Oktiabr'*. The authorized Posev *Rasskazy* of 1976 retained the Soviet title, which was not restored until the appearance

of *Vermont Sobr. soch.* III (see the textual note in that volume). This story has the distinction of being the first literary work which Solzhenitsyn wrote specifically for publication rather than "for the drawer" (*The Oak*, 55, 47). He also notes (*ibid.*) that the writing came easily to him.

16. "For the Good of the Cause" ("Dlia pol'zy dela"). *Vermont Sobr. soch.* III, with a textual note identifying some of the principal characters. Written in Spring 1963, it first appeared in *Novyi mir*, 1963, No. 7. The author describes it as "a story which I felt no inner compulsion to write. (...) In this story I began to slip back from the position I had taken up. Signs of conformity were creeping in" (*The Oak*, 77, 66-67). He was aggrieved to discover that Zaks, a member of the *Novyi mir* editorial board, had introduced changes without consulting him (*ibid.*). Of the authorized text included in the 1976 Posev *Rasskazy*, Artemova writes that "the author has discarded the entire first section and changed the beginning of the second, making it into the first. In the fourth section, the scene where the intrepid Val'ka Rogozkin calls for a strike is restored": A. Artemova, "Novoe izdanie rasskazov A. I. Solzhenitsyna," *Posev*, 1976, No. 4, p. 60. The text is further pruned for *Vermont Sobr. soch.*, though much less drastically. English translations do not yet reflect these revisions.

17. "Zakhar-Kalita." *Vermont Sobr. soch.* III. Written in Fall 1965. Before it finally appeared, in *Novyi mir*, 1966, No. 1, it had been, in turn, accepted by *Literaturnaia Rossiia* and *Ogonek*, seriously considered by *Pravda* and even set up in type by *Izvestiia* (*The Oak*, 136-41, 120-25). The authorized text, first published in Posev's 1976 *Rasskazy*, omits the final two paragraphs.

Published outside the Soviet Union:

18. *The First Circle* (*V kruge pervom*). *Vermont Sobr. soch.* I-II, with an important textual note by the author. [*According to Reshetovskaia, the title evolved from *V pervom kruge ada* (*Veche*), but elsewhere (*V spore*) she refers to it as *Sharashka*.] This novel has a complex textual history and provides the most vivid and best publicized instance of Solzhenitsyn's self-censorship. He distinguishes

Krug-87 (the version known in *samizdat* and in the West) from *Krug-96*, "the real 'circle'" containing 96 chapters (*The Oak*, 239, 218). He believes that the latter version could, if discovered in the years before his literary debut, have put his life in jeopardy (*The Oak*, 11, 6, fn. 2). Interviewed soon after his exile to the West, he disclosed that:

> When I decided to show it to *Novyi mir* it at once became apparent that it was impossible *even to show it* to the editorial board of an official Soviet journal, still less to get it printed. And I undertook the following procedure: I broke this edifice of 96 chapters down into bricks, into chapters, half-chapters, sometimes paragraphs, and built another, *new* novel out of what was still presentable. And that is how the 87-chapter variant came to exist . . . (*Udgaard*)

In another account of this reconstruction Solzhenitsyn described how a necessary alteration to the plot came to affect his treatment of many characters and scenes quite apart from the question of the missing chapters. He also spoke of literary, as distinct from political, reworking (Paris Press Conference, item 135).

Speculation about *Krug-96* was further fueled by the appearance of four of the missing chapters in the émigré press during 1974:

Ch. 88—"Dialectical Materialism Is a Progressive World-View" ("Dialekticheskii materializm—peredovoe mirovozzrenie"), *Kontinent*, No. 1 (1974), 125-42.

Ch. 44—"In the Open" ("Na prostore"), *Vestnik RSKhD*, No. 111 (1, 1974), 70-89.

Ch. 61—"An Uncle from Tver'" ("Tverskoi diadiushka"), *Vestnik RKhD*, No. 112-113 (2-3, 1974), 160-73.

Ch. 90—"The Word Will Smash Concrete" ("Slovo raszrushit beton"), *Vestnik RKhD*, No. 114 (4, 1974), 193-203.

(Solzhenitsyn had released the first two of the above-listed chapters into *samizdat* in September 1973 with a covering note setting out his expectation that he would be protected against unauthorized publication of his works now that the Soviet Union had acceded to the International Copyright Convention.) For a discussion of the new chapters see: Thomas Weiss, "Solzhenitsyn Publishes the Missing Chapter from 'The First Circle,'" *Radio Liberty Research*, RL 13/75 (10 January 1975); Laszlo Tikos, "Solzhenitsyn Publishes Two More Missing Chapters from 'The First Circle,'" *Radio Liberty Research*,

RL 306/75 (25 July 1975); and K. Filips-Juswigg, "New Chapters for Solženicyn's *V kruge pervom*: Indirect Modes of Expression," *Russian Language Journal*, Vol. 29 (Fall 1975), pp. 95-106.

With the publication of the full authorized text in *Vermont Sobr. soch.* in 1978, together with Solzhenitsyn's own textual note, it has become possible to summarize the history of the various versions:

First redaction (96 chapters)—begun in exile in Kazakhstan in 1955 and completed in Mil'tsevo in 1957.

Second and third redactions—Riazan' 1958. (All three of these first versions were later destroyed for reasons of security.)

Fourth redaction—1962, the then "final" version of *Krug-96*.

Fifth redaction—Winter 1963-1964. The lightened 87-chapter version submitted to and accepted, but never published, by *Novyi mir*. This was the text which the KGB confiscated in Fall 1965, and which circulated in *samizdat* from 1967 on. Meanwhile, Solzhenitsyn had, in Summer 1964, prepared a:

Sixth redaction—which, while still essentially the 87-chapter version, took back some of the concessions made in the fifth redaction. It was sent to the West on microfilm in Fall 1964, was published in Russian in 1968 by Harper and Row, forming the basis for all Western translations at that time.

Seventh redaction—the full and final 96-chapter version, prepared in Summer 1968. It did not circulate in *samizdat* and first appeared in Fall 1978 as volumes one and two of *Vermont Sobr. soch.* This seventh redaction (due to appear in English translation in 1982 or 1983) is described by the author as principally a "restoration" of the novel to its state before the distorted fifth redaction. He does, however, note in a preface that "in restoring it, I also introduced certain improvements *[ia koe-chto i usovershil]*; after all, I was forty years old then and now I am fifty" (*Vermont Sobr. soch.* I, 7). The differences between the familiar version of *The First Circle* and the new one are discussed in the present volume by Georges Nivat ("Solzhenitsyn's Different *Circles*"); also in Edgar H. Lehrman, "Solzhenitsyn's 'New' View of Stalinist Russia," *St. Louis Post Dispatch*, 18 November 1979, p. 4D; and Rosalind Wells, "The Definitive Solzhenitsyn?" *Irish Slavonic Studies*, No. 1 (1980), pp. 115-20.

It is interesting that, among the items listed as part of Solzhenitsyn's literary archive confiscated in 1965 is: "Stepan Khlynov, 'Ulybka Buddy' ['Buddha's Smile']" (*Zil'berberg*, 75). That this chapter of *The First Circle* might once have had an independent existence was also suggested by the tape-recording of Solzhenitsyn reading it which reached the West in the late 1960s.

19. "Miniature Stories" ("Krokhotnye rasskazy" or "Krokhotki"). "Written at various times between 1958 and 1960 (i.e., earlier than some previous estimates], many in connection with the author's bicycle trips through Central Russia" (note to *Vermont Sobr. soch.* III). Solzhenitsyn showed several of the "more harmless" ones to Tvardovskii in December 1961, but the latter was not very impressed (*The Oak*, 33, *26*). In Spring 1964, Solzhenitsyn allowed them to be unofficially disseminated, his first experience of the effectiveness of *samizdat* "publication" (*The Oak*, 100, *87*). The journal *Sem'ia i shkola* failed in a bid to publish some of them in Fall 1965 (by which time they had already appeared in the West). The first authorized publication was in the 1976 Posev *Rasskazy*.

20. "The Right Hand" ("Pravaia kist'"). According to a note in *Vermont Sobr. soch.* III, it was written in 1960 and is based on a real incident in Tashkent. Solzhenitsyn appears to be particularly fond of this story. It was rejected in November 1965 by the editors of *Novyi mir*, *Literaturnaia Rossiia*, *Ogonek*, and *Moskva* (*The Oak*, 129 & 139; *114 & 123-24*). Solzhenitsyn personally encouraged its *samizdat* circulation (*The Oak*, 136, *121*). On textual variants in two of the early Western editions of the story, see: Michael Nicholson, "Solzhenitsyn's *The Right Hand*. An Early Variant?," *Scando-Slavica,* tomus XVIII (1972), 97-111. The authorized text first appeared in the 1976 Posev *Rasskazy*.

21. "What a Pity" ("Kak zhal'"). *Vermont Sobr. soch.* III. Even the title of this story was generally unknown in the West until the appearance of *The Oak* in 1975. Although the story is mentiond in the text of Solzhenitsyn's 1967 letter to the Fourth Congress of the Soviet Writers' Union which he appends to *The Oak* (Document No. 2), previous versions of the letter which reached the West had not included that title. In *The Oak*, he names the story as one of the four which he offered to several editorial boards in November 1965. He had completed it in the Fall of 1965, but a passage in *The Oak* suggests that it had been begun earlier (p. 136, *121*). It was rejected for publication (*The Oak*, 136 & 139, *121 & 123-24*). The story is, in effect, a literary treatment of a true episode involving Professor V. A. Vasil'ev, which is discussed in *Gulag*, Part VI. It first appeared in

1979 in *Vermont Sobr. soch.* and has not been published in English translation.

22. "The Easter Procession" ("Paskhal'nyi krestnyi khod"). *Vermont Sobr. soch.* III. The story bears the date 10 April 1966. It was written in Peredelkino and circulated in *samizdat* in the Soviet Union. A. Artemova notes that there are minor corrections in the authorized text, first published in the 1976 Posev *Rasskazy* (see her "Novoe izdanie rasskazov..." details in item 16).

23. *Cancer Ward* (*Rakovyi korpus*). *Vermont Sobr. soch* IV. Tvardovskii proposed two less offensive titles, *Patients and Doctors* (*Bol'nye i vrachi*) and "something like *The Ward at the End of the Path* (*Korpus v kontse allei*)" (*The Oak*, 81 & 153; 70 & 136). The first conception of the story (*povest'*)—the strand involving Kostoglotov— dates from the day in Spring 1955 when Solzhenitsyn was discharged from a Tashkent cancer clinic. (A textual note in *Vermont Sobr. soch.* IV includes information concerning the prototypes of several characters in the story.) Solzhenitsyn began working on it in January 1963, returning to Tashkent the following year to renew acquaintances and check medical details. Not until Fall 1965, however, did he devote himself to completing the story. Part I was finished in Spring 1966 and allowed to circulate in *samizdat* when *Novyi mir*'s plans to publish it were frustrated. According to the note in *Vermont Sobr. soch.*, Part II was completed "during 1966," though the text of the whole work is dated in that volume (as in earlier Western editions) "1963-1967." In 1974, Solzhenitsyn told Udgaard that he had "softened" the version intended for publication "in many places." Specific details of criticisms and proposals made by the editors of *Novyi mir* are given in *The Oak* (e.g., pp. 149-53, 191 & 194-95; *132-36, 172 & 175-76*). The version which Solzhenitsyn allowed to circulate in *samizdat* was free of these cuts (*The Oak*, 154, *137*). First publication of the authorized text was in Summer 1979 in *Vermont Sobr. soch.* No systematic study of the texts of *Cancer Ward* has yet been published. Earlier Russian-language editions brought out in the West had displayed frequent, but generally comparatively minor, variants. A very selective comparison of the new authorized version with the text published in Aleksandr Solzhenitsyn, *Sobranie sochinenii*, II (Frankfurt/Main: Posev, 1969) suggests that the latest variants do not begin to match in extent and significance those found in *The First Circle*.

Although the major part of the following item has yet to appear in print, publication may be regarded as proceeding:

24. *The Red Wheel* (*Krasnoe koleso*), *Revolution* (*Revoliutsiia*), *R-17*. These titles have all been used by Solzhenitsyn to designate an "epopee," "historical narrative," or "cycle of knots (*uzly*)," of which *August 1914* (*Avgust Chetyrnadtsatogo*) is the first "knot." [*Reshetovskaia refers to two further titles which she apparently associates with the early versions of this project: they are *Russians in the Vanguard* (*Russkie v avangarde*) and *Black in Red* (*Chernoe v krasnom*) (*V spore*, 35).] By the end of the 1970s, *The Red Wheel* had established itself as the overall title. In *Gulag I* Solzhenitsyn writes: "Ever since I was a child I have somehow known that my objective is the history of the Russian revolution, and that other things are no concern of mine" (p. 219, *213*). The earliest design dates from 1936: "I had planned my big epopee (*August 1914* and the works which are to follow it) by the time I was 18. I have never had to modify this plan. In about 1938-1939 I started putting it into effect. Then came the war, the camps, and so on. When I came back I re-read those chapters, which by then I had almost forgotten. I didn't change anything in them. They fitted straight into the place I had allocated to them" (*Le Point* interview, item 162). In 1937 and 1938, while he was still at the university Solzhenitsyn researched Samsonov's defeat at Tannenberg and wrote an undergraduate paper on it. The project was interrupted for some 30 years, during which time Solzhenitsyn's world-view and attitude to his subject changed drastically. After his reputation was established in the early 1960s he collected materials systematically. In a note appended to *Vermont Sobr. soch.* IV, he mentions that he began writing *Cancer Ward* in January 1963, but that it was interrupted by the start of his work on *The Red Wheel*. When he began writing *August 1914* in 1969, he considered that he had now absolved all his other literary tasks and could at last devote himself to what he has repeatedly described as his "main" work. By the time of his exile from the Soviet Union, he had already mapped out many "knots" in advance (*The Oak*, 480, *452*). At one stage, he was thinking in terms of no less than twenty "knots" (*The Oak*, 339, *313*), while doubting that his lifetime would be sufficiently long for such a project. It is clear that the number and relative weight of the different "knots" altered considerably in the course of the 1970s. For example, Solzhenitsyn reports having abandoned, as an "economy" measure, a

"knot" entitled *August 1915*, which had the effect of increasing the size of the following "knot" (*The Oak*, 353, *328*). A further "knot," *April 1917*, which in 1978 had been tentatively announced as volume XVIII of *Vermont Sobr. soch.*, now appears to have been discarded as well. Thus, reality seems at last to be in step with those many commentators over the last decade who, through ignorance, have described the project as a "trilogy." That it should (for the time being at least) stop short of the October revolution is consistent with Solzhenitsyn's well-publicized interest in the February revolution and the lessons embodied in it. As regards the publication schedule of the cycle, he wrote in Summer 1980: "(...) I am presently completing an account in eight volumes which will begin appearing in Russian in 1982 and perhaps three years later in English" ("The Courage to See," item 223). The component "knots" will be:

i. *August 1914* (*Avgust Chetyrnadtsatogo*). *Vermont Sobr. soch.* XI-XII. A version of this "knot," written between 1969 and 1970, was published in Russian in 1971 (YMCA-Press, Paris) with an author's afterword, dated May 1971. A second, slightly emended edition came out later in the same year, and under the same imprint, with the English translation following in 1972 (New York: Farrar, Straus and Giroux; London: Bodley Head). In the English-language editions Solzhenitsyn's afterword is replaced by a shorter foreword. He evidently continued to work on *August 1914* during the seventies, and the text scheduled to take up two volumes of *Vermont Sobr. soch.* will supersede the familiar version, expanding it considerably. For the fate of Chapter 22, omitted from the published editions, see the next entry (*Lenin in Zurich*). An additional chapter, devoted to Tsar Nicholas II, has appeared separately, in Russian only:
Chapter 67 (A Study of the Monarch) [Etiud o monarkhe], *Vestnik RKhD*, No. 124 (1, 1978), 153-249.
(The familiar version of *August 1914* goes no further than Chapter 64.)

ii. *October 1916* (*Oktiabr' Shestnadtsatogo*). *Vermont Sobr. soch.* XIII-XIV. There have been various brief references during the 1970s to this "knot" as substantially complete, but information is too scant to permit any useful dating. No less than fifteen chapters had been pre-published by mid-1981. Seven "Lenin-chapters" from this "knot" were included in *Lenin in Zurich* (see the next entry). In addition, the following chapters were individually published in Russian (the apostrophe after a chapter number indicates a "survey chapter" ["obzornaia glava"], without fictional elements and intended to illuminate the overall historical context):

Chapter 24 (October 17th, 1916) [17 oktiabria 1916], *Vestnik RKhD*, No. 131 (1-2, 1980), 85-108.

Chapter 25' (Origins of the Cadets) [Kadetskie istoki], *Vestnik RKhD*, No. 129 (3, 1979), 97-123.

Chapter 42' (Aleksandr Guchkov), *Vestnik RKhD*, No. 130 (4, 1979), 188-213.

Chapter 56' (The Progressive Bloc) [Progressivnyi Blok], *Vestnik RKhD*, No. 126 (3, 1978), 53-77.

Chapter 62 (October 31st) [31 oktiabria], *Vestnik RKhD*, No. 132 (3-4, 1980), 71-98.

Chapter 63' (The State Duma, November 1st) [Gosudarstvennaia Duma, 1 noiabria], *Vestnik RKhD*, No. 127 (4, 1978), 85-104.

Chapter 68 (November 2nd) [2 noiabria], *Vestnik RKhD*, No. 132 (3-4, 1980), 99-114.

Chapter 68' (The State Duma, November 3rd and 4th) [Gosudarstvennaia Duma, 3 i 4 noiabria], *Vestnik RKhD*, No. 128 (1-2, 1979), 147-65.

iii. *March 1917 (Mart Semnadtsatogo)*. *Vermont Sobr. soch.* XV-XVIII. No less than four volumes of the new *Collected Works* have been set aside for this "knot." Three chapters were pre-published as part of *Lenin in Zurich* (item 25), in addition to the following chapters which have appeared in Russian only:

Chapter 1' (The Grain Noose) [Khlebnaia petlia], *Vestnik RKhD*, No. 133 (1, 1981), 121-43.

Chapters 5-7 (February 27th) [Dvadtsat' sed'moe fevralia], *Russkoe Vozrozhdenie*, No. 14 (2, 1981), 5-26. The numbering of these chapters is tentative. They show Tsar Nicholas II at his General Headquarters.

25. *Lenin in Zurich: Chapters (Lenin v Tsiurikhe: Glavy)*. Although this book has enjoyed a separate existence since 1975, it is unique among Solzhenitsyn's published works, in that it represents a compilation of chapters from *The Red Wheel* (see preceding item), namely:

from *August 1914*: the omitted Chapter 22;

from *October 1916*: Chapters 38, 44-45 and 47-50;
from *March 1917*: three chapters, provisionally numbered L-1, L-2, L-3.

The first edition (Paris: YMCA-Press, 1975) also contains: a loose-leaf prefatory statement; an afterword (datelined Moscow 1971/ Zurich 1975), which refers the reader to selected works by Lenin and acknowledges certain Western studies; and the author's own glossary of names. The English translation by H. T. Willetts, published in 1975 (New York: Farrar, Straus and Giroux; London: Bodley Head), adds a supplementary translator's glossary of proper names. Solzhenitsyn has emphasized that Lenin is one of the central figures in *The Red Wheel*: "I have been thinking about him from the very first moment that I conceived the epopee—that's forty years already—and I have been collecting everything I could find about him (...)" (interview with N. Struve, item 175). The first chapter is an integral part of *August 1914*, showing "just what Lenin was doing on that day of August 13th when Samsonov was transferring his headquarters to Neidenburg and Nechvolodov was holding a defensive line at Roth-fliess" *(Udgaard)*. At the beginning of the 1970s, his plan had been to complete and authorize Western publication of the first three "knots," but without their Lenin chapters. At that time, each of those "knots" contained a single such chapter. It would have been impossible, however, to adopt a similar procedure with the proposed fourth "knot" *(April 1917)*, which was to have shown Lenin in action in Petrograd. Accordingly, Solzhenitsyn intended, if events had not overtaken him, to arrange simultaneous publication abroad in the mid-1970s of *April 1917*, the hitherto omitted Lenin-chapters, in the form of free, insertable supplements, and *The Gulag Archipelago*, whereupon he would have awaited the consequences *(The Oak, 339, 314*; and *Udgaard)*. In his preface, he describes how the materials which he discovered in Zurich after his expatriation caused him to augment the already written Lenin chapters. We can trace something of this process: in his interview with Udgaard of August 1974, the number of Lenin chapters in *October 1916* had risen to two; by the time *Lenin in Zurich* was complete, there were seven of them. *Lenin in Zurich* is not scheduled for separate inclusion in *Vermont Sobr. soch.*, and it will presumably dissolve back into its parent "knots."

26. Somewhat difficult to place by genre is : *The Gulag Archipelago 1918-1956: An Experiment in Literary Investigation (ARKHI-*

PELAG GULag 1918-1956: Opyt khudozhestvennogo issledovaniia).
Vermont Sobr. soch. V-VII. This work is the culmination of that part
of Solzhenitsyn's life's work which he distinguishes from his "main"
project, The Red Wheel. Its composition spans a period of ten years.
The initial conception, plan, and title date from Spring 1958, and
several chapters were written at that time, only to be set aside for
some years, for want of adequate materials and evidence. This
deficiency was remedied after the appearance of Ivan Denisovich in
November 1962, when Solzhenitsyn was inundated with letters from
labor camp veterans. During 1963 and 1964 he accumulated (by
correspondence and personal meetings) the testimony of the 227
witnesses acknowledged at the beginning of Gulag. In this connection, he has disclosed that the collection of extracts from readers'
letters interspersed with mordant "editorial" observations, known as
"They Are Reading Ivan Denisovich" ("Chitaiut Ivana Denisovicha"), began life as a chapter of Gulag. Solzhenitsyn excised it
during one revision and, rather than waste it, allowed it to enter
samizdat circulation (The Oak, 223, 203). In fact, a much reduced
selection of these readers' responses is retained in Gulag III (Part 7,
Chapter 1). By 1964, the plan of the book was finalized. Parts 1 and 5
were written during the winter of 1964-1965. Solzhenitsyn's clandestine work on this vast project was made even more difficult and
dangerous after the KGB confiscated a portion of his literary archive
in Fall 1965. By March 1967, a second redaction of the first six parts
had been completed, and by May 1968, after further research and
rewriting, the entire book was typed up in its final form and sent
abroad on microfilm. It underwent only minor alterations between
then and the appearance of the Russian edition of the first volume
(Parts 1-2) in December 1973 (Paris: YMCA-Press). Solzhenitsyn had
delayed publication in order to proceed as far as possible with The
Red Wheel, but he was forestalled by the KGB's seizure of a copy of
an earlier redaction of the book, an event which precipitated his
expulsion from the Soviet Union. The second volume of the YMCA-
Press edition (Parts 3-4) came out in August 1974, and the third
(Parts 5-7) in February 1976 (copyright date given as 1975). The
volumes of the English translation appeared in 1974, 1975, and 1978,
respectively (New York: Harper and Row; London: Collins and
Harvill). The last of these volumes contained the author's "Preface
to the English Translation," dated November 1977. An excerpt from
the final part (overall title "Stalin Is No More" ["Stalina net"]) had

already appeared in *The New York Times*, 13 February 1974. A Russian text of this excerpt had circulated in 1974 as part of the *samizdat* volume *Zhit' ne po lzhi* (see item 80). In the West, Solzhenitsyn continued to make alterations and additions, in the light of further correspondence and published materials to which he had not formerly had access, and an expanded and corrected version of Part I, Chapter 6 (pp. 257-68 of the YMCA edition) was published in *Vestnik RKhD*, No. 115 (1, 1975), 164-82. Solzhenitsyn regards the text in *Vermont Sobr. soch.* as final. His textual note to volume VII of that edition gives valuable information on the history of the writing of *Gulag*.

B. Poetry

Although Solzhenitsyn did try his hand at verse in his youth (see the section on "Juvenilia"), he has repeatedly emphasized that he regards himself first and foremost as a writer of prose. Compelled by the circumstances of his internment to confine his literary efforts to what he could compose and retain in his head, he turned naturally to verse forms. In the late 1940s he composed poetry in the Marfino *sharashka* and by the time he left Ekibastuz labor camp in 1953 he had committed to memory some twelve thousand lines of original verse (*Gulag III*, 109, *101*). None of it has been officially published in the Soviet Union, with the exception of a secret, limited edition of the verse-drama *Feast of the Victors*. Tvardovskii reportedly felt that at least some of Solzhenitsyn's poetry was worthy of publication (*The Oak*, 33, *26*). Since 1974, the volume of Solzhenitsyn's early verse available in print in the West has increased dramatically, and a clearer picture is emerging of the unpublished parent opus. For his plays in verse, see Section C. "Drama." In addition, some of the titles listed, and manuscripts described in the official report of items confiscated from Zil'berberg's apartment, are very likely to be examples of labor camp verse (see Section E. "Miscellaneous").

27. *The Highway* (*Dorozhen'ka*, a hypocoristic diminutive form, found in folk verse), also known as *Highway of Enthusiasts* (*Shosse Entuziastov*, the Soviet name given to the Moscow end of the notorious "Vladimir Road," the route taken by convicts bound for Siberia). In *The Oak*, Solzhenitsyn uses the title *Highway of Enthusiasts* to

describe a tale *(povest')* in verse, consisting of a number of chapters
(76, *66*). In *Gulag*, he speaks of a "long poem" which occupied all his
spare moments in the Ekibastuz camp *(Gulag III,* 106, *98*). The
existence of a single, vast poem is further attested by acquaintances
of Solzhenitsyn. In his memoirs, *Zapiski Sologdina* (Frankfurt/Main;
Posev, 1973), Dimitrii Panin describes how, over a period of time and
by a prodigious feat of memory, Solzhenitsyn composed in his head a
long poem, "rather more than twice the length of Pushkin's *Evgenii
Onegin,* which itself contains about 5,400 lines of verse" (p. 479).
Elsewhere, Panin estimates the number of lines as "some 13,000"
("Kinofil'my po romanam Solzhenitsyna," *NRS,* 12 May 1974). Panin
(who calls the poem "Doroga," rather than "Dorozhen'ka") recalls
speaking to Solzhenitsyn about it in 1957. The latter reportedly
expressed dissatisfaction with it, considering it to be drawn-out and
repetitious. He spoke of reworking it *(Zapiski Sologdina,* p. 480).
Furthermore, Anna Akhmatova has given an account of a visit which
Solzhenitsyn paid her (probably in 1963), in the course of which he
read her "a long poem—over-long, in fact—10,000 lines, which had
saved his life in the camps" (cit. in N. Struve, "Vosem' chasov s
Annoi Akhmatovoi," A. Akhmatova, *Sochineniia,* II [Inter-Language
Literary Associates, 1968], 343). Akhmatova told him not to publish
it, but to keep to prose, in which he was "invulnerable." He apparently took the advice in good part. In *The Oak* he tells how Tvardovskii "rightly rejected" some modified, toned-down chapters of
The Highway which he had submitted for Tvardovskii's consideration
(76, *66*). On the basis of available published information, it would
seem that this one poem, written between 1948 and 1953, constitutes
the bulk of the 12,000 lines of labor camp verse to which Solzhenitsyn
refers. It appears to be heavily autobiographical, and to cover his
wartime experiences as well as the period of his imprisonment. The
possibility that other fragments of camp verse itemized below form,
or once formed, a part of *The Highway* is great, especially since
Solzhenitsyn's disclosure (in a note on *Feast of the Victors* appended
to *Vermont Sobr. soch.* VIII) that *Prussian Nights* originally made up
Chapter 9 of *The Highway,* while *Feast of the Victors* was Chapter 10.
(This note also appears to mark the first appearance in print of the
title "Dorozhen'ka.") In *Gulag III* he gives a remarkable account of
the mechanics of composing poetry in captivity (106 ff., *98* ff.) and
reproduces five lines which, the context suggests, are part of *The
Highway* (109, *101*). This fragment, "Our losses all will be made

good..." ("Vse nashe nam vospolnitsia"), is in iambic meter and is in the form of a stanza rhyming abaab. It is based on Solzhenitsyn's experience of returning from the front line under arrest in 1945. In *Gulag III* he describes a dangerous moment at Ekibastuz when he was caught with this fragment in his possession (109-110, *101-102*). A further 240 lines, headed "On the Soviet Frontier" ("Na sovetskoi granitse") and explicitly identified as an excerpt from *The Highway*, appeared in *Vestnik RKhD*, No. 117 (1, 1976), 148-54, together with a brief author's introduction. The verses, amphibrachic trimeters, are dated 1951, Ekibastuz, Steplag. The poet, returning to Russia under escort, reflects on what he sees at the frontier railway station and upon the fate of his homeland in general. *The Highway* is listed among the works which were to appear in the West in the event of Solzhenitsyn's death or arrest in the Soviet Union (*The Oak*, 449, *421*). There appear to be no immediate plans for publication of the remainder of *The Highway*.

28. A group of 69 lines of iambics, very probably part of *The Highway*. The lines are of varying length and are arranged in three sections, beginning respectively:

"It has not been! And never shall, this world that sparkles!..." ("Ne budet! Ne bylo sverkaiushchego mira!...")—four lines in all.

"The enfeebled pick-axe striking sparks against the frozen earth..." ("Iskrit o zemliu merzluiu bessil'naia kirka...")—20 lines.

"Though verses pound within—be still..." ("Pust' b'iutsia stroki—ne shepni...)—45 lines.

They are dated 1948-1950 and first appeared in an article by D. Blagov (pseudonym of V. L. Teush, an acquaintance with whom Solzhenitsyn stored part of his literary archive), "A. Solzhenitsyn i dukhovnaia missiia pisatelia," *Grani*, Nos. 64-65 (1967), reprinted in Aleksandr Solzhenitsyn, *Sobr. soch.*, 2nd ed., VI (Frankfurt/Main: Posev, 1973), 503-505. For an English translation of the verses, by Michael Scammell, see *Index*, Vol. 1, No. 2 (Summer 1972), pp. 149-51. (Scammell suggests the later dating of 1950 to 1953.) They tell of the suffering and desperation out of which poetry is born in the camps. Composing them is an act of liberation and helps the poet cling to his sanity. It is also an obligation to those who have died around him. He dreams of some day easing his burdened memory by writing down this tale (*povest'*) and hiding it in his place of exile.

Pushkin's line "God grant I do not lose my mind!" is used as a refrain.

29. *Prussian Nights* (*Prusskie nochi*). Dated 1950, at which time Solzhenitsyn was still in Ekibastuz labor camp. The poem consists of about 1,200 lines, written in trochaic tetrameters, except for one short passage in dactyls, and has a varying rhyme scheme. It contains pronouncedly autobiographical elements. The poet sweeps into East Prussia with the advancing Red Armies in the closing stage of World War II. He witnesses, and becomes involved in an orgy of retribution and license, which his conscience struggles in vain to accommodate. Superficially, at least, the form recalls Tvardovskii's long poem *Vasilii Terkin*. Indeed, when a written fragment of *Prussian Nights* was discovered on him during a search in Ekibastuz Solzhenitsyn managed to persuade the warder that he had been trying to recall some lines from that very work (*Gulag III*, 111-12, *103*). The context appears to suggest that *Prussian Nights* was once part of *The Highway*. This is confirmed in an authorial note on *Feast of the Victors* in *Vermont Sobr. soch.* VIII, where *Prussian Nights* is described as having once formed Chapter 9 of *The Highway*. In *The Oak*, Solzhenitsyn tells the story behind the appearance of an excerpt from *Prussian Nights* (not from *Feast of the Victors*, as was reported at the time) in *Die Zeit*, 5 December 1969 (*The Oak*, 295-96 & 350-51; *273* only). First complete publication in Russian was in 1974 (Paris YMCA-Press) together with a recording made in 1969 in the Soviet Union of the author reading his poem. Robert Conquest's translation appeared in 1977 in a Russian-English parallel edition (New York: Farrar, Straus and Giroux). This work has not so far been allocated a place in *Vermont Sobr. soch.*

30. "The Man above the Cowering Crowd" ("Chelovek nad sognutoi tolpoi"). The title may not be Solzhenitsyn's. The first line reads: "Our convict column marched. And more than once..." ("My shli etapom, I ne raz..."). Date unknown. This 44-line poem or fragment was first published, anonymously and untitled, in *Grani*, No. 57 (1965), pp. 3-4. It appeared above Solzhenitsyn's name in the Paris-based Cossack émigré monthly, *Rodimyi krai*, No. 112 (1974), pp. 6-7. Punctuation differed slightly in the later version and the fourth line ("Prikazyval konvoi") was printed before the first, clearly in error. The verses are in iambic meter, tetrameters alternating with trimeters, and rhyme abab. They describe what happens when one

zek in the column refuses to sit down when ordered to do so by the escort. The possibility of this being a further fragment of *The Highway* remains open for the present. A similar episode figures in the film scenario *Tanks Know the Truth*.

31. "The Stone-Mason" ("Kamenshchik") "Here I am—a mason. Poet-like, creatively..." ("Vot—ia kamenshchik. Kak u poeta slozheno..."). A 26-line poem in trochaic meter, the lines varying in length from five to seven feet. The rhyme-scheme is abaab or abab with dactylic rhyme predominating. Solzhenitsyn wrote it soon after his arrival in Ekibastuz in 1950 when he was engaged in building the camp's internal prison. The poem comments on the ironies of this situation and the passivity of the prisoners. The text was published in *Gulag III*, 79-80, 74), and Solzhenitsyn has described the loss and "miraculous" recovery of a copy of the poem in the camp (*ibid.*, pp. 111-12, *103-4*). Panin reports the same incident in *Zapiski Sologdina* (pp. 480-81).

32. "But when was it that I so completely..." ("Da kogda zh ia tak dopusta, dochista..."). Composed in a hospital bed in Ekibastuz labor camp (probably in February 1952), the poem or fragment is quoted in *Gulag II*, 601-2, *614-15*, and comprises 24 lines in anapestic trimeters, rhyming abab. It tells of the poet's loss and rediscovery of religious faith.

33. "Russia?" ("Rossiia?"). A poem of 80 lines, dated 1952, Ekibastuz, Steplag and written in amphibrachic trimeters grouped in four-line stanzas rhyming abab. The poet longs for the true Russia which flickers only occasionally behind the many faces of his tormented motherland. *Vestnik RKhD*, No. 117 (1, 1976), 155-157, with a brief author's introduction, *ibid.*, p. 148.

34. "To smite us like hammer on anvil..." ("Chtob srazu, kak molot kuznechnyi..."). A 10-line epigram, "albeit rather a long one" which Solzhenitsyn composed in February 1953 upon receiving notification that he had been exiled in perpetuity to Kok-Terek (Kazakhstan). The poem, which is in amphibrachic trimeters rhyming ababaaabab, makes play with the concept of "eternity." It is quoted in *Gulag III*, 432-33, *413*.

35. Solzhenitsyn refers to a poem, entitled "The Fifth of March"

("Piatoe marta"), the day of Stalin's death, which he wrote on 6 March 1953 (*Gulag III*, 442, *422*). The text has not been published.

36. On one occasion (*The Oak*, 440, *411*) Solzhenitsyn cites three lines of his own verse, but does not indicate their source beyond saying:

> As I myself wrote concerning my first arrest: Upon my body and my bones/ Descends a new tranquility,/ As tranquil as a man led to the block.
> ("Na telo mne, na kosti mne/ Spuskaetsia spokoistvie,/ Spokoistvie vedomykh pod obukh.")

37. [*Several times in her book, *V spore*, Reshetovskaia speaks of poetry which Solzhenitsyn wrote *before* his imprisonment, but she cites none of it. She does, however, quote two lines from a poem of the early 1950s entitled "The Prisoner's Right" ("Pravo uznika"), which she ascribes to Solzhenitsyn (p. 123). The theme is revenge. In addition she includes three undated fragments (nine lines in all) of the poetry which he had written to or about her during their years of separation (p. 138).]

38. An example of ephemeral verse is quoted by I. Kashkadamov, who in 1962 visited the school in Riazan' where Solzhenitsyn was teaching. In the photographic darkroom Kashkadamov found a four-line jingle on display, in which Solzhenitsyn exhorted his pupils not to be profligate or untidy when using chemicals ("Uchitel' s ulitsy Revoliutsii," *Uchitel'skaia gazeta*, 1 December 1962, p. 2).

C. Drama

39. *Feast of the Victors* (*Pir pobeditelei*). *Vermont Sobr. soch.* VIII, with a note on its provenance. A four-act play in verse, designated a "comedy." Solzhenitsyn composed it in Ekibastuz camp during 1951, often without the aid of pen and paper. He memorized it, rehearsing the whole text monthly until his release from camp. He himself has called *The Feast of the Victors* "seditious" (*The Oak*, 121, *107*), and he had a narrow escape when a written fragment of it was discovered during a routine search in the camp (*Gulag III*, 110-11, *102*). In 1953 he was able to write the play down and conceal

it in Kok-Terek, his place of exile. Originally, it had formed Chapter 10 of the long poem *The Highway*, but Solzhenitsyn came to regard it as a separate work, and from 1954 on as part of the dramatic trilogy *1945 (1945-i god)*—together with *The Captives* and *Republic of Labor*. After his move to metropolitan Russia, Solzhenitsyn kept the play hidden. When a copy had to be destroyed in 1964, only one remained, and in Fall 1965 it was discovered and confiscated by the KGB. Solzhenitsyn experienced its loss almost with relief: "For whatever I might think now, there was no way it could be worse or harsher than the angry things I had written in my labor camp play" (*The Oak*, 147, *130*). The confiscated copy was reproduced and selectively distributed for use in the campaign against Solzhenitsyn in the late 1960s. For the official reaction to the play, see the transcript of Solzhenitsyn's 1967 meeting with the Secretariat of the Writers' Union, appended to *The Oak* (Document No. 4). There appears to have been an attempt to have the play published abroad as part of the same campaign (*The Oak*, 247-48, *226-27*). In his note to *Vermont Sobr. soch.* VIII, Solzhenitsyn explains that: "The lost text was later restored by the author." There too, he writes that: "The play draws upon the author's personal experiences as commander of a sound-ranging battery, as well as reminiscences of the reconnaissance division in which he served, of various adjacent units, and of the January days in Prussia [in 1945]." Readers of *The First Circle* and *Republic of Labor* will recognize among the *dramatis personae* the figure of "Captain Nerzhin, commander of a range-finding battery." The first open publication of the play in any language was in 1981, in *Vermont Sobr. soch.* VIII.

40. *The Captives (Plenniki)*, earlier title *Decembrists without a December (Dekabristy bez dekabria)*. A "tragedy" in twelve scenes (*kartiny*). *Vermont Sobr. soch.* VIII, with a note by the author. Scenes 1, 2 and 12 are in verse. These Solzhenitsyn composed in his head in Ekibastuz camp during 1952, together with four of the scenes in prose (Scenes 3, 4, 5, and 11). The play was completed in Kok-Terek in Spring 1953, under circumstances described in *Gulag III* (Part 6, Chapter 6). Solzhenitsyn came to regard it as part of the dramatic trilogy *1945*. *The Captives* did not circulate in *samizdat* and never fell into the hands of the KGB. Before its appearance in *Vermont Sobr. soch.* in 1981 scarcely anything was known about it, although the title *Decembrists without a December* had figured in *The Oak*. It was

listed there among the works which Solzhenitsyn sent to the West, intending that they be published "automatically" should he be killed or imprisoned. A minor incident from the play was recalled in *The Oak*, 468, *441*. The action spans 24 hours and takes place on 9 July 1945 in one of the prisons of Smersh, the Red Army's counterespionage service. We see the interplay between prisoners of widely differing backgrounds and their captors and judges. Solzhenitsyn draws upon his own analogous experience in February 1945, as well as his wider prison and camp encounters, There are familiar names among the *dramatis personae*: Lev Rubin and Valentin Prianchikov (*The First Circle*) and Georgii Vorotyntsev, "a colonel in the Imperial Russian Army" (*August 1914*), whose death had been prophesied for 1945.

41. *The Republic of Labor* (*Respublika truda*). *Vermont Sobr. soch.* VIII. A four-act drama, dedicated to Ania Breslavskaia. It has been available in the West since 1969 in a variant entitled *The Tenderfoot and the Camp Whore* (*Olen' i shalashovka*), also rendered as *The Lovegirl and the Innocent*. In its original version it was written in Kok-Terek in Spring 1954—Solzhenitsyn's first new work since leaving the camps—and it formed the third part of the dramatic trilogy *1945* (*The Oak*, 9, *4*; and notes to *Vermont Sobr. soch.* VIII). In December 1962 (according to *Vermont Sobr. soch.*), he prepared a toned-down version, changing the title from *Republic of Labor*, but in *The Oak* he writes that "at the end of November" the Sovremennik Theater in Moscow was already anxious to stage the "lightened" version, and outlines the circumstances which led to this opportunity being missed (61-64, *52-54*). A copy of *Republic of Labor* was among the items confiscated by the KGB in Fall 1965, but until the appearance of *Vermont Sobr. soch.*, the uncensored version had been published only in German by Luchterhand (1977); it was staged in Essen in 1974. All other editions and performances in the West were based on the "lightened" variant, which had circulated in *samizdat*.

42. *The Light within You* (*Svet, kotoryi v tebe*). *Vermont Sobr. soch.* VIII. Solzhenitsyn now prefers this title to the one better known in the West, *Candle in the Wind* (*Svecha na vetru*), which, however, he retains as a subtitle in *Vermont Sobr. soch.* (Part of the reason is his reported belief that his first title was plagiarized by a Soviet playwright.) Solzhenitsyn has been extremely frank in admitting the weakness of this play, which he has described as his least successful

work. In a note to *Vermont Sobr. soch.* he speaks, in particular, of the loss of "the expressive features of the Russian language and Russian dialogue," as a result of his abstract, "de-nationalized" treatment of his theme. He began the play in 1960—the first of his works which he did not have to keep hidden—and returned to it four or five times (*The Oak*, 18-19 & 127-28; *12-13 & 112-14*). In 1964 he tried to interest "several theaters" in it (*The Oak*, 100), but without success: "*Novyi mir* could not publish it (1964), and it could not be staged by the Lenin Komsomol Theater in Moscow (1965), the Leningrad Comedy Theater (1966) and the Vakhtangov Theater (1967)" (note in *Vermont Sobr. soch.*). It reached the West via *samizdat* and was first published in 1969. In the new edition Solzhenitsyn confirms that he drew upon his own experiences and those of several Moscow families in writing the play.

43. *Den of the Fortunate* (*Vertep schastlivykh*), "a drama in seven scenes." This item is listed among the works confiscated with Solzhenitsyn's literary archive in Fall 1965 (*Zil'berberg*, 76). The confiscated copy was 49 pages long. No other information is known. (It is, of course, conceivable that this is an earlier title of one of the works listed above. For example, the version of *The Captives* which Solzhenitsyn brought out of the camps in his memory apparently also contained seven scenes.)

D. Film Scenarios

44. *Tanks Know the Truth* (*Znaiut istinu tanki*). "A film scenario for screen with variable dimensions." *Vermont Sobr. soch.* VIII. This is a "literary" film scenario, written in order to create in the reader the illusion of watching a cinema screen, at a time when there was no prospect of its ever being filmed. It is thus related to the "cinematographic" passages in *The Red Wheel*. The scenario was written in Fall 1959 in Riazan'. "I almost wept when I had to destroy the original of the scenario; it had been written in a special way. But one anxious night I had to burn it" (*The Oak*, 11, 6, fn.). "It tells of how, after the death of Stalin, a rising by unarmed prisoners in the Special Camps was crushed by tanks, by a regular unit of the Soviet Army" (CBS-TV Interview, item 107). More specifically, it combines Solzhenitsyn's first-hand experiences of the events surrounding the Eki-

bastuz strike in 1951-1952 with what he learned about the 1954 uprising in Kengir (note to *Vermont Sobr. soch.* VIII). (The fact that these events are described in the third volume of *Gulag* inspired rumors in the West in the mid-1970s that Solzhenitsyn was planning to film *The Gulag Archipelago*.) In his letter of 16 May 1967 to the Fourth Congress of the Soviet Writers' Union, he mentioned that he had been unable to find either a publisher or a film studio willing to accept the scenario. Although he did consider allowing it to be filmed in the West after his expulsion from the Soviet Union, no such film has been made, and *Vermont Sobr. soch.* VIII (1981) is the first publication of the work in any language. An English translation is expected to appear in the early 1980s.

45. *The Parasite (Tuneiadets)*. "A comedy film." *Vermont Sobr. soch.* VIII. This scenario is unusual among Solzhenitsyn's works in that it was commissioned, by the Soviet film studio "Mosfil'm" in about 1966. He delivered it in November 1968 with no real hopes that it would ever be filmed, and it was indeed halted on Demichev's injunction. Tvardovskii told Solzhenitsyn, after reading the scenario (and in jest), that he ought to be "locked up, and as quickly as possible" (*The Oak*, 244 & 263; *223 & 241*). The scenario is based on certain real-life events: for example, Solzhenitsyn's attempt to have his car repaired in Riazan' "on the side," and various features of a Soviet election campaign. He does not appear to hold this scenario in very high regard, mentioning it infrequently and on one occasion referring to *Tanks Know the Truth* as "my only original film scenario" (CBS-TV Interview, item 107). *The Parasite* has not been filmed and was first published in 1981 in *Vermont Sobr. soch.*

E. Miscellaneous

A number of items listed in the KGB record of its search and confiscation at the home of Il'ia Zil'berberg in Fall 1965 have been incorporated into the bibliography. There remain several titles whose genre cannot be confidently identified:

46. *An Unhappy Tale (Neveselaia povest')*. A typescript or manuscript of 60 pages bearing Solzhenitsyn's name, confiscated in Fall 1965 with his literary archive (*Zil'berberg*, 76). Nothing

further is known about it. (The title may be a variant masking a familiar work, and the *povest'* may not even be in prose at all.)

47. *The Heart beneath the Convict Jacket* (*Serdtse pod bush-latom*);

48. *Losing Count of the Years. Grieg, "Solveig's Song"* (*Kogda teriaiut schet godam. Grig, "Pesnia Sol'veig"*).

In addition, several manuscripts are described only by their opening and closing words (*Zil'berberg*, 75-76).

49. In November 1965, Solzhenitsyn offered *four* stories to various editorial boards: "The Right Hand," "What a Pity," "Za-khar-Kalita," "and one other" *(The Oak, 136, 120)*. If this "other" story is a familiar one, it seems odd that Solzhenitsyn should not refer to it by its title.

In his 1976 interview with Nikita Struve (item 175), Solzhenitsyn refers to plots which he has begun, but which he does not expect to have time to complete. Projects about which a little more is known include:

50. An account of the "unforgettable" night of 26-27 January 1945, when Solzhenitsyn's sound-ranging battery was encircled by the enemy. "How often I have felt the urge to describe it. My first attempt, while still in labor camp, was in trochaic tetrameters, as a sequel to *Prussian Nights*. I did get some of it written, but then I lost it and none of it has stayed in my memory. Next, in exile, I was going to try it in prose, but other, more important themes took precedence, and I never really got started" *(Skvoz' chad, 35)*. He makes up for the omission in the pages which follow *(ibid., 35-39)*.

51. "Verses on the Beauties of Exile" ("Stikhi o prekrasnoi ssylke"). Under the first impressions of his journey into exile in 1953, Solzhenitsyn planned to write a cycle of poems under this title *(Gulag III, 427, 408)*.

52. "The Spoilt Wife" ("Isporchennaia zhena"). "I have had the subject of a story, 'The Spoilt Wife,' for a long time. But I shall evidently not get round to writing it, so here it is" *(Gulag I, 160, 151, fn. 12)*. There follows a summary, some 150 words in length, of a rather macabre episode demonstrating the omnipotence of even a

relatively junior officer in the state security forces. Solzhenitsyn regards other incidents in *Gulag* as potential material for literary treatment (e.g., *Gulag I*, 164, *156*, fn. 15 and 323, fn. 41, *317*, fn. 39).

53. Contemplating the possibility of arrest in 1974, Solzhenitsyn thought that he might even be able to write while in prison: "What could I write? A history of Russia in short stories for children, written lucidly and without embellishing the subject. (I had thought of this ever since my first sons were born, but will I ever get down to it?)" (*The Oak*, 429, *401*).

One piece of negative information about Solzhenitsyn's plans is his promise on French television, 11 April 1975, that he will never write a serious work of literature about the West.

II. NON-BELLETRISTIC WRITINGS AND STATEMENTS

Many of the items in this section were published almost the whole world over. The full extent of the response since 1974 cannot be recorded in the present brief listing, but every effort has been made to indicate a reliable Russian and English text where available.

Apart from volumes IX and X of the Vermont Collected Works, and the documentary appendix to *The Oak and the Calf* (see item 133), the following new anthologies or new editions of older anthologies have appeared since 1974:

54. L. Labedz, ed., *Solzhenitsyn: A Documentary Record*, 2nd, expanded ed. (Harmondsworth: Penguin, 1974).

55. Aleksandr Solzhenitsyn, *Mir i nasilie* (Frankfurt/Main: Posev, 1974). In addition to an interview and an article from 1973, the collection includes items 103, 105, and 107.

56. A. I. Solzhenitsyn, *Amerikanskie rechi* (Paris: YMCA-Press, 1975). Contains items 141, 142, and 145. French and German translations appeared in the same year, as *Drei Reden an die Amerikaner* (Neuwied: Luchterhand) and *Discours américains* (Paris: Seuil). See also the following two items.

57. Alexander Solzhenitsyn, *Warning to the West* (New York: Farrar, Straus & Giroux, 1976). Comprises the three "speeches to the.

Americans'' (see item 56), together with two ''speeches to the British'' (items 166 and 167).

58. *Alexander Solzhenitsyn Speaks to the West* (London: Bodley Head, 1978). Contains the three ''speeches to the Americans,'' together with the 1978 Harvard Address (item 200).

59. Aleksandr I. Solzhenitsyn, *East and West* (New York: Harper and Row, 1980). Reprints the Nobel Lecture, as well as items 76, 200, and 208.

A. Before 1974

The following *new* information about Solzhenitsyn's earlier publicistic and essayistic writings has become available since 1974:

60. [*Reshetovskaia refers to Solzhenitsyn's work on the preliminary outline of ''A Teacher's Day'' (''Odin den' odnogo uchitelia''), apparently at some time before May 1959. It is not clear whether the projected work was to have been literary or essayistic in form (*V spore*, 154).]

61. [*An article on earth satellites, written in 1957 for the Obkom's *Notebook of an Agitator* (*Bloknot agitatora*). It was not published (*V spore*, 145).]

62. [*''Post Office Curiosities'' (''Pochtovye kur'ezy''), a note (*zametka*) on delays in postal delivery, published in *Priokskaia pravda* in March 1959. If Reshetovskaia is correct, this was Solzhenitsyn's first appearance in print, some three and a half years before *One Day in the Life of Ivan Denisovich* (*V spore*, 164).]

63. [*Another such piece (feuilleton?) complaining about irregularities in booking railway seats was sent to the newspaper *Trud* in 1960, but was not published (*V spore*, 164).]

64. An article criticizing the recent spate of literary autobiographies, in particular those of Erenburg and Paustovskii. Solzhenitsyn submitted it to more than one editorial board in Fall 1960 but without success. ''My article took the form of a criticism of literary memoirs in general, but in reality it expressed my irritation at the way writers who had witnessed a great, somber epoch kept trying to skim over it,

without telling us any of the main things (...)'' (*The Oak*, 18, *12*). [*Reshetovskaia adds a title, "Epidemic of Autobiographies" ("Epidemiia avtobiografii") and tells how Solzhenitsyn sent the article to *Literaturnaia gazeta* in November 1960 (*V spore*, 164-65).]

65. "It Is Not Customary to Whiten Soup with Tar..." ("Ne obychai degtem shchi belit'"). This short article, printed in *Literaturnaia gazeta*, 4 November 1965, has been heavily relied upon in the West as Solzhenitsyn's only programmatic statement of his attitude towards the Russian language. All the more noteworthy is his own subsequent assessment: "It is true that I had been collecting material on the literary language for some time, but here I made a hash of it, presenting it hastily, superficially, unconvincingly (...)" (*The Oak*, 135, *119*). The article was first published in English in *Russian Literature Triquarterly*, No. 11 (Winter 1975). *Vermont Sobr. soch.* X.

66. 1966. "Reply to a Young Scholar" ("Otvet molodomu uchenomu"). Hitherto unpublished, but due to appear in *Vermont Sobr. soch.* X.

67. 26 June 1967. Letter to Kirill Simonian, a childhood friend, on the latter's belated charges that Solzhenitsyn had denounced him. Facsimile of holograph in Kirill Samjonovitsj Simonjan, *Hvem er Solsjenitsyn?* (Skaerbaek, Denmark: Melbyhus, 1976), p. 15, with a translation into Danish. Although the book appears to have been inspired at least in part by the Novosti Press Agency, Solzhenitsyn has not challenged the authenticity of this letter.

68. 13 August 1971. Letter to Aleksandr Gorlov, informing him of his decision publicly to protest against Gorlov's treatment at the hands of the KGB. In A. M. Gorlov, *Sluchai na dache* (Paris: YMCA-Press, 1977), pp. 24-25.

69. Date unknown. "Notes for *Chukokkala*" ("Zametki dlia Chukokkaly"). Hitherto unpublished reflections on literature. *Vermont Sobr. soch.* X.

70. April 1972. Statement to the Swedish Academy of Science on Nabokov. *Vermont Sobr. soch.* X.

71. May 1972(?). Letter to a Western correspondent praising Father Aleksandr Shmeman's broadcasts over Radio Liberty. It contains an interesting reference to Pushkin. The text, which is

apparently incomplete, was first published in *NRS*, 9 August 1972, with a brief editorial introduction and reprinted (in an article on Father Shmeman) In *NRS*, 16 September 1973.

B. 1974 and After

In citing sources within any given entry, the year is given only where it differs from that which heads the entry.

72. 6 January 1974. Letter to Sarra Emmanuilovna Babenysheva enlisting help in "actively resisting" the impending expulsion from the Soviet Writers' Union of Lidiia Chukovskaia and Vladimir Voinovich. The same letter was apparently sent to other members of the Writers' Union. Cited in full in Lidiia Chukovskaia, *Protsess iskliucheniia (Ocherk literaturnykh nravov)* (Paris: YMCA-Press, 1979), p. 140. English translation first published in the present volume.

73. 15(?) January 1974. Statement in support of Lidiia Chukovskaia, following her expulsion from the Writers' Union. English (excerpts only) as: "Solzhenitsyn Deplores 'Revenge,'" *Times* (London), 16 January, p. 4; "Soviet Official, on TV, Urges That Solzhenitsyn Go Abroad," *NYT*, 16 January, p. 10.

74. 18 January 1974. Press statement in response to the campaign against him in the Soviet media ("Birnam Wood...shall come"). *Vermont Sobr. soch.* X; *The Oak*, 609-11, *531-32*; *RM*, 31 January, p. 1. English in the *Times* (London), 19 January, p. 6; *NYT*, 19 January, p. 4; latter text repr. in *CR*, vol. 120, Pt. 1 (22 January), pp. 221-22, and in *A Chronicle of Human Rights in the USSR*, No. 7 (January-February 1974), pp. 7-8.

75. 19 January 1974. Interview with *Time* Magazine. Written answers to pre-submitted questions, concerning his attitude to the proposals of Sakharov and the Medvedev brothers, TASS's recent charges, radio broadcasting of *Gulag*, possible official reprisals against him, etc. *Time*, 28 January, p. 45 cites only a portion of the interview. Solzhenitsyn published the text in *The Oak*, 612-14, *532-34*, and in *Vermont Sobr. soch.*, X. What appears to be a somewhat fuller text was released to foreign correspondents on 21 January and appeared in English as "The Lie Is a Pillar of the State," *Times*

(London), 22 January, p. 14, and, in extensive excerpts, in Christopher S. Wren, "Solzhenitsyn Calls on Russians to Reject 'the Lie,'" *NYT*, 22 January, p. 12.

76. January 1974. "Letter to Soviet Leaders." Written in August 1973, it bears the date on which it was sent to its addressees: 5 September 1973. In January 1974 Solzhenitsyn revised the Letter, furnished it with a preface and sent it abroad. He was obliged to delay publication (*The Oak*, 415, *387*), but after his deportation the Letter appeared widely and in many languages. Russian: as *Pis'mo vozhdiam Sovetskogo Soiuza* (Paris: YMCA-Press, 1974); and in *Vermont Sobr. soch.* IX. Full English text in *Sunday Times* (London), 3 March, pp. 33-36; repr. in *CR*, vol. 120, Pt. 5 (8 March), pp. 5999-6006. Book editions in English by Index/Fontana (London) and Harper and Row (New York), both 1974. The preface, omitted from all the English-language editions cited, was restored in the collection *East and West* (item 59). Alleged variants in the texts of September 1973 and January 1974 are discussed in: Nan Robertson, "Letter Softened by Solzhenitsyn," *NYT*, 5 March, p. 9.

77. January 1974. "The Secret Must Out" ("Nevyrvannaia taina"), foreword to D*, *Stremia "Tikhogo Dona" (Zagadki romana)* [*A Current of the "Quiet Don" (Enigmas of a Novel)*] (Paris: YMCA-Press, 1974). Solzhenitsyn also provides a biographical note on the writer F. D. Kriukov (*ibid.*, pp. 190-93). Russian text of the foreword also in *Vermont Sobr. soch.* X. English in *Times Literary Supplement*, 4 October, p. 1056.

78. 2 February 1974. Statement on the official campaign against him (notably a denunciatory statement to the Novosti Press Agency by his former friend, Vitkevich), and on the messages of support he has received. *Vermont Sobr. soch.* X; *The Oak*, 617-19, *535-37*. A text published in the Western press shows variants: "Excerpts from Solzhenitsyn Statements," *NYT*, 4 February, p. 14 (includes excerpts from both Vitkevich's statement and Solzhenitsyn's response).

79. 11 February 1974. Statement to the Public Prosecutor of the Soviet Union, refusing to comply with repeated summonses to appear. *The Oak*, 621, *537-38*. English also in Hedrick Smith, "Solzhenitsyn Disregards 2nd Summons," *NYT*, 12 February, p. 5; and *A Chronicle of Current Events*, No. 32 (17 July 1974), p. 9 (different translation).

80. 12 February 1974. "Live Not by Lies!" ("'Zhit' ne po lzhi!'"). An appeal to his compatriots. The final version was completed on the date cited, but according to a bibliographical note in *Vermont Sobr. soch.* IX, where the full Russian text is reprinted, Solzhenitsyn "prepared" the appeal during 1972 and 1973. Elsewhere, he states that by early 1974 it had already been "languishing" unpublished for four years (*The Oak*, 415, *387*). He arranged for the text to be released automatically in the event of his arrest. The first of many publications appear to have been in English in the *Washington Post*, 18 February, repr. in *CR*, vol. 120, Pt. 3 (18 February), pp. 3119-20; and in the *Daily Express* (London), 18 February, p. 11 (same translation). The Russian text also appeared in *RM*, 21 March, p. 3; and in the *samizdat* anthology of materials on Solzhenitsyn which was circulating in the Soviet Union by March 1974, and which eventually came out as *Zhit' ne po lzhi: Sbornik materialov, avgust 1973—fevral' 1974* (Moscow: Samizdat. Paris: YMCA-Press, 1975), pp. 194-98.

81. 13 February 1974 (written in August 1973). Statement to be released in the event of arrest, refusing to cooperate in any proceedings or to recognize the authority of any Soviet court to prosecute Russian literature. The text was "activated" by Solzhenitsyn's wife after his arrest: see the account in *The Oak*, 457-58, *430*. Full text *ibid.*, 622, *538*; and in *Vermont Sobr. soch.* X. English also as "Solzhenitsyn Bars Aid to Judges or Jailers," *NYT*, 13 February, p. 12 (late eds. only); and *A Chronicle of Current Events*, No. 32 (17 July 1974), p. 10 (different translation).

The massive news coverage of Solzhenitsyn's movements following his arrival in West Germany on 13 February continued throughout that month. Reporters attributed to him various brief statements and remarks, some of which were no more than refusals to grant interviews or expressions of irritation at the importunities of the press; other observations concerned, for example, the similarity between the winter landscape of Norway and that of Russia. While of interest to the biographer, such fragmentary utterances would not seem to justify individual inclusion in the present bibliography. Exception is made for the following two rather more substantial items:

82. 14 February 1974. A ten-minute meeting in Langenbroich with Janis Sapiets of the BCC Russian Service. Although this was not

an interview and Solzhenitsyn specifically asked that Sapiets not take notes, accounts of the meeting give some idea of Solzhenitsyn's concerns at this time and of the circumstances in which he found himself one day after his expulsion. Janis Sapiets, "Solzhenitsyn Face to Face," BBC Current Affairs External Broadcasting talk, CAR 31/74, 14 February; and Nicholas Carroll, "Solzhenitsyn 'under Dreadful Strain, Yet So Inwardly Calm'" (consisting largely of an account by Sapiets), *Sunday Times* (London), 17 February, p. 9.

83. 16 February 1974. Brief meeting in Zurich with a former inhabitant of Riazan', who had sent him flowers and a proverb. Henry Kamm, "Solzhenitsyn Goes Downtown in Zurich," *NYT*, 17 February, p. 3; also described in "Solzhenitsyn Takes a Trip in Hills around Lake Zurich," *IHT*, 18 February.

84. 18 February 1974. Interview in Zurich (in the form of type-written answers to questions) with Associated Press correspondent Frank Crepeau. The questions concerned Solzhenitsyn's experiences in exile and his literary and domestic plans for the future. Full text (in German) as "Die Wunder hören nie auf," *FAZ*, 20 February, p. 22. Excerpts: "Solzhenitsyn, Still Defiant, Eager to Get on with Work," *NYT*, 19 February, p. C3. For an account of the circum-stances attending the interview, see "Frank, What Are You Doing Here?" *Stars and Stripes*, 20 February.

85. 19 February 1974. Typewritten statement sharply criticizing recent Western press reports about him which were "irresponsible," "childish" and mendacious. It was read out to journalists and copies were distributed. Reports (mixed quotation and summary): "Solzhe-nitsyn Assails Press," *NYT*, 20 February, p. 2; "Solzhenitsyn Says Press in West Invented Stories," *IHT*, 20 February; "Solschenizyn und die Sensationspresse," *NZZ*, 21 February.

86. February 1974 (not later than 21st). Telegram from Zurich, thanking the West German government for its "great and speedy assistance" in the period following his expulsion. The thirty-word German text was read out to the Bundestag during question time on 21 February. "Solschenizyn dankt der Bundesregierung," *FAZ*, 22 February, p. 1; "Der Dichter dankt der Bundesregierung," *Süd-deutsche Zeitung*, 22 February.

87. 25 February 1974. Brief interview in Oslo for Norwegian TV,

in which he expressed admiration for Norway, but said that he had not decided where to settle. "Norwegian Aides See Solzhenitsyn about Residency," *IHT*, 26 February; "Erstes Fernsehinterview Solschenizyns," *NZZ*, 27 February.

88. 5 March 1974. Letter in reply to Sen. Jesse Helms. Solzhenitsyn thanks him for proposing him for honorary US Citizenship, but declines an invitation to visit America. Russian (facsimile of typescript): *East Europe*, Vol. 23, No. 27 (July 1974), p. 4. English (together with Helms's original letter to Solzhenitsyn): *ibid.*, pp. 2-3; (Solzhenitsyn's letter only) *CR*, vol. 120, Pt. 5 ((11 March), p. 6088.

89. 8 March 1974. "These Aren't Stalin's Times" ("Ne stalinskie vremena"). Joint statement with Igor' Shafarevich protesting against the continuing detention of Petr Grigorenko. Russian: *RM*, 30 May, p. 4; Radio Liberty "Arkhiv Samizdata," No. 1683 (annotated); and *Vermont Sobr. soch.* X. English (summary and brief quotations): "Solzhenitsyn Asks Release of Inmate," *NYT*, 9 April, p. 4.

90. 1974, before 14 March. Letter to George Meany of the AFL-CIO (American Federation of Labor-Congress of Industrial Organizations). "Solzhenitsyn Declines an Offer from A.F.L.-C.I.O. to Tour U.S.," *NYT*, 15 March, p. 12 (full text in English). For the text of Meany's original letter to Solzhenitsyn, see: *CR*, vol. 120, Pt. 5 (14 March), p. 6903.

91. 22 March 1974. Letter to Sen. Jesse Helms on the dilemmas facing America and, more especially, Russia, on non-violent social change, and on difficulties of mutual comprehension. English (extensive excerpts): *CR*, vol. 120, Pt. 7 (1 April), p. 9025.

92. 31(?) March 1974. Interview in Zurich with Fred Luchsinger, editor-in-chief of the *Neue Zürcher Zeitung*, published as "f. l.," "Gespräch mit Solschenizyn," *NZZ*, 3 April, p. 5. Some of the circumstances attending the interview, as well as Solzhenitsyn's reaction to the finished article, are described in Herbert Riehl-Heyse, "Wohl aufgehoben und verschlossen," *Süddeutsche Zeitung*, 22 October.

93. 31 March 1974. Written answer to a question by AP correspondent Rodger Leddington. Russian: *Vermont Sobr. soch.* X. Solzhenitsyn stresses the need for mutual understanding between

the Russian and American peoples, and accuses the American press of having misrepresented his "Letter to the Soviet Leaders": Rodger Leddington, "U.S. Press," *New York Post*, 1 April; "Solzhenitsyn: U.S. Press Misread Call," *Washington Post*, 2 April; "Solzhenitsyn Accuses Press of Distortion," *IHT*, 2 April, p. 1.

94. March 1974. "To Live Without Losing One's Dignity" ("Zhit', ne teriaia dostoinstva"). Critical reply to an essay by "X. Y." (Boris Shragin) which had proposed changes in the journal, *Vestnik RSKhD*, No. 111 (1, 1974), p. 7; also in *Vermont Sobr. soch.* X.

95. 3 April 1974. Letter to Rep. Benjamin Rosenthal and Rep. Donald Fraser, Chairmen of the House of Representatives Subcommittees for, respectively, European Affairs and International Organizations, declining an invitation to participate personally in House discussions of détente, but warning at length against the dangers of "pseudo-détente." Russian in *RM*, 23 May, p. 2; and *Vermont Sobr. soch.* X. Full English text was made public as part of the House hearings on détente beginning 8 May and was extensively cited by Jack Anderson in his syndicated column, which appeared, e.g., as "Warning on False Detente Given by Solzhenitsyn," *Poughkeepsie Journal*, 28 April.

96. 5 April 1974. Statement on the recent treatment of Viktor Nekrasov and Aleksandr Ginzburg as examples of "serfdom" in the Soviet Union today. The 220-word statement was telephoned to the BBC from Zurich and broadcast over the BBC's Russian Service. Russian: *RM*, 11 April, p. 2; *Vermont Sobr. soch.* X. English (full text): Richard Davy, "Solzhenitsyn Denounces Serfdom in Russia," *Times* (London), 6 April, p. 1; (excerpts only) "Solzhenitsyn Says Soviet Is 'Serfdom,'" *NYT*, 6 April, p. 6.

97. 8 April 1974. Press statement, thanking his well-wishers in the West. Russian: as "Solzhenitsyn svoim druz'iam" ("Solzhenitsyn to His Friends"), *RM*, 18 April, p. 1. English (brief, untitled report, without quotations): *NYT*, 9 April, p. 4.

98. 10 April 1974. Letter in reply to greetings from Tolstoi's daughter, Aleksandra L'vovna Tolstaia, recalling how he almost sent his works to her for publication during the 1950s. Russian: *NRS*, 5 July, p. 1. English (incomplete): Israel Shenker, "Alexandra Tolstoy,

at 90, Is Honored...," *NYT*, 2 July, p. 37. (Solzhenitsyn refers to a "letter" from Tolstaia. The text of a *telegram* which she sent to him on the day of his expulsion was printed in *NRS*, 14 February, p. 1.)

99. 23(?) April 1974. Solzhenitsyn briefly reported as having told a representative of Deutsche Welle in his Zurich home that Deutsche Welle is the most popular foreign radio station in the Soviet Union. "Solschenizyn: Deutsche Welle in SU populärster Sender," *Die Welt*, 25 April, p. 23.

100. 1974, not before mid-April. Essay in response to Sakharov's criticism of "Letter to Soviet Leaders." Publication of the response was delayed until after the appearance of *From Under the Rubble* and the text reflects Solzhenitsyn's awareness of the difficulties facing Sakharov in the Soviet Union (from the textual note in *Vermont Sobr. soch.* IX). The Russian text had first been published in *Kontinent*, No. 2 (1975), pp. 350-59. English (preceded by Sakharov's original essay) in *Kontinent* (London: Hodder and Stoughton, 1977), pp. 30-38 (U.S. ed. Garden City, N.Y.: Doubleday, 1976).

101. 3 May 1974. Interview with *Time* magazine, published as "Eternally Bound to the Homeland," *Time*, 27 May. It apparently took the form of written answers to pre-submitted questions (omitted in *Time*) on his reaction to Sakharov's criticism of the "Letter to Soviet Leaders," on his life in exile and his attitude to the Soviet practice of deporting intellectuals. In replying, Solzhenitsyn quoted at length from the preface to his "Letter" (its first publication in English; see item 76). A Russian text which included the questions, together with several paragraphs of Solzhenitsyn's response not found in the *Time* version, was published in *RM*, 30 May, p. 5; also in *Vermont Sobr. soch.* X.

102. 3 May 1974. Statement on a KGB attempt to compromise him in 1972 by sending forged letters in his name to V. Orekhov, a prominent émigré and Russian nationalist. The statement, which includes examples in facsimile, was published in English as "Solzhenitsyn v. the KGB," *Time*, 27 May, p. 51. A slightly fuller text appeared in Russian as "Gosbezopasnost' ne unimaetsia" ("The Irrepressible KGB"), *RM*, 30 May, p. 5, and was corroborated in a letter from Orekhov in *RM*, 6 June, p. 5.

103. 25 May 1974. Letter to *Aftenposten* (Oslo) on recent repri-

sals against Gabriel' Superfin and Efim Etkind. Norwegian: *Aften-posten*, 27 May. Russian: *RM*, 6 June, p. 2; *Posev*, No. 7, 1974, p. 11 (as "Rastianutyi Miunkhen"); in the collection *Mir i nasilie*, pp. 46-48; and in *Vermont Sobr. soch.* X.

104. 25 May 1974. Brief interview with *Aftenposten* correspondent Per Egil Hegge, discussing *Tanks Know the Truth*, *Prussian Nights* and his impressions of the West. Norwegian: *Aftenposten*, 27 May. Russian: broadcast by Radio Liberty, 28 May, together with the preceding item. English (short untitled report): *IHT*, 28 May.

105. 31 May 1974. Speech in a Zurich hotel, upon receiving the Italian press's "Golden Cliché" Prize for 1973, on the subject of individualism, materialism and the need for an "ethical revolution." Russian: *Vestnik RSKhD*, No. 111 (1, 1974), pp. 66-69; in the collection *Mir i nasilie*, pp. 97-102; *Vermont Sobr. soch.* IX.

106. 31 May 1974. Remarks to Ennio Caretto. Although Solzhenitsyn refused to hold a press conference after the award of the "Golden Cliché" Prize, Caretto quotes a number of his comments during the reception which followed. Ennio Caretto, "Come vive a Zurigo il russo del dissenso," *La Stampa*, 1 June.

107. 17 June 1974. Wide-ranging one-hour CBS-TV interview with Walter Cronkite in Zurich. Russian: *RM*, 11 July, pp. 6-7; in the collection *Mir i nasilie*, pp. 49-96; *Vermont Sobr. soch.* X. Full English text: *CR*, vol. 120, Pt. 16 (27 June), pp. 21483-86. Extensive excerpts: *The Listener*, 4 July, pp. 8-9.

108. June 1974. Message to accompany the first issue of the journal *Kontinent*. Russian: *Kontinent*, No. 1 (1974), pp. 7-8; *Vermont Sobr. soch.* X. English in: *Kontinent* (London: Hodder and Stoughton, 1977), pp. 11-12 (U.S. ed. Garden City, N. Y.: Doubleday, 1976).

109. Late June-early July 1974. Telegram to Aleksandra Tolstaia with congratulations on her 90th birthday. Reported without text in Israel Shenker, "Alexandra Tolstoy, at 90, Is Honored...," *NYT*, 2 July, p. 37.

110. Mid-1974. Reply of some 85 words, declining an invitation to address participants at a course in Munich in July 1974, arranged by the Ukrainian Free University and Central Michigan University.

Solzhenitsyn writes of his connections with and affection for the Ukrainian people. Ukrainian: *Suchasnist'*, No. 11 (167), November 1974, p. 124. English: *Svoboda, The Ukrainian Weekly*, 31 August, repr. in *CR*, vol. 121, Pt. 1 (23 January 1975), p. 1186; *The Ukrainian Quarterly*, vol. 30, No. 3 (Autumn 1974), pp. 332-33 (same trans.).

111. 23 August 1974. Letter from Zurich to the *New York Times* on its report of the persecution of Svetlana Shramko, printed as "How Things Are Done in the Soviet Provinces," *NYT*, 30 September, p. 34. Original text, as "Ne dadim pogibnut' Svetlane Shramko" ("Let Us Not Allow Svetlana Shramko to Perish") in *Vermont Sobr. soch*. X.

112. C. August 1974 (before 28th). Interview in Zurich with Norwegian correspondent Nils Morten Udgaard. Includes Solzhenitsyn's first substantial discussion of how he self-censored his works. Norwegian: N. M. Udgaard, "Også Solsjenitsyns romaner i utlandet har han selv sensurert," *Aftenposten*, 28 August, p. 4. German: "Solschenizyn im Exil," *Die Zeit*, 6 September, p. 19. Russian: apart from a paraphrase of the *Die Zeit* text in *RM*, 10 October, p. 5, the only published source is *Vermont Sobr. soch*. X. No English text was published, but see Hedrick Smith (item 126).

113. 30 August 1974. Letter to the editor of the newspaper *Nasha strana* (Tel-Aviv), protesting against unjustifiably high prices being charged in Israel for the Russian edition of *Gulag*. *Nasha strana*, 5 September.

114. August 1974. Letter replying to an invitation to attend the Third Council of the Russian Orthodox Church Abroad in Jordanville, N.Y., 8-22 September. The lengthy text discusses the fate of the Church under the Soviet regime, the Church's persecution of the Old Believers, and the problem of reunification. *NRS*, 27 September, p. 2 and *Vestnik RKhD*, No. 112-113 (2-3, 1974), pp. 99-111 (both also give Metropolitan Philaret's reply), *Vermont Sobr. soch*. IX. English in *Eastern Churches Review*, No. 1, 1975, pp. 40-51; and Niels C. Nielsen, *Solzhenitsyn's Religion* (Nashville: Nelson, 1975; London: Mowbray, 1976), pp. 142-58.

115. 11 September 1974. "A Worthy Commentator" ("Dostoinyi istolkovatel'"). Letter criticizing various recent public statements by Zhores Medvedev. Originally intended for the London *Times*, it first

appeared in Norwegian in *Aftenposten*, 20 September, p. 7. Russian: *RM*, 26 September, p. 2; *NRS*, 3 October; *Posev*, No. 10, 1974, p. 15; *Vermont Sobr. soch.* X. English (trans. from Norwegian): *Foreign Broadcast Information Service*, III, 1 October, pp. R1-R2. Medvedev replied in *Aftenposten*, 26 September, p. 7. His letter appeared in Russian in *NRS*, 12 October and in English in *FBIS*, III, 3 October, pp. R3-R5; a somewhat different text was printed in *RM*, 10 October, p. 4, and a third in *The Daily Telegraph*, 3 October.

116. 10 October 1974. Statement on judicial persecution of Aleksandr Ginzburg. Reuters report from Zurich, 11 October.

117. 29 October 1974. Press statement released in Solzhenitsyn's name by his lawyer, protesting against allegations in the journal *Der Spiegel*, that he was planning a kind of Vietnam-tribunal against his homeland. German: *Der Spiegel*, 18 November, p. 130 (full text). Incomplete English text in an untitled note in *IHT*, 31 October.

118. 30 October 1974. Letter of thanks to the US Senate for adopting a resolution that honorary American citizenship be conferred upon him. Russian: *RM*, 12 December, p. 2; *Vermont Sobr. soch.* X. English (full text): *CR*, vol. 121, Pt. 4 (24 February 1975), pp. 4080-81. Brief summary in "Notes on People," *NYT*, 12 November, p. 21.

119. November 1974 (before 7th). Brief message welcoming the formation of an Action and Mutual Aid Committee to coordinate efforts to assist those persecuted for their beliefs in Czechoslovakia and the Soviet Union. Reported in *RM*, 14 November, p. 2.

120. 6 November 1974. Letter to Rudolf Augstein, publisher of *Der Spiegel*. Augstein had replied to a letter from Solzhenitsyn's lawyer concerning allegations printed in his journal (see item 117) and had rejected the charges made against him. Solzhenitsyn responded, spelling out his objections to the report. This letter, in a facsimile of the Russian typescript and in German translation, was published, together with the related correspondence, including Augstein's response, in *Der Spiegel*, 18 November, pp. 130 & 132-33.

121. 14 November 1974. *Samizdat* publication in Moscow of *From Under the Rubble: A Collection of Essays* (*Iz-pod glyb: Sbornik statei*), which contains a preface (written 1973) and three essays by

Solzhenitsyn, who is co-editor of the collection with Igor' Shafarevich. The essays are:

"As Breathing and Consciousness Return" ("Na vozvrate dykhaniia i soznaniia"), a polemic with A. Sakharov originally written in 1969. Solzhenitsyn intended to circulate it through *samizdat*, but did not do so (*The Oak*, 398-99; *371*).

"Repentance and Self-Limitation in the Life of Nations" ("Raskaianie i samoogranichenie kak kategorii natsional'noi zhizni").

"The Smatterers" ("Obrazovanshchina").

The last two were written between 1972 and 1973 and finally revised shortly before Solzhenitsyn's expulsion. He collaborated on this volume with Shafarevich over a period of some three years. Publication was originally intended for March or April 1974, a schedule which was interrupted by Solzhenitsyn's deportation. First Western publication was by YMCA-Press (Paris) in 1974, in Russian. The essays by Solzhenitsyn are also included in *Vermont Sobr. soch.* IX, and the preface *ibid.*, X. English translation of the volume: Little, Brown (Boston) and Collins & Harvill (London), both in 1975.

122. 16 November 1974. Four-hour press conference in Zurich to mark the appearance of *From Under the Rubble*. Approximately half of the conference was taken up by Solzhenitsyn's description of the collection, the remainder by questions and answers on such topics as détente, emigration, political versus ethical revolutions, his alleged "chauvinism," etc. Full Russian text: *Dve press-konferentsii (K sborniku "Iz-pod glyb")* (Paris: YMCA-Press, 1975); *Vermont Sobr. soch.* X. An apparently full translation into English appeared as a supplement to Radio Liberty Research Bulletin of 14 February 1975. Another translation, without Solzhenitsyn's opening speech and based on a transcript which differs at some points from the authorized Russian text, is A. I. Solzhenitsyn, *Press Conference on the Future of Russia, Zurich, 16 November 1974*, trans. with intro. and notes by D. Pospielovsky (Ontario: Zaria, 1975).

123. 17 November 1974. Conversation in Zurich with Janis Sapiets of the BBC Russian Service. Solzhenitsyn elaborated at length upon the themes raised at the previous day's press conference. Russian text was broadcast to the Soviet Union. English: BBC Current Affairs Research & Information Section Report No. 16/74 (3 December 1974); as "Conversation with Solzhenitsyn," *Encounter*, vol. 44, No. 3 (March 1975), pp. 67-72.

124. November 1974. Preface to his publication of an account of a 1918 meeting of Petrograd workers' representatives. *Kontinent*, No. 2 (1975), pp. 383-84; and *Vermont Sobr. soch.* X. English in *Kontinent 2* (London: Hodder and Stoughton, 1978), p. 211 (U.S. ed. Garden City, N.Y.: Doubleday, 1977).

125. Late November—early December 1974. Reading from *Gulag* followed by a conversation with Ernst Kux of Swiss TV (some 50 minutes in all). First broadcast ("several weeks" after it was recorded, according to *NZZ*) in Switzerland on 19 December. Repeated in Germany on 22 December and Austria around 19 January 1975. Reports: "Solschenizyn liest und erzählt," *NZZ*, 21-22 December, p. 40; "Solschenizyn liest im ZDF," *Die Welt*, 17 December; untitled notice, *Die Presse* (Vienna), 20 January 1975.

126. 1 December 1974. Meeting in Zurich with Hedrick Smith of the *New York Times*. The most substantial part of this report coincides with the details of the textual history of Solzhenitsyn's works given in an earlier interview with N. M. Udgaard (see item 112). Hedrick Smith, "Solzhenitsyn Puts Back Parts of Self-Censored Works," *NYT*, 4 December, p. 32.

127. 10 December 1974. Brief speech in Stockholm upon receiving the insignia for his Nobel Prize. Russian: *RM*, 26 December, p. 2; *Posev*, No. 1, 1975, p. 16 (with variants); *Vermont Sobr. soch.* IX. English (full text): *CR*, vol. 121, Pt. 4 (24 February 1975), p. 4081 (provided by the Swedish Embassy). Substantial excerpts: Mark Goldsmith, "Solzhenitsyn Says Nobel Prize 'Saved Me,'" *Guardian*, 11 December, p. 3.

128. 12 December 1974. Wide-ranging four-hour press conference in Stockholm. Russian: *RM*, 16 January 1975, pp. 6-7; *Posev*, No. 2, 1975, pp. 12-23 (slightly edited text); *Vermont Sobr. soch.* X. English (translation of *Russkaia mysl'* text): *National Review*, 6 June 1975, pp. 603-609, repr. in *CR*, vol. 121, Pt. 13 (4 and 5 June 1975), pp. 17137-39 and 17476-78.

129. 2 January 1975. Inscription in the guest book during a visit to the Paris offices of *Russkaia mysl'*. *RM*, 9 January, p. 1.

130. 3 January 1975. Brief remarks to the press during his visit to Paris. UPI report from Paris, 3 January gives quotations. See also

"Solzhenitsyn on First Visit to Paris Leaves the Press Out in the Cold," *IHT*, 4-5 January.

131. 7 January 1975. Letter to the Zurich Canton Police. Hitherto unpublished. *Vermont Sobr. soch.* X.

132. January 1975 (before 15th). "The End of a Soviet Decade" ("Konets odnogo sovetskogo desiatiletiia"). A letter to the *Neue Zürcher Zeitung* on the new strategy of suppressing information from the Soviet Union. "Das Ende eines sowjetischen Jahrzehnts," *NZZ*, 15 January. Russian in *Vermont Sobr. soch.* X. Report in *NYT*, 16 January, p. 8.

133. February 1975. Publication of the Russian edition (YMCA-Press, Paris) of *The Oak and the Calf: Sketches of Literary Life in the Soviet Union* (*Bodalsia telenok s dubom: Ocherki literaturnoi zhizni*). The English translation (New York: Harper and Row; London: Collins and Harvill, 1980) contains some new material. This autobiographical account of events since about 1961 was begun in 1967 and continued in four supplements over the next seven years. There are several letters or excerpts from letters to and from Solzhenitsyn within the body of the text, some of which have not hitherto been available either at all, or in reliable form. They include correspondence with Tvardovskii (e.g., pp. 52-54, *44-45*), unpublished 50th birthday greetings (pp. 245-46, *224-25*), and a message from inmates of Vladimir prison on the occasion of the Nobel award (p. 332, *307*). The bulk of the documents included in the extensive appendix is familiar, but a number of texts which reached the West in varying stages of completeness are here presented in full. Solzhenitsyn has spoken more than once of a sequel to *The Oak* revealing aspects of the story which, for conspiratorial reasons, may not yet be disclosed. An excerpt from the Sixth Supplement was separately published in 1979 as *Skvoz' chad* (item 204).

134. February 1975. Letter in reply to Pavel Litvinov's criticism of several of his recent public statements. *Vestnik RKhD*, No. 114 (4, 1974), pp. 261-64 (preceded by Litvinov's original letter); *Vermont Sobr. soch.* X.

135. 10 April 1975. Press conference in Paris to mark the publication of the French edition of *The Oak and the Calf*. *RM*, 17 April, pp. 1-2, and 24 April, p. 3; *Vermont Sobr. soch.* X. Extensive cover-

age in *Le Monde*, 12 April, p. 4; and Jean-Claude Lamy, "Soljéni-tsyne: 'C'est au contact de la souffrance humaine que je suis devenu écrivain'," *France-Soir*, 12 April.

136. 11 April 1975. Appearance on French TV program, "Apos-trophes." *Vermont Sobr. soch.* X. *Contrepoint*, No. 21, 1976, pp. 143-62. For reports and excerpts see "A. I. Solzhenitsyn vo Frantsii," *RM*, 24 April, p. 3; Claude Sarraute, "Soljenitsyne en direct," *Le Monde*, 13-14 April, p. 11; Nan Robertson, "Solzhenitsyn Speaks Out on Paris TV," *NYT*, 13 April, p. 10.

137. 28 April 1975. "A Third World War?.." ("Tret'ia miro-vaia?.."). Short essay on the West's loss of courage and influence, written during the flight to North America. First published in *Le Monde*, 31 May, p. 8. Russian: *RM*, 12 June, p. 3; *Vestnik RKhD*, No. 115 (1, 1975), pp. 255-57; *Vermont Sobr. soch.* IX. English, as "The Big Losers in the Third World War," *NYT*, 22 June, Section IV, p. 15.

138. 4(?) May 1975. Tape-recorded Easter message to Ukrainians in Canada. The recording (three and one half minutes long) was beamed abroad over Radio Canada International and for the domestic audience over CFMB's "Ukrainian Time" program, on Sunday, 4 May. Full text in *Vermont Sobr. soch.* X. Excerpts and background: "A. I. Solzhenitsyn v Kanade," *NRS*, 10 May, p. 1; John Richmond, "Solzhenitsyn Breaks Silence," *Montreal Star*, 5 May; Roman Rakhmanny, "Solzhenitsyn Airs Grievance at West," *Gazette* (Montreal), 5 May.

139. June 1975. Inscription made during a visit to the Hoover Institution in California, praising their special collections and library materials. Back cover of the Hoover Institution pamphlet, *Solzheni-tsyn Speaks* (undated, but probably 1976).

140. Late June 1975. Remarks to Senator Jesse Helms on the West's defeat in World War III, cited by the Senator in two slightly different versions. *CR*, vol. 121, No. 105 (7 July), p. S11882 and No. 106 (8 July), p. S11956.

141. 30 June 1975. Speech, delivered from notes at a dinner in Washington under the auspices of the AFL-CIO. Widely published, e.g.: *NRS*, 8 July, pp. 2-3; *RM*, 17 July, pp. 3-5; *AFT-KPP Novosti svobodnykh profsoiuzov*, vol. 30, Nos. 7-8 (July-August 1975), pp.

4-16; *Vermont Sobr. soch.* IX. English in *Washington Star*, 6 July; *CR*, vol. 121, No. 106 (8 July), pp. S11951-S11956; *Survey*, vol. 21, No. 3 (96), Summer 1975, pp. 114-32; *AFL-CIO American Federationist*, July 1975. Anthologized in items 56, 57 and 58.

142. 9 July 1975. Speech given from notes at an AFL-CIO luncheon in New York City. The second of the major "American speeches." *NRS*, 13 July, pp. 2-3; *AFT-KPP Novosti svobodnykh profsoiuzov*, vol. 30, Nos. 7-8 (July-August 1975), pp. 17-32; *Vermont Sobr. soch.* IX. English in *AFL-CIO American Federationist*, August 1975. Anthologized in items 56, 57 and 58.

143. 13 July 1975. Thirty-minute live interview on NBC-TV's "Meet the Press." The interviewers were Norman Cousins (*Saturday Review*), Peter Lisagor (*Chicago Daily News*), Bill Monroe (NBC), and Hedrick Smith (*New York Times*). Transcript due to appear in *Vermont Sobr. soch.* X. Reports: *New York Post*, 14 July; and Norman Cousins, "Brief Encounter with A. Solzhenitsyn," *Saturday Review*, 23 August, especially pp. 5-6.

144. 14 July 1975. Recorded forty-minute interview with Barbara Walters on NBC-TV's "Today" program, broadcast with some cuts on 22 and 23 July. The questions concerned the collection *From Under the Rubble* as well as more general topics. Due to appear in *Vermont Sobr. soch.* X(?). Reports and summaries: A. B., "A. I. Solzhenitsyn o vozvrate k religii," *RM*, 31 July; *Posev*, No. 8, 1975, p. 8. Excerpts were broadcast in Russian over Radio Liberty on 22 and 23 July.

145. 15 July 1975. Speech read to a gathering of Senators and Congressmen in Washington, at the invitation of a group of Senators. *NRS*, 19 July, p. 1; *Vermont Sobr. soch.* IX. English in *CR*, vol. 121, No. 111 (15 July), pp. E3823-E3824. Anthologized in items 56, 57 and 58. Account with quotations: William Greider, "Hill Audience Hears Solzhenitsyn," *Washington Post*, 16 July, p. A3.

146. 21 July 1975. Brief message of congratulations and good wishes in the visitors' book at the Tolstoy Foundation Center. *NRS*, 23 July. Definitive text (facsimile of holograph), together with an English translation, in *Tolstoy Foundation, Inc.: History, Aims and Achievements* (New York, 1976), pp. 20-21.

147. 21 July 1975. Statement declining to meet President Ford,

telephoned from the Tolstoy Foundation Center, in Russian to *Novoe russkoe slovo* (publ. 22 July), and in English to the *New York Times* (publ. 22 July, pp. 1 and 9). The *NYT* account includes further explanatory remarks made by Solzhenitsyn during the telephone conversation.

148. 27 July 1975. During a four-day visit to Norwich University, Vermont, Solzhenitsyn inscribed a program at a performance of Slavic music: "I am impressed with your efforts to preserve Russian culture without the Soviet imprint." "Solzhenitsyn Ends Visit to Vermont Campus," *IHT*, 31 July; more briefly in *NYT*, 31 July, p. 19.

149. July 1975. "Letter from America" ("Pis'mo iz Ameriki"), on Russian Orthodox Church unity. *Vestnik RKhD*, No. 116 (2-4, 1975), pp. 121-31 (dated "June 1975", apparently in error), together with a response by Nikita Struve. *Vermont Sobr. soch.* X.

150. 27 August 1975. Reply to an invitation to participate in the International Sakharov Hearing in Copenhagen. The bulk of the text was quoted in *Posev*, No. 11, 1975, p. 10.

151. 25 September 1975. Statement protesting against the trial of Vladimir Osipov. *Vestnik RKhD*, No. 116 (2-4, 1975), p. 257; *Vermont Sobr. soch.* X.

152. 27 September 1975. Message of support to the Strasbourg Conference of Nations Enslaved by Communism. *RM*, 16 October, p. 3; *Vestnik RKhD*, No. 116 (2-4, 1975), p. 252; *Kontinent*, No. 6 (1976), p. 66; *Novyi Amerikanets*, No. 72 (5-11 July 1981), p. 13; *Vermont Sobr. soch.* X. UPI report with quotations, Strasbourg, 5 October.

153. September(?) 1975. Statement on a fabricated "interview" with him in the *Deutsche Nationalzeitung* of 8 August. "Ich bin noch nicht tot," *FAZ*, 16 September.

154. 1975. Preface to Russian ed. of *Lenin in Zurich* publ. October 1975 (see item 25).

155. Early October(?) 1975. Statement on recent press fabrications and misrepresentations concerning him. "Solschenizyn wehrt sich gegen Fälschungen," *NZZ*, 7 October; "Soljenitsyne et *le Monde*," *Le Monde*, 8 October, p. 3 (followed by an editorial response to his charge against *Le Monde*).

156. 9 October 1975. Brief statement congratulating Andrei Sakharov on winning the Nobel Peace Prize for 1975. *Posev*, No. 11, 1975, p. 3; *Vermont Sobr. soch.* X. English text carried by Reuter and UPI from Oslo, 9 October (differing translations). Report in *NYT*, 10 October, p. 13.

157. July-October 1975. On the work of Radio Liberty. First publication in *Vermont Sobr. soch.* X(?).

158. 14 October 1975. Statement on repressive measures against Igor' Shafarevich. *Vermont Sobr. soch.* X; *Vestnik RKhD*, No. 116 (2-4, 1975), p. 258.

159. Mid-November (between 15th and 18th) 1975. Statement on a false press agency report that he was suffering from severe depression. *NZZ*, 19 November.

160. November(?) 1975. "Schlesinger and Kissinger." An article for the *New York Times*. *NYT*, 1 December, p. 31. *Vermont Sobr. soch.* X.

161. December 1975. "Appeal to Russian Émigrés Born before the Revolution" ("Obrashchenie k russkim emigrantam, starshim revoliutsii"), asking for personal reminiscences of the period 1917-1922. *RM*, 25 December, p. 2; *Vermont Sobr. soch.* X.

162. December 1975. Substantial interview with Georges Suffert in Zurich. *Le Point* (Paris), No. 171 (29 December 1975), pp. 32-37. Russian in *Vermont Sobr. soch.* X. English in *Encounter*, April 1976, pp. 9-15.

163. February 1976(?) Conversation with students in the Slavic Department of Zurich University on literary themes. First publication in *Vermont Sobr. soch.* X.

164. Late February 1976. Informal conversation with George Mikes, including a brief report of Solzhenitsyn's comments at a Pen Club meeting. George Mikes, "Lunching with a Legend," *To the Point International*, 22 March, p. 54.

165. 26 February 1976. Talk with the BBC's Russian Service, offering general and specific criticisms. *Kontinent*, No. 9 (1976), pp. 210-23; *Vermont Sobr. soch.* X. Abridged, but extensive report

and paraphrase in *East-West Digest*, December 1976, pp. 910-12; summary in *Daily Telegraph*, 18 October, p. 17.

166. Late February 1976. Recorded fifty-minute interview with Michael Charlton for BBC-TV's "Panorama" program, broadcast on 1 March. A slightly abridged soundtrack was transmitted over the BBC Russian Service on 9 March, and the whole interview was shown in the USA on William F. Buckley Jr.'s PBS-TV program "Firing Line" on 27 March. Russian in *Vermont Sobr. soch.* X. Full English text in item 57, and also in the booklet: Alexander Solzhenitsyn, *Warning to the Western World* (London: Bodley Head and BBC, 1976). Edited version: *Listener*, 4 March, pp. 260-61. For an account of the "Firing Line" broadcast, see Benjamin Stein, "Words of Warning from Solzhenitsyn," *Wall Street Journal*, 26 March.

167. 26 February 1976. Recorded forty-minute talk for BBC-Radio 3, broadcast on 24 March and over the BBC Russian Service on the same day. Russian in *Vestnik RKhD*, No. 117 (1, 1976), pp. 136-47; and *Vermont Sobr. soch.* IX. Full English text in London *Times*, 2 April, p. 9; also in item 57 and in Alexander Solzhenitsyn, *Warning to the Western World* (London: Bodley Head and BBC, 1976).

168. Late February 1976. Letter to the Director General of the BBC expressing qualified appreciation of the TV film "The Last Secret" (on the forcible repatriation of Soviet citizens by the allies after World War II). *Vermont Sobr. soch.* X. English in *House of Lords Debates*, vol. 369, No. 47 (17 March 1976), col. 342.

169. Early March 1976. Conversation on political themes in Paris with C. L. Sulzberger. Two parts: C. L. Sulzberger, "Gloomsayer or Soothsayer," *NYT*, 7 March, Section IV, p. 15, and "Does National Marxism Exist?" *NYT*, 10 March, p. 39.

170. 9 March 1976. Solzhenitsyn replies to questions telephoned in by viewers of French TV's program "Les dossiers de l'écran" after a showing of the film "One Day in the Life of Ivan Denisovich." The exchanges reportedly lasted some two hours. *Vermont Sobr. soch.* X. Excerpts and summary in *Le Monde*, 11 March, pp. 1-2; and as "Solschenizyn am französischen Fernsehen," *NZZ*, 12 March.

171. 10(?) March 1976. Interview in Paris with Jean-Claude Lamy. "Soljénitsyne aide les détenus du Goulag avec ses droits

d'auteur," *France-Soir*, 12 March. Excerpts in *Vermont Sobr. soch.* X.

172. 20 March 1976. Forty-five minute appearance on Spanish TV's "Directisimo" program, replying to questions pre-submitted by journalists. *Kontinent*, No. 8 (1976), pp. 429-40 (misdated); *Vermont Sobr. soch.* X. Extensive coverage in *Informaciones* (Madrid), 22 March, pp. 20-22. Much briefer reports on same day in *NYT*, London *Times*, *Guardian*. Full Italian text in Aleksandr Solženicyn, *Dialogo con il futuro: Discorsi e interviste* (Milan: La Casa di Matriona, 1977).

173. 20 March 1976. Press conference in Madrid. *Kontinent*, No. 11 (1977), spetsial'noe prilozhenie, pp. 19-28 (with author's emendations); *Vermont Sobr. soch.* X. Report with quotations: Juan Pedro Quinonero, "Solzhenitsyn anuncia el apocalipsis," *Informaciones*, 22 March, pp. 20-21. Full Italian text (misdated) in *Dialogo con il futuro* (see preceding item).

174. 25 March(?) 1976. Recorded interview with Robert Robinson for BBC-TV's "Book Programme" on *Lenin in Zurich*, broadcast on 27 April. *Vermont Sobr. soch.* X. English in *The Listener*, 29 April, pp. 546-47.

175. March 1976. Exensive interview on literary themes with Nikita Struve. *Vestnik RKhD*, No. 120 (1, 1977), pp. 130-58; *Vermont Sobr. soch.* X. A color film, apparently of this interview, has been shown in Paris: see announcement in *RM*, 16 February 1978, p. 14. English text first published in the present volume.

176. March 1976. Interview for Japanese TV. To appear in *Vermont Sobr. soch.* X. [In his *Soljénitsyne* (Paris: Seuil, 1980), Georges Nivat cites a 1976 interview with G. Uchimara (Uchimura?), it is not clear whether these items are connected.]

177. Mid-April(?) 1976. Letter to the Russian Orthodox Bishop of Sitka and Alaska with Easter greetings and congratulations on the restoration of the St. Mikhail Cathedral in Sitka. *NRS*, 22 April, p. 3.

178. Spring 1976. Foreword to Igor' Shafarevich's book, *The Socialist Phenomenon*. First published as *Sotsializm kak iavlenie mirovoi istorii* (Paris: YMCA-Press, 1977). English by Harper and Row (New York, 1980). The foreword appeared separately in *Vestnik RKhD*, No. 121 (2, 1977), pp. 192-94; and in *Vermont Sobr. soch.* X.

179. 18 May 1976. Statement on a new KGB forgery depicting him as an informer while in labor camp. *NRS*, 23 May, p. 1; *Posev*, No. 7, 1976, p. 15. Full German text as "Eine Presseerklärung Alexander Solschenizyns," *NZZ*, 30-31 May. Brief report in English in *NYT*, 20 May, p. 34.

180. 24 May 1976. Speech on the study of Russian history in the West, prepared during May and read at a dinner in his honor at the Hoover Institution. *Vestnik RKhD*, No. 118 (2, 1976), pp. 166-72; *Novyi zhurnal*, No. 123 (1976), pp. 195-201; *Vermont Sobr. soch.* IX. English in *Russian Review*, vol. 36, No. 2 (April 1977), pp. 184-89; and in the Hoover Institution pamphlet *Solzhenitsyn Speaks* (1976).

181. 1 June 1976. Speech at the Hoover Institution upon receiving the Friendship Prize of the American Freedom Foundation. *Vestnik RKhD*, No. 118 (2, 1976), pp. 172-75; *Vermont Sobr. soch.* IX. English in the Hoover Institution pamphlet *Solzhenitsyn Speaks* (1976).

182. June(?) 1976. Remarks on the Italian Communist Party, reportedly made to a correspondent of *La Nazione* (Florence). AFP dispatch from Florence, published, e.g., as "Solschenizyn: Ich traue der KPI nicht," *Die Welt*, 18 June.

183. 18 June 1976. Letter to the Parliamentary Committee of the Israeli Knesset in reply to an (unspecified) invitation and speaking of religion as a unifying force in a threatened world. *Sion* (Tel-Aviv), No. 16 (1976), p. 215 (Russian text).

184. October(?) 1976. Letter of thanks for the cultural prize awarded to him by the Cultural Circle of the Federation of West German Industries (BDI). "Ehrengabe für Alexander Solschenizyn," *FAZ*, 18 October.

185. 21 January 1977. Very brief impromptu interview with Elizabeth Slater of the Barre-Montpelier *Times Argus*, on his plans to found a non-profit publishing company. Reported in *NYT*, 23 January, p. 14; and *Washington Post*, 25 January, pp. B1-B2.

186. 22 January 1977. Governor of Vermont briefly reports Solzhenitsyn's intention to settle in the State, expressed at a meeting with him to discuss the State's publishing laws. UPI report from Washington, 25 January.

187. 4 February 1977. Statement to the press on the arrest of Aleksandr Ginzburg. *NRS*, 5 February; *RM*, 24 February, p. 3; *Vermont Sobr. soch.* X. English in *NYT*, 6 February, p. 6.

188. February 1977. Letter to Edward Bennet Williams, asking him to be Aleksandr Ginzburg's legal representative. Released to the *Washington Post* and published, together with a background story by Robert Kaiser, on 1 March.

189. 28 February 1977. Twenty-minute address to some 200 of his "friends and neighbors" at a Cavendish Town Meeting. Fullest English text in Ned Lamont, "Solzhenitsyn: Dear Friends," *Black River Tribune* (Ludlow, Vermont), 2 March, pp. 1 and 5. Also reported in *Christian Science Monitor*, 2 March, p. 3.

190. 25 May 1977. Reply to Tat'iana Khodorovich and Mal'va Landa, executrices of his Russian Social Fund for the relief of political prisoners and their families. *RM*, 2 June, p. 2; *Vestnik RKhD*, No. 121 (2, 1977), p. 382; *Kontinent*, No. 12 (1977), p. 259; *Vermont Sobr. soch.* X.

191. Late May 1977. Statement, released through Mutual Broadcasting System correspondent, Philip Clarke, on increasing reprisals against Soviet dissidents. UPI report (with quotations) from Washington, 29 May; brief untitled report in *Guardian*, 30 May.

192. Early June 1977. Brief statement on recent reprisals against a Soviet sculptor, reported as having been made through Vermont Congressman, James Jeffords. *NYT*, 17 June, p. 10.

193. September 1977. Statement on his newly founded All-Russian Memoir Library, with a request for materials. Widely published in the emigre press, e.g.,: *NRS*, 27 September, p. 3; *RM*, 29 September, pp. 1-2; *Vestnik RKhD*, No. 122 (3, 1977), pp. 283-85. Also in *Vermont Sobr. soch.* X. English (slightly abridged) in *The Sun* (Baltimore), 18 October, p. A19; summary and quotations in Raymond H. Anderson, "Solzhenitsyn Seeking Chronicles..," *NYT*, 19 November, p. 14.

194. September 1977. Letter to the editor of *Vestnik RKhD*, objecting to the recent publication, without comment, of "russophobic" materials *Vestnik RKhD*, No. 122 (3, 1977), pp. 6-9; *Vermont Sobr. soch.* X.

195. November 1977. Message to the Second International Sakharov Hearing in Rome. *NRS*, 26 November; *RM*, 1 December, p. 1; *Posev*, No. 11, 1977, pp. 12-13; *Vermont Sobr. soch.* X. Excerpt in *NYT*, 26 November, p. 7.

196. November 1977. Preface to the English translation of *The Gulag Archipelago* (see item 26).

197. January 1978. Brief message of support to the Coalition for a Democratic Majority, read out at a ceremony on 26 January to honor Human Rights groups in the Soviet Union. *Posev*, No. 4, 1978, p. 11 (back-translation). *Vermont Sobr. soch.* X.

198. 17(?) March 1978. Statement on the occasion of Mstislav Rostropovich and Galina Vishnevskaia's deprivation of Soviet citizenship. *RM*, 23 March, p. 1; *Kontinent*, No. 16 (1978), spetsial'noe prilozhenie, p. 6; *Tret'ia volna*, Nos. 3-4 (April 1978), p. 234; *Vermont Sobr. soch.* X.

199. 8 June 1978. Statement on the trial of Aleksandr Ginzburg. *Vermont Sobr. soch.* X.

200. 8 June 1978. Harvard University Commencement Address, "A World Split Apart" ("Raskolotyi mir"). Written during May. Very widely published and reported. *Vestnik RKhD*, No. 125 (2, 1978), pp. 275-91; *Russkoe Vozrozhdenie*, No. 2 (1978), pp. 85-109; *Novyi zhurnal*, No. 131 (June 1978), pp. 305-16; *Posev*, No. 9, 1978, pp. 14-22; *Vermont Sobr. soch.* IX. Bi-lingual book edition: Aleksandr I. Solzhenitsyn, *A World Split Apart* (New York: Harper and Row, 1978). English also in *Harvard Magazine*, vol. 80, No. 6 (July-August 1978), pp. 21-26; *Times* (London), 26 July, p. 6; *Washington Post*, 11 June, pp. C1 and C5 (somewhat abridged). Anthologized in items 58 and 59. The Address was broadcast over PBS-TV.

201. 12 June 1978. Interview with Hilton Kramer, chiefly on his current literary projects. "Solzhenitsyn in Vermont," *NYT Book Review*, 2 July, pp. 2 and 14.

202. 12 June 1978. Statements made in an interview with Hilton Kramer criticizing Ol'ga Carlisle's role in the publication of his works in the West. Hilton Kramer, "Book about Him Irks Solzhenitsyn," *NYT*, 13 June, p. C3.

203. June(?) 1978. Letter to *Prospettive nel Mondo* (Rome) on

conditions in Soviet labor camps, apparently published 15 July. UPI report from Rome, 15 July.

204. September 1978. *Through the Fumes (Skvoz' chad)*. A sixty-page excerpt from the unpublished Sixth Supplement to *The Oak and the Calf* (item 133), discussing the accusations of a former friend, as well as various KGB concoctions. In Russian only: *Skvoz' chad* (Paris: YMCA-Press, 1979).

205. 27 October 1978. Reply to a question from the émigré Polish journal *Kultura* (Paris) on the significance of the election of a Polish Pope. Russian in *RM*, 16 November, p. 1; *Vermont Sobr. soch.* X.

206. 1978. Preface to the new Vermont Collected Works. Separately published in *RM*, 2 November, p. 7; *Vestnik RKhD*, No. 126 (3, 1978), p. 311; and in *Vermont Sobr. soch.* I.

207. 31 December 1978. Letter in reply to A. Kniazev et al., on the recent suicide of I. V. Morozov, a leading figure in the Russian Student Christian Movement. *Sovremennik* (Toronto), No. 42 (1979), pp. 157-58.

208. 3 February 1979. Lengthy radio interview in Vermont with Janis Sapiets of the BBC, on the fifth anniversary of his exile. Broadcast over the BBC's Russian Service in two installments, 13 and 18 February. *Vestnik RKhD*, No. 127 (4, 1978), pp. 279-95; *Russkoe Vozrozhdenie*, No. 6 (2, 1979), pp. 50-75; *Posev*, No. 4, 1979, pp. 20-28; *Vermont Sobr. soch.* X. English in the *Listener*, 15 February, pp. 240-41 and 22 February, pp. 270-72 (abridged); *Kenyon Review*, New Series, vol. 1, No. 3 (Summer 1979), pp. 8-17 and No. 4 (Fall 1979), pp. 3-11. Anthologized in item 59. Sapiets gives background information in his "Solzhenitsyn: Three Years in the Country," *Spectator*, 3 March, pp. 12-13.

209. June 1979. Statement on behalf of Igor' Ogurtsov to the Coalition for a Democratic Majority on the occasion of its annual "Friends of Freedom" Awards Dinner in Washington, 12 June. *NRS*, 15 June, p. 1; *RM*, 21 June, p. 1; *Posev*, No. 7, 1979, p. 17; *Vermont Sobr. soch.* X.

210. July 1979. "On the Old Believers, Yet Again" ("I vnov' o staroobriadtsakh"), a letter to the Editor of *Vestnik*. *Vestnik RKhD*, No. 129 (3, 1979), pp. 311-12; *Vermont Sobr. soch.* X.

211. September 1979. Appeal on behalf of Igor' Ogurtsov, read by Solzhenitsyn's wife to the International Sakharov Hearing in Washington. *Khronika zashchity prav v SSSR*, No. 35 (July-September 1979), pp. 51-52; *NRS*, 9 October, p. 2; *RM*, 11 October, p. 1; *Vestnik RKhD*, No. 129 (3, 1979), pp. 290-91; *Posev*, No. 10, 1979, p. 4; *Vermont Sobr. soch.* X. English in *A Chronicle of Human Rights in the USSR*, No. 35 (July-September 1979), pp. 54-55; *Spectator*, 3 November, p. 8

212. October 1979. "The Persian Trick" ("Persidskii triuk"), replying to allegations of religious authoritarianism and nationalism. *NRS*, 20 November, p. 2; *RM*, 22 November, p. 3; *Novyi zhurnal*, No. 137 (1979), pp. 195-96; *Russkoe Vozrozhdenie*, No. 9 (1, 1980), pp. 12-14; *Vermont Sobr. soch.* X. English in *Jerusalem Post*, 20 December, p. 8 ("The Persian Ruse"); and *Encounter*, vol. 54, No. 2 (February 1980), pp. 34-35 ("I Am No Russian Ayatollah").

213. 1979. Preface to the series "Studies in Modern Russian History," published by YMCA-Press, Paris, of which he is general editor. V. V. Leontovich, *Istoriia liberalizma v Rossii 1762-1914* (Paris: YMCA-Press, 1980), pp. i-ii; *Vermont Sobr. soch.* X.

214. 1979. Foreword to the first volume in the series "Studies in Modern Russian History." V. V. Leontovich, *Istoriia liberalizma v Rossii 1762-1914* (Paris: YMCA-Press, 1980), pp. iii-v; *Vermont Sobr. soch.* X.

215. Early 1980(?). Interviewed by Hilton Kramer on his literary views and plans. "A Talk with Solzhenitsyn," *NYT Book Review*, 11 May 1980, pp. 3 and 30-31. Russian in *Vermont Sobr. soch.* X.

216. January 1980. Essay commissioned by *Time* magazine and published as "Solzhenitsyn on Communism. Advice to the West, in an 'Hour of Extremity,'" 18 February, pp. 48-49. Russian, as "Communism Is Visible to All, Yet Not Understood" ("Kommunizm u vsekh na vidu—i ne poniat"), in *NRS*, 17 February, p. 3; *RM*, 21 February, pp. 1 and 3; *Vestnik RKhD*, No. 130 (4, 1979), pp. 391-96; *Russkoe Vozrozhdenie*, No. 9 (1, 1980), pp. 3-11, and other émigré journals; *Vermont Sobr. soch.* IX. Some editorial cuts were required for the *Time* version, see "Strannye kupiury," *Posev*, No. 5, 1980, p. 25.

217. February 1980. "Misconceptions about Russia Are a Threat

to America" ("Chem grozit Amerike plokhoe ponimanie Rossii"). To some extent an elaboration of the themes in the *Time* essay (see preceding item), begun in November 1979, set aside, resumed in January 1980 after the occupation of Afghanistan. The essay was written for *Foreign Affairs* and appeared in vol. 58, No. 4 (Spring 1980), pp. 797-834; then as Aleksandr I. Solzhenitsyn, *The Mortal Danger: How Misconceptions about Russia Imperil America* (New York: Harper and Row; London: Bodley Head, both 1980), in a slightly revised translation. Russian in *Vestnik RKhD*, No. 131 (1-2, 1980), pp. 182-216; *Russkoe Vozrozhdenie*, No. 10 (2, 1980), pp. 5-56; *Vermont Sobr. soch.* IX.

218. 11 February 1980. Letter to Boris Souvarine, author of an extensive critique of the historical foundations of *Lenin in Zurich*. *RM*, 17 April, p. 5; *Vestnik RKhD*, No. 131 (1-2, 1980), pp. 217-20; *Vermont Sobr. soch.* X. English text in the present volume.

219. 20 March 1980. Statement on the arrests of Priests Dmitrii Dudko and Gleb Iakunin. *NRS*, 25 March, p. 1; *RM*, 27 March, p. 1; *Russkoe Vozrozhdenie*, No. 9 (1, 1980), pp. 147-48; *Posev*, No. 5, 1980, p. 26; *Vermont Sobr. soch.* X. English in *Christianity Today*, vol. 24, 6 June, p. 13.

220. April 1980. Letter to David Atkinson declining an invitation to attend British Conservative Party Congress and reiterating some of the points in his Spring *Foreign Affairs* essay. First publication due in *Vermont Sobr. soch.* X.

221. 14 May 1980. Statement on behalf of Iosif D'iadkin, arrested for circulating a study of unnatural mortality in the USSR. The appeal was released, together with a description of D'iadkin's study, by the Center for Appeals for Freedom, New York. *NRS*, 20 May, p. 1; *RM*, 22 May, p. 1; *Kontinent*, No. 24 (1980), p. 238; *Vermont Sobr. soch.* X. A summary in English appeared in the *Guardian*, 21 May, p. 14 ("Soviet Scholar Arrested"). For a detailed review of D'iadkin's research, see James Ring Adams, "Revising Stalin's Legacy," *Wall Street Journal*, 23 July, p. 22.

222. 18 June 1980. "On the Fragments by Boris Souvarine" ("O fragmentakh Borisa Suvarina"), a short essay, continuing his

exchange over *Lenin in Zurich* with the French historian. *RM*, 18 December, p. 7; *Vestnik RKhD*, No. 132 (3-4, 1980), pp. 266-67; *Vermont Sobr. soch.* X. English text in the present volume.

223. July 1980. "The Courage to See" ("Imet' muzhestvo videt'"). A response to the generally hostile letters from readers of his essay in *Foreign Affairs* that Spring. *Foreign Affairs*, vol. 59, No. 1 (Fall 1980), pp. 196-210. Russian in *Vestnik RKhD*, No. 132 (3-4, 1980), pp. 233-51; *Russkoe Vozrozhdenie*, No. 12 (4, 1980), pp. 5-31; *Vermont Sobr. soch.* IX.

224. 20 August 1980. Brief telegram expressing admiration for the striking Polish workers. Released in English and Russian by the Center for Appeals for Freedom, New York. *NRS*, 22 August, p. 1; *RM*, 28 August, p. 1; *Vermont Sobr. soch.* X. UPI report from Cavendish, Vermont, 20 August.

225. 25 August 1980. Statement on the trial of Father Gleb Iakunin. *NRS*, 27 August, p. 1; *RM*, 4 September, p. 1; *Vermont Sobr. soch.* X. English text made available through the Center for Appeals for Freedom, New York.

226. October(?) 1980. Letter criticizing Sergei Rafal'skii's memoirs of the revolution. *RM*, 13 November, p. 14. (Rafal'skii replied in *RM*, 27 November, p. 15.)

227. 4 December 1980. Letter continuing the exchange with Sergei Rafal'skii. *RM*, 29 January 1981, p. 14.

228. 4 December 1980. Brief statement "On the Threat to Poland" ("Ob ugroze Pol'she"). *RM*, 11 December, p. 1; *Novyi Amerikanets*, vol. 1, No. 44 (10-16 December 1980), p. 2; *Vermont Sobr. soch.* X. English text released through the Center for Appeals for Freedom, New York.

229. 1980. Preface to the Chinese edition of *The Gulag Archipelago*. First publication in Russian due in *Vermont Sobr. soch.* X.

230. 1980(?). Reflections on Grammar. First publication due in *Vermont Sobr. soch.* X.

231. 22 January 1981. Statement on the persecution of Sergei

Khodorovich. *RM*, 29 January, p. 3; *NRS*, 30 January, p. 1; *Vermont Sobr. soch.* X. English text released by the Center for Appeals for Freedom, New York.

232. April 1981. Lengthy open letter to the organizers of a conference in Toronto on Russo-Ukrainian relations. *NRS*, 21 June, p. 2; *Russkoe Vozrozhdenie*, No. 14 (2, 1981), pp. 246-52; *RM*, 18 June 1981, p. 3.

233. 14 May 1981. Telegram with birthday greetings to Andrei Sakharov. *RM*, 21 May, p. 1. English text released through the Center for Appeals for Freedom, New York.

Index of Titles

Titles of all literary works and of a small selection of publicistic works listed in the bibliography are given in English and Russian. Untitled poetry is identified by first line in Russian only. Numbers indicate the relevant item in the bibliography.